ALSO BY JOHN KEAY

Into India

India Discovered

Eccentric Travellers

Explores Extraordinary

Highland Drove

The Honourable Company: A History of the English East India Company

Indonesia: From Sabang to Merauke

Explorers of the Western Himalayas, 1820–1893
(first published as *When Men and Mountain Meet* and *The Gilgit Game*)

The Royal Geographical Society's History of World Exploration
(general editor)

The Robinson Book of Exploration (editor)

Collins' Encyclopedia of Scotland (co-editor with Julia Keay)

EMPIRE'S END

A HISTORY OF THE FAR EAST
FROM HIGH COLONIALISM TO HONG KONG

JOHN KEAY

SCRIBNER

SCRIBNER
1230 Avenue of the Americas
New York, NY 10020

Published by arrangement with John Murray (Publishers) Ltd.
First published in Great Britain as *Last Post*

SCRIBNER and design are trademarks of Simon & Schuster Inc.

Set in Garamond No.3

Manufactured in the United States of America

3   5   7   9   10   8   6   4   2

Library of Congress Cataloging-in-Publication Data
Keay, John.
Empire's end : a history of the Far East from high colonialism to Hong Kong / John Keay.
p.   cm.
Previously published as: Last post.
Includes bibliographical references and index.
1. Asia, Southeastern—History. 2. East Asia—History. 3. Imperialism.
I. Keay, John. Last post. II. Title.
DS526.6.K43   1997
950—dc21   96-39725
CIP

ISBN 0-684-81592-3

For Nell and Sam

Contents

Contents

Illustrations

(*between pages 210 and 211*)

Illustrations

The author and publishers wish to acknowledge the following for permission to reproduce illustrations:

1, *Yearbook of the Netherlands East Indies*, n.p., 1920; 2, 4, J. Stewart Lockhart Collection (see bibliographical note); 3, Louis Salaun, *L'Indochine*, Imprimerie National, Paris, 1943; 5, A. Wright, *Twentieth Century Impressions of British Malaya*, Lloyds, London, 1908; 6, Robert Payne, *The White Rajahs of Sarawak*, Robert Hale, London, 1960; 7, 14, 17, Imperial War Museum; 8, 10, 11, 12, 15, 16, 18, 19, 20, Hulton Getty Picture Collection; 9, reproduced in *The US Army in World War Two* (Pictorial Record), Department of the Army, Washington DC, 1952, vol.2, from a captured Japanese publication; 13, 22, Popperfoto; 21, 23, Raymond Flower, *Raffles: The Story of Singapore*, Croom Helm, Beckenham, 1984; 24, Associated Press.

Note on Place Names

Place names are rendered and spelled so as to be recognisable to English-speaking readers. This means that in most cases, but not all, they appear in the form used by colonial writers at the time. For alternative forms and spellings the reader should refer to the Glossary at the end of the text.

Acknowledgements

My principal debt is to the numerous colonial officials, soldiers, academics and authors whose works are quoted in the text and listed in the Bibliography.

Additionally, I would like to extend belated thanks to all those in Vietnam, Cambodia, Malaysia, Singapore, Indonesia, the Philippines and Hong Kong whom I interviewed in the 1980s during several protracted tours as a writer and presenter of radio documentaries, principally for the BBC's Radio 3. That experience emboldened me to undertake this book and the opinions of those contributors, sadly far too numerous to list, inform the result.

For more specific assistance I am also most grateful to Shiona Airlie, Charles Allen, Janie Cottis, Michael Gill, Brian Lapping, Norman Lewis, Sarah Markham and the children of Duncan Stewart. Austin Coates kindly read and commented on the text. My sincere thanks to him should not be taken to imply his concurrence with all the views expressed. From Gail Pirkis of John Murray and Scott Moyers of Scribner the text has benefited from some exceptionally perceptive editing; my debt to them is great. Finally Anna, my daughter, undertook some of the research and Julia, my wife, commented on the text. I hesitate to thank them. Formality somehow demeans family. The advantages of being the father of a formidable historian and the husband of a stylish author should be obvious. If not, the fault is mine.

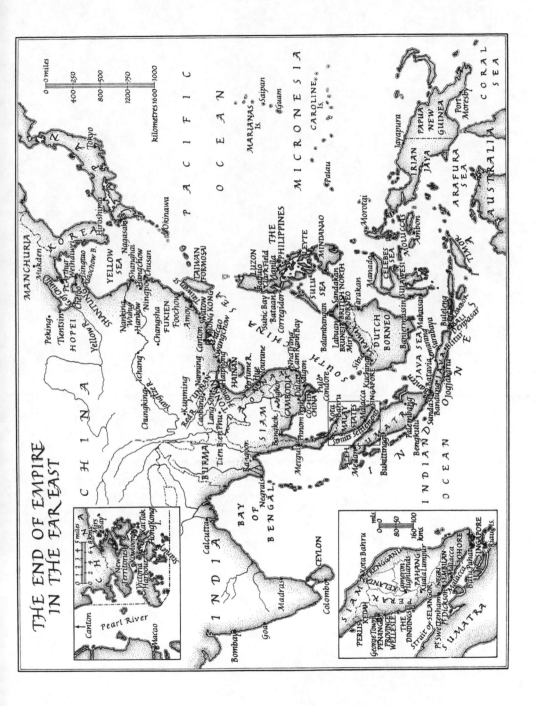

THE END OF EMPIRE
IN THE FAR EAST

Last Post

In the British army a particularly haunting bugle call was once used to sound the retreat at the end of the fighting day. The same call was subsequently adopted for the nightly ritual of the lowering of the flag and the mounting of the guard. It acquired a suitably conclusive title – 'Last Post'; and it also came to be used as a sombre requiem at ceremonies of remembrance like the one held annually at the Cenotaph in London's Whitehall.

Sounded by a solitary bugler, all present standing hushed to attention, the staccato phrasing seems to echo like a plaintive valedictory across the parade grounds of memory. Even as its final cadenza dies away on the breeze, it catches the unwary with a last, long drawn-out note. The flag is lowered and furled and, like a sentence unfinished, the note lingers on the stilled air. Long after the bugler has about-turned and marched away, this tune that has no words troubles the mind, evoking the ghosts of places past.

In the tropical East, where the sun sets at much the same time throughout the year, the evening's 'Last Post' often coincided with the Muslim call to prayer or the gongs and bells of a nearby temple. Together they came to comprise a reassuring recessional at day's end. The scent-laden air, once the sting of its heat had been drawn by the lengthening shadows, seemed at last to stir in moist sympathy with these serenades to silence and repose. Somewhere the flag had been furled and the watch had been set. Peace reigned; empires came off duty. Into crystal glasses tinkled ice cubes while rattan roofing reawoke to the first tut-tuts of the pale nocturnal lizard which Malays call the chik-chak. 'You might think', wrote the novelist Somerset Maugham, 'that it was chuckling with amusement at the white men who come and go and leave all things as they were.'

And so it seemed when Maugham was writing in 1922. Almost all the countries of the East, over half of the world's population if one included India as well as China, were somewhere subject to a form of colonial rule. The European naval powers, on the scene for three hundred years, had been regulating the affairs of the Far East for the past century. The Americans, though latecomers, were no less part of the colonial mechanism. Individual white men came and went but their supremacy had become a cast-iron feature of the unchanging Orient.

Then, in about 1930, the rust began to show and the first cracks to appear. Just twenty years after Maugham was writing, very few things were 'as they were'; forty years later almost nothing was as it had once been; and sixty years later all that remained of the West's empires in the East was Hong Kong, a last post counting the sunsets until its own 'Last Post'.

In the English-speaking world the demise of empire is inseparably linked with Edward Gibbon's concept of 'decline and fall' as applied to the Roman empire. The phrase, suggestive of a descent from civilisation and rationality to barbarism and superstition, has a certain apocalyptic appeal, but it is inappropriate as a description of the demise of empire in the East during the mid-twentieth century. The decline of British, French and Dutch power was more marked before 1930 than after it; American power and influence were actually in the ascendant even as the US withdrew from formal empire.

Empire's end, though often fraught and in Indo-China tragic, was ultimately a catastrophe neither for the colonial powers nor for their erstwhile subjects. Barbarism did not ensue. On the contrary, in east and south-east Asia decolonisation triggered the most dramatic economic advances of the late twentieth century while in Europe the shared experience of colonial disengagement contributed to the momentum for a more peaceful, integrated and prosperous European community. In short, the 'Last Post' of empire sounded a retreat that was as welcome to the economies and the liberal consciences of the West as it was to the self-esteem and the nationalist ambitions of the East.

Nationalism plays a prominent part in the story of decolonisation in Asia, much more so than in, say, Africa. As empire-builders like Thomas Stamford Raffles had been at pains to point out, barbarism was no more a feature of the East's pre-colonial past than it would be of its post-colonial future. Places like Java, Cambodia and, of course, China boasted long and rich traditions of civilisation which, besides making a nonsense of the civilising mission sometimes assumed by the colonial powers, gave to these countries a ready-made focus of identity, and hence a sense of nationhood.

At the height of the Vietnam War American generals sometimes talked of 'bombing North Vietnam back to the Stone Age'. They were unaware that going back to the Stone Age was official policy in Hanoi. Improbably, North Vietnam, though experiencing desperate shortages, subject to the heaviest bombardment in history, and taking 10,000 casualties a month, still found the resources and personnel to fund an ambitious programme of archaeological research. Professor Cao Xuan Pho was then excavating the pre-historic Hoa Binh culture. His work, occasionally helped but more often hindered by US carpet bombing, went on regardless. As he recalled, even Ho Chi Minh acknowledged the importance of archaeological study.

> We were telling our people that they were going into war with 4,000 years of history behind them. What does this mean? It is a matter of tradition. We are poor, OK, desperate; but we have to divert some expenditure into archaeology to prove to our people that once we were an independent nation with a social organisation of our own and that after that we were oppressed by foreigners.

History in the case of Indonesia and geography in the case of Malaya and the Philippines served much the same purpose as archaeology in Vietnam. In varying degrees most of the peoples of the Far East had some pre-colonial claim to a nucleus of national pride and cohesion which awaited only a catalyst – economic collapse, world war, revolution, all of which were waiting in the wings – to excite mass support and become a righteous demand for national liberation.

No less important than nationalism in the anti-colonial equation, according to the Hanoi professor, was another feature shared by most of the peoples of the Far East. They all ate rice, a lot of it and not much else; and nearly all the rice was grown on irrigated land. Until the third millennium BC Vietnam's Stone Age people had lived in upland caves and knew nothing of irrigation.

> The sea then came up to Dien Bien Phu and the delta was inundated. But when the sea receded, the people came down to the plain and had to close ranks, to support one another and to work together to build an irrigation system for wet rice cultivation. So the first characteristic of our people is solidarity, the solidarity learnt from working together to clear, and make fertile with water, the land.

Constructing and operating a system of water management makes exceptional demands on the collective will of a community. The consequent tradition of peasant 'solidarity' is seen as a distinctive feature of most east and south-east Asian societies and, in Vietnam, as the bed-rock of resistance to both the French and the Americans. The enemy had more sophisticated weapons but, in Cao Xuan Pho's opinion, the Vietnamese had the more cohesive society 'which, in a people's war, is what counts'.

It was also, of course, a Communist society. Whether or not Marx had anything to teach the Vietnamese about solidarity, and whether or not one subscribes to the idea that Communist ideology, originally tailored to an industrial proletariat in Europe, found an Asian equivalent in the equally organised and exploited masses in the rice fields, the fact remains that in the Far East Communism was as much a part of the colonial challenge as nationalism.

This complicated the end of empire considerably. Scrutinising the fabric of anti-colonialism so as to distinguish strands of Communist ideology from those of nationalist resurgence would so obsess the imperial powers that their final hour seemed as much about Cold War containment as about sponsoring successor states. Initially in China and Malaya, and eventually in Indonesia, nationalists came out against the Communist challenge, but in Indo-China the strands proved indistinguishable and the US found itself in the anomalous position of waging a colonial war in defence of the free world.

The vigour of nationalism, then, and the wide appeal of Communism distinguished the process of decolonisation in the Far East from that elsewhere and considerably hastened empire's end. Additionally and crucially, the colonies of the Far East, though totally dissimilar and firmly rooted in the very different imperial cultures of France, the Netherlands, Great Britain and the USA, nevertheless underwent a common historical experience in the mid-twentieth century. All suffered from the worldwide depression of the 1930s, and all witnessed the defeat of their colonial overlords by the Japanese in the 1940s. The myth of colonial prosperity was wrecked by the depression; that of imperial invincibility was exploded by the war. Within weeks of Pearl Harbor the erstwhile master races were to be seen being marched off to prison camps in the midday sun, their bags and bundles slung about them, without a servant in sight.

Regaining their colonies would be as much about restoring pride as restoring empire. Indeed restoring anything looked to be a formidable challenge. The Japanese occupation, though a short and variable experience, had heightened Asian expectations of independence and in some cases provided a passing acquaintance with self-rule. An appetite for freedom, once whetted, demands to be satisfied. The colonial powers were welcomed back only in Malaya, rent by ethnic tension, the Philippines, to whose independence the US was already committed, and outlying areas of the Indonesian archipelago. Elsewhere the returning colonialists were either opposed, as in Vietnam and most of Indonesia, or greeted with indifference, as in Hong Kong where in any case British rule looked to be imminently doomed. As for Sarawak and North Borneo, their attitudes were uncertain and probably ambivalent; those twin constitutional dinosaurs, the corporate entity known as the British North Borneo Company and the family fief known as the 'White Raj' of Sarawak, had been casualties of the war; if their peoples resented the new colonial regime it was more from nostalgia for the feudal past than from expectations of an independent future.

Much had been changed by the war. It had betrayed the fragility of empire, bankrupted most of the imperial powers, stiffened the resolve of their colonial subjects to be rid of them, and provided these same subjects with powerful new sponsors in the USA, the USSR and the UN. It had also furnished new means of contact and communication which internationalised their struggle and which would, in the final analysis, make empire redundant.

Autopsies of empire, particularly by British writers for whom the subject is of great forensic interest, tend to focus on the shared experience of colonies scattered throughout the world. In that the entire British empire was wiped out in the space of a few decades, they understandably look for tell-tale lesions common to British colonial rule worldwide. Perhaps, for instance, the British electorate, enamoured of social spending at home, had come to recognise empire as an imposition, the *pax Britannica* as a 'tax Britannica'. Perhaps the failings of Britain's class-ridden society with its élitist educational system had finally betrayed the empire by precluding the innovative compromises that twentieth-century dominion demanded. Or perhaps reliance on the now largely obsolete concept of naval power had fatally reduced imperial clout.

These and many other causes for the demise of the British empire make good sense. But it was not only the British empire that succumbed in the space of a few decades. So did all the West's other colonial enterprises. There may, therefore, be some merit in dissecting not a particular empire but a particular arena of empire. Comparing the cadavers of British, Dutch, French and American empire in the Far East may focus attention on contributory causes of a regional nature and may reveal failures in the very concept of empire.

If there was one major surprise about decolonisation in the East it was the speed with which it came about. In the 1930s, although few expected empire to last indefinitely, a couple more generations still looked a safe bet. As late as 1950, with India, the Philippines and Indonesia already independent, Europeans and Asians in Malaya, Singapore, Vietnam and Borneo were still thinking in terms of decades rather than months. Decades, in the case of Hong Kong, would prove right; but for the rest it was as if some unforeseen force had taken over, depressing the accelerator of history and scattering empire to the winds.

The force in question seems to have been that cliché of the period, the 'revolution in communications'. Impossible to quantify and difficult to incorporate into a historical narrative, the twentieth century's catalogue of advances in long-distance transport, mass media and instantaneous communication would make the structures of formal empire look antiquated and superfluous. This applied, of course, throughout the world; but in the East the impact was particularly dramatic, partly because of the war and partly because of existing traditions of travel, trade and migration around the west Pacific rim.

The war brought to the East the whole paraphernalia of a modern communications infrastructure, something which to this day some parts of the once colonial world lack (notably most of sub-Saharan Africa). Malayan and Javanese villages received their first radio sets courtesy of Tokyo's propaganda effort. Airstrips were built, under both Allied and Japanese direction, in places which even now scarcely justify an air service. Roads and rail tracks, like the notorious 'death railways' of Sumatra and Siam, were carved through the jungle. Wharves, dockyards and ferries opened up whole archipelagoes in the Philippines.

And then came American *matériel*. Vehicles, ships and planes, radios, telephones and radar flooded the East courtesy of the US war effort and then continued coming under a variety of aid and reconstruction programmes. Whole airlines sprang into existence using superfluous US army transports and whole automotive industries were jump-started by the maintenance requirements of US army vehicles. Later a country like Laos, though still awaiting a television service, would find itself inundated with television receivers. South Vietnam's airports would briefly become the busiest in the world.

The ease of contact, and the ability to exert long-range influence which resulted, might have been superfluous elsewhere. Not so in the Far East. To the peoples of the west Pacific rim, the island-girt Java and South China Seas have always formed an integrated trading basin, like the Mediterranean, criss-crossed by routes of migration and exchange. Vietnamese, Malay, Bugis, Chinese, Indian and Arab navigators have travelled and traded within and beyond the region since 2000 BC. Their movements can be traced in the distribution of bronze, porcelain, spices, drugs and, above all, peoples. When Europeans first ventured round the Cape of Good Hope and across the Indian Ocean they blundered into a world of already thriving markets linked by sophisticated systems of travel and finance. They were duly impressed and, ostensibly there to participate in this trade, they augmented and eventually engrossed it.

The augmenting was as significant as the engrossing. Under colonial auspices new products and new markets brought a dramatic increase not only in the region's external trade but also in its internal trade. American emphasis on the 'Open Door' in China, British obsessions with free trade and free ports, and the inability of the Dutch to withhold free access to their island world in the Indies encouraged a highly competitive and uniquely open trading climate. Migration also boomed, especially of Chinese and Javanese labourers to the plantation economies of Malaya and Sumatra. The Chinese commercial networks which dominate the region today were as much a product of empire as the great European- and American-owned 'hongs' of the China coast.

Ascribing the Far East's late twentieth-century economic 'miracle' to the liberation of its peoples from the tentacles of empire may, therefore, be simplistic. There seems to be a continuum in the history of the East to which, albeit for its own purposes, empire substantially contributed. In this sense the white men did 'come and go leaving all things as they were'. And when they went, it was not because their empires had collapsed; like sailing ships and sealing wax they had simply become outdated. If there are those who still cannot listen dry-eyed to the 'Last Post', perhaps this narrative of empire's end in the Far East may help reconcile them to the pulse of history and so lay to rest the ghosts of places past.

PART ONE

Flying the Flag

1930

I

Lords of the East

Empires, like tides, flow and ebb at different times in different places. Globally the high-water mark of Western imperialism is usually put at around the year 1900, by which time Germany and the USA had joined the older imperial powers in pushing the white man's rule out into the blue wastes of the Pacific and deep into the heart of Africa's 'Dark Continent'. Seventy years earlier empire had scarcely lapped at these areas; seventy years later it had largely receded from them.

In the East, though, this timetable scarcely applied in that the whole cycle was much more protracted. Here the imperial tide had been running since the eighteenth century and remained in flood until 1930, the year when the story of empire's end begins. And the antecedents of eastern empire go back much further, to the late sixteenth century in the case of the Dutch and the British, and to the late seventeenth in the case of the French and the Americans. All four, moreover, had been preceded by the eastern empires of Spain and Portugal. The West's intervention in the East started early and lasted long. It was yet remarkably consistent, rising and falling on the same swell of commercial ambition and naval supremacy for hundreds of years.

That a search for markets resulted in the acquisition of dominions and that an obsession with sea power resulted in the creation of land-based empires may seem contradictory. How it happened, though, is important to an understanding both of empire in the East and of its demise. A longish perspective is essential. It alone reveals the limitations of empire and the regional continuities which may account for Asian resurgence.

The Portuguese, undisputed masters of east-west trade back in the sixteenth century, had largely avoided the complication of territorial responsibilities in the East (although not, of course, in the Americas and Africa). Following Vasco da Gama's pioneering voyage of 1497 from Lisbon to India, they had established a maritime empire which commanded the sea lanes from a chain of port-cities in the Persian Gulf, India and Malaya. Outside of these they rarely aspired to authority. When their maritime supremacy was overthrown by the Dutch, they thus quickly disappeared from the scene, lingering on only in the irrelevant enclaves of Goa, Macao and East Timor. As early as 1793 Lord Macartney, a British emissary in the East, could declare the Portuguese to 'have been long exanimated and dead in this part of world'.

The West's intervention had, nevertheless, begun with port-cities and, exactly five hundred years after da Gama's voyage, it would end with a port-city as the British relinquished Hong Kong. Like the Portuguese, the British had been wary of territorial responsibilities and remained so, disguising their dependencies under a variety of constitutional expedients. That they nevertheless made the transition from traders to empire-builders was largely due to the example of the Dutch in the East Indies.

The Netherlands, Europe's foremost sea power in the early seventeenth century, pioneered landward empire in the East. The East Indies, or today Indonesia, a 5,000-mile archipelago between the Asian mainland and Australia, includes three of the world's four largest islands (Borneo, Sumatra and New Guinea). Its considerable population is largely concentrated in the smaller islands of Java and Bali. And its original attraction to the Dutch, and previously to the Portuguese, lay in the even smaller 'spice islands', or Moluccas (Maluku), at the eastern extremity of the archipelago. Here, in groves of nutmeg and clove, were sown the seeds of Holland's empire. Sprouting and spreading prodigiously, they eventually smothered the whole archipelago, making the Netherlands East Indies the largest, the oldest, and the most profitable of the empires in the Far East. Latterly it was also the most vulnerable; and to all but Dutchmen, it was ever the least understood. Yet just as the East Indies were the first to succumb to the tide of empire, so they would be the first to re-emerge from it.

The Last Paradise

In 1928, while scouring a vicious world in search of somewhere free from avarice and exploitation, Hickman Powell, a disillusioned

American newspaperman, fetched up at Buleleng (Singaraja) on the north coast of the island of Bali. He was not impressed. Buleleng had been under direct Dutch rule for nearly a century; it was just another dull colonial port. It was nevertheless where André Roosevelt had taken up residence. Closely related to President Theodore Roosevelt and more distantly to soon-to-be-President Franklin Delano Roosevelt, the work-shy André was 'doing his best to live down the family's association with "the strenuous life"'. He took photographs, planned to make a movie, and owned a car. In the young Powell he recognised both a fellow drop-out and an able publicist. Together they drove south up into the mountain spine of the island.

As the tangled hillsides gave way to a grey volcanic wilderness, Roosevelt rambled on about the unique charms of Balinese culture. It must be preserved; 'Bali for the Balinese' was his motto. The Dutch must be persuaded to restrict access by tourists; the Balinese must be convinced that galvanised sheeting was not an aesthetically acceptable substitute for palm-thatch. Some sort of campaign, he thought, was needed. And in the tragically misguided belief that only international awareness could save an endangered society, he offered his contacts and his photographs if Powell would write the first ever book on Bali in English.

Meanwhile Powell's eyes were being opened by Bali itself. The cloud-mist thinned and the road began its tortuous descent; sunlight danced on a mirror-work of flooded paddy fields below. There was a tinkle of music on the breeze. Waterfalls tumbled into deep ravines where lissom brown bathers splashed and laughed. 'Chaste dryads in a tropic Arcady,' noted Powell. He saw a village woman with an earthenware pot on her head. She walked with sublime indifference and, as they passed, her shawl slipped carelessly from her shoulders, baring a young Balinese bosom. So the topless, or 'shirt-less', reputation of the island's womenfolk was not, after all, a traveller's fantasy. Powell's reservations about Bali and books were crumbling. 'The bronze bowls of her maiden breasts projected angular, living shadows,' he recalled.

All the carefree and exotic promise of an island Elysium seemed to be embodied in this woman. She was 'part of a vast spreading wonderland'. Those magnificent Balinese breasts, much photographed by Roosevelt and others, proclaimed incomparable fertility; her artless grace epitomised the ubiquitous aesthetic of a people for whom 'life is art'; and as for history, 'in her eyes', according to

Powell, 'burned the afterglow of fallen empires'. He was thinking, presumably, of the Javanese empire of Majapahit which had ruled Bali in the fifteenth century. More plausibly, if eyes really can reflect imperial conflagrations, hers shone not with some ancient afterglow but with the bright kindling of more immediate imperial bonfires. In the islands that comprised what would soon be Indonesia, the assault on colonial rule had already begun.

Seemingly unaware of this, Powell called his book on Bali *The Last Paradise*. With an introduction by André Roosevelt it was published in 1930 and became immensely popular, adding much in the way of romance and titillation to the established image of Bali as a repository of art and culture. A world rent by depressions and revolutions badly needed a new paradise myth, and in this island in the back of beyond it found it. Here art transcended dogma, and abundance obviated toil. Social tensions and sexual constraints were unknown; spontaneous communal bonds and all-pervading rituals alone modified personal liberty; only poverty and oppression were taboo.

'The Balinese are a very happy people' confirmed the usually waspish Geoffrey Gorer five years later. A dilettante Englishman and the author of a classic account of West Africa, he had come east immune to Powell's sentimentalism, indignant at the presumptions of colonialism and ready to exult over any evidence of falling empires. Instead he witnessed in Bali 'the nearest approach to Utopia that I am ever likely to see'. It was downright disorientating. Like the film-makers who would place Krakatoa *east* of Java, Gorer introduced Bali as being *west* of Java. Getting things wrong in the topsy-turvy lands on the other side of the world was all too easy. It was also easy to forget that these 'very happy people' laboured under what Gorer himself had decried as 'an overwhelming burden of crushing and continuous taxation which covers every part of their lives'.

By now, the mid-1930s, Bali's trickle of travellers was giving way to a flood of touring celebrities and jaded aesthetes. Like Roosevelt, Powell and Gorer, they readily subscribed to the paradise myth, oblivious of the contradiction that placed this heaven-on-earth in the midst of the most blatantly exploitative colonial empire in the Orient. It was a contradiction familiar to other colonialists in the Far East. Neither the French in Indo-China nor the British in Malaya or the Americans in the Philippines were indifferent to the romance of their surroundings. Even the Japanese would succumb; an Imperial officer dispatched to occupied Indonesia at the height of the Pacific

War would call it 'a passport to Paradise'. Exotic peoples, beguiling cultures and tropical profusion seduced them all and lent to a Far East posting a touch of glamour not to be found in Africa or India. Reconciling this allure with the stern business of empire could be a problem; reconciling it with the relinquishment of empire posed an even greater challenge.

According to Gorer, in 1934 the Dutch in the East Indies were already in a panic. In this sprawling archipelago of 14,000 islands lived more Muslims than anywhere else in the world except India. As waves of early twentieth-century Islamic modernism and revivalism broke on their shores, the religious became politicised and the politicised became nationalists.

Coincidentally Communism had also made its appearance. A Javanese Communist party had been founded as early as 1920 and in 1926–7, just a year before Powell's visit to Bali, Communist uprisings had flared in both Java and Sumatra. Prompt Dutch action suppressed them, but the religious awakening and the advent of ideological certainty continued to attract a population exposed to worsening commercial and agrarian conditions. By 1933 mass movements with pronounced nationalist agendas were being contained only by the summary arrest and deportation of their leaders. In the same year, in a widely publicised affair, the largely Indonesian crew of a Dutch naval cruiser mutinied in apparent sympathy with the nationalists. It seemed that Holland's naval power, the foundation on which her empire had been built, was vulnerable; and it was this incident which convinced Gorer that panic was already besetting the erstwhile 'Lords of the East'.

They stood to lose more than paradise. Not possessed of an extensive empire anywhere else in the world, and liable to profound humiliation whenever continental Europe erupted in another bout of conflict, the little Netherlands set immense store by their eastern possessions. Their investment in the region was proportionately much larger than that of any other colonial power and it had generally been much more profitable. More Dutchmen had made their home in the Indies than had Britons in Malaya, Hong Kong and north Borneo combined. And by 1930 the number of Dutch Eurasians, the result of mixed marriages, probably exceeded that of all other Eurasian pedigrees in the East. Only the Portuguese had intermarried so freely and only the Portuguese had been in the East for longer. But Portugal had long since ceased to rank as an imperial power. It was the Netherlands East Indies which in terms of its territorial extent, its population, its antiquity and its wealth, constituted the senior empire of the east.

'This Other India'

'We have ruled here for 300 years with the whip and the club,' declared Bonifacius de Jonge, the hard-line Governor-General at the time of Gorer's visit and the man responsible for the recent clampdown on the nationalists, 'and we shall be doing it for another 300 years.' Right about the accoutrements of authority, he was over-optimistic about its duration. It was true that a fleet of vessels from what was then the United Provinces (of the Netherlands) had first reached the archipelago in 1595. In Java they bought pepper and in Bali, a Hindu haven in a then rapidly Islamicising world, they duly scented paradise. Indeed the entire crew of one ship absconded, some of them for good. Thereafter Dutch skippers tended to give the island a wide berth. It was bad for morale; worse still, it produced no spices.

Affording profits of over 1,000 per cent, spices were what had brought the Dutch to the East. Although the first fleet returned only a modest profit, the possibility of obtaining a world monopoly of this sensational trade ensured a regular armada of vessels in subsequent years. To the same end in 1602 was formed the Vereenigde Oost-Indische Compagnie (United East India Company) which in the Moluccas, the 'spice islands', quickly took the offensive against both Portuguese incumbents and English rivals. The former were eliminated in 1605, the latter were dispersed by 1625 following a sustained offensive by Governor-General Jan Pieterzoon Coen. Coen, a scruple-free oppressor of whom de Jonge heartily approved, is the man usually credited with having founded the Dutch empire. Hence the '300 years' of Dutch rule. To make his Company's monopoly of clove and nutmeg production smuggler-proof, Coen was also pleased to assert direct control over some of the spice-producing islands. On others, with a view to maintaining prices, he forcibly eliminated both spice production and spice producers.

Like the Portuguese, whose example was closely followed, the Vereenigde Oost-Indische Compagnie (VOC) tailored its political responsibilities to the requirements of its trade. Throughout the seventeenth century and most of the eighteenth Holland's territorial 'empire' in the Indies was effectively limited to a scatter of forts in the Moluccas, plus a string of ports flanking the Java Sea. From these, thanks to its naval supremacy, the VOC could police the shipping of the archipelago and protect the corridor leading to the Moluccas. The ports, each commanded by a fortress and its garrison, stretched from the Malay peninsula's Malacca (captured from the Portuguese in 1641) to south Sulawesi's Makassar (captured with local assistance in 1666) and so to Ambon in the heart of the Moluccas. Along with their connecting sea lanes they comprised, in effect, the bones of empire; but as yet the skeleton lacked both flesh and muscle. Normally the small Dutch garrisons were in no position to foist VOC rule on the hinterlands; often their forts were more places of refuge than springboards for aggression.

There was, however, an exception. On the north coast of the island of Java, the port-city of Jayakarta (Jakarta) had in 1619 been destroyed by Coen during the course of his vendetta against the English and their local allies. He then selected the site as the VOC's eastern headquarters. It was renamed Batavia and, as the administrative and commercial centre of the archipelago's new maritime masters, it grew rapidly. Malay and Chinese traders flocked to the low-lying estuary which flanked its port. Dutch renegades and retired VOC servants stayed on to savour its opportunities for private initiative. Naturally the VOC's administrative costs spiralled; so did the city's dependence on the rice, timber and labour of its Javanese neighbours.

Unwittingly the Company thus invited political complications in Java that were not directly connected with the spice trade. Siting a large and thriving Dutch city on the most heavily populated and volatile island in the archipelago was asking for trouble. It was as provocative as, somewhat later, the English East India Company's choice of Calcutta as its Indian headquarters. Java and Bengal had much in common. Both seethed with dynastic rivalries; successions were invariably contested; adventurers and mercenaries waited to take their chance. But the prospect of these contending parties uniting against the newcomer, however alien and infidel, could safely be discounted; more often they vied for the newcomer's favours since, better led and better drilled, European troops enjoyed a tactical superiority.

The VOC's century of involvement in Java's dynastic tussles, from 1670 to 1770, also paralleled that of the English Company in India.

Early endeavours to defend Batavia and its trade served only to destabilise neighbours; the search for more stable, that is amenable, neighbours necessitated still wider political commitments; and the more ambitious these commitments, the more insistent the Company's demand for commensurate compensation and the more extravagant its servants' expectations of personal enrichment. Military expeditions seldom involved more than a few hundred Dutch troops who were invariably deployed on behalf of supposedly grateful native protégés. But in a pattern familiar to all rising coloni-alisms, each round of hostilities elicited further concessions and indemnities, the realisation of which necessitated a further assertion of authority.

Substantial territorial gains did result. They included the Priangan, or highlands, of west Java plus a narrow strip running the length of the island's populous north coast and embracing all its major port-cities from Bantam (Banten) and Batavia (Jakarta) to Semarang and Surabaya. Together these acquisitions represented something between a third and a quarter of the total island and, along with the Moluccas and that string of ports, constituted the maximum extent of VOC rule. Though sometimes called 'the first Dutch empire' in the Indies, this was a modest affair compared with the second. Sumatra, Borneo and New Guinea formed no part of it. Neither did the remaining two-thirds of Java, most of Sulawesi (the Celebes) and all of Bali, Lombok and the stepping-stone islands of the south-east (excluding an outpost in West Timor).

Arguably the VOC's informal, or commercial, reach was more significant and extensive than its territorial holdings. A trading company should, after all, be judged by the places where it can profitably trade rather than by the acres it reluctantly administers. But herein lay the real failure of the Company. For by 1770 profits from the spice trade had dramatically declined. Far from being poised on the threshold of empire, the VOC, thanks also to the expenses of its Java policy and the legendary corruption of its servants, faced imminent bankruptcy.

It was delayed only by the political turmoil in Europe when in 1795 the Netherlands succumbed to republican France. The British, at war with France, promptly appropriated the Moluccas and the other outlying Dutch establishments in the Indies. Three years later the VOC was duly declared insolvent in one of the most spectacular bankruptcies of all time. Its responsibilities were assumed by the government of what was now the 'Batavian Republic'. To head this puppet state Louis Bonaparte, the younger brother of Napoleon, was appointed in 1806. He in turn appointed Herman Willem Daendels, 'the Iron Marshal', as Governor-General of the Indies.

Pruned by the British so that it now consisted simply of the VOC's Java territories, it was a colony which Daendels inherited rather than a trading empire, and he proceeded to treat it as such. Local recruitment more than quadrupled the size of the army; new roads, including a Grand Trunk Road running the length of the island, were constructed; Batavia was rebuilt; the troublesome neighbours of old, relieved of more territory, were reduced to feudatory status; and a barrage of reforms was designed to transform the native bureaucracy into an effective colonial administration.

These reforms had barely taken effect when Anglo-French hostilities prompted a further British move to deprive the Batavian Republic, and so Napoleon, of its remaining, possibly menacing, outpost in the East. Organised from Calcutta by the English East India Company, an expeditionary force was assembled at Malacca and duly overran Dutch Java in 1811. The occupation lasted six years during which Thomas Stamford Raffles, as the English Company's Lieutenant-Governor for Java, identified closely with the island. His wild predictions of its economic potential, his bold offensives, grandiose reform programmes and generous recognition of Java's cultural distinction were designed to discredit Dutch rule and so make an unanswerable case for the indefinite British retention of what he called 'this other India'. It was not to be. Napoleon's defeat at Waterloo ended French influence in the Netherlands and so removed the only good reason for the British occupation of Java. Averse to further territorial commitments and aware that British commercial interests could be well served without them, London ordered the restoration of all Dutch possessions in the East.

In retrospect it was the ease of the Anglo-Indian conquest and the reluctance with which Javanese levies fought for their Dutch masters that were most revealing about this episode. It was beyond Holland's capacity to defend even Java against an outside aggressor, never mind the rest of the sprawling archipelago. So it remained throughout the next century and a half of Dutch rule. Here was an empire which could survive only with the connivance of other imperial powers. In due course Tokyo would take note. So would Indonesia's nationalists. One who had the measure of his opponents in the independence struggle was Sutan Sjahrir, first prime minister of the future republic.

> [Since the nineteenth century] the Dutch have remained in our country not on the basis of their strength but by favour of the English on whose policies they have been wholly dependent . . . Dutch power has been a pawn in the political chess-game that the British have been playing.

It was no surprise that, soon after this diagnosis, Indonesian nationalists would find themselves fighting the bloodiest battle of their 'freedom struggle' not against Dutch troops but against the British.

No such direct British intervention had been necessary in the century since Raffles. Under the spreading parasol of the *pax Britannica*, epitomised by the masts and funnels that filled the anchorages of Raffles' post-Java foundation at Singapore, the Dutch across the Malacca Strait enjoyed a sheltered existence. It meant making concessions. Coen's vision of sealing the Indies so that their sea lanes became Dutch waterways was doomed. There could be no more monopolies of the archipelago's trade nor, later, of its cash-crop plantations. Singapore would replace Batavia as south-east Asia's entrepôt. The Royal Navy would assume the role of protector of the Indies. And should Britannia's parasol, faded and frayed with time, be whisked away by an errant typhoon, fair Dutch skins would suffer. Isolated from the competitive uncertainties of mainland Asia and hence regarded with an often patronising indulgence by the other colonial powers, the senior empire in the East was also its most dispensable.

Adjusting to their role as colonisers rather than maritime traders, in the 1820s the Dutch completed their conquest of Java. They also began to assert their authority in parts of the outer islands. Creation of the second Dutch empire, less ambitious as to sea power but more so as to territory, was under way. An 1824 agreement with the British saw the Dutch surrender all claims on the Malay peninsula (including Malacca) in return for British withdrawal from Sumatra. The Dutch in effect were to be given a free hand in the archipelago. Sumatra's numerous sultanates were laboriously subdued, annexed or conquered between 1820 and 1900. A similar process of piecemeal acquisition brought most of Sulawesi and the coastal areas of much of Borneo under indirect Dutch rule. And in 1846–9 offensives on the north coast of Bali gave them a toe-hold in paradise.

Raffles, during his brief rule in Java, had also visited north Bali. The island's main exports he reported as pigs and female slaves, both in great demand amongst the wealthy Chinese and European communities now settled in Batavia and other Javanese ports. Slaves were plentiful because the Balinese kingdoms were in a state of constant civil war. Raffles was not minded of paradise. But he did, as both scholar and imperialist, investigate the island's Hindu credentials, portraying it as a valuable archive of ancient Indic traditions and so naturally susceptible to rule by those who best understood Hindu subjects, namely the British.

The Dutch assault on north Bali in 1846–9 was designed partly to scotch any such ambitions by Raffles' successors; and in this it succeeded. But battles were lost, casualties were heavy and only the northern kingdom of Buleleng was effectively subjugated. There cash crops like coffee were introduced, although never on a scale to justify the full paraphernalia of Dutch economic exploitation. Instead of European planters, Buleleng was opened to European missionaries and scholars. The rest of the island was left to stew in its rich cultural juices, enjoying the secluded status of a timeless, and topless, reservation. Miraculously preserved from the strictures of Islam, the teeming kingdoms of south Bali were now spared the rod of colonialism. Romantics like André Roosevelt would look back to this time as the golden age of Bali. It would last only fifty years and end in a cataclysm of violence which, however unexceptionable it might have been in the nineteenth century, would challenge the colonial conscience of the twentieth century.

How to Manage a Colony

Elsewhere in the archipelago, and especially in Java, economic priorities dictated more consistent intervention. In the eighteenth century, as the importance of spices declined, new crops had been tried. Coffee, mostly grown in the west Javan Priangan, soon showed a handsome return and so did sugar from central and east Java. The problem facing the colonial government was how to assert the tight control exercised over the production of spices in respect of the more scattered production of these much bulkier crops. Only by regulating supply and monopolising export would it be possible to turn them to national account and so restore profitability.

As it happened, this ambitious turnaround was achieved with such speed and success that it became the envy of other colonial powers. In spite of further war in Java (1825–30), by 1831 the colonial budget had been balanced. Soon after that, the 35.5 million guilders of debt accumulated by the VOC were paid off and by 1860 the Indies were providing almost a third of the Netherlands' state revenues. By 1877 it was estimated that Holland had benefited from its Far Eastern empire to the tune of an amazing 832 million guilders in 45 years. 'These revenues kept the domestic Dutch economy afloat,' notes the historian M. C. Ricklefs, 'debts were redeemed, taxes reduced, fortifications, waterways and the Dutch state railway built, all on the profits forced out of the villages of Java.'

Other colonial powers agonised over distractions like the strategic importance of their possessions in a global scheme of defence and trade. They promoted the idea of their colonies as vital export markets for the manufactures of their domestic industries, and they muddied their colonial accounts with a host of invisible and unquantifiable considerations. Conscious of the self-evident superiority of their own civilisations, they also acknowledged a moral responsibility to impart to their colonial subjects some appreciation of their religious beliefs, social ethics and cultural achievements. Thus a minor Vietnamese functionary who went to Mass, took the occasional Pernod and hankered after Paris represented a greater asset to France than whatever his ancestral lands might yield in the way of taxes. Empire was a complex equation; it was not susceptible to the simple profit-and-loss calculations of farm accounts.

The Dutch disagreed. For them the Indies meant just that, farming. Empire, shorn of imperial responsibilities, became essentially an agricultural enterprise. Subject territories were reckoned in *bouws* (that is, acreage) of forest and of wet and dry *sawah* (rice fields); subject peoples were the labour pool which, like water rights, came with the fields and were essential to their working. While colonial governments elsewhere liked to think of empire as an exercise in tutelage, partnership or, as in the Philippines, even brotherhood, the government of the Netherlands East Indies saw it simply as an exercise in resource management. Hence, and perfectly logically, in 1829 Johannes van den Bosch had formulated and, as Governor-General, soon implemented not an administrative system but a 'Cultivation System', the notorious Cultuurstelsel.

Ostensibly this changed the heritable burden on agricultural lands from a cash rent to an equivalent 'set-aside' of both labour and land.

The time and land so set aside were to be used for producing a commercial crop designated by the government and delivered to it in lieu
of rent. Thus the village would continue to be self-supporting while
contributing to the cash-crop economy, and thus the state would
acquire marketable produce at minimal cost plus the desired control
over its supply and its export. It was a sensible and ingenious solution and in the likes of A. R. Wallace, the great English naturalist who
explored the archipelago in the 1860s, it won the approval of a disinterested observer.

From another visitor of the same period, the Calcutta-born
Englishman J. W. B. Money, it won even more extravagant praise.
Money's *Java or How to Manage a Colony* regarded the system as a colonial panacea and strongly recommended it to the British authorities
in India. It would benefit the government but, equally important, it
made for contented subjects. Natives did not want rights, regulations
and means of redress. They wanted a chance to prosper and that was
precisely what the system offered in that it guaranteed the purchase
of any surplus. It also thus encouraged the circulation of money, said
Money, and so improved native purchasing power. Although these
views never found favour amongst the British in India, they seem to
have appealed to their fellow countrymen in China. In Hong Kong,
then and for a hundred years thereafter, the received wisdom held
that the local people were interested only in making money and that
they would willingly forego rights and representation so long as the
currency was strong and the market open.

Re-examination of the Cultivation System as practised in the
Indies has tended to support Money's optimism. It did usher in the
cash economy; its success eventually convinced the colonial government to accord a higher priority to the well-being of the cultivator;
and some Javanese did prosper. But more starved; and the pattern of
repeated famines and migrations cannot simply be swept under the
carpet of rapid population growth. In practice the land rent was
seldom abolished while the quota for set-aside labour was arbitrarily
increased. To minimise administrative costs, the government farmed
out its operation to 'Regents' or local aristocrats who in turn
co-opted district and village headmen. Each was entitled to a
commission on the produce collected and so had a vested interest in
maximising, by fair means or foul, the burden on the peasantry.

To a disgruntled Dutch official like Edward Douwes Dekker,
author (as 'Multatuli') of the influential novel *Max Havelaar* which

exposed the iniquities of the system, the obligation to work for no return looked much like forced labour and the obligation to render specified produce looked much like forced deliveries. The Cultivation System thus bore an uncanny resemblance to the much disparaged expedients associated with the VOC's rule. But whereas the VOC's operations had extended only to the Moluccas and latterly to the Priangan, the Cultuurstelsel affected all Java and soon spread beyond. There were wide local variations but overall it had the effect of destroying rural initiative, entrenching authoritarian attitudes and reducing a vast population to a state indistinguishable from rural bondage.

A Nation of Coolies

Such was the unlikely setting for the world's 'last paradise'. 'The Dutch', declared André Roosevelt in words faithfully echoed by the young Hickman Powell, 'are the greatest of colonialists.' It was not a criticism. Americans, like the Englishmen Wallace and Money, generally approved of Dutch rule. Even President Franklin Roosevelt, whose Second World War rhetoric would do more than anyone's to undermine French and British colonialism, was unusually restrained on the subject of Dutch rule. That the Roosevelts, whose ancestors had settled in New York when it was still New Amsterdam, were themselves of Dutch colonial descent, may be relevant.

André, of course, would have claimed that his beloved Bali was quite different from the rest of the Netherlands Indies; and FDR would have snorted that conditions had improved dramatically since the days of the Cultivation System. Both were right. Yet Bali, an integral part of the Netherlands East Indies by the 1930s, was no longer that different; and until the end, the Dutch empire remained essentially an agricultural enterprise, ill-equipped to effect the redress of social grievances, however desirable, let alone to negotiate political freedoms.

Edward Douwes Dekker's objective – 'protection of the Javanese against the rapacity of his Chiefs in complicity with a corrupt Dutch administration' – remained elusive long after the bombshell of his *Max Havelaar*. Indeed it remains doubtful whether the embittered Dekker would have been satisfied even with the concessions of the twentieth century. 'It must be emphasised that the effects of the Company and Cultivation systems were not transitory,' wrote the

Cornell historian George Kahin in 1952. 'They were strongly in evidence until the end of Dutch rule in early 1942 and are still very much felt today.' To them may be ascribed that reputation for supine submission which prompted a Dutchman to call Indonesia 'a nation of coolies and a coolie among nations' and which obliged even Sukarno to chide his followers as 'a bean-curd people'.

The Cultivation System was dismantled piecemeal from about 1860 onwards. In a rare but significant example of intervention by the home government, pressure came from an occasionally liberal parliament in the Netherlands which was as keen to oblige private entrepreneurs by abolishing state monopolies as it was to alleviate the burden on Java's peasant farmers. Not used to such directives, the Batavian authorities responded sluggishly. The first crops to be freed from the system were spices which had become an irrelevance ever since both the French and the British had successfully broken the Indies monopoly before and during the Napoleonic Wars. Forced deliveries of sugar-cane did not end until the 1880s and of coffee, long the most lucrative crop of all, not until 1919. Forced labour, on the other hand, though progressively reduced and increasingly directed towards public works, remained a feature of many areas outside Java until 1942. In the end it took the occupying Japanese, with their unrivalled genius for antagonising potential allies, so to extend and exploit the system as to discredit it irredeemably.

The years 1870–1900 in the Netherlands East Indies are sometimes characterised as 'the liberal period'. The term is used purely in an economic sense and does not imply social liberalisation. It meant simply that state monopolies were dismantled in favour of private European ownership while some attempt was made to reform and standardise the administrative system. These changes coincided with an uncertain period for Java's sugar and coffee; but Dutch colonial history being essentially about crop management, alternatives were quickly found. Tobacco, then palm oil and rubber, transformed large tracts of Sumatra and Borneo into plantation economies; many were managed by Singapore-based companies and all depended on bonded labour imported from China and Java.

The dismal conditions in north-east Sumatra, where Medan became the focus of a late nineteenth-century tobacco bonanza that was south-east Asia's nearest equivalent to a gold rush, rivalled those anywhere in the colonial world. 'Men died like flies,' wrote Ladislao

Székely of the clearance programme necessary to transform virgin forest into virginia leaf; 'the fit ones cleared away the dead and continued the life-and-death struggle'. Székely had heard of the bonanza in his native Budapest and gambled all on a voyage to Medan. He found unimaginable brutality, described it in appalling detail, yet stayed on long enough to acquire the expected reward.

Apologists emphasise that to their credit the Dutch made no attempt to institutionalise a 'white settler' economy. Land for plantations could be leased by Europeans but never acquired outright. In law native rights were respected and racial presumption was not a major irritant. With the Indonesian élite heavily involved in the worst manifestations of colonial rule there was little risk of the clash of interests between Dutch settlers and indigenous peoples that occurred in South Africa and spawned apartheid. Travelling in Java in the 1930s, the Dutch scholar J. C. van Leur was horrified by the deference shown to a *tuan*, 'a lord'.

> I've been in regions where I rode as a knight on horseback down the road, followed by Javanese officials on foot and on horseback; all other traffic I met would stop; everyone bared his head, many squatted alongside the road . . . when you arrive the entire village goes along with you; eighty people Indian file behind you; when you stop you are the only one standing; everybody else squats on the ground.

But, as van Leur noted, this deference was to the pallor not of his skin but of his uniform. The colonialist's high-buttoned white suit, the 'stengah-shifter' of Malaya, had become the symbol of a cold and awesome authoritarianism which was proving as disastrous for the 'Tuans of the East' as for their downtrodden subjects.

A Question of Honour

Wars being a costly distraction from the business of crop management, the Dutch had acquired their second empire with minimal military expenditure. Few territories had been conquered outright and none without substantial local assistance. Scarcely a land battle worthy of the name enlivens the annals of Dutch colonialism. Moreover, since defence had ceased to be a serious option, there was no need for a large standing army. The KNIL, the Royal Netherlands Indies Army, was recruited from peripheral and long-Christianised areas like the Moluccas, north Sulawesi and parts of Java. It was deemed a modest and effective peace-keeping force but not a formidable instrument of colonial aggression.

That, however, was the role it came to play as the Dutch, emboldened by their imperial ranking and seduced by the deference of their subjects, finally extended their authority to the extremities of the archipelago at the end of the nineteenth century. There were usually good local reasons for intervention – removing an autocratic anomaly here, quashing a piratical trouble-maker there. But in the 1880s, in the context of the world-wide scramble for colonies, especially in Africa, this expansion was also a precaution against outside intervention. Even if the Netherlands could no longer monopolise the wealth of the Indies, they must monopolise their territory. Indeed it was suspicions of desultory British and then American interest in the northern tip of Sumatra which induced the first assault on its still independent sultanate of Aceh (Acheh, Acheen) in 1873.

It was not the last assault. The war, or wars, with Aceh dragged on for a good thirty years, providing the KNIL with by far the sternest test it would ever face. Ten thousand troops, the largest expedition ever mounted in the Indies, incurred appalling casualties and failed to dent the resolve of the fiercely Islamic Acehnese. Reinforcements were summoned, an elaborate network of defences and communications constructed. Yet an assessment of 1881 which declared the war conclusively won – 'one of the most fanciful pronouncements of colonialism' according to M. C. Ricklefs – served only to transform feudal and ethnic resistance into an anti-colonial *jihad*. Sympathy for the Acehnese extended from Penang and Singapore to London and Washington, and throughout the Islamic world. Suddenly the Dutch in the Indies, so seldom challenged and so apparently successful, were revealed as scarcely less oppressive than their French counterparts in Indo-China.

An expensive policy of conciliating moderate Islamic opinion and buying off the feudal aristocracy eventually brought to Aceh an uneasy peace in 1903. Two years later it was the turn of Sulawesi, a vast and neglected island which cartographers, under the misapprehension that it was in fact an archipelago, still called 'The Celebes'. Here a series of bloody engagements and military sweeps between 1905 and 1907 ended the independence of the proud Bugis, Makassarese and Toraja peoples. Dutch rule, hitherto limited to a southern enclave round Makassar (Ujung Pandang) and a northern one round Manado, was extended deep into the island's interior and then out to its flailing extremities.

That left just Bali. The final act in the drama of Dutch colonial expansion looked like being a formality. So bitter were the rivalries between the handful of petty rajahs who lorded it over south Bali's crowded rice terraces that a united resistance was unthinkable. Cowed by the Dutch defeat of Balinese forces in neighbouring Lombok in 1894, the squabbling princelings pursued their flower-strewn vendettas with a frantic abandon that further divided their minuscule states and provoked their scandalised Dutch neighbours at Buleleng. It was as if, far from oblivious of impending disaster, they were anxious only to settle all outstanding scores and leave no theme unplayed before the final curtain.

In 1906 an inflated Dutch claim for compensation in respect of a wrecked and plundered schooner provided the pretext for intervention. The rajah of Badung (Denpasar), whose subjects were held responsible, loftily dismissed the claim. 'It was a very small amount of money, about 7,500 guilders,' according to Dr Ide Anak Agung Gde Agung, the last rajah of neighbouring Gianyar. 'But, you see, the prince of Badung found it unjust. He thinks "I have no reason to pay you Dutch." So only for $700 there was a quarrel.'

At Sanur, now a tourist beach, where the schooner had grounded, KNIL artillery, infantry and cavalry began disembarking from troop carriers. The Balinese offered no resistance. Badung seemed deserted but smoke was seen rising from the palace as the expedition converged upon it down dusty streets which muffled the tramp of boots and the clatter of waggons and guns.

> It was a question of his [the rajah of Badung's] honour, you see. He thought 'I don't like to be put under pressure by these Dutch people; I like better to die.' So he marched out through the gates of his *puri* [palace], you see, followed by all his court, his wives, his sons, his nephews, his cousins, everybody dressed in white and the ladies with flowers in their hair as if they were going to a temple festival. And music and drums. And they marched through the gates. And the Dutch thought this is some kind of procession. But instead of a procession to the temple, they marched into the fusillades of the Dutch forces. Everybody was killed. And he who wasn't killed, killed himself. This is *puputan*, the ending.

Over a thousand died at Badung. At nearby Pemacutan the awesome ritual was repeated, then again at Klungkung, home of the most exalted rajah. The whole of Bali was overrun by 1908. As the cream of its ancient aristocracy fell to the grape-shot of the KNIL artillery and the self-administered thrusts of bejewelled Balinese daggers, the island's cherished independence was finally extinguished.

But to Balinese like Dr Ide, all was not lost. The *puputan* had been a triumph, 'an unbelievable expression of defending one's honour'. To the limpid notes of the royal gamelan the old order went out in a blaze of glory which dramatically enhanced Bali's cultural self-image. It also went out in a blaze of publicity which inflamed international opinion. News reports of unarmed priests and demure princesses offering themselves for slaughter 'shocked private citizens, religious groups and governments from The Hague to London, Paris and New York' according to the American historian Willard Hanna. Worse still, the carnage was captured on film. Through the smoke of battle KNIL gunners in their slouch hats were seen crouched beside the spoked wheels of their field pieces in what looked like scenes from the Boer War. Their adversaries, gaily dressed and blood-spattered, lay strewn about the palace lawns as if stricken in the midst of a garden party; the rajah's gilded palanquin stood empty nearby; troopers rummaged through the tangle of raven hair and golden limbs for jewelled heirlooms and silken souvenirs.

Such scenes probably provoked as much revulsion against colonialism as any other incident in the twentieth century. The Dutch authorities stood accused of grotesquely overreacting to a minor provocation and of betraying their colonial trust. They responded by protesting that the carnage was self inflicted and that the Balinese had been given every encouragement to surrender peacefully. But even Batavian consciences were now troubled.

The cumulative effect of diatribes like Dekker's, exposés like Székely's, unease over the Aceh and Sulawesi wars and continued agrarian unrest in Java was at last beginning to tell. In 1899 a distinguished Dutch lawyer had advanced the novel argument that in return for their contribution to the Dutch economy, Holland owed the peoples of the Indies what he called 'a debt of honour'. Enquiries were set up and with the 1909 appointment as Governor-General of Alexander Idenberg, previously a reform-minded Minister for Colonies in The Hague, Dutch colonialism abruptly disowned the habits of Company and Cultuurstelsel to embrace an 'Ethical Policy'. Indonesian intellectuals, like the outstanding novelist Pramoedya Ananta Toer, hailed a new dawn.

[Idenberg] descended on the Indies like a prince from the heavens, relaxed and as if without a care in the world. He had a big heart and his brain was full of a million plans for humanitarian improvement . . . The [preceding] epoch of triumphant cheers of victory, and of the tormented wailing of defeat disappeared like a thief scuttling off to find his own grave.

It was somehow typical of Holland's single-minded approach to empire that ethical considerations were so belatedly entertained and then so proudly proclaimed. Typical too that, rather than being a spontaneous reaction to conditions in the *kampung* (villages) or to casualties in the field, they took the form of a series of carefully drafted directives from above.

Public health programmes, rural credit schemes and irrigation projects were given a high priority under the Ethical Policy. Yet they proved difficult to implement amongst a cowed and dislocated population suspicious of its local hierarchies and predisposed to shun Dutch initiatives. Nor was it obvious to their Dutch employers that change was needed. Ten years into the 'ethical' era, Richard Winstedt, a visitor from British Malaya, found things much as they had been under the Cultuurstelsel.

Java in 1916 was the Java of sugar-kings, of free gin in the hotels and of mountainous *rijst-tafel* ['rice-tables', gargantuan curry buffets]. The value of sugar exported was nearly four times that of rubber. The development of planting and the wages paid had increased the purchasing power of the Javanese and of the local Dutch till the value of exports by 1920 was to be nearly ten times as great as it had been in 1900 . . . There were more than crumbs for the natives from this rich man's table. Not yet had the Dutch come to worry about communism, and adverse balances, about over-production or over-eating, and not yet had prosperity led to much change in old colonial habits.

Education, another 'ethical' priority, was more successful. As elsewhere, though, it tended to create greater expectations than either the schools, the job market or the political system could satisfy. Students typically became teachers, teachers typically became nationalists. The Ethical Policy contained the seeds of its own destruction. It was also too late. Japan had already pioneered an Asian form of resurgence; Filipino revolutionaries had rejected Spanish rule; Sun Yat-sen's nationalist revolution was getting under-way in China. 'The times', wrote Pramoedya Ananta Toer, 'were choosing their own direction, buffeting [the Governor-General's] humanitarian face like a stalking whirlwind. It was hard, hard for Idenburg . . .'

He managed, however, to rescue the Balinese. 'Ethical' remorse over events there secured for the island the privilege of lenient rule and minimal interference. 'The scar on the liberal imagination of the Netherlands produced by the massacres', writes Adrian Vickers, an Australian authority on Balinese culture, 'had to be healed, and the preservation of Balinese culture, in combination with tourism, were the most effective balms for the healing process.'

An eccentric philologist, H. N. van der Tuuk, had pioneered Balinese studies in the late nineteenth century. Amongst his disciples F. A. Liefrinck anticipated 'ethical' indulgence by exalting the supposedly democratic nature of traditional Balinese villages while Dr Julius Jacobs is credited by Vickers as being 'the man who discovered the Balinese female breast'. About bare breasts and other manifestations of Bali's lack of sexual taboos Jacobs wrote at length; and the word spread. By 1914 KPM, the inter-island shipping line, was issuing Bali's first tourist brochure and anticipating the paradise tag.

> You leave this island with a sigh of regret
> And as long as you live you can never forget
> This Garden of Eden.

The First World War then intervened. Though Holland stayed neutral and the Indies were little affected, tourism had to wait. It was the publication in 1920 of Dr Gregor Krause's *Bali*, written in German but lavishly illustrated with photographs of Balinese physiques, that alerted early visitors. Amongst them were the American André Roosevelt and the German Walter Spies who would succeed Roosevelt as the island's unofficial impresario during the 1930s. KPM opened the first luxury hotel in 1925 and the first movies were shot in Bali in 1926–7. Celebrity was assured; the *puputan* was exorcised; paradise beckoned. Access and imagery, the twentieth century's twin catalysts of change, had worked their magic.

A Faint Glow

The ease and speed of twentieth-century communications and the immediacy and emotive power of its media imagery are fundamental to the story of imperial eclipse. KPM was complemented by KLM whose intercontinental air services also began in the 1920s. Contemporary imaginations were as exercised by the photos of bare-breasted Balinese belles as, later, they would be by those of the napalm-scorched waifs of Vietnam; those grainy scenes on Badung's untidy lawns anticipated the lurid chaos of Tiananmen Square. In a cheap berth and an oriental pin-up there could lie as much revolutionary potential as in an 'ethical' manifesto, or in a nationalist diatribe.

To assist him in his work, H. N. van der Tuuk, the father of Balinese studies, had used the part-time services of Sukemi, a teacher from Java who was working in Buleleng. This man married a Balinese and in 1901 their marriage was blessed with the birth of a son. They called him Kusno Sosro Sukarno. As plain Sukarno, the future president would retain a soft spot for his mother's homeland and eventually do much to enhance Bali's international popularity. In the meantime he had other interests.

It was as if the Ethical Policy had been introduced specially for him. Benefiting from its educational openings he secured one of the few places now available to natives in a Dutch-language secondary school. The school was in Surabaya, Indonesia's second city, where he boarded with a family friend who happened to be chairman of an organisation which the Ethical Policy had made possible. This was Sarekat Islam, originally a commercial pressure group but since 1912 committed to a varied agenda and acting as a mass movement umbrella for a host of other interests, religious, nationalist and Communist. It was like lodging with the Nehru family in the early days of India's Congress Party. The house was the hub of nationalist debate and Sukarno's political apprenticeship had begun.

It continued, after 1921, in Bandung in west Java where he studied engineering, developed his skills as an inspirational if long-winded demagogue, and formulated a revolutionary credo. Though heavily influenced by Marxist theory, Javanese mysticism and Islamic solidarity, this gave primacy to secular nationalism and the anti-colonial struggle. Unlike many of his gifted contemporaries, Sukarno had not taken advantage of the new opportunities for attending a university in Holland. 'The ship which will carry us to free Indonesia is the ship of unity', he declared.

Sarekat Islam had just split with the Communists whose subsequent risings in Java and Sumatra had been easily crushed by the Dutch authorities. The struggle demanded a sinking of such sec-

tional and ideological interests and to this end Sukarno's newly
formed PNI (Indonesian National Party) forged a broad alliance
across the political spectrum. Under the now assured leadership of
the one man who harboured no doubts about either Indonesia's
future or his own ability to achieve it, the PNI grew in stature and
numbers. By 1929, strengthened by the first batch of intellectuals
returning from Dutch universities, it was demanding full independence. Non-cooperation was being applauded, strikes encouraged. The authorities decided that they had seen enough. 'Ethical' or
not, Sukarno was arrested.

His trial was held in late 1930. Just as Hickman Powell's book was
announcing 'the last paradise', Sukarno was delivering from the dock
a damning indictment of its colonial setting. In a two-day harangue
he made sure that it was capitalist imperialism, not the leader of the
PNI, that stood accused. If his party was associated with unrest it
was because unrest was the people's inevitable response to exploitation and colonial injustice. 'The people's movement is the product of
the people's suffering,' he declared. It was the same all over the
world. But in India and China, the Philippines and Japan the
exploited masses were at last rousing from their slumber. So was the
Indonesian nation. A nationalist organisation like the PNI was
merely the creature of this awakening, not its creator. 'The sun does
not rise because the cock crows; the cock crows because the sun
rises.' A rosy-fingered future beckoned; according to Sukarno, paradise, far from sinking astern, lay full ahead.

> Today Indonesia's future is discernible only as a faint glow, like the gentle
> light of daybreak. We can just hear the promise it holds, like the melody of
> a distant gamelan on a moonlit night ... We hear a promise that millions
> worth of income will not be drained off to another country. We hear the
> promise of a life for our people that will be happy and safe, of social ben-
> efits which will meet and fulfil our needs, of an open and democratic
> system of political life, of unbounded progress in the arts, sciences and
> culture. We hear the promise of the future united Republic of Indonesia
> at one in friendship and respect with other nations, of an Indonesian
> national flag adorning the Eastern sky, of a nation strong and healthy ...

It was a classic statement of nationalist objectives which confirmed the authorities in their worst suspicions. For 'recommending
the disturbance of public order and the overthrow of the established
Netherlands Indies Authority' Sukarno was sentenced to four years'
detention. He served only two but was arrested again in 1933 along

with other nationalist leaders. This time there was to be no trial. All were summarily exiled to far-flung corners of the archipelago. There they would remain for the best part of a decade. Indonesian nationalism had seemingly been nipped in the bud. But emotions surface gradually, if extremely powerfully, in Indonesia. The social anthropologist Clifford Geertz cites a Javanese proverb: 'The crocodile is quick to sink but slow to come up.'

2

The Malay World

Philatelic Fantasies

Just as the North Sea separates the Dutch and the English in north-west Europe so in south-east Asia they were separated by the Malacca Strait, an equally busy and even more strategic waterway between the Asian mainland and the offshore Indies. Naval rivals since the sixteenth century, the two nations had grown accustomed to eyeing one another's expertise with a mixture of envy and contempt, like anglers on opposite banks of a river. Initially the Dutch were mostly contemptuous and the English envious, but by the twentieth century it was the other way around. For whilst Holland without the Netherlands East Indies scarcely rated as an imperial power, Britain without Malaya still boasted the largest empire the world had ever seen.

If asked in, say, 1930 to list the various lands that comprised this empire, few outside the Colonial Office in London's Whitehall could have obliged. Basic information about such a global agglomeration was not readily available. Other empires might be reducible to a tally of territories but no squalid inventory could do justice to Britain's. Its spectacular diversity was part of its mystique. Three hundred years of cruising the high seas had resulted in a mixed haul from all five continents comprising everything from barely inhabited atolls to a teeming subcontinent.

Here was an empire, less formal than the French, less systematic than the Dutch, that had, in the words of the historian D. K. Fieldhouse, 'absolutely no unity of character and no necessary imperial function'. Apologists liked the idea that it had been 'acquired in a fit of absent-mindedness' or had 'fallen into England's lap while she was sleeping'. Similarly it was quite consoling that bits of it had no sooner been graciously received than they were absent-mindedly mislaid, like not very useful souvenirs. All those Caribbean territories, or the Pacific islands – there were just too many to name. Unless you could recall why and when they had been acquired, they got forgotten.

Of the British public only stamp collectors had some inkling of the empire's diversity. Stamps in those days were issued sparingly; and places which generated little mail, like the more obscure colonies, required few. Their value to collectors, as listed in pounds, shillings and pence in Stanley Gibbons' annual catalogues, was correspondingly enhanced. While poring over their stamp collections, school-boy philatelists, like the young John Davis, learnt of the existence of otherwise unsuspected territories. '[It was] the fact that I was a stamp collector and they had very lovely stamps with tigers on them that determined me to go for the Federated Malay States,' recalled Davis. Each of the Malay states had its own stamps and they all had tigers on them. After a wartime career in insurgency and a post-war career in counter-insurgency, Davis would eventually serve in Kedah, the most northerly of the Malay states. To Stanley Gibbons and his predecessors, the Colonial Office owed some of its most distinguished recruits including Sir Richard Winstedt, Principal of Singapore's Raffles College in the 1920s and a prolific scholar of all things Malay.

It is doubtful, however, whether even the young Davis or the bookish Winstedt could have correctly itemised the entire British portfolio in the Far East. For reasons that will appear, here more than anywhere the geography of empire bristled with territorial pin-pricks and constitutional oddities. Everyone knew about Singapore and Hong Kong; and thanks to Somerset Maugham, quite a few knew that the Malay peninsula was divided into Federated Malay States and Unfederated Malay States. But what, if any, was the imperial status of Sarawak, Johore or Shanghai? And what, indeed where, were Labuan, the Dindings and Weihaiwei?

Technically the first three were not colonies at all in 1930; Shanghai was a treaty port while Sarawak and Johore were protectorates, sovereign states under British protection; only Sarawak would ever become a crown colony. Yet, of the other three, Labuan and the Dindings, though decidedly less prominent, were very much colonies while Weihaiwei, though of ambiguous status, was treated as one.

Labuan, a disappointing island off the north-west coast of Borneo, had been a crown colony since 1846 and had had its own stamps since 1879. It was now administered, along with places of more moment like Singapore and Penang, as one of the Straits Settlements. That it was far removed from the Malacca Strait, to which this designation referred, seems not to have mattered.

Also bundled into the Straits Settlements was the entity known as the Dindings, an inconsequential estuary plus adjacent islands on the west coast of the Malay peninsula. The existence of the Dindings was not widely appreciated and their potential seems to have escaped even music-hall gag writers. All that could be said for them was that they, at least, were located on the Strait.

Weihaiwei, with the distinction of being a crown territory in mainland China, was of greater moment. It was also so remote and of such uncertain status that even the tidy minds at the Colonial Office could find no handy administrative hold-all into which to bundle it. Opposite the Korean peninsula and commanding access to the Gulf of Chihli and so to Peking (Beijing), its 300 square miles had been leased from the Chinese authorities in 1898 to offset similar concessions extracted by the Russian empire. Weihaiwei (pronounced 'Way-high-way') had its own post office and its own stamps. 'A fascinating but complex subject' says Stanley Gibbons of the postal markings used in Weihaiwei before the advent of adhesive stamps. The latter arrived in 1917 and were actually Hong Kong's stamps but overprinted, very boldly, with the word CHINA. A full colonial administration of Commissioner, Assistant Commissioner and District Magistrates had by then been installed, and the colony's port and commercial hub had been renamed Port Edward.

At the same 1898 round of Anglo-Chinese negotiations which produced the Weihaiwei lease in northern China, occasion had been taken to expand British possessions in southern China with the addition of another 300-square-mile plot. Adjacent to Hong Kong but very much larger, this area became known as Hong Kong's 'New Territories'; and whereas Weihaiwei's lease was contingent on the Russian presence at what they called Port Arthur (Lushun), the New Territories were the subject of a fixed-term lease. It was set at 99 years. Fatefully if distantly, the New Territories would thus revert to China at midnight on 30 June 1997.

As a matter of principle the British negotiators would have preferred indefinite rights, although it was not yet foreseen that reversion of the New Territories would ultimately, like pulling the plug on the baby's bathwater, mean the loss of Hong Kong as well. Nor was it obvious that the New Territories would necessarily outlast Weihaiwei. With the Russians rejoicing over having gained access to the warm waters of Port Arthur, it was quite possible that Weihaiwei would remain in British hands forever.

As it happened, Russia was obliged to relinquish its concession in 1905 following unexpected defeat in the Russo-Japanese War. The British, though, stayed on in Weihaiwei. It was partly policy; no empire liked to be seen relinquishing territory. And it was partly habit; Weihaiwei's fine beaches and cooler climate appealed to holiday-makers from Shanghai and the other treaty ports. With a sanatorium and supply base, Weihaiwei thus became the China coast's equivalent of India's salubrious hill-stations and looked likely to remain so. Yet by 1922 the situation had changed again. Under pressure from Japan and the USA, Britain conceded that Weihaiwei was not actually one of its global priorities. Finally in 1930, when the British empire was of apparently unassailable extent, further pressure would result in Weihaiwei being quietly evacuated. For the first time since the revolution in their north American colonies a century and a half earlier, the British would find themselves surrendering territory to a nationalist government.

Thus, by an odd coincidence, of the two territories leased in 1898, one would become the first to slip from the imperial grip while the other would be the last. Weihaiwei's handover in 1930 would signify the beginning of Britain's imperial disengagement; the New Territories' (and so Hong Kong's) handover in 1997 would signify the end. In the Netherlands East Indies and French Indo-China, 1930 found the colonial powers cracking down on idle talk about independence; Sukarno was standing trial in Bandung and the French Sûreté was hot on the trail of the elusive Ho Chi Minh. Even in the Philippines people were having second thoughts about a head-long dash from American tutelage. The British, though, were already giving ground.

They had more ground to give. In due course eight years would suffice to remove the Dutch from the East Indies and nine to excise the French from Indo-China, but it took a couple of generations for the British to vacate their scattered lines, haul down their faded flags and hand over their cherished traditions. Decolonisation, a short and painful post-war postscript for others, was for them so spun out as to become one of the themes of the century, rich in opportunities for historical analysis, personal nostalgia and national introspection. Rationales were propounded, debate raged, mythologies mushroomed. So overwhelming has been the attention lavished on Britain's imperial retraction that an Anglocentric view of other retracting empires becomes almost unavoidable.

More Chinese than China

Of those who grappled with the implications of Britain's colonial role in the East two men, both formidable minds, were also close friends. With careers that offer a commentary on the anomalies of the empire in the Far East during the inter-war years, they will feature repeatedly in the next few chapters. Cecil Clementi and Reginald Johnston had met at Oxford when both went up to Magdalen College as Demies (scholars) in 1894. Johnston read history, Clementi Classics plus Sanskrit. Both then joined the colonial service, were posted to Hong Kong and there, lodging together, studied Manchu and Mandarin. They also immersed themselves in Chinese literature and each made long solitary journeys on the mainland. Clementi, a willowy figure of considerable charm, translated Cantonese love-songs; Johnston, stockier and more eccentric, wrote on Chinese drama and Buddhism.

Between 1903 and 1906 it fell to Clementi to assess and register the 300,000 often conflicting land claims of the residents of the recently acquired New Territories. According to a fellow scholar, Sir Richard Winstedt, 'Every ingenious device was used to establish baseless titles, but there was not a single appeal against his decisions, and the country people remained his firm friends for life.' Meanwhile Johnston was sent north to similar work as a District Magistrate in Weihaiwei.

It was the first of Johnston's two sojourns in what he would call 'that delectable territory'. He took a jaundiced interest in the Chinese revolution, cultivated contacts with Peking, endorsed Buddhist precepts and formed a lifelong friendship with Sir James Stewart Lockhart who was then Commissioner for the colony (and so his boss) as well as being another eccentric Sinophile. London was nonplussed. Run by a Confucianist with a Buddhist as his assistant, Weihaiwei, it was said, was more Chinese than China.

Official doubts about Johnston's suitability appeared to be confirmed when he published a spirited attack on the methods adopted by Christian missionaries in China. His career prospects suffered, but compensation was on hand when in 1919 an unthinkable opportunity arose; he was invited to take up residence in Peking's Forbidden City as the only foreigner in the direct employ of the last Manchu emperor who, though he had abdicated in 1912, still enjoyed the perquisites of office. Nonplussed again, the Colonial Office offered no objections. Johnston said farewell to Weihaiwei and duly entered a world of medieval make-believe as one of the Celestial Emperor's most exalted counsellors.

> My position is a peculiar and rather interesting one . . . I was appointed *Ti Shih* or *Shih-fu*, which for want of a better term must be translated Imperial Tutor; but 'tutor' does not exactly convey the proper idea. It is a court appointment of very great dignity, only conferred upon officials of very high standing, such as governors of provinces . . . A tutor of the Son of Heaven . . . is also the emperor's confidential adviser (even in affairs of state), and is practically the only person who can be treated by the emperor as a friend. At court he takes precedence of everyone except some – but not all – princes of the blood. The emperor always stands when his tutor stands; and a tutor is the only official who, as a matter of right, sits in the emperor's presence.

In this letter of 1923 to Sir Herbert Warren, the president of his old college, Johnston also urged the idea that the 18-year-old Emperor might, like the Prince of Wales, benefit from a sojourn at Magdalen.

> This is by no means impossible; for I have inspired in him a proper respect for Oxford, and . . . he knows what Magdalen looks like from the photographs I have shown him . . . He has learnt a fair amount of English history, and I have been trying to teach him something about the English constitution and theory of kingship.

There were problems, though. The Son of Heaven's English was not good enough for him to sit any kind of entrance exam and, more seriously, China was now a republic whose squabbling leaders, far from launching the Emperor on the international stage, were more disposed to slash his few remaining privileges. So it proved. After five years, during which Johnston became his most trusted adviser, the Son of Heaven was obliged to flee his palace. Johnston smuggled him, plus a bag of jewels and little else, to the apparent safety of the Japanese Legation in Peking.

It was not the last that would be heard of Henry Pu-yi, as the

Emperor was now called; but it did preclude Johnston's idea of bequeathing to the Celestial Empire a proper regard for constitutional monarchy. In time other ideals dear to British hearts, like racial harmony, representative government and the free market, would take its place. The notion of assuaging Britannia's imperial bereavement by making a bequest to the successor states of some priceless memento of British rule would loom large in the years ahead. It would still be current in the 1990s when, during the countdown to withdrawal from Hong Kong, democratic representation suddenly became an essential souvenir of British rule. Decolonisation, though often prolonged as a result, could ultimately be gratifying even to the decoloniser.

Redundant in Peking following the flight of the Emperor, Johnston sought the advice of Clementi who, after postings elsewhere, had just been appointed Governor of Hong Kong. The ex-tutor evidently fancied another academic posting, but with Clementi's encouragement he was eventually directed back to Weihaiwei. It would thus be Johnston who, as the colony's Commissioner from 1927 to 1930, would preside over that first surrender of crown territory since the American War of Independence. The surrender itself, an event rich in symbolism for the future, belongs to the next chapter. Johnston would manage it well after his own fashion. Knighted in 1930 for his services there, he would finally return to academia and England as Professor of Chinese at the London School of Oriental Studies.

Clementi, too, would leave China in 1930. By then a stooped and awesome figure with a doom-laden reputation for thinking the unthinkable about imperial disengagement, he would proceed to Singapore as Governor of the Straits Settlements and High Commissioner for the Malay States. There, as in Hong Kong, he would stir up trouble. As yet, even minor constitutional reforms designed to rationalise the British presence and make government marginally more representative of the governed were treated with suspicion by the colonial communities. There was no official endorsement, as in Holland, of 'a debt of honour' to the colonies, no espousal of a determinedly 'Ethical Policy'. Pragmatic as ever, British policy assumed that its governors and commissioners would respond to circumstances as they saw fit. It had always been so. The empire was essentially the product of individual initiative aided by the threat, and occasional use, of force. In Francis Light, Stamford

Raffles and James Brooke, men who between them had created the British presence in south-east Asia, Clementi would find ample precedent for going it alone.

Country Trade

Historically the British empire, despite its debt to individual empire-builders, and despite that myth about its falling into Britannia's lap while she was sleeping, was not wholly devoid of logic. In the Far East the disposition of its possessions reflected a clear maritime imperative. All flanked the main sea route from the Indian Ocean to the China coast. Just as the Dutch East India Company's first landward bases were located to cover the sea approaches to the spice islands, so the English East India Company's Far Eastern establishments were designed to command the approaches to China. It was the China trade which first necessitated a British presence in the Far East and, later, it was as a result of French and American commitments in China that other empires came to cluster round the South China Sea. That empire's end would both start and finish on the China coast would be appropriate.

In 1600, when applying to Queen Elizabeth I for a founding charter, the would-be directors of the English East India Company had indicated a commercial interest in several eastern kingdoms none of which looked more promising than 'the most mighty and wealthy empire of China'. Its might suggested a worthwhile patron and its wealth, epitomised in silks and porcelain, suggested an exciting market for Tudor England's principal export, namely woollen textiles.

Nothing much came of these plans in the seventeenth century. Fustian tweeds and blankets of broadcloth were not sufficiently exotic to persuade Chinese merchants to risk the wrath of their xenophobic mandarins. Moreover the Portuguese, whose settlement at Macao was then the only foreign trading post recognised by the Chinese empire, proved unhelpful. The English Company was soon committing most of its limited investment to Indian and Persian manufactures. Some Chinese goods were obtained via agencies in Japan, Siam and Formosa (Taiwan), and on the China coast at Amoy (Xiamen) and Chusan (Zhoushan), but all these establishments proved vulnerable to political change and were short-lived.

The credit for opening China to English trade on a more permanent basis, and so triggering the creation of a Far Eastern empire, belongs not to the East India Company but to its employees and rivals acting in a private capacity. Under the terms of its royal charter the Company enjoyed a monopoly of all trade with the East; 'out-and-back' only Company ships carrying Company consignments could legally operate. But within the East the very extensive inter-port carrying trade was by the late seventeenth century acknowledged as open to all. By investing in vessels engaged in this 'country trade', or in the cargoes which they carried, Company men transformed their miserly salaries into the princely fortunes which excited so much jealousy at home. Undoubtedly they benefited from the protection afforded by the Company's acknowledged naval supremacy in the Indian Ocean; but there was a reciprocal advantage in that the Company itself stood to benefit should their endeavours open new markets for English exports or discover new commodities which could command a sale in Europe.

Typical of this rugged breed of trader-officials were the brothers Thomas and Elihu Yale. American-born and no great respecters of monopolies, they operated from Madras where Elihu, whose fortune would endow the Connecticut college which bears his name, was president of the Company's establishments on India's Coromandel coast. He was also the prime mover in a pioneering endeavour to open trade with Canton (Guangzhou). 'We are of the opinion [that it] will be very advantageous to Your Honours', he told the directors in London; 'that port [Canton] much exceeding Amoy in all sorts of China commodities . . . is a greater and better government.' Eighty miles upstream from Macao at the mouth of the Pearl River, Canton was southern China's major metropolis and probably the busiest port in Asia. Elihu Yale had chosen the right place and he had just the ship to make a formidable impression. For it so happened that the *Defence*, the most heavily armed Company vessel in Indian waters, was available for such a voyage and that Thomas Yale, following an ill-fated venture in Siam, was available to direct her operations.

The *Defence* duly reached the mouth of the Pearl River in late 1689. There Yale and two companions went ashore and were conveyed up to the city by junk and wheelbarrow ('more convenient than our English ones but somewhat more noisy'). They met Canton's customs official and were authorised to bring their ship up-river. Unfortunately the *Defence*'s captain had other ideas. He declined to risk his vessel among the shoals of the Pearl River and preferred to refit at its mouth while trading on his own account at Portuguese Macao.

Fuming at his 'hot-headed, wrong-headed, capricious and futile, feather-brained skipper', Yale nevertheless found a cargo and was loading the ship in Macao when his captain suffered another rush of blood to the head. In a dispute over a new mast he ordered his men to fire on the Chinese carpenters. One man was killed outright, others injured. In the mêlée the ship's doctor was also badly wounded and taken hostage. He and nine ratings were left to their fate. Anticipating hefty compensation and long delays, Yale immediately ordered the ship to sea.

Although the Company's directors later gloated over the failure of this initiative, it may not have been the financial disaster that they imagined. From Madras the Yales continued to trade eastwards as did other private syndicates, both English and Indian. Valuable lessons were being learnt about China's system of trade and its maritime regulations. In 1699 one of Thomas Yale's companions on the *Defence* returned to Canton aboard the *Macclesfield* which was probably the first English vessel actually to sail up the Pearl River and conclude her business without hostilities. Although she failed to find a market for her English exports and was delayed for nearly a year, she still made a 100 per cent profit, mostly on silks, 'which is more than our Company expected and more than any ship from India or China had done this year'.

The year was 1700, from when may be dated the regular annual intercourse with Canton, but the Company responsible was not the old East India Company. The *Macclesfield* belonged to a rival 'New Company' largely comprised of men who as private 'interlopers' had challenged the old Company's monopoly on the high seas and were now testing it in the courts. In 1702 the two companies, in effect, merged, and the resultant United Company would prove as jealous of its 'out-and-back' monopoly as its predecessor. After 1720, as the value of the trade escalated thanks to the growing demand for China's tea, the monopoly of homeward-bound sailings from Canton would become its most valued asset.

Yet the part played by private traders, particularly in supplying Canton with imports from India and south-east Asia, would also escalate. Free trade, the hallmark of nineteenth-century British imperialism, was not incompatible with mercantilist monopolism as practised by the chartered companies of the seventeenth century. In the East, where trade was traditionally open to all-comers, the two had never been mutually exclusive, and the Company grudgingly accepted this situation. It did little to discourage competition within the East and it looked to private traders not only to open new markets but also to offset imbalances in its own trade. The private traders for their part looked to the Company for a degree of protection and for the commercial authorisation which its pre-eminence at Canton alone ensured. Far from being the outcome of a long struggle between the two, British empire in the Far East was the result of a fruitful if bad-tempered collaboration between corporate authority and private initiative and between regulated trade and free trade.

Throughout the eighteenth century Europe's new-found thirst for hot beverages, both as refreshing stimulants and as an agreeable way of imbibing the Americas' massive sugar production, waxed insatiable. Coffee from Java appealed to bourgeois tastes, especially in continental Europe, and came to dominate the Amsterdam market. Tea made a greater impact on the English-speaking world and rapidly found favour with all social classes. By 1770, in spite of the heavy duties on tea imports which would soon account for 10 per cent of the British government's total revenues, and in spite of the large-scale smuggling which resulted, the Company's China trade was beginning to exceed its trade with all other markets.

Ironically this commercial success in China coincided with a dramatic upgrading of the Company's political responsibilities in India. There, in the second half of the eighteenth century, erratic conquests and painful adjustments transformed it from a society of seafaring merchants into a continental superpower. Empire-builders of the British raj like Robert Clive and Warren Hastings began their careers wading through cotton piece-goods and poring over ledgers, but ended them waging wars and administering a subcontinent. The collection of consignments for export was superseded by the collection of revenue as the Company's main Indian preoccupation. Its employees continued trading, but in concessions, prize money and patronage rather than in commodities. These last were increasingly left to private enterprise as local syndicates, successors of the Yales and their like, organised themselves into powerful trading houses. Still banned from the 'out-and-back' trade, they concentrated on supplying Canton with Asiatic produce. Offshoots of these 'agency houses' would set up business in Macao and eventually spawn such illustrious names as Dent's and Jardine Matheson.

In the 1780s Bombay's agency houses profited substantially from the export of raw cotton to Canton. Calcutta followed suit as its agency houses bought up Bengal's opium crop and then exported it to south-east Asia or smuggled it into China. Not to be outdone, Madras's private traders specialised in exporting finished cottons and batiks to south-east Asia and then shipping from that region to Canton the exotic produce so dear to the Chinese – birds' nests from Borneo, sandalwood from Timor, pepper from Sumatra, spices from wherever they could buy them, pearls and sea-slugs from the Arafura Sea. By 1772 the 'Madras Association', previously Jourdain, Sulivan and de Souza, dominated this trade and had begun actively to promote the need for a permanent settlement in the vicinity of the Malacca Strait. Aceh, on the northern tip of Sumatra, was one possibility. Alternatively, across the Strait on the Malay peninsula there were inviting sites in the territory of the hard-pressed sultan of Kedah, amongst them the island of Penang.

An Eastern Entrepôt

The Company was not unsympathetic. Though driven from the spice islands 150 years earlier by Jan Pieterzoon Coen and the Dutch VOC, it had never quite given up on the south-east Asian archipelago. Originally inspired by the profits in pepper, cloves and nutmeg, it had continued to seek spices wherever a chink in the Dutch monopoly appeared. It had also managed to maintain a territorial toehold in the region, first in west Java and then, since 1685, at Bengkulu (Benkulen) in south Sumatra.

Bengkulu still boasted a jaunty little fort from which flew the Company's flag, but it was on the wrong side of Sumatra to be of much relevance to the booming China trade. Facing out into the Indian Ocean, its windswept anchorage attracted little commerce from the archipelago and served only as a run-down outlet for the region's pepper crop. The climate was vile, the mortality rate astronomical. To Bengkulu were sent convicts, debtors and drunkards. It was not an enviable posting. Pacing its forlorn sand dunes only an incorrigible megalomaniac like Raffles would dare to dream of empire.

The case for some alternative base east of India had accordingly been under active consideration for the best part of a century. It would need to be accessible to shipping from all over south-east

Asia, and to afford shelter, protection and refitting facilities for vessels plying to and from Canton. Moreover, should Canton be closed to British shipping, it should also be easily accessible to Chinese junks and thus able to serve as an entrepôt for a relocated China trade. For just such a purpose in the late seventeenth century the Yales had been amongst those exploring the potential of various sites in Siam. Mergui, near the top of the long Malay isthmus, had been briefly occupied and so, in the early eighteenth century, had Pulo Condore off the coast of south Vietnam, and Banjermassin on the south coast of Borneo.

In the 1750s, with the Company in India locked in a life-and-death struggle with the French wherein both sides depended on the support of their navies, attention had refocused on the sheltered havens and ample teak supplies to be found on the opposite side of the Bay of Bengal. Mergui was not retaken but, further north, the island of Negrais off the south-west tip of Burma was occupied by Madras men and promoted as a future naval base and entrepôt. The Negrais settlement lasted only five years but in the early 1760s another scion of the Madras establishment, the eccentric antiquarian and cartographer Alexander Dalrymple, embarked on a series of more ambitious reconnaissances. His 'secret service' surveys, ranging from Vietnam to Manila and the Moluccas, eventually concentrated on the Sulu Sea and resulted in the choice of Balambangan, an island sandwiched between Borneo and the Philippines and so in the colonial no man's land between the Dutch and Spanish spheres of influence. In 1763 it duly became the Company's first possession in the South China Sea; and in words that would be echoed by Raffles in respect of his own foundation of Singapore, the indefatigable Dalrymple declared Balambangan's virgin sands and matted jungle the future British entrepôt for the trade not only of China and the Dutch archipelago but also of Japan, Korea, Australia and the south Pacific.

Had Dalrymple's dream been realised, Singapore might still be a tiger-infested swamp and Hong Kong a navigational hazard frequented largely by Chinese buccaneers. The crossroads of the East, ablaze with the high-rise neon of corporate finance, its waters crammed with freighters and criss-crossed by hydrofoils, would be on the other side of the South China Sea. Adjacent areas of north Borneo and the southern Philippines, forlorn Cinderellas in the late twentieth century, would be landscaped with the shopping malls and leisure facilities of a new 'growth triangle'. But arbitrary are the ways of human geography. Balambangan was never endowed even with a waterfront of shop-houses.

Today the pirate-ridden Sulu Sea remains much as Dalrymple found it more than 200 years ago. It was partly his own fault. 'So rich a jewel' as Balambangan, he insisted, required the disinterested devotion which only he, as absolute ruler on behalf of the Company, could bestow. The Company thought otherwise and eventually sent one of Bengkulu's notoriously alcoholic officials. Within two years the settlement 'exhibited a scene of irregularity, duplicity and presumption not to be equalled upon the records of the Company'. Funds intended for the construction of a fort disappeared without trace; so did vast quantities of liquor. Trade was negligible, the climate hideous and the natives hostile. When in 1777, the latter eventually succeeded in burning down the Company's house and forcing its inmates back to sea, there was a sigh of relief even in London. The natives of Sulu, sneered the Company's directors, had done everyone a favour.

Washing their hands of Balambangan, they reviewed the Madras Association's plea for a settlement at Aceh in Sumatra. Its sultan determinedly resisted such overtures but amongst those involved in them were two ex-naval officers, Captain Thomas Forrest and Captain Francis Light. Forrest, after an unhappy stint at Balambangan, had assumed Dalrymple's role as a one-man reconnaissance. Mindful of the strategic considerations that had prompted the Negrais settlement in Burma, he urged the continued need for a naval station on the leeward side of the Bay of Bengal and reinvestigated the possibilities of Mergui, the Siamese port on the west of the Malay peninsula. Light, on behalf of the Madras Association, was thinking more in terms of a south-east Asian entrepôt. In place of Aceh he suggested the Riau (Rhio) islands, just off modern Singapore, and then Penang in the territory of Kedah, with whose sultan he was on good terms. The Company baulked at the military support demanded by the Sultan as his price for Penang, but Light continued to urge the advantages of a deal with Kedah while Forrest noted that Penang would also serve well as the required naval base.

Both men got their way when a French squadron reappeared in the Bay of Bengal in 1782. While the Royal Navy was obliged to retire to Bombay to refit, the French briefly had the run of the Bay and threatened Calcutta itself. As Forrest had foreseen, a naval station sheltered from the south-west monsoon had become a strategic imperative. Warren Hastings, India's Governor-General, agreed and finally gave the go-ahead to take up the offer of Penang. On 11 August 1786 Francis Light duly took possession of the island on behalf of George III and the Honourable East India Company, renaming it Prince of Wales Island and designating its new settlement as George Town.

Thereafter the creation of British south-east Asia proceeded apace. In 1794 the port of Malacca, near the tip of the Malay peninsula, was temporarily acquired from the Dutch along with other parts of their island empire to pre-empt their use by Napoleonic France. Three years later Arthur Wellesley, the future Duke of Wellington, assembled an expedition in Penang for an attack on the Philippines. The expedition was aborted but, on Wellesley's recommendation, in 1800 the first territory on the Malay mainland was acquired when the Sultan of Kedah was persuaded to cede what became known as Province Wellesley (after Arthur's brother Richard, then Governor-General of India). In 1805 Penang and adjacent Wellesley were upgraded to the status of a Company presidency, equivalent to Bombay or Madras. The young Thomas Stamford Raffles came to Penang as part of the new establishment, and from Penang and Malacca he masterminded the 1811 invasion of Java.

Eight years later he would sail again from Penang, this time to lay claim to Singapore. From there in the 1840s one of his disciples, James Brooke, would visit Borneo and acquire Sarawak while Palmerston authorised the annexation of the nearby island of Labuan. In little over half a century the sea route to China became marked by a string of flanking British positions.

Just off Brunei, Labuan supposedly boasted substantial coal deposits, a new and important consideration as steamships made their eastern début. For this reason it was chosen in preference to Balambangan of unhappy memory. The latter was, nevertheless, revisited. Of the earlier settlement the only trace to be found was the island's rather superior breed of cattle. Now wild and somewhat degenerated, these descendants of stock from Madras served as a useful reminder of all those earlier attempts to establish an eastern settlement.

The British empire in the Far East was not, as so often represented, an afterthought to India; nor was it tangential to some supposedly preordained progress towards a British raj in India. For a century before Penang and Singapore, in a dozen different locations from Mergui to Balambangan, the necessity for an eastern entrepôt and settlement had been relentlessly pursued. At first private traders took the lead in these initiatives, with the Company an interested spectator. Latterly, as the value of its China trade grew, the Company itself became a prime mover.

In India, British merchants deserted their warehouses to lead armies and ape the grasping ways of their oriental adversaries. Further east their contemporaries and successors remained truer to their commercial vocation. India meant continental responsibilities, a massive land-based army and direct political intervention on an unprecedented scale, all of which were anathema to traditional British policy. The raj, in short, was the aberration. On the other hand, the maritime, mercantile empire of trading settlements and city-states that grew up in the Far East afforded precisely the informal hegemony to which both Company and country had so long aspired.

The Lion City

This distinction between territorial responsibilities and trading ambitions was not, however, drawn at the time. Britain's informal empire in the East seems to have been as fortuitous and unorchestrated as its formal empire in India. Raffles, the man often credited with creating the free-trade ideal of informal empire, planned something totally different. Installed as Lieutenant-Governor of Java following its successful invasion in 1811, he quite forgot about commercial priorities and, marvelling at Java's fertility, its vast population and its ancient civilisation, thought of it as 'this other India'. His flurry of reforms was designed both to discredit Dutch rule and also, by boosting the revenue and streamlining the administration, to lay the foundations for another raj.

Denied any such thing by the return of the island to the Dutch after the final defeat of Napoleon, a smarting Raffles retired to the Sumatran irrelevance that was Bengkulu. Being himself of obscure origins, modest stature and boundless ambition, he liked to identify with Napoleon; he now compared his situation to that of the Emperor in exile. But Bengkulu was not his St Helena; it was 'my Elba'. Raffles was planning a comeback.

In the interior of Sumatra he identified the Minangkabau people as the original Malay race and dreamt of recreating a Malay empire under British tutelage. Sumatra being a thousand years behind Java in terms of civilisation, he asked for 10,000 immigrants and planned something less like the raj and more like the 'white settler' colonies of Australia and Canada. It was still empire-building and the scheme, like others, was firmly repudiated. Raffles dreamt on. The Company, though totally opposed to expansion in south-east Asia, remained concerned about its China trade. Penang was failing to live up to its billing either as a naval dockyard (the local timber was found unsuitable) or as an entrepôt (it was too far from the archipelago). In 1818 Raffles persuaded the Governor-General in Calcutta to authorise another reconnaissance in the Malacca Strait. Like Light and Forrest forty years earlier, he was to try Aceh, Riau and any other suitable sites not already claimed by the Dutch.

Singhapura, an overgrown island in the territory of Johore, may already have been in his sights. The name, meaning 'Lion City', identified it as the site of an ancient metropolis. Raffles liked a place to have a pedigree. Moreover skippers *en route* to Canton had been reporting on its pivotal position and sheltered anchorage for more than a century. Raffles recognised its wider potential as the service station of both the China trade and that of the archipelago and the west Pacific. 'What Malta is in the West, that may Singapore become in the East.' In 1819 he blatantly exploited a complex succession crisis in Johore to engineer the island's cession. Then he pre-empted all objections by such rapid development of the site that the city was a *fait accompli* before its existence could be questioned or its status defined. Free trade, the key to this success because it instantly attracted settlers, had been Dalrymple's dream for Balambangan and had since produced dramatic early growth in Penang. Raffles endorsed the idea not out of ideological conviction but because it was essential to the overnight success of his creation. As with Singapore itself, a mere 'Malta' rather than 'another India', he made a virtue, then a dogma, out of necessity.

Possessed now of three Malacca Strait settlements – Penang, Province Wellesley and Singapore – the Company promptly acquired a fourth when the Dutch abandoned claims to the port of Malacca in return for British withdrawal from Bengkulu. The 1824 Anglo-Dutch treaty also endorsed the British claim to Singapore, already upstaging Penang, and gave to Raffles' successors a free hand in the Malay peninsula. In return the British acknowledged Holland's exclusive rights in the archipelago 'south of the straits of Singapore'. This cleared the political air but, despite Dutch undertakings to afford British shipping favourable access throughout the archipelago, left ample scope for commercial grievances. Where it left Borneo, much of which was in latitudes north of Singapore, was also uncertain – though not for long.

More pressing were the Siamese (Thai) government's claims to suzerainty over Kedah and other sultanates in the north of the Malay peninsula. Kedah supplied Penang and Province Wellesley with food and its sultan insisted that his cessions had been contingent on the British affording him protection. Neither Calcutta nor London recognised this obligation and they remained totally opposed to any involvement in the Malay interior. It was thus left to the authorities in Penang and Singapore to counter persistent Siamese intrigues and encourage the various Malay states to assert their independence (of one another as well as of Siam), all without deploying force or committing the British government. In fact they did both, incurring much censure but gradually creating a climate of dependence favourable to the extension of trade.

Trade in Malaya meant tin, principally from the west coast sultanates, which had long been the peninsula's main export. Industrial processing now boosted demand just as more settled conditions and more sophisticated mining techniques permitted increased production. Singapore's Chinese immigrants provided the management and the capital, China's Chinese the labour. Faced with this growing and often unruly immigrant community, the Malay sultans looked expectantly towards their British neighbours while London began to accept that their territories might not after all be a total liability. In 1867 it transferred the Straits Settlements from the India Office to the Colonial Office and was soon looking more favourably on interventionist policies. Seven years later, when the Dutch were pouring troops into Aceh and the French pushing north into Tonkin, the British endorsed the spirit of this acquisitive era with the so-called Pangkor Engagement.

This Engagement, an agreement rather than a military encounter, was made initially with the Sultan of Perak, the Malay state immediately south of Kedah. It was soon extended to the neighbouring states of Selangor and Pahang and then piecemeal to what Winstedt called 'that delightful little state of lost causes and incredible beliefs' known as Negri Sembilan ('The Nine States'). In return for guarantees of British protection of his sovereignty, plus substantial annuities, each sultan agreed to accept the guidance of a British Resident in all matters of government. State budgets, courts of law, legislative councils, police forces, railway lines and all the other paraphernalia of progress followed. The Resident needed a staff and the staff became an administration. To co-ordinate the four state administrations which resulted, in 1896 they were grouped into a federation and so became the Federated Malay States (FMS). Federation necessitated a new tier of government with a Resident-General, later High Commissioner, based in Kuala Lumpur. He too acquired a staff, council and the rest which progressively supplanted the state administrations. To the latter were left only such vital functions as 'sanitary boards, museums, bands, game wardens, and a few other things'; to the sultans there remained only their sovereignty.

It was otherwise with those states outside the Federation, the so-called Unfederated Malay States (UMS). Exhibiting much greater variety, they ranged from Johore, Singapore's neighbour, with a comparatively developed economy, a vast immigrant population and an independent-minded sultan, to backward states like Kelantan and Trengganu which had only lately been prised from Siamese suzerainty. Each eventually accepted a British Adviser whose counsel, in practice if not in theory, had to be followed. He thus resembled the Resident in a Federated Malay State. State councils, administrative departments and so on followed. But spared the additional tier of the Federal government, a UMS retained considerably greater autonomy. To a newcomer like Sir Cecil Clementi, the UMS would appear to embody the spirit of the Pangkor Engagement more closely than did the FMS and to afford a more promising basis for an eventual union of all the Malay states.

Forged from the demand for tin plate, Malaya's customised conjunction of FMS, UMS and Straits Settlements sped into the twentieth century on rubber. Forest produce, especially gums, lacs and resins, were as much a traditional Malay export as tin. But the Brazilian rubber tree was a British introduction. Unlike tin, the creation of rubber plantations and rubber processing facilities depended entirely on European capital and expertise. The planters were mostly British and the labour came mostly from British India. Something like the settler colony which Raffles had envisaged for Sumatra resulted. But instead of pandering to Western fancies with spices and coffee, Malaya found itself calling the shots in the automobile age.

By the 1920s, as well as about a third of the world's tin, much of it smelted in Singapore, the Malay states were producing over half the world's rubber. The long neglected and chaotically organised peninsula had become, and would remain, what the economic historian L. A. Mills has called 'the wealthiest and, strategically and economically, the most important possession of Great Britain in the tropics'.

The White Raj

The same could not be said for Borneo, the other theatre of British endeavour in south-east Asia. Impenetrable except by river, and with a hundred acres of forest for every human being, the island of Borneo rivalled Amazonia and the Congo as quintessential jungle. Such places were principally of interest to naturalists for, though they invariably aroused mercantile expectations, rarely did they reward them. Rumours of gold deposits and diamonds, like those of ape-men, were not without substance but somehow never withstood commercial scrutiny. Birds' nests for China's favourite soup, antimony for lead pencils, and latterly some latex were poor compensation. The much vaunted coal deposits in Borneo's satellite island of Labuan had proved equally disappointing, and it was not until a black sludge on adjacent beaches of the main island betrayed the presence of oil that Borneo's promise would be rewarded.

The island was nevertheless as big as Mexico and, forming the angle between the South China and Java Seas, had considerable strategic value. Its southern shores, facing Java, offered secure anchorages and had formed part of the Dutch empire since the seventeenth century. Similarly its long north-western coastline faced the Malay peninsula and had been colonised and Islamicised by Malays. It, also, was blessed with many jungle-shrouded estuaries and inlets whence, managed by Malays and Arabs, Borneo's Sea Dayaks pursued their ancient calling of piracy.

Such self-evident proof of the need for more effective government applied equally to much of what the Dutch considered their sector of Borneo. The island, in other words, was fair game, and in the imaginations of men like Dalrymple and Raffles it had figured more prominently than Malaya. Encouraged by Raffles, in 1812 Alexander Hare, an enterprising Englishman, had set up home and harem as the 'white rajah of Moluko' in the territories of the Sultan of Banjermassin on the island's south coast. Rajah Hare's reign ended ignominiously with the return of the Dutch in 1817; but with the 1824 Anglo-Dutch treaty leaving doubt over how much of Borneo fell within the Dutch 'sphere of influence', further British endeavours were anticipated. Obligingly, the Sea Dayak corsairs provided the perfect pretext for such intervention.

Then, as now, those offshore impositions which, though sanctioned by local tradition, the international community chose to construe as piracy were seen as the 'scourge' of the South China Sea and the archipelago. They did not directly threaten the China trade or European vessels. But to buccaneers, for whom a laden schooner was as a chubby swimmer to a shoal of ravenous sharks, the rich pickings to be had amongst the local shipping which increasingly converged on Singapore proved irresistible.

It was on the grounds that a section of the Perak coast (south of Penang) accommodated particularly ferocious pirates that a zealous Captain Low had accepted the cession of what became known as the Dindings in the late 1820s. Thereafter the place scarcely merited a mention until it was returned to the Sultan of Perak in 1935. (Had 'the Sultan of Iraq' actually been consulted, enquired a member of the British Parliament whose hearing must have been as defective as his geography.) Technically the Dindings thus became the second territory (Weihaiwei being the first) to be decolonised. But with Perak itself being a protectorate within the Federated Malay States, the Colonial Office had merely to refile the Dindings.

More serious was the annual armada of corsairs which issued from north-west Borneo and from the Sulu Sea beyond. North-west Borneo consisted largely of the sultanate of Brunei, a Malay foundation once of such formidable authority that the whole island bore its name. Now, with its consonants rearranged, Brunei counted for little in Borneo. It was hard-pressed to control even its Sea Dayak, or Iban, subjects and their Arab-Malay backers.

Enter James Brooke, a one-time cadet in the East India Company's army who had invested his sizeable inheritance in a second-hand schooner and who now, full of Rafflesian fantasies, cruised the eastern seas. In 1839 a visit to Brunei paid unexpected dividends when the Sultan's uncle enlisted his help in suppressing the Sea Dayaks of the Sarawak River. Brooke's services were rewarded with the governorship of the district and the title of rajah. His firm administration and undoubted abilities won the loyalty of his subjects; vigorous action against his piratical neighbours, often in collaboration with British naval squadrons, won the approval of the Colonial Office; and such shows of force, plus heavy cash subsidies to Brunei, brought further favours from the impoverished sultanate. They included recognition of Brooke as sovereign ruler of Sarawak and no less than seven territorial cessions which extended Sarawak territory from Kuching, its capital, up to and around the dwindling enclave that was Brunei.

Returning to London in 1847, Brooke was popularly acclaimed as Sarawak's 'White Rajah'. His exploits, according to the *Illustrated London News*, constituted 'a remarkable union of romantic adventure and of usefulness'. He had rid the Malacca Strait of its most cutthroat pirates and from his capital at the misspelt 'Kucking' he had carved out a kingdom for himself amongst the primitive headhunters of Borneo. He had also realised the fantasies of a whole generation of school-boy imperialists.

> Mr Brooke contemplates a sojourn of six months in England. He is now residing at Mivart's Hotel, where he entertained a select party at dinner on Tuesday evening. On the same day Mr Brooke conducted business at the Colonial Office, the Admiralty and the Board of Trade.

To bolster his improbable position, Brooke needed all the support he could get. Buckingham Palace obliged by creating him Sir James and the Colonial Office rewarded him with the posts of Consul-General in Brunei and Governor of Labuan. It refused, however, that which the Rajah most wanted, namely British recognition and protection for Sarawak. A decade later it still declined to regard Sarawak as other than a dependency of Brunei and Brooke as other than a British subject who, by definition, could only be an independent sovereign if so designated by the British crown. This was galling to Brooke's patriotism, to his security and to his purse, cash being the normal compensation for the diminution of suzerainty which British protection would imply.

To disprove the government's contention, he proceeded to endow his creation with the trappings of sovereignty. The Rajah acquired a *rajah muda* (crown prince, his nephew), 'Kucking' got an *istana* (palace) and Sarawak got a flag, a currency, a national anthem and postage stamps (which, like Her Britannic Majesty's, always featured the sovereign, in other words a Brooke). The Rajah also sought assistance elsewhere, making overtures at different times to the Dutch,

French, Belgian, Italian and even Greek governments. Not until the 1860s did Whitehall relent to the extent of recognising Sarawak's sovereignty and not until 1888, twenty years after the first Rajah's death, was the state welcomed into the imperial fold as a protectorate. Even then uncertainties over its 'international personality' and the precise status of its Rajah remained. These would resurface with bewildering and tragic effect in the 1940s when, with the British crown assuming whatever sovereignty the raj did possess, Sarawak at last became a crown colony. Having been refused colonial status when colonisation was all the rage, the Brookes achieved it when decolonisation was all the rage. An anachronism as well as an anomaly, Sarawak nicely encapsulated the contradictions of British empire in the East.

Similar confusion surrounded two other Bornean territories to which protectorate status was extended, also in 1888. North and east of Brunei, Sabah was about the size of Ireland and had also been part of the Brunei sultanate. As in Sarawak, the Sultan had sold concessions there, initially to an American syndicate. These were acquired by an Austrian and then by the Hong Kong company of Dent's which secured a charter for its British North Borneo Company in 1881. Gladstone's agreement to this extension of British activity – although he later claimed never to have been consulted – was only slightly less surprising than the reappearance of the chartered company, a device for acquiring territory at no expense to the government which, supposedly incompatible with the idea of 'free-trade empire', had long since been discredited.

In the frenzied colonial climate of the 1880s, with the Dutch and the Americans disputing its claims and the Germans grabbing whatever territorial crumbs remained, the British North Borneo Company (BNBC) was not unduly bothered by such inconsistencies. Like the Brookes, its deadly rivals, the BNBC welcomed the security which protectorate status implied and continued to gobble up more Brunei fiefdoms. It also issued much the most colourful stamps which featured a veritable menagerie of Bornean fauna. (This tradition continued until the BNBC was no more; a last issue of 1960 featured an orang-utan cavorting beside the head, apparently severed, of Elizabeth II.)

Briefly the BNBC also assumed responsibility for the island colony of Labuan just off Brunei. Far from becoming 'a second Singapore', Labuan was now 'a decaying settlement'. It proved no more rewarding to the BNBC than it had to the Brookes and, like an unfancied relish, was returned to the crown larder in 1906 to be administered as one of the Straits Settlements.

Meanwhile Brunei itself, squeezed between the white raj and the chartered company, looked sure to be snapped up by one of them. For its sultans the nineteenth century had been 'one long record of unrelieved disaster'. 'At the end of it the sultanate's prospects, economically as well as politically, had never looked bleaker,' writes D. J. M. Tate in *The Making of Modern South East Asia*. Indeed it was only the 1888 grant to Brunei of British protection (against the Brookes and the BNBC as much as the international community) which preserved it from extinction.

Twenty years later the first oil reserves were discovered in adjacent areas of Sarawak. A delicious irony subsequently revealed that the few acres of Borneo that were still Brunei happened to contain the major deposits. The reversal of the sultanate's appalling decline, the survival through war, occupation and post-colonial federalisation of this minute enclave, its continuance as a British protectorate until 1984 and its current status as an independent Islamic city-state with the highest per capita income in the world is the stuff of fairy tales. Sarawak, Sabah, Labuan, Penang, the other Straits Settlements and, briefly, even Singapore would be absorbed into Malaysia. Of Britain's territorial pin-pricks in the East the only one to retain its distinct status throughout was Brunei – and, of course, Hong Kong.

3

The China Coast

Seeing Pink

To British schoolboys whose notions of the empire derived from the classroom wall-map the Far East was something of a disappointment. East of India there was the solid purple of French Indo-China, the perforated green of the American Philippines, and the long orange trail that was the Netherlands East Indies, but there seemed to be very little British pink. The Malay peninsula was so narrow and so cobwebbed with incomprehensible state boundaries that the pink was barely visible. The north Borneo states, because of their ambiguous status, merely had pink stripes. And China, despite the number of uncles and cousins who were always being posted there, was yellow.

When such maps were reduced for the school atlas, even the rosy little dots which represented Hong Kong and Weihaiwei disappeared. Instead, a thin pink line ran under their names. In the context of a country as vast as China, the existence of these underlined locations appeared scarcely more damaging to national integrity than that of anomalies like the principality of Monaco in France or the San Marino republic in Italy.

China's nationalists were equally dismissive of the colonial presence. According to them, these enclaves of empire had never even passed from Chinese sovereignty. The treaties which said otherwise all dated from the nineteenth century when the Celestial Empire was in its death throes. For 300 years it had been ruled by the Manchu (or Qing) emperors, an alien and conservative dynasty whose energy and ambitions had largely expired in a prolonged struggle to assert their authority from Tibet to Formosa. Success in this venture encouraged arrogance and complacency. Peking had turned its back on the

59

world. Isolated and ennervated, it scarcely took cognisance of the barbarian merchants whose shipping queued to enter the Pearl River; and when in the 1840s it did take note, it was too late. Possessed of warships, artillery and effrontery of an unexpectedly high order, the barbarians repeatedly terrorised the coastal provinces and each time imposed their own terms for a cessation of hostilities.

Such were the so-called 'treaties'. Because they had been signed under duress, they were obviously 'unequal'; and in Chinese eyes, this made them invalid. In signing them, the Manchu dynasty stood accused of having connived with the foreigners. Accordingly, the Chinese people soon repudiated both their emperors and the treaties by staging a revolution from which, eventually, there emerged a Communist People's Republic. Naturally a People's Republic could not endorse treaties which the people had so emphatically rejected. It followed that no part of China had been legally alienated to any of the Western powers. The thin pink line under places like Hong Kong might indicate a foreign presence but not foreign sovereignty. At the cost of a long and bloody revolution the Chinese people had triumphed over the imperialists' machinations to dismember their country.

On the other hand, the Communists in particular did make much of the fact that the Chinese masses had suffered mercilessly from capitalist imperialism's exploitation. To pay for the contraband opium foisted upon them, to meet the indemnities which resulted from abortive attempts to stop this illegal traffic, and to service the loans needed to pay such indemnities and acquire new technology, China's peasants had been subjected to ruthless oppression. Widespread dislocation and famine resulted; and whole sectors of the Chinese economy passed under foreign control. Lost territories like Hong Kong and Weihaiwei were but the tip of an iceberg of concessions – jurisdictional, diplomatic, fiscal and religious but mostly economic and financial. In everything from the construction and operation of railways to the distribution of domestic fuel the rapacious foreigner had secured preferential access and monopolistic control.

Ironically, this economic penetration of Asia's largest market corresponded, more or less precisely, with what pioneers like the Yale brothers would have deemed a favourable trading climate and with what later historians dubbed 'informal empire'. Whether demonised as imperialist exploitation or applauded as a cheap and comparatively restrained form of dominion, it was much the same thing. It concentrated on securing the economic advantages of empire without incurring unnecessary responsibilities, like governing peoples and administering territory; it was grounded in ideas about free trade and open markets, ideas which invited competition from other imperial powers and also provided a basis for collaboration amongst them; it relied heavily on military, and especially naval, supremacy; and it found its classic expression in China.

A Community in Search of a Colony

'Commerce was the beginning, the middle and the end of our life in China,' recalled a Shanghai Englishman in the nineteenth century; 'if there were no trade, not a single man, except missionaries, would have come there at all.' Popularly, trade followed the flag as, for example, in Raffles' Singapore. Alternatively, the flag followed trade as it had for the Dutch in the East Indies and the British in India; first came the 'factory', a warehouse plus accommodation, then the fort. In China, however, trade often seemed to flourish regardless of flags. It did so at Canton for 140 years before the British acquisition of Hong Kong. Thereafter, despite the colonial presence in Hong Kong, it did so in Shanghai. Perversely the trading fraternity seemed much to prefer Shanghai whose International Settlement, though providing immunity from Chinese exactions and a degree of security, fell far short of being a colony.

Yet it was this same trading fraternity, the Canton-based successors of the Yales, who had been foremost in urging the necessity of occupying Hong Kong. Controlling the tea trade, on the receipts from which the British economy was so dependent, plus the opium trade, reckoned the most valuable in any single commodity in the world, the Canton merchants had acquired a dazzling importance. By 1830 they numbered about 200 of whom roughly half were British. They included a permanent chaplain, a doctor and interpreters. They had their own newspapers and periodicals; they had their Chamber of Commerce, their banking and insurance arrangements; and in the Select Committee of Supracargoes composed of the East India Company's senior representatives, they had an embryonic government. Its president affected the airs of a governor; its last president would in fact become one of Hong Kong's first governors.

Here then was a ready-made colonial community; all it lacked was a territory. Legitimate trade (that is, excluding opium) had come to be conducted from a spit of riverside frontage in Canton where the East India Company's factory was flanked by those of other nations. Like exhibitors at an international trade fair, they hoisted their flags during business hours, dispensed hospitality, and fretted over the lack of exercise. The Chinese authorities permitted their presence only during the trading months. Supervision was strict; no guns and no women were allowed in the enclave, and the rest of Canton was usually out of bounds. Home comforts were to be found only down-river, either aboard the ships moored in the estuary or in the only slightly less cramped confines of Portuguese Macao. To men who were forever pacing jetties and clambering in and out of sampans, China remained an unwelcoming foreshore where their reception bore absolutely no relationship to their self-importance as masters of the world's most flourishing long-distance commerce.

To this thriving if embattled community the 1841 occupation of the island of Hong Kong would give a new identity, a legal title and a degree of security. Colonial institutions further bolstered the impression of a distinct territorial entity. Yet to the British public even in the 1920s Hong Kong was still commonly 'China'. 'I have to go back to China,' announces the sad hero of Somerset Maugham's *The Painted Veil* when returning to Hong Kong. Dwarfed by British investments elsewhere in China, especially in Shanghai, the island served primarily as what *The Economist* in 1851 had called 'a kind of bonded warehouse for the opium trade'. Since the opium all went to China and since from China came most of the island's people and provisions, its dependence on the mainland was absolute.

So it continued. A century later it could still be said that Hong Kong was worthless without the market of south China. Its population not only remained overwhelmingly Chinese but at any one time the majority were migrant workers from the mainland to whom the idea of a distinct Hong Kong identity was meaningless. According to Frank Welsh, the island's biographer, Hong Kong was 'a Chinese colony that happen[ed] to be run by the British'. Similarly Shanghai was a Chinese port that happened to be run by the British. Amongst those who made good in Shanghai and then removed to Hong Kong was the Kadoorie family, originally from Iraq. To Lord Kadoorie, the colony's first British peer, 'Shanghai was London';

Hong Kong, on the other hand, was merely 'Hastings', a sleepy seaside resort.

Later perceptions of Hong Kong as a distinct city-state whose status and interests had less in common with China and more in common with other thrusting independent Asian economies arose principally as a result of changes on the mainland. As the Chinese empire became a stuttering republic and then an erratic experiment in Marxist-Leninist socialism, the glaring differences between island and mainland generated profound suspicion and came to overshadow their common ties. Foreign withdrawal from Shanghai and the other treaty ports severed further links, thus emphasising this divergence and making Hong Kong's status unique; even the Japanese made no attempt to reintegrate an occupied Hong Kong with occupied China.

After the Second World War the breakaway of Taiwan further challenged the idea of China as an indivisible whole. If there were to be several Chinas, Hong Kong's sovereign status became more plausible. Finally, while China proper languished, sensational growth in the 1960s–1980s propelled the colony into the economic superleague. The sleepy satellite became a soaring international metropolis whose dynamism revitalised adjacent areas of the mainland and whose example triggered economic liberalisation throughout China.

Unsurprisingly this clamorous finale has induced some retrospective distortion. It needs to be emphasised that, for most of its colonial incarnation, dynamism was not a word readily associated with Hong Kong. To Reginald Johnston it was certainly less easygoing than his 'delectable' Weihaiwei; on the other hand, it could scarcely compare with Singapore, the next rung on Cecil Clementi's career ladder. In the Colonial Office's ragbag of responsibilities it rated on a par with Malta or Gibraltar, somewhat above the Gambia or Mauritius but below Ceylon or the Straits Settlements.

Queen Victoria had liked the name, had fancied the title of 'Princess of Hong Kong' for the Princess Royal and, like many of her subjects, had been tickled – pink, naturally – by the addition to her terrestrial empire of a Celestial appanage. It was always, though, a far-flung dependency at the extremity of the imperial sea-ways, prestigious and commercially viable but a political and strategic liability. In the early days, in spite of inheriting that ready-made community of semi-aquatic China traders, its future had been less assured than

Singapore's; ever after, its existence owed more to the distracted state of the mainland and the forbearance of its international rivals than to any defensive capabilities. It was useful to the China trade and, latterly, pivotal; but it was not indispensable. It never had been.

Delivering Briskly

The China trade as established at Canton during the eighteenth century had been managed by the English East India Company whose tea purchases together with those of its foreign rivals constituted the main item of Chinese export. Private traders contributed purchasing power in the form of raw cotton and opium from India, plus south-east Asian produce. The balance was made up by the Company's sale of mechanical curios, mostly clockwork, and, above all, of silver bullion.

Canton's Co-hong, the consortium of merchants with whom the foreigners dealt, was generally well-regarded; commercial relations, though heavily circumscribed, were amicable. Tensions usually resulted from Peking's refusal to consider foreign merchants as other than low-born supplicants and from conflicting ideas about criminal justice – as when, for instance, a Chinese subject was struck, inadvertently or otherwise, by a foreigner's bullet. To adjust and redress such matters, a succession of official initiatives, beginning with Lord Macartney's mission in 1793, attempted to open diplomatic relations with the Manchu court in Peking. They failed dismally. As usual the Company picked up the pieces and trade resumed on the original basis.

What triggered the dramatic interventions of the mid-nineteenth century was not Peking's obtuse attitude to foreign trade and international diplomacy but a sudden escalation in the opium traffic and the commercial demise of the East India Company. The first destabilised trading patterns just at a time when the second removed the only regulating authority capable of readjusting them.

Opium had long been grown in India, mainly for export to Chinese communities in south-east Asia. Recognising its value, in India the Company endeavoured to establish a monopoly of its production while in China, where the drug was officially proscribed, the Company was obliged to practise prohibition. This anomaly threw the trade wide open. Since private traders considered themselves less inhibited by the Chinese proscription, agency houses in Calcutta could legitimately purchase the Company's Indian production, ship it east (as if destined for south-east Asia), and then invite their counterparts in Macao to dispose of it surreptitiously on the China coast. By the 1790s between 3,000 and 4,000 chests a year were being thus smuggled into China to the benefit of all – the agency houses who handled them, the Company which disposed of its Indian crop and could offset opium credits in India against tea debits in China, and the Co-hong merchants and their Canton mandarins who derived considerable income from connivance in the traffic.

Thanks largely to opium, the need to finance tea purchases with bullion ended in the early 1800s when the British balance of payments deficit at Canton became a surplus. Now it was China that was being drained of silver, although the effects were not apparent until the 1820s. In that decade opium exports quadrupled and in the next decade they doubled again. The demand in China seemed insatiable. Production in India, so profitable in itself, was stepped up accordingly. In China the illicit distribution web operated by the private traders drew in ever more officials and began to extend both up and down the China coast. Thus in 1832 James Innes, one of Jardine Matheson's most active skippers, was exploring the opium potential of Fukien (Fujian).

> *Nov 29.* Chinchew Bay, just before daylight I sent ashore two Chinese servants with a list of twenty-eight opium dealers to ask them to come off and do business . . .
> *Dec 2.* Employed delivering briskly. No time to read my bible or to keep my journal.
> *Dec 5.* Still delivering briskly. Today several small mandarin junks sailed round us once or twice when some smuggling boats were alongside, but whether they did not like our look, or remembered the reception they got from the little *Kronberg*, I know not. They gave us no trouble and the opium boats came and went easily close to them.

'Chinchew' was near Amoy, 300 miles round the coast from Canton. Opium was succeeding where legitimate trade had failed in introducing foreign traders to all the great estuarine ports – Foochow (Fuzhou), Ningpo (Ningbo), Shanghai and Tientsin (Tianjin). Their commercial potential was assessed, their inadequate defences noted, their mandarins suborned.

Meanwhile Captain Innes's colleagues in the employ of Jardine Matheson and other agency houses were beginning to make inroads into the Company's ancient monopoly of the intercontinental 'out-

and-back' trade. In 1813, supported by British manufacturing interests who felt that the Company was less than enthusiastic about pushing their exports, the agency houses of Bombay and Calcutta had secured an end to the Company's monopoly of the India trade. Its monopoly of the China trade remained, but in the 1820s this too was severely dented as China firms set up shop in Raffles' newly founded Singapore. Singapore was administratively under the Governor-General in Calcutta and so, for trading purposes, was regarded as part of India. Its trade with Britain was now, therefore, open. By shipping China goods to Singapore and then quickly switching papers for onward shipment to London, the Company's China monopoly could be neatly circumvented. Singapore grew sensationally as a result; the Company's share of the China trade shrank proportionately. When in 1833 another alliance of British manufacturing interests and China traders bullied Parliament into at last terminating the Company's 'out-and-back' China monopoly, the agency houses gratefully eased themselves into the driving seat and trade was barely disrupted.

What was disrupted was the centuries-old system of accreditation whereby the Company, as represented by its august Select Committee of Supracargoes, had acted as guarantor, regulator, liaison and sole agent for the whole foreign trading community of Canton. It was 'The Select' who could alone deal with the Hoppo, the senior Manchu commercial functionary, and it was they who adjusted the terms of trade and resolved endless minor disputes. Their demise therefore left a sizeable gap. Private traders, in cut-throat competition with one another and ill-regarded by the Chinese authorities, proved incapable of filling it. So did Lord Napier, an official Superintendent of Trade who was dispatched from London in 1834. Napier's ignorance of conditions in China and his insistence on introducing himself as a government official, rather than a trader, elicited total suspension of the trade that he was supposed to be superintending. Although a resumption was arranged, a trial of strength looked inevitable.

The conflict duly came in 1839–40 and again in 1841–2. These were the Opium Wars and, though a host of other British demands – unrestricted residence at Canton, access to Chinese ports other than Canton, diplomatic relations with Peking, jurisdictional rights over British subjects, and the settlement of debts incurred by members of the Co-hong – clouded the issue, opium provided both the underlying grievance and the initial pretext. Moral outrage over the spread of such a pernicious drug, plus alarm over that drain of Chinese silver, had finally prompted Peking to attempt a crackdown. Commissioner Lin Tse-hsu had been dispatched to Canton in early 1839 and the China traders were ordered to surrender all stocks and sign an undertaking to forgo all future opium trading. Until they obliged, they were detained in Canton and all legal trade was again stopped. It goes without saying that Peking's action was both legitimate and responsible. When 20,000 chests of opium, over 1,000 tons and commonly regarded as the largest drug haul ever, was handed over and destroyed, Commissioner Lin felt vindicated.

This was not how the likes of William Jardine and James Matheson saw it. Nor, since Jardine was now active in Whitehall and since his colleagues had handed over the opium only on the understanding that compensation would be made by the British government, was it how the British government saw it. Faced with a stoppage of trade and a bill for £2 million, Lord Palmerston, the Foreign Secretary, identified a case for military intervention. An expedition of 3,000 troops from India plus ships of the Royal Navy headed for the Pearl River.

By the time it arrived in June 1840, hostilities had already commenced. Captain Charles Elliot, Lord Napier's successor, had ordered British traders not to sign the required undertaking to refrain from opium trading; they had accordingly resumed 'delivering briskly'. Refused access to Canton or even Macao, they operated from Manila in the Philippines and from vessels moored amongst the islands at the mouth of the Pearl River in what would become Hong Kong harbour. Chinese efforts to prevent provisions from reaching these vessels in October 1839 produced the first exchanges of fire. A more serious fire-fight resulted when Chinese junks went to the support of individual traders who preferred to sign Commissioner Lin's bond rather than forgo legitimate trade.

Directed by Elliot, the newly arrived expedition soon established the awful superiority of European firepower; while the Pearl River was blockaded, the main expedition sailed up the coast, capturing the island of Chusan and blockading Amoy, Ningpo and the mouth of the Yangtze (Chang Jiang). Finally at Tientsin, the port for Peking, Elliot was promised a settlement, later concluded (after more fighting) at Chuenpi near Canton in early 1841. A large indemnity was exacted, trade was to be resumed, diplomatic relations upgraded and an 'insular station' near the mouth of the Pearl River was to be ceded to the British. This was Hong Kong island. Captain Edward Belcher quickly took possession at a flag-raising ceremony on 26 January 1841.

In other respects this agreement proved a dead letter. Since Peking found the Chinese concessions wholly unacceptable and London found them wholly inadequate, both withheld ratification. Further hostilities loomed. Elliot's campaign had been merely a rehearsal. He would return home in disgrace, his failure to secure access to ports other than Canton being deemed a wretched gaffe while his preference for 'the desert island of Hong Kong' over thriving Chusan seemed utterly incomprehensible. It was so barren that, according to Palmerston, it could never be 'a mart of trade'. Nor, for some time to come, would it. It was, however, dry land possessed of fresh water. To it that ship-bound colony of traders rapidly repaired without waiting for ratification.

Elliot's replacement, Sir Henry Pottinger, joined them in August 1841 and, learning of further hostilities at Canton, proceeded to wreak vengeance. This time there was no jabbing round the coastline. Pottinger went straight for the jugular. Storming the central ports of Ningpo, Hangchow (Hangzhou) and, eventually, Shanghai he sailed boldly up the Yangtze to train his guns on Nanking (Nanjing). Nor did he relent at the negotiating table. With its supplementary treaties the 1842 Treaty of Nanking took over a year to negotiate and gave the British all they wanted. To Canton were added four new ports at which foreigners might trade, including Shanghai. At these 'treaty ports', as they became known, foreign trade would be subject to an agreed tariff of reduced duties, and foreign merchants would be under the protection of their own guns and under the jurisdiction of their own consuls. In addition, Hong Kong would be retained. Opium continued to be banned from the treaty ports but, since nothing was said about its 'brisk distribution' elsewhere, smuggling continued. In fact, it expanded, drawing in ever more officials and finding ever more openings. Palmerston was delighted.

> The conditions of peace imposed upon the Emperor are precisely those we had instructed our plenipotentiaries Elliot and Pottinger to obtain . . . This event, which will form an epoch in the progress of the civilisation of the human races, must be attended with most important advantages to the commercial interests of England.

It was 'an epoch in the progress of the human races' because, as Rutherford Alcock, one of the new consuls, fervently believed, commerce was 'the true herald of civilisation . . . the human agency appointed under a Divine dispensation to work out man's emancipation from the thralldom and evils of a savage existence'. Missionaries were also to be given greater access under the treaties; but trade was to be the real emancipator, the more and the freer the better.

According to J. K. Fairbank, the American authority on the China trade, the British knew 'what they wanted but [were] only half aware of what they were obtaining'. They had laid down a framework of treaty law on the assumption that the Chinese authorities were willing and able to implement it. It was soon clear that this assumption was wrong. The tariff system at the ports collapsed while internal transit duties proved a new and formidable obstruction to the penetration of Western manufactures. Rebellion by the Taipings and associated Triad groups during the 1850s soon threw Shanghai and the Yangtze into chaos; meanwhile in Canton an ancient quarrel about British rights of access to the Chinese city simmered ominously. By now American, French and other foreign competitors had negotiated their own favoured status and did not feel bound by the more restrictive clauses in the British treaties. Moreover the British, when two of the treaty ports degenerated into smuggling stations, simply demanded to swap them. They were also having second thoughts about Hong Kong, whose commercial potential remained doubtful while its expenses mounted.

Always ready, as he put it, 'to strike another blow [against] half-civilised governments such as China, Portugal, Spanish America', it was again Palmerston, now Prime Minister, who made renegotiation of the treaties, access to Canton city and, once again, diplomatic links with Peking a *casus belli*. There followed the desultory engagements of the 'Arrow' War of 1856–60 (so-called because the Chinese detention of a vessel named the *Arrow* precipitated it). It began with the storming of Canton and ended with the looting and destruction of the imperial summer palace at Peking.

In the resultant Treaty of Tientsin and the Peking Convention, all Palmerston's objectives were again met. Henceforth there would be foreign legations in Peking and no more trouble in Canton. Ten more treaty ports were opened, most significantly up the Yangtze where British shipping, having already engrossed most of China's coastal trade, now obtained entry to her most important inland waterway and so her internal trade. To improve Hong Kong's security, three square miles of the Kowloon peninsula, opposite Hong Kong island and commanding its main anchorage, were ceded. And perhaps most important of all, a system, established in 1854 in Shanghai, whereby the responsibility for collecting all China's customs duties on foreign trade had been assumed by a British-run Inspectorate, was confirmed and extended to the opium trade. This arrangement at last ended the commercial confusion which had dogged and discredited the China trade for decades. It also boosted the revenues of Peking's imperial treasury, thus reassuring the British, French and other interested parties that indemnities imposed on Peking would actually be met. In the operation of what became the Chinese Imperial Maritime Customs the British had acquired an interest in the maintenance, rather than the dismemberment, of China's territorial integrity.

Apart from Kowloon, Hong Kong's gain from these events consisted mainly of personnel. War brought an influx of British officers and largely Indian troops while the disturbances caused by the Taiping rebellion resulted in the first major migration of Chinese capital and entrepreneurs from the mainland, an event hailed by James Legge, a contemporary missionary, as 'the turning point in the progress of Hong Kong'. The agency houses had been the island's pioneers and for similar reasons – free trade and comparative security – Chinese business began to follow.

Although Hong Kong's trade figures rocketed, the trade in question was mostly re-export as the island became a convenient distribution centre for coastal shipping. Business and banking were more important. The Hongkong and Shanghai Bank was founded in 1865. A year later the trade and transport conglomerate of Butterfield and Swire, Jardine Matheson's mighty rival, began life in Shanghai and soon opened a branch in Hong Kong.

Yet already Britons were more numerous in the treaty ports than in the colony. Compared to the stuffy little island, Shanghai was especially appealing and its International Settlement – basically a pooling of real estate concessions won by the British and the Americans – soon housed the most powerful trading community in the East. It, and not Hong Kong, was the true successor to the Company's Canton establishment. Without Shanghai's trade, Hong Kong would have been worthless. But as the number of treaty ports multiplied and as their trade escalated, Hong Kong's function as counting-house and parlour of the China traders won grudging acceptance.

The Vultures Gather

Enjoying an overwhelming share of China's overseas trade, and having at last removed the main obstacles to its unlimited expansion, the British after 1870 were mainly concerned with keeping rivals at bay. The first to make a move were the French. Lately established in the south of Indo-China, in the early 1880s, as will appear, they moved north into Annam and Tonkin, roughly north Vietnam. This meant infringing ancient Chinese claims to suzerainty over these areas and opening a back door into Chinese Yunnan by way of the Red River. Peking's objections were met by tearing a leaf from the Palmerstonian manual of statecraft. In 1884 French troops landed in Formosa while at Foochow on the mainland a Chinese fleet was routed and the port bombarded.

Although Paris subsequently settled for a free hand throughout Indo-China, the lesson was obvious: the British had a serious rival in the south. If Hong Kong were to avoid the fate of Foochow, its defences needed to take account of new developments in naval gunnery. It was also obvious that China's ability to defend its territory was still negligible and that neither the British nor the Americans were willing to risk war on its behalf. To an industrialised power short of colonial outlets like Germany, the situation looked promising. To neighbours like Japan and Russia, with conflicting strategic and demographic interests in east Asia as well as commercial ambitions, it presented a veritable imperative for expansion.

A newly modernised and militarised Japan had the most to prove. Exploiting assorted grievances in Korea, in 1894 Japan's forces decisively defeated the Chinese on land and sea, grabbing in the process the Liaotung (Liaodong) peninsula of Manchuria and the extremity of the Shantung (Shandong) peninsula. Both were eventually to be relinquished under the terms of the Treaty of Shimonoseki (1895), but only after intervention by the European powers, notably France, Russia and Germany, and only in exchange for recognition of Japan's claim to Formosa plus an indemnity ten times that extracted by the British in 1842. To meet this financial obligation, Peking needed foreign loans; the price of foreign loans was more concessions, both territorial and commercial.

As the British historian D. K. Fieldhouse has noted, 'the vultures quickly gathered round what they thought was a dying empire'. In the north, Germany extracted a 99-year lease of Kiaochow Bay (Jiaozhou Wan), including its port of Tsingtao (Qingdao), on the underside of the Shantung peninsula; in the south France got a similar lease of the Kwangchow (Leizhou) peninsula in the Gulf of Tonkin; and in the extreme north Russia added to its already considerable control of Manchuria the major naval facility of Port Arthur (Lushun) at the tip of the Liaotung peninsula.

The British might, for once, have stayed aloof. Apart from the treaty ports of Tientsin and Chefoo (Yantai), their interests in northern China were inconsiderable. If anything, Japan's presence in that region was to be preferred to that of European rivals, and the British had therefore played no part in curbing Japanese demands in 1895. The subsequent scramble for concessions was a different matter. A strong British protest was registered.

The Chinese replied by offering Weihaiwei, midway between German Tsingtao and Russian Port Arthur and so a potential challenge to either. At first it was refused; official British policy was still in favour of preserving the integrity of China, not infringing it. Then it was accepted, and an additional demand was lodged for that tract of similar size in southern China, namely what became the New Territories of Hong Kong. Strategic considerations had triumphed over political reservations. The Royal Navy relished the facilities and defence capabilities of Weihaiwei, and Hong Kong's military supremo had made a good case for the New Territories being imperative to the defence of the colony.

As already noted, neither place was ceded outright. Since both were supposed to offset corresponding concessions to the other powers, the New Territories were the subject of a 99-year lease, like the French and German acquisitions, while Weihaiwei's lease was to run 'for a period as long as Port Arthur shall remain in the possession of Russia'. Although the Russian lease was for just 25 years, few expected the Russians to withdraw so soon and Weihaiwei's lease was therefore potentially open-ended.

In fact the Russians lasted only seven years. Their defeat in the 1904–5 war with Japan meant that Port Arthur then became Japanese. Arguing that it was still alienated from China, the British stayed on in Weihaiwei and, on this basis, could have endeavoured to remain there until 1945. They recognised no legal obligation for the surrender over which Reginald Johnston would eventually preside. Nor, to his chagrin, would they recognise any moral obligation to the people of Weihaiwei. It would be exactly the opposite when the future of Hong Kong's New Territories came up for review in 1982. Though ceded on such similar terms, the British would choose to treat these extremities of imperial disengagement as if one were soft chalk and the other hard cheese.

Meanwhile, China plunged deeper into chaos. Peking's support for the anti-Western Boxer rebellion of 1900 brought a crushing response from the treaty powers as an international force occupied the capital's Forbidden City, humiliated its imperial household and imposed another crippling indemnity. In despair, reform-minded Chinese, many of them temporarily resident in Hong Kong like Dr Sun Yat-sen, instigated a series of risings against their now ineffectual and discredited Manchu rulers. These climaxed in the revolution of 1911. The last emperor, soon to be Johnston's pupil, officially abdicated; he was allowed to stay on in the Forbidden City. Outside, elections were proclaimed. In what was probably the nearest thing to a legitimate and unengineered poll ever to be held in China, the Nationalist Kuomintang party claimed victory and was promptly outlawed. Whole provinces now rejected central authority as assorted warlords and Nationalists disputed among themselves.

They were joined, in the early 1920s, by Bolsheviks fired by Russia's revolution. At Nanning on the upper reaches of the You Jiang, the novelist Stella Benson and her husband, an official in the Maritime Customs, were due to leave for Hong Kong in April 1930. 'Buckled round with wars', as she put it, it was not that easy.

> Up-river are insurgent Communist peasants, most rough . . . Down river are brigands – also ill-bred to excess. Between are our rebel soldiers – Chang-Fat-Kwei and his famous Ironsides – but we are getting quite used to them and indeed fraternise . . . A warlord called Huang Shao Hsiung came to our tennis tournament the other day, and I sat side by side with him, making myself a new pair of camiknickers . . . As soon as there is the least chance of not being sunk by gunfire, we set off in a little motor launch victualled with the last White Man's food left in besieged Nanning – ie two tins of sausages, one bottle of gin and three boxes of petit beurre. It should be rather fun . . .

All these insurgent groups espoused modernisation and national revival. Many acknowledged a debt to the West and were not necessarily hostile to foreigners. Their aggression was directed at one another and at any vestiges of the Manchu empire, including its treaties. The 'queue' or pigtail, the detested symbol of Manchu subjugation, was succumbing to the snip of machine-made scissors.

Such chaos brought to Hong Kong, as well as fleeing Europeans, another wave of influential Chinese settlers and another brief boom; but the two were not obviously connected. The boom owed more to the island's original function as an opium warehouse. Once again well-meaning attempts to outlaw opium had merely resulted, as in the 1840s, in an escalation in the trade. The revenue deriving from it leapt from about 30 per cent of the colony's total in 1905 to nearly 50 per cent in 1918. The University of Hong Kong was founded. The new railway from Kowloon to Canton was opened. In the booking office in Hong Kong's Victoria you could now reserve a sleeping compartment right through to London's Victoria. Otherwise it was business, and not much else, as usual.

Back to Weihaiwei

'Via Siberia' scrawled Reginald Johnston on the envelopes of his first letters home from Weihaiwei. It was much quicker than via Suez. Sometimes *The Times* arrived at Government House only two weeks late. Weihaiwei no longer seemed 'the most absolutely forgotten of [British] imperial outposts', as James (later Jan) Morris, author of the *Pax Britannica* trilogy, would later describe it.

News of Johnston's reappointment to Weihaiwei as its Commissioner (or Governor) had come in 1926. In London at the time, he hastily packed his bags and sailed for New York, thence west by rail to Vancouver and by sea to Hong Kong. It was an eccentric way of reaching the East but it spared one the jingoistic horde of soldiers, planters, memsahibs and fortune-hunters who steamed out via Suez on the P&O ships.

Johnston enjoyed the journey, savouring its opportunities for study and reflection while contributing with un-Buddhist gusto to Canadian Pacific's on-board festivities. Now 52 years old, happily unmarried, and wholly devoted to Chinese scholarship, his only anxiety was lest Weihaiwei might have ceased to be British before he could get there. As will be seen, by 1926 negotiations for the surrender of its lease had been underway for some years. In 1924 agreement had actually been reached, only for contacts to be broken off when the political chaos which led to the young Emperor's flight from the Forbidden City removed any chance of an immediate hand-over.

Fortunately Johnston was somewhat reassured on this point as soon as he reached Hong Kong. He stayed with its Governor, his old Oxford friend Cecil Clementi. 'An excellent governor', he thought, 'but I am not sure that I care much about his wife.' He went up in an aeroplane for the first time and he learnt that, though the 'rendition' (the prefered euphemism for the 'surrender') of Weihaiwei was still imminent, he could expect at least 'a few remaining weeks or months of British rule'.

This estimate was probably based on the current state of the Hong Kong Governor's forward planning for the New Territories. Clementi, it will be recalled, was the man who twenty years earlier had been responsible for the registration of land claims in the New Territories – 'The country people remained his firm friends for life.' Now, as Governor and with 30 of the 99 years on the New Territories lease already gone, he was anxious about their future. He was also anxious about the colony in that he already feared for its future development if no land in the New Territories could be sub-let for longer than the term remaining on the main lease.

This may have seemed a legalistic and unnecessarily abstruse concern for one as eminent and patrician as Governor Clementi. In fact it was typical. Thinking the unthinkable was Clementi's forte; he would do the same in Malaya. Immensely charming, delightfully cultivated but uncannily prescient, Clementi was in effect posing the lowering question that would hang over Hong Kong like a thundercloud for the next half century: what would happen to the colony when the New Territories lease ran out in 1997?

His answer was simple. If in Weihaiwei the British had a disposable asset, why not make its surrender conditional on the Chinese converting the lease of the New Territories into a permanent cession, like that of Hong Kong island? This was the proposal he was about to put to the Colonial Office. Given that any subsequent negotiations with the Chinese would take time, it was safe to assume that Weihaiwei would be British for 'some weeks or months' to come.

Reassured if not convinced, Johnston had sailed north from Hong Kong to Tientsin courtesy of Butterfield and Swire's China Steam Navigation Company. Tientsin was one of the larger international treaty ports and that to which the Japanese had removed his old pupil, now plain Henry Pu-yi. The ex-Emperor was so excited to hear of his ex-tutor's return that, confounding convention, he sped round to the Tientsin Club where Johnston was staying. Later he insisted on coming on board to see him off, 'much to the excitement of the crew'.

The new steamer – Johnston's fourth and this time one of Jardine Matheson's – worked its way round the ice-encrusted Gulf of Chihli. It was March. They called at Chefoo, another treaty port, and then finally drew abreast of a low featureless island near the utmost extremity of the Shantung peninsula. Liukungtao still served as a summer station for the British China squadron. It was also the focus of the extensive but treeless promontory beyond – 'that delectable territory' to which Johnston was returning so happily. Bulky figures wearing greatcoats and fur hats with ear mufflers awaited him on the quay with a mittened guard of honour. Shaggy ponies steamed beside a *shenzi*, China's equivalent of the covered waggon. From scattered cottages sheltering half-hidden in the folds of the rock-strewn heath, an icy wind snatched at the smoke of coal fires. Scots like Johnston and Stewart Lockhart, his predecessor and mentor, were sometimes reminded of Sutherland; to others it was simply 'a colder Aden'.

In the spartan conditions of one of the British empire's more modest gubernatorial residences, Johnston set up home. There was still neither running water nor electricity. One storey high with a lot of roof, elaborate chimneys, casement windows and some intricate lattice-work, Government House could have passed for a well-kept station on the West Highland Line. It smelled of saddlery and beeswax. Day and night for six months a year pigtailed men in padded coats stoked the fires, one in every room. Roses rambled prolifically over the porch. For a bachelor of simple tastes and scholarly bent it was agreeably adequate.

Old friendships were soon renewed. Like the mandarins he so much admired, Johnston toured his 300-square-mile domain, commending the ground-nut crop, ascribing the fall in mortality to small-pox immunisation and dispensing his usual mixture of Confucian homilies and colonial justice. 'Rendition', he wrote in a letter to Stewart Lockhart, though apparently unavoidable, was not welcome.

> The longer it is postponed the better I will be pleased as it is delightful to be back in the old place and to find the people as friendly as ever. The place is prospering and the revenue is now nearly [a] quarter of a million dollars . . . Weihaiwei is no longer the tranquil *wu wai* place that it used to be.

The long summer months brought more than the normal invasion of holiday-makers from Hong Kong. A British regiment arrived for garrison duty together with several hundred venereally diseased convalescents from the Shanghai Defence Force. The fleet came and went. So did assorted Bolshevik agents and Nationalist spies. Planes occasionally passed across Weihaiwei's empty azure skies. On the ground the wheel-less *shenzi*, so well adapted to a largely roadless territory (being in effect a horse-borne palanquin with shafts fore and aft) was no longer the only means of transport. Up the new road from Port Edward to Government House there ground, with increasing frequency, the first motor cars.

Such were the demands on Johnston's annual entertainment allowance that it was exhausted within a matter of weeks. The Emperor himself wanted to come and stay. Johnston would have been delighted but, as he had tactfully to explain, 'His Britannic Majesty's Government would not approve'. Attracting attention to what he always called 'the place' was the last thing the government wanted. Even its assets were now just an embarrassment. As Johnston had written in his *Lion and Dragon in Northern China*,

> The greatest advantage that Weihaiwei possesses – from the naval as well from the civilian point of view – is its good climate. It is perhaps not so superlatively excellent as some writers, official and other, have made out: but none will deny that the climate is 'a white man's', and most will agree that it is on the whole, the finest on the coast of China.

Equally favourable was the political climate. With Chiang Kai-shek's Kuomintang Nationalists, Moscow-backed Communists and assorted warlords running riot throughout the erstwhile empire, Johnston was right in calling Weihaiwei 'probably the safest place in China today'. Thanks to his and Stewart Lockhart's reverence for Chinese tradition and their allegiance to Confucian principles, the place, unlike the weather, was not 'a white man's'. In fact it was probably the most traditional enclave in China and the one least troubled by reform or revolution. Peace and comparative prosperity reigned. The strife elsewhere had not been reflected within Weihaiwei society.

Pigtails and Hair-nets

In the 1919 Treaty of Versailles which ended the First World War, Japan's wartime support of the victors had been generously recog-

nised with the award to Tokyo of defeated Germany's ex-colonies in
the East. These comprised some islands in the west Pacific, of which
more will be heard, plus Tsingtao, Germany's territorial concession
on the Shantung coast. Such high-handed shuffling of a bit of
Chinese territory amongst the imperial powers had not been untypical during the last days of the Manchu empire; in the post-revolution
climate it was less acceptable. Student demonstrations in Peking's
Tiananmen Square protested the award and ignited anti-foreign
feeling throughout the country. Weihaiwei, no great distance from
Tsingtao and an eminently suitable target, did not escape altogether.
Here, however, the well-behaved protests and boycotts were directed
solely at Japanese nationals and Japanese trade.

Similarly, in 1925–6 Shanghai and Hong Kong were crippled by a
boycott of British trade inspired by left-wing Nationalists. In Hong
Kong the boycott included a general strike against both of which
Clementi stood firm, although the effects were disastrous. Opium
sales were now declining anyway, but in addition textile exports, previously something of a staple, dwindled to retail dimensions. The
colony's total trade was almost halved and would barely recover for a
decade.

Yet up the coast in Weihaiwei, strikes were unknown and the
1920s witnessed a steady and impressive rise in both trade and
government revenue. True, compared to Hong Kong's revenue of
23.5 million dollars in 1929, Weihaiwei's 0.4 million was not sensational. It was growing, though – in fact it doubled during Johnston's
tenure – while Hong Kong's was dwindling. A good peanut harvest
was crucial to this success. So was Port Edward's free-trade status.
Additionally Weihaiwei's dedicated administrators liked to emphasise
that the territory had incipient industries; silk thread was being produced for the China market, lace and stockings for the tourists; yet
more of Weihaiwei's nimble-fingered ladies were employed turning
the discarded pigtails of China's Nationalists into the finest of hair-
nets for America's housewives.

For this modest but steady advance, the Sinophile Johnston and
his predecessor Stewart Lockhart deserve every credit. They would,
though, have been the first to admit that Weihaiwei's tranquillity
owed as much to its Chinese citizens as to its British rulers. When
Stewart Lockhart had retired in 1921, Weihaiwei's district headmen
had composed a farewell address about how Commissioner 'Lo-
Kung' had 'been kind and polite to scholars, and treated the peasants

bounteously'. Perhaps such phrases were standard, and perhaps Stewart Lockhart's reply was the standard response by a departing mandarin. It was certainly not the standard valedictory of a British colonial governor.

> I regard myself as fortunate in having always had to deal with the affairs of such an eminently reasonable and lovable race as the Chinese whom I have always found as loyal as the Highlanders of my own country and ever ready to lend me their assistance in sunshine and storm.

Such sentiments were unthinkable in stiff and stuffy Hong Kong. There, according to Clementi, racial prejudice retarded 'the social, moral, intellectual, and even the material and commercial progress of the colony'. In 1926 he had proposed changing the colony's seal. Instead of the badly executed beach scene of an Englishman and a Chinaman trading what could have been either opium or tea, he suggested an elegant composition including the Chinese characters for 'Hong Kong'. This was rejected out of hand; a representative of Jardine Matheson summed up opinion when he proudly insisted that there were not ten Europeans in the colony who could recognise the Chinese characters. Two years later, against fierce opposition from both the colony's British community and the Colonial Office, Clementi did just succeed in changing the constitution of his Executive Council so that he could appoint its first ever Chinese member. There was no possibility of the incumbent being elected and so enjoying any kind of democratic mandate; the Council, anyway, was little more than a rubber stamp. And all this in a colony where the Chinese accounted for 97 per cent of the population and 90 per cent of colonial revenue, and where all residents, regardless of their race, were technically British subjects.

Herein lay the principal difference between Weihaiwei and Hong Kong. Unlike the treaty ports, which were not British territory (although foreigners had territorial rights there) and whose relations with the British government were therefore handled by the Foreign Office, Weihaiwei and Hong Kong (including Kowloon and the New Territories) were colonies administered by the Colonial Office. Yet whereas the New Territories had been quickly incorporated into Hong Kong as if they had originally formed part of it, Weihaiwei had not been incorporated into anything. The New Territories lease was taken to imply a cession of territory and a transfer of sovereignty from the Chinese Emperor to the British crown; the population thereby became British subjects. Weihaiwei's lease was taken to mean exactly the opposite, that no territory was ceded, that Chinese sovereignty remained and that the people therefore retained their Chinese citizenship. Hence Hong Kong, in legal jargon, would one day have to be 'retroceded', Weihaiwei being merely rendered – or, as Johnston preferred, 'rendited'.

The distinction seems to have been made purely on the grounds of expediency. The New Territories were vital to Hong Kong's defence, to its supplies (especially of water) and to its amenities, a new cemetery and a new rifle range being amongst the first developments slated for the area. Weihaiwei, on the other hand, was vital to no one. Russia's displacement at Port Arthur left the Japanese as the dominant power in the Yellow Sea. The British and the Japanese were in alliance until 1922 and the strategic argument was therefore irrelevant. Moreover the Royal Navy, prime supporters of the 1898 leasing arrangement, had since decided against developing the base at Liukungtao as other than a sanatorium and a 'flying station' (a temporary facility). Weihaiwei, as one of Stewart Lockhart's correspondents had put it, was to be 'a local Margate instead of a Portsmouth' – a foreshore for bathing machines rather than battleships. The uncertainty and lack of enthusiasm which had characterised the territory's acquisition were not going to go away.

As Stewart Lockhart and Johnston repeatedly pointed out, this uncertainty did the place no favours. Talk of rendition had been in the air ever since 1905. It had been agreed in principle in 1922 when, following US pressure, the British reluctantly accepted that the only way to assuage Chinese fury about that Versailles transfer of Tsingtao was to get the Japanese to give it up; and the only way to get the Japanese to give it up was for Britain to make a similar gesture in respect of Weihaiwei.

Subsequently Clementi's idea of a swap – linking the trade-in of Weihaiwei's lease with the replacement of that on the New Territories by an outright cession – added another good reason for 'rendition'. Clementi was the first to explore the dire consequences of the New Territories lease for Hong Kong as a whole, and the late 1920s was probably the latest date at which such a swap might have been made. Fatally for the colony's future, this golden opportunity was allowed to slip. Advancing an argument that would become all too familiar in the years ahead, London discouraged the idea on the grounds that it would attract attention to the existing lease which could be even more damaging to the colony's development than ignoring it. In the case of Hong Kong the uncertainty would merely be compounded by its recognition.

For Weihaiwei, however, this argument worked the other way. The shortcomings of the lease were positively trumpeted; uncertainty had thus become as much an acknowledged feature of 'the place' as its bracing breezes. Poised for imminent extinction for the best part of a decade, it was hardly surprising that entrepreneurs and investors from Hong Kong and Shanghai had not beaten a path to Port Edward's waterfront. In fact it was something of a miracle that it enjoyed that modicum of prosperity, let alone its enviable stability. Johnston, though, remained philosophical.

> There is no local demand for rendition – quite the reverse – but I think it is bound to come very soon . . . The Chamber of Commerce has no desire to be handed back to China. Unfortunately no one is likely to consult them in the matter . . .

Local opinion was irrelevant. So were business interests. So was the fact that, against all odds, Weihaiwei was finally paying its way. This last meant that the place would be handed over in good running order. It was definitely a plus, perhaps the only plus, but it had no bearing on the act of rendition or its timing. These were being decided elsewhere and on principles with which Johnston had no quarrel. As with Hong Kong seventy years later, Weihaiwei's fate had long since acquired a crushing inevitability. Johnston's role would be simply to manage it with dignity.

Having Done with It

As Weihaiwei was being quietly written out of the imperial drama, only the continued influx of tourists kept it on the map. Passing celebrities enlivened Johnston's summers in Government House and, though the winters were quieter, in late 1928 the Clementis came to stay. 'Lady C' could still be a trial; but to one as given to dotty intellectual fantasising as Johnston, the Clementi children were a rare delight. With Sir Cecil he discussed his future. Chances of succeeding to the latter's governorship of Hong Kong never looked rosy. The Colonial Office had written Johnston off for what, he admitted, he was – 'a deranged old man'. Clementi's suggestion of a Doctorate of Letters at the University of Hong Kong had possibilities, not least that of 'the hilarious delights of becoming "Dr Johnston"'.

One thing was certain; he would soon be moving on. In early 1929 he learnt that the Foreign Office had recognised the Nationalist regime established by Chiang Kai-shek in Nanking. Here at last was a legitimate government, if not exactly a stable one, to whom the lease could be surrendered. There was now no excuse for delay. Nearer to hand, radical Nationalists at the treaty port of Chefoo were demanding immediate withdrawal. Johnston sympathised.

> I think it is a great pity that H[is] M[ajesty's] G[overnment] does not get the thing put through and have done with it. This continual postpone-ment may end in our having to go under humiliating circumstances. However the C[olonial] O[ffice] can't say that I haven't warned them.

This was in a letter to Stewart Lockhart of February 1929. A year later Johnston was still at Government House. A small detachment of troops, deemed necessary because of the continued influx of 'Bolsheviks' and 'bandits', now over-wintered in the territory. In 1930 it was the turn of the Argyll and Sutherland Highlanders, the first kilted regiment to be stationed there. 'If rendition takes place this year, I expect to have a piper to pipe me down to the pier,' wrote Johnston. In the New Year's Honours he had just been created Sir Reginald. That, surely, presaged the end. Discussions about compensation for foreign-owned businesses were well advanced. The Chinese soon agreed to the Royal Navy having continued access to Liukungtao, and in July they announced that after rendition Weihaiwei would become a Special Administrative Area under central government control.

August brought a visit from Stella Benson who had stayed with Johnston, 'one of the most cherished creatures in the world', in happier days when he was the Emperor's tutor. Tongues might wag over the sylph-like novelist sharing Johnston's bachelor home but, as she explained, Johnston did not consider himself unattached.

> He has a pretence lady-friend called Mrs Walkinshaw whose outrageous and improper sayings he constantly quotes, even on the most icely [*sic*] official occasions. It must be very puzzling for an orthodox place like Weihaiwei to be governed by a non-existent but very improper Mrs Walkinshaw.

Other fantasy figures – the 'Earl of Dumbarton' ('always a bit of a saucy puss') and 'The Trouserless One' (alias the Moon) – were helping him prepare a programme for the handing-over ceremony. No doubt the fair Stella added a few telling flourishes. The date was set for 1 October 1930. No less exciting, 'Government House is now ablaze with electric light!'

If, in the light of later imperial disengagements, Weihaiwei's rendition was of somewhat low wattage it was because questions of nationhood scarcely arose. Barely fifty non-Chinese looked like wanting to stay on; provision for them posed no problem. As for the 120,000 Chinese, since they had never become British subjects, no special arrangements were needed. For them thirty-two years of British rule had changed little. In fact such dedicated Sinologists as Stewart Lockhart and Johnston, far from trying to modernise the place, had prided themselves on reviving the old imperial system and being the very model of traditional Chinese mandarins. They had retained the existing fiscal system whereby the village, rather than individual villagers, was responsible for taxes; they encouraged the traditional village headmen in their role as keepers of the peace; and in their own role as magistrates they consciously replicated the traditional *hsien* magistrate of Manchu times. Certainly there was an element of trusteeship in this, but they acted less as improving colonial trustees and more as conservative Confucian trustees. Unlike the Dutch in Indonesia or the French in Indo-China, no one could accuse the British in China of destroying local self-governing structures in the interests of authoritarian or central rule. Instead of changing Chinese practice in this remote corner of the Celestial kingdom, British rule had mothballed it.

It was China that had changed. In the generation during which Weihaiwei had been under British rule, the moribund Manchu empire had been transformed into a turbulent republic. How the law-abiding folk of this remote extremity of Shantung would fare under the multiple dispensations of provincial warlords and radical Nationalists deeply concerned Johnston. True to the mandarin code, he would be obliged to hand over his office with a dignity bordering on indifference. He was, nevertheless, relieved to find that his successor, Commissioner Hsu, was sympathetic and as well-intentioned as he could wish.

Rendition Day began with the hoisting of two flags, the British and that of Nationalist China. They flew throughout the full-dress parades, the speeches and the presentations. Hsu thanked the British for ruling wisely and well, the Chamber of Commerce extolled the virtues of the British Commissioners, and Johnston lauded the good people of Weihaiwei, wishing both them and his successor well. 'Mrs Walkinshaw' did not get a word in. Salutes were fired, bands played, the Last Post was sounded, and as Johnston and Hsu, both in top hat and tails, walked to the pier four abreast with the Argylls' Commanding Officer and the senior naval officer, the bagpipes played. Both flags were still flying as the launch left the pier. Not until sunset was the Union Jack quietly lowered for the last time.

As early as 1915 Johnston, when invited to summarise the reasons for the British presence in Weihaiwei, had argued for immediate rendition. Fifteen years later, and only six weeks before Rendition Day, he expressed the same view in a letter to the Colonial Office.

> If asked the question, what specific British interests are served by our retaining our territorial jurisdiction over the mainland of the Leased Territory of Weihaiwei [that is, excluding the naval facility at Liukungtao], I should be obliged to reply that I am aware of none.

The Colonial Office had hoped that he might insist on special provisions for the local inhabitants; 'but with our own Commissioner against us,' minuted an under-secretary, 'it seems hopeless to try to postpone rendition for their sake'. Weihaiwei was discarded not just because it served no purpose but because its Commissioner deemed this absence of purpose sufficient reason for relinquishing it. For once Johnston was arguing not as a mandarin but as a pragmatic colonial governor. To the British in the East territory had never been of paramount importance. Weihaiwei's rendition provided a timely reminder of this cardinal principle which, in marked contrast to the territorial obsessions of its European rivals, would so facilitate Britain's imperial disengagement over the next four decades.

4

Indo-Chinoiserie

Ho Who Enlightens

While Governor of Hong Kong, Sir Cecil Clementi was wont to describe his crown colony as a mere municipality. 'I regard myself as in effect Mayor of Hong Kong,' he announced. In a touchy society already distrustful of his Chinese sympathies, this mildly derogatory attitude was not well received. To cut the Governor down to size, residents insisted that, whether colony or municipality, Hong Kong was actually run by 'the Jockey Club, the Hongkong and Shanghai Bank, and the Governor, *in that order*'.

The Royal Hong Kong Jockey Club staged race-meetings at Happy Valley. It was also known for its obsession with social blood-stock and unassailable bank balances. Discriminating against not only Asians and most Europeans but also most British, it epitomised the exclusive nature of Hong Kong's colonial élite. Coupled with the intimacy of life in a cramped municipality, it made the island far and away the stiffest, stuffiest colony in the East. 'England at last,' sighs a character in one of Stella Benson's novels as he lands in a Hong Kong of red-faced subalterns isolated in their own complacency. When Somerset Maugham's *The Painted Veil* appeared in 1925, British residents were outraged. Writs were issued, one being from the Assistant Colonial Secretary who believed himself and his office maliciously libelled because his fictional counterpart had been por-trayed as a liar and seducer. Self-mockery, like dynamism, was not something readily associated with the 'tin gods' up on their Peak. It was too much like sedition.

It is thus somewhat surprising that away from the hallowed turf of Happy Valley and below the mist-shrouded heights of the salubrious Peak, there lurked in the crowded bazaars of Central and Kowloon a

veritable hot-bed of revolution. Here Dr Sun Yat-sen, lately graduated from the Hong Kong College of Medicine, planned his first
rising on the mainland. It failed as did the half dozen more that followed, but when he eventually became president of the Republic of
China he acknowledged the colony as his nationalist nursery where
he had imbibed his 'revolutionary and modern ideas'.

In late 1897, two years after the doctor's abortive rising, a more
exotic revolutionary found sanctuary in the colony. Emilio
Aguinaldo had been 'generalissimo' of the recent rebellion against
Spanish rule in the Philippines. Temporarily banished in exchange
for a hefty subsidy, Aguinaldo came to Hong Kong to spend the
money on arms and plan the next phase of his revolt. While there he
made contact with the US armada being assembled by George
Dewey in nearby Mirs Bay for an assault on Manila. With the help of
Aguinaldo's partisans, in 1898 Dewey would overthrow Spanish rule,
then claim for the United States its first Asian colony.

Thirty years and a Russian revolution later, Hong Kong served as
a conduit for Asian Communism. Following the suppression of
Indonesia's first Communist uprisings, Tan Malaka, the mercurial
figure from west Sumatra who would come to represent the only
serious challenge to Sukarno's leadership, seems to have briefly oper-
ated from Hong Kong as a south-east Asian representative of the
Comintern. For other Indonesian exiles Singapore provided a
handier haven. Hong Kong was better sited as a refuge for
Vietnamese activists. In 1930, when Clementi was nearing the end of
his governorship and Weihaiwei the end of its colonial interlude,
Hong Kong provided an unlikely venue for the founding of the
Vietnamese Communist Party. Soon renamed the Indo-Chinese
Communist Party, it would in 1941 become the nucleus of the
Vietminh.

The venue in question was in fact Hong Kong's football stadium
and the crucial meeting is said to have taken place on 3 February
during the course of a match. Convened, possibly at half-time, by a
senior activist who went by the name of Nguyen Ai Quoc ('Nguyen
the Patriot'), it brought together delegates of two recently formed
Communist cells, one representing Tonkin and north Annam (north
Vietnam), the other south Annam and Cochin-China (south
Vietnam). They were informed of the Moscow Comintern's requirement that they unite round a new programme and dutifully obliged.
It seems to have been a short meeting. Soon after 'Nguyen the

Patriot' published a ten-point manifesto, its first pledge being the overthrow of 'imperialism, the feudal system and the reactionary bourgeoisie of Vietnam'. There followed calls for Indo-Chinese independence, government by the proletariat, confiscation of estates, nationalisation of banks, and other social and industrial measures conducive to a broad-based revolution. Henceforth, in spite of the French crackdown which had driven these delegates into exile, the party was to operate within Vietnam in close touch with the masses, as orthodox principles demanded.

The Comintern, with 'Nguyen the Patriot' as its trusted agent, was insisting on a close supervision of the Vietnamese struggle. In Indonesia the PKI (Communist Party of Indonesia), with a ten-year start on Vietnam's Communist Party, had demonstrated the futility of premature armed struggle when the 1926–7 risings in Java and Sumatra had been easily quelled by the Dutch authorities. Similar mistakes must be avoided in Indo-China. As it was, within a week of the meeting in the football stadium, a serious revolt took place at the military base of Yen Bay in the vital Red River corridor from Tonkin into China. The French responded with customary aplomb, strafing the base and rounding up for execution many of the supposed leaders. To 'Nguyen the Patriot' and his colleagues this was a salutary lesson though not an unmitigated disaster. The Yen Bay mutiny had been the bungled result of a call to arms by the VNQDD, their bourgeois Nationalist rivals. Now obliged to seek refuge in China, the VNQDD's exodus conveniently cleared the field for the Communists and their 'orthodox principles'.

These, however, proved scarcely less disastrous. In September 1930 peasant farmers in north Annam began staging hunger marches and commandeering local estates. To run them they elected people's committees known as 'Xo-Viets', a neatly Vietnamised version of the more orthodox 'soviets'. Evidently party activists were busy in the ranks, although the peasants' principal motivation seems to have been extreme impoverishment rather than Marxist-Leninist indoctrination. The French bothered little about such distinctions. More air and ground offensives inflicted 10,000 casualties and were followed by the arrest and detention of many of the Party's luminaries. Its general secretary died in captivity; Pham Van Dong, one of his aides and later prime minister, was banished to the penal settlement of Pulo Condore, an experience which may have contributed to his later reputation as 'an austere personage whose rare and wintry smile', according to the British diplomat Donald Lancaster, 'seemed out of place in a countenance otherwise set in lines of bleak and permanent disapproval'.

Of 'Nguyen the Patriot' there was no sign. Nevertheless he was known to be a native of the region as well as the founder of the Party. He was therefore tried in his absence and condemned to death. In fact he was still in Hong Kong but living under a new name – information of which Monsieur Louis Arnoux of the French Sûreté was well aware.

Arnoux had been on 'the Patriot's' trail for over a decade. In Paris during the early 1920s he had stalked the lonely Annamite through a succession of cheap lodgings, expatriate cafés and left-wing publishers' offices. In Asia he had subsequently tracked his progress from Bangkok to China, Tashkent and Singapore. They had actually met on more than one occasion. According to Arnoux, 'he knew me well enough to realise that as long as I was alive and had a free hand there was no chance of his returning to Indo-China . . .' Involuntarily, that is. For in June 1931 the British authorities suddenly arrested 'Nguyen the Patriot' along with other Comintern agents. Applications for their extradition followed immediately, and it may be that the French authorities actually instigated the arrests. Anglo-French co-operation in China had a long pedigree. Since under Hong Kong law there was nothing illegal about belonging to the Party or holding Comintern office, the prisoner faced charges which were clearly false, namely prejudicing the security of Hong Kong. He was accordingly acquitted, but he remained in detention pending extradition.

The legal tussle that followed goes some way towards explaining Hong Kong's popularity as a refuge for revolutionaries. Respect for the law was something on which even witless assistant colonial secretaries prided themselves. Simply bundling the prisoner aboard a French ship was out of the question. Left-wing organisations quickly adopted him as a prisoner of conscience; appeals were forwarded to London; the affair became a *cause célèbre*. Extradition seemed certain to lead to the prisoner's death yet it was far from clear whether he had been other than very indirectly involved in the Annam disturbances. Described at the time as so thin and lithe as to be quivering like a bow-string, and with a lifestyle of unimpeachable austerity to match, 'the Patriot' simply did not conform to criminal type. Referred to the Privy Council in London, his case was presented by Sir Stafford Cripps, then Solicitor-General in Ramsay

MacDonald's Labour government. An abler advocate and a more sympathetic government could not have been found. Extradition was refused.

By now it was 1932 and 'Nguyen the Patriot' had been moved to Hong Kong's prison hospital suffering from malaria. There, according to Sûreté records in Hanoi, he died in 1933. Certainly no one called 'Nguyen the Patriot' ever troubled the Sûreté again. But, twelve years later, they would be troubled by a man, admittedly a lot older looking, called Ho Chi Minh. It meant 'Ho who enlightens', another alias. Evidently the man had been using this name since 1942. His colleagues quickly, and the French eventually, conceded that his just perceptible resemblance to 'Nguyen the Patriot' was no coincidence. It was confirmed when Frank Loseby, a British lawyer who had adopted 'the Patriot's' case in 1931, averred that in 1932 he and his wife had been responsible for smuggling the prisoner out of Hong Kong, first to Singapore and then, after his recapture, up the coast to Amoy. There, while recuperating in a safe house arranged by the Losebys, the spectral revolutionary adopted the improbable disguise of a prosperous merchant. In 1933 he was in Shanghai dodging Chiang Kai-shek's Communist purges and renewing contacts with the Comintern. A year later he was spirited aboard a Russian liner to Vladivostok, and then by train to Moscow.

A Cobra Rearing its Head

Myth and mystery obscure many stages of Ho Chi Minh's life but it seems fairly certain that he was born in the year 1890. This was a mere seven years after Annam became a French protectorate and only twenty years after the first French settlement in Indo-China was established at Saigon. Compared to Dutch rule in the archipelago or British rule in India, French rule in Indo-China was a fleeting affair, scarcely more permanent than America's colonial flirtation in the Philippines. There was no plateau of empire, no dog-days of commercial speculation and administrative tinkering. Having scaled the path to paramountcy, the French were almost immediately faced with a slippery descent towards disembarkation. Retraction threatened even as expansion peaked.

Ho's father had been a mandarin in the service of the Annamite emperor and also a locally revered scholar. His victimisation and dismissal by the first French officials to penetrate Ha Tinh province made a profound impression on his son. 'Thus,' explains the intrepid Inspector Arnoux, 'Ho's life was begun in an atmosphere of injustice, of anger and bitterness, of hatred towards France . . .' More significantly, the family provided a good example of how the pre-colonial order was separated from the post-colonial order by just a single generation. It was as if Mahatma Gandhi had been the son of an official in the employ of the Great Moguls. One minute the French were riding to the rescue of an ignorant peasantry exposed to the brutalities of an unreconstructed oriental despotism, the next they were executing the Communist leaders and machine-gunning the revolutionary cadres of the self-same peasantry.

As for nationalism, the usual response to oppressive foreign rule, no gradual awakening was either possible or necessary. Vietnam already had national spirit in abundance. This was not the case throughout Indo-China. As late as the 1950s it was reported that more than half the population of Laos did not know they were living in Laos. Since Laos had often been divided into two or more principalities and since communications were almost non-existent, this was not altogether surprising. Cambodians, better informed thanks to the monumental relics of their Khmer ancestors at Angkor, did know about Cambodia, although they may have been wondering what had become of it. So severely had its frontiers been pruned, and so relentlessly had its Siamese and Vietnamese neighbours bullied the kings of Phnom Penh, that both its extent and its sovereignty were no longer certain.

Vietnam was very different. Its historians insist that patriotic Nguyens had been fighting for its national identity ever since the Trung sisters, veritable Boadiceas, had challenged Chinese rule in the first century AD. Peking's authority had since been reimposed but, by the fifteenth century, had been successfully rejected in favour of occasional tribute missions and a vague recognition of Chinese suzerainty. Latterly, following expansion into the Mekong delta at the expense of the Khmers, the country whose borders were roughly those of today had acknowledged the supremacy of an emperor based at Hue. In the early nineteenth century Gia Long of the Nguyen dynasty pursued a policy of unification reminiscent of, and contemporary with, the efforts of Daendels and Raffles in Java. Hanoi and Saigon were linked with the completion of a road running the length of the country. Impressive fortifications were constructed and irrigation works undertaken. Like Java, where Raffles had detected 'a strong sense of nationality . . . [which] supports a hope of future independence', Vietnam could claim that its nationhood already had substance.

Geography, on the other hand, had done the place no favours. Vietnam's configuration has been variously described as that of a cobra rearing to strike, two rice bowls suspended at opposite ends of a bent carrying pole, or two semi-submerged flood-plains totally unconnected by 500 miles of impenetrable forest and unclimbable mountain. Shared language and a common but not exclusive ethnicity helped to overcome these problems; so did those two millennia of resistance to Chinese rule and the Confucian acculturation which, as in Japan, nevertheless characterised them.

These common features were not, however, immediately apparent to seafarers approaching points at opposite ends of a 1,500-mile coastline. To the Portuguese, Dutch and English who first ventured to trade with Vietnam in the seventeenth century, the cobra's head ('Tonkin, the northern or Red River flood-plain) was a different country to the cobra's tail (Cochin-China, the lower part of which comprises the Mekong delta). In between, the long neck, the pole between the two rice bowls, was known as Annam. This was the Chinese designation for the whole country but one which Europeans applied only to the elongated and mountainous central spine where was sited the imperial capital of Hue. All three sections had at various times hosted rebellions against the central authority but it was the French, pursuing the imperialist cliché of 'divide and rule', who chose to exploit and institutionalise the political potential of these regional differences.

Mission Accomplished

French interest in Vietnam is somewhat optimistically dated to the late seventeenth century when both traders and clerics entered the South China Sea. The Compagnie des Indes, like other East India Companies, reconnoitred commercial prospects at Vietnam's ports but failed to establish any permanent links. In India the Compagnie enjoyed dazzling if short-lived success when in the mid-eighteenth century Dupleix and de Bussy very nearly established a French raj; but in the Far East it signally failed to compete with either the Dutch or the English. It was the other way round with the Société des Missions Etrangères – little impact in India but dogged endeavour

further east. To serve the Christian congregations originally converted by Portuguese missionaries, the Société, founded in 1663, was
soon dispatching vicars apostolic to both China and Vietnam.

A pattern of proselytisation was thus set and would remain
unchanged until the late nineteenth century. Missionaries, not merchants, spearheaded French activity in the Far East. Their work
constituted the only obvious reason for a French interest in the
region and their welfare provided the leading pretext for diplomatic
and military intervention. The flag belatedly followed the cross.
British apologists might waffle about how trade provided the means,
under some divine dispensation, for civilising the savage; but trade
could hardly compete with the true faith as a divinely dispensed
commodity. To the French in the East belonged the high moral
ground. They never relinquished it and their much proclaimed *mission
civilisatrice*, begun as just that, a Christian mission, retained its crusad-
ing overtones long after the missionaries had become irrelevant.

The first political openings did not appear until the second half of
the eighteenth century and came, as elsewhere, courtesy of dynastic
rivalry and rebellion within the country. Both the British in the 1770s
and the French in the 1780s exploited approaches from dispossessed
Nguyen claimants to the throne of Hue, and dispatched small
expeditions from India to assist them. That from Calcutta was nearly
a total disaster but that from Pondicherry should have been a sensational success. Pigneau de Behaine, vicar apostolic to Cambodia and
Cochin-China, had espoused the cause of the eventual winner in
Vietnam's dynastic stakes and arrived back in Cochin-China to find
him already possessed of Saigon and poised to make a push for Hue.
The small French contingent was able to provide invaluable technical and military assistance for which Gia Long, as he became,
was duly grateful, affording protection for both French missions
and trade. Uncharacteristically this promising opportunity was
completely wasted. Something more serious than dynastic rivalry
had overtaken France itself. A country in the throes of a revolution
and then of a succession of demanding wars could not afford oriental
distractions.

It was fifty years before contacts with the country were successfully revived. During this period the British extended their rule
throughout India, acquired Ceylon (Sri Lanka) and part of Burma,
founded Singapore and consolidated their commercial supremacy
throughout the Far East. France could never compete on equal

terms. Her trade with the East was virtually non-existent and her Indian possessions had long since shrunk to forgotten enclaves. All that remained as the basis for an eastern policy were her missionary responsibilities in China and adjacent countries like Vietnam. Since there was no hope of challenging British supremacy, and since the protection of missions and the protection of trade seemed to complement one another, such a policy could be best pursued in collaboration with the British.

Anglo-French collaboration did not, of course, exclude the possibility of pursuing national advantage. 'The taproot of French imperialism in the Far East from first to last was', according to the French American historian J. F. Cady, 'national pride – pride of culture, reputation, prestige, and influence.' But until the 1870s this concern with national pride was largely for domestic consumption. As monarchies, empires and republics succeeded one another in Paris, colonial activity came to be regarded as a way of boosting a regime's credentials. It assuaged powerful clerical interests and, by asserting national prestige, it gratified a volatile populace. The convulsions of French domestic politics had, and would continue to have, a far greater bearing on overseas policy than was the case with Britain or the Netherlands. If the empire that resulted was more susceptible to metropolitan control than any of its rivals, an explanation may as well be found in the erratic nature of French politics as in any inherent French tendency towards centralisation.

Missionary activity in China revived following the 1839 papal recognition of the Société des Missions Etrangères as the leading China mission in succession to the Portuguese. A host of new vicariates and ecclesiastical prefectures were established in the 1840s. To support and protect them from occasional persecution, ships of the French navy began calling at Chinese ports with the agreement of the British following the Sino-British Opium Wars. At the same time French diplomatic representatives, seeking from Peking guarantees of religious toleration and unimpeded travel, began associating themselves with the treaty demands emanating from Hong Kong, while at the same time tempting the Chinese authorities with suggestions of French assistance and mediation in resisting such demands.

The only exception was a powerful expedition of 1844 whose objectives included commercial concessions from the Chinese and the seizure of an island to rival Hong Kong. Basilan, the island so designated, lay off the north coast of Borneo and French plans for it closely resembled those of the British for its neighbour, Balambangan, in the previous century. Like Balambangan, Basilan proved an unmitigated disaster. French sailors were taken hostage, the Sultan of Sulu defied the French marine, and the Spanish in the Philippines claimed that the island was actually theirs. French prestige was badly shaken and further attempts at territorial aggrandisement were temporarily vetoed. Consolation was sought in bullying Peking into more concessions to the Catholic missions and in the French consul's insistence that in Shanghai France should have its own settlement, distinct from the International Settlement of the British and the Americans. By 1850 there were still only ten French citizens in Shanghai, five of them members of the consul's family; but eventually the French settlement would acquire a cathedral and in the twentieth century, much grown, it would become noted for its distinctive night-life.

Meanwhile contacts with Vietnam were limited to occasional visits, mostly to Tourane (Da Nang), the sea port nearest to Hue. Maltreated missionaries were uplifted, replacements smuggled ashore, and protests over the treatment of Vietnamese Christians delivered. The latter were then left to face the still worse persecution which such visits invariably provoked.

Opportunities for more effective intervention came to nothing until a large French force appeared in Chinese waters in 1857. The execution of a French missionary in China together with the imperialist ambitions of Louis Napoleon had prompted participation in the new British offensive against Peking that began with the *Arrow* incident. In subsequent operations at Shanghai and Tientsin the French played a significant role since part of the British contingent had been diverted to India to deal with the 1857 Mutiny. The effect of the Treaty of Tientsin, however, was to confirm British pre-eminence in China. Obliged to seek success and prestige elsewhere, the French expedition turned its attention to Vietnam.

The need for tangible results from such a major expedition, and the possibility that Tourane might fulfil the role envisaged for Basilan as a base and entrepôt, had ensured the inclusion of Vietnam in the expedition's official instructions. For public, that is British, consumption, it was emphasised that only a show of strength and the acquisition of a guarantee, be it territory or a cash indemnity, would ensure the future safety of missionaries and their Vietnamese converts. As if to emphasise the point, a Spanish missionary had just been sentenced to death. This fortuitously provided an immediate pretext for the landing at Tourane in 1858. It also enlisted support from Spain whose administration in the Philippines provided a small contingent of Spanish and Filipino troops.

From Tourane, the joint expedition was supposed to force its way up-river to Hue, just as the British had to Canton and Shanghai. Unfortunately the Perfume River was a lot shallower than the Pearl River or the Yangtze. Vessels of minimal draught were needed and the French did not have any. The Vietnamese, though slow to materialise, eventually put up a stout resistance and, as with the Dutch in Aceh, disease and exposure decimated the French ranks. After five fruitless months, stalemate had been reached with the French barely able to hang on to their Tourane bridgehead. By way of diversion the expedition's missionary advisers, backed by the Spanish contingent, urged a move north to Tonkin. There, they insisted, disaffection with Hue's rule and a greater concentration of Catholic converts would ensure a more favourable reception. Admiral Rigault de Genouilly had heard such promises before. Disillusioned about the strength of anti-Nguyen sentiment and desperate for tangible results, he opted instead to sail south and grab Saigon. It was a defining moment for France in the East. Saigon's Christian community was small and, unlike those in Annam and Tonkin, it had not been notably oppressed. The Admiral had put the imperial option before the clerical option. Support of missionary endeavour was no longer the priority.

Saigon was taken against strong resistance in February 1859. A garrison, left to hold it, barely survived until reinforcements arrived in 1861 while negotiations back at Tourane proved abortive. Time eventually ran out for the expedition when it was recalled to China in 1860 for the Anglo-French offensive which ended with the burning of the summer palace in Peking. The reinforcement of Saigon in 1861 proved more decisive. Three adjacent provinces were brought under French control and were recognised as such by an 1862 treaty with the Emperor Tu-Duc. The treaty also promised an indemnity plus better treatment for missionaries, and it gave the French exclusive commercial access in Annam.

For three years of considerable expense and heavy fatalities, concessions of such doubtful value and limited extent were seen as a poor return. In the light of British gains in China, they merely confirmed France's subordinate role in the East. The reputation of French arms had scarcely been enhanced and the acquisition of Saigon, whose trade consisted largely of rice exports, did little for national or dynastic prestige. Tiring of the enterprise, Louis Napoleon looked elsewhere. The development of what would soon be recognised as 'the Pearl of French Empire' was left to the initiative of those, mostly sailors, who had accompanied the original expeditions. As with the British experience in India and Malaya, less direction from on high meant more progress on the ground.

Instead of hammering again at the gates of hostile Hue, enterprising officers at Saigon addressed themselves to the possibilities of the Mekong River. In 1863 Lieutenant Doudart Lagrée travelled up-river to Phnom Penh and found the Cambodian king open to any arrangement which might secure his country from further encroachment by Siam. After several scares, Cambodia thus became a French protectorate with scarcely a shot being fired. Three years later Lagrée pushed further up-river, this time in command of a supposedly scientific expedition. In what became one of the great epics of nineteenth-century exploration, the expedition forced its way up cataracts to Laos, then Burma and finally, sixteen months after leaving Saigon, into Yunnan in China. There Lagrée died, leaving François Garnier, his able assistant, to lead the penniless remnant of the party down the Yangtze to Shanghai and so back to Saigon. Garnier also published a lavish account of the expedition which awakened his fellow-countrymen to the exotic potential of their south-east Asian colony. The Mekong might be a navigational nightmare but so was the Niger. What mattered was that Cochin-China lay on the threshold of a vast tropical interior which cried out for development by a civilising and beneficent power. Moreover, if the Mekong was not navigable, Tonkin's Red River was and it provided an even more direct route into China.

As an empire-builder, Garnier clearly modelled himself on Dupleix. The dominion that Dupleix had so nearly realised in India Garnier saw ready and waiting in what French writers now called 'Indo-China'. Even the name was artfully chosen; baulked in both India and China, France found consolation in the semantically engineered hybrid of Indo-Chine. Thanks to Garnier's encouragement, the means for realising this empire lay to hand in the exploits of Jean Dupuis, an enterprising trader based in Yunnan. In 1872 Dupuis undertook to open the Red River route from Haiphong through

Tonkin and up into Yunnan. On his second run he was detained at Hanoi. He appealed to the French Governor in Saigon for assistance against the Emperor's officials. The Emperor also appealed for assistance, but to expel Dupuis. Ostensibly in response to the latter request, Garnier was dispatched to Hanoi with a force of 200.

Acting on his own initiative, Garnier seized the citadel of Hanoi and declared the river open. Dupuis' expectations of popular support proved well-founded as the coastal districts rejected Annamite authority and rose in support of the French. 'Truly,' wrote the chastened Emperor in Hue, 'one does not know what to say or what to do to help the subjects of the empire . . . I tremble and blush at one and the same time.'

Opposition in Tonkin came principally from the 'Black Flags' (marauding bands of Chinese who soon claimed the life of Garnier himself) and from the cautious, cost-conscious authorities in Saigon and Paris. 'You have let yourself be seduced, deceived and led by this Dupuis,' Garnier was told by Monsieur Philastre, the man sent to arrange a disengagement. The Tonkin expedition had been intended merely as a means of extracting more political concessions from Hue, not as 'odious aggression' aimed at the conquest of Tonkin. The river was to be kept open and a consul left at Hanoi, but Dupuis was disgraced, all French troops were withdrawn, and their local supporters were abandoned to horrific retaliatory oppression.

It would take another decade and another much more savage war before Tonkin was brought under French protection. The withdrawal had merely served to spare Hue's blushes and control the Emperor's trembling. For help in restoring its authority the Annamite court now turned to Peking. Tributary relations were renewed and imperial Chinese troops were sent to quell the assorted freebooters and warlords who continued to pour out of Yunnan. To the 'Black Flags' were now added 'Red Flags' and 'Yellow Flags', all of them operating in kaleidoscopic confusion along the side valleys of the Red and Black Rivers.

In 1882 the danger to French nationals in Tonkin, plus the adoption in Paris and elsewhere of an aggressive imperialism, heralded the end of French restraint and the renewal of Garnier's civilising imperative. Expeditions of an unprecedented size stormed up the Perfume River to Hue, engaged the various Flags in Tonkin, suppressed revolts in Cochin-China and Cambodia, and met China's intervention with an attack on Formosa and the bombardment of

Foochow. Bloody disasters gave way to even bloodier victories. Out of them was born the 1887 Union, later Fédération, Indo-Chinoise consisting of the colony of Cochin-China, the protectorates of Annam and Cambodia, and Tonkin (which was somewhere between a protectorate and a colony). It remained only to add Laos in the early 1890s.

Muddled Enterprises

Arriving at Hanoi in late 1894, Colonel Hubert Lyautey, later revered as the Marshal who would bring Morocco under French protection, looked back on this period with some dismay.

> When our trader, Dupuis, about 1875, alone with a few employees, had conquered Tonquin, we disowned him, disavowed him, pursued him with the Navy, the War Office, the Quai d'Orsay, almost as if he had been a criminal. A man without gold braid, without a definite mission, an adventurer! Horrors! Scandal!

Compare, said Lyautey, the British attitude towards Rajah Brooke in Sarawak. Having just enjoyed the company of the Rajah's niece on the voyage out, Lyautey felt well-informed.

> What was he [Brooke]? An English adventurer, of modest standing, who went to Borneo as a pirate[?]. No sooner did he arrive and enforce his sovereignty on the inhabitants than the English flag appeared to defend and cover him [at the mast-head of ships of the Royal Navy], his country knowing well that in the end it would be the nation rather than the individual which would profit.

Imperial expansion might now be nearing its natural limits, but still, according to Lyautey, the British showed a greater awareness of the importance of their colonies. They responded to local conditions, acted with initiative. In Ceylon and Singapore Lyautey had marvelled at the efficiency of British administration. For a Frenchman and a patriot the East was truly a sobering experience. No one took them seriously.

> The anarchy of our government, our muddled enterprises, the extraordinary way in which our overseas functionaries are recruited, give strangers the impression of an even worse backsliding than is the case.

British officials were well-schooled and hand-picked. They were 'gentlemen' with principles and clear objectives. 'But with us there is no colonial school, no principles and as many methods as persons, and often what persons!'

Sent out to join the Headquarters Staff of the Army of Occupation, Lyautey soon experienced something of the general confusion when within days of landing he found himself Acting Chief of Staff for the whole of Indo-China and responsible only to a Commander-in-Chief who 'likes all his food served ready-cooked'. Eighteen months later, many of them spent pursuing bands of Chinese 'brigands' in the formidable mountain terrain along the Chinese frontier, he had nothing but praise for his fellow officers and their improvised methods of pacification. Any appreciation of their efforts, though, any continuity of command, or political support he still found wanting.

So was Indo-China worth having? Cochin-China, where land reclamation and irrigation south of the Mekong delta were already boosting rice yields, looked profitable; Cambodia and perhaps Annam too. But Tonkin was 'an absolute waste of money'. Its retention could only be justified on the grounds that it was 'the shield, the frontier and at the same time the outlet to China'. For the real value of Indo-China lay not in the Fédération but in Siam and in that Red River access to inland China which had inspired Garnier and Dupuis. Pushing west or north the French could truly create 'a twin of India . . . an empire *à la Dupleix*'. But 'if Siam passes into the possession of the English, if the whole thing merely results in supplying jobs for functionaries – then, yes, it is better to leave quickly'.

Lyautey was writing in 1895 when the future of Siam appeared to hang in the balance. The French navy had blockaded Bangkok and French claims in Laos extended well into Siamese territory. The British, however, were alerted. In return for Bangkok making concessions along the Laotian border, they insisted on guarantees of Siamese independence. The Anglo-French Agreement of 1896 probably saved Siam from becoming another component of French Indo-China. Similarly, though a railway was eventually built from Tonkin up into Yunnan, no great carve-up of Chinese territory materialised and no significant political advantage resulted from this 'outlet' into the crumbling Celestial Empire. On the contrary, the thankless struggle against marauding bands of freebooters and then Nationalists from China's turmoil continued unabated. In the jungle-choked ravines where Lyautey and his mentor, Colonel Gallieni,

chased 'brigands', their successors would chase Vietnamese nationalists, then revolutionaries.

The Great Exhibition

The show-piece of French colonialism was Saigon. Here, Lyautey
was told, his reservations about France's impact on the East would
be confounded. A gracious city of tree-lined boulevards and pavement cafés, it embodied the ideal of an exportable culture. No one
who had witnessed the massive investment in Saigon could claim
that French colonialism was exploitative. Given thirty years of uninterrupted French rule in the rest of Indo-China, a similar transformation could be expected.

Lyautey duly noted the imposing government monuments, the
finely executed caryatids, the familiar stucco and the plentiful gold
braid; but he was not impressed. Where were the financial institutions and the business houses? Where was the wealth that derived
from other than government salaries?

> The general appearance of all this cardboard decoration is very satisfying
> and rejoices the eye. One quickly feels that it is better not to scratch
> beneath the surface, and that if the functionaries, the military and the
> immense power of those who protect the place were withdrawn, every-
> thing would collapse. I had not this impression in Singapore.

Forty years later much the same point was made by the English
writer Osbert Sitwell, brother of the be-ringed poetess Edith. The
great 1930 Colonial Exposition at Vincennes on the outskirts of
Paris had just been dismantled. Saigon, thought Sitwell, looked as if
'it had been constructed as its antithesis, a French Imperial
Exhibition arranged for the colonies'. By now there were plenty of
banks and many more public buildings, each 'ticketed all over in gold
letters with the three world-famous tags of the Third Republic
[*Liberté, Egalité, Fraternité*]'. The shops and restaurants still rejoiced
the eye, though their prices were exorbitant; the trees along the
boulevards were grown to true magnificence.

> [But] except for the trees, all the rest of it – the theatre, the Palace, the
> Post Office – might disappear in an instant; an order might come at any
> minute, it seemed, for the Exhibition (which could not now be counted as
> altogether a financial success) to be wound up, and for the gay, exotic
> exhibits – and those responsible for them – to be packed immediately and
> sent home.

Sitwell was particularly taken by a florist's shop. Its frontage was of green marble brought from Europe and it framed a plate-glass window down which cascaded a continuous sheet of water. Before this miracle Vietnamese families, out for a stroll round the 'exhibition', stood for hours in fascinated amazement. They were particularly amazed because inside there were only a few very un-obtrusive, very expensive blooms, mostly 'consumptive-looking daisies', 'nostalgic sweet-peas' and some rosebuds 'all evidently chlorotic'. In a land ablaze with dew-fresh hibiscus, oleander and orchids, where the air dripped with the scent of jasmine and gardenia and where 'jungle flowers, lolling their large heads from tubs of water, could be bought, twelve a penny', such anaemic fare seemed quite inexplicable. Like the French themselves, their flowers wilted the moment you took them outside. Sitwell imagined the Vietnamese onlookers wondering what it was all about. What were these strange people with their strange exhibits doing here? 'How long will they stay? And when will all these funny buildings be taken down?'

Yet 'leaving quickly' as per Lyautey's suggestion was never a serious option. Prestige was involved. So, increasingly, were eco-nomic and moral considerations. Ninety thousand Indo-Chinese troops and factory workers came to France's aid during the First World War. Rice in Cochin-China, new rubber plantations mostly in the south, and the coal mines in Tonkin had begun to make a signif-icant budgetary contribution. Colonies like Indo-China were now seen not merely as prestigious appendages or forward positions on some global chessboard but as vital national assets which could be as valuable to France as the Indies had been to Holland and as Malaya was proving to be to the British.

Albert Sarraut, Governor-General of Indo-China from 1911 to 1920 and subsequently a minister in numerous French governments, encapsulated this new attitude when he enunciated a colonial policy of *mise en valeur*, that is 'development'. Development was to take the place of proselytisation and/or trade as the civilising imperative. Its object was to expand and promote the resources of the colonies (mainly raw materials) so that they complemented those of France (mainly manufactured products and technical expertise). Thus would the *metropole* and the colonies be integrated in a co-operative endeav-our aimed at economic and social expansion.

A lofty sense of mission informed this policy. To all but Marxists those republican ideals emblazoned on Saigon's buildings pro-

claimed credentials that uniquely suited France to the task of liberating less favoured peoples from exploitation and oppression. Belief
in personal liberty, in the equality of man regardless of race or colour,
in popular sovereignty, and in the liberal traditions of French culture
combined to make French rule a truly emancipating and so, surely,
an enviable experience. The Dutch directed their colonial subjects,
the British merely administered them, but the French insisted on
embracing them. French education was promoted, so was travel to
France.

By way of a seaman's ticket and a short spell of dish-washing in a
London hotel, 'Nguyen the Patriot' had arrived in Paris in 1917.
Amongst those who would follow him were Chou En-lai and Pol
Pot. For them and for all the other Asian emigrants, Paris was indeed
a liberating experience. They learnt about union rights, about social-
ism and national self-determination, about freedom of expression
and of political debate. But if these were the proud results of the
republican tradition, why were they not available in Indo-China? For
a speech demanding just such rights which he delivered as Indo-
China's representative to the 1920 Tours conference of the French
Socialist Party, 'Nguyen the Patriot' would have been arrested in
Vietnam and probably exiled to the penal settlement on Pulo
Condore. But in Tours he was applauded.

Economic and social co-operation were worthless if they
excluded both basic human rights and the possibility of economic
self-sufficiency. For somewhere like Lower Tonkin, with its coal
mines and its abundant labour, Sarraut's 'development' should have
meant industrialisation. Yet an industrial capacity would undermine
the market for the manufactures of the *metropole* – just as orchids did
the market for sweet-peas. It was not therefore on offer. Man was not
free, equal or fraternal; nor were political economies. When the
Tours conference voted in favour of the Third International and so
split the French left into Socialists and Communists, 'the Patriot'
duly joined the Communists. Thereafter Monsieur Arnoux began to
tail him. Three years later he went to Moscow, a year later he
appeared in Canton, and after various assignments in south-east
Asia, five years later he surfaced in Hong Kong for that historic
meeting in the football stadium.

5

Fixing the Philippines

Flannel and Petticoats

If France pioneered the idea of empire as a civilising mission, the United States was quick to appropriate it. Neither country was exactly indifferent to commercial advantage or to ready sources of primary produce; indeed it was somewhat marvellous how often a sense of mission turned out to be advantageous for the domestic economy. Yet the fact remained that, in marked contrast to the Netherlands and Great Britain, both France and the US professed to be concerned with what they could do for their colonies, not with what their colonies could do for them.

Instead of the stern demands of 'free trade' or a 'cultivation system', the talk was all of 'assimilation', 'association' and 'attraction'. Although the prospect of their subjects thus sharing in the glories of French civilisation would be ungratefully rejected in Indo-China, on the other side of the South China Sea, in the archipelago of the Philippines, the chance of participating in the American way of life would ultimately receive a ringing endorsement. Americans, even those opposed on principle to empire, would have nothing to be ashamed of.

Looking back over the formative years of American rule in the Philippines, Paul V. McNutt, US High Commissioner in Manila in the late 1930s, expressed the satisfaction felt by many Americans over their first colonial venture in Asia. 'We built well,' he declared.

> Our work is a monument to American idealism and enterprise, a living monument of 15 millions rescued from tyranny, rebellion, ignorance, poverty and disease, and set upon the path to free government, peace, education, prosperity and health. With all seriousness, no nation in the world can boast of so grand a monument.

Literacy rates in the Philippines were the highest in Asia; so probably was the provision of dispensaries; democratic principles and local autonomy were taken for granted; most Filipinos had come to feel genuine affection for the Americans and their way of life. In fact the 'monument' was so very grand that McNutt made no secret of wanting to retain it indefinitely. Giving the Philippines their independence would be a mistake, he thought, since it would consign their people to poverty and would deprive the US of its hard-won salient in Asia.

The doubtful logic of such sentiments was not untypical; later it would fatally ensnare US policy on the other side of the South China Sea. In the 1930s safeguarding America's salient in Asia implied ulterior motives that had nothing to do with Filipino welfare; and if America had really built so well, how come withdrawal would be such a disaster for the Filipinos? Anyway, 1938 was too late for second thoughts. The US had been committed to Filipino independence for two decades; only its terms and timing were still uncertain. Notwithstanding imminent Asian upheavals, there could be no going back on the road to independence.

McNutt was quite sure that most Filipinos did not want independence and, if one may judge by the ambivalence of their leaders, he may well have been right. President Franklin D. Roosevelt, however, most certainly did want it. It had been Theodore Roosevelt, then the hawkish Navy Secretary largely responsible for dispatching US warships to Manila in the first place, who on maturer consideration had feared that the islands might become 'our heel of Achilles'. Forty years later FDR had no doubts about it. Indifferent or disaffected colonial subject were a nation's undoing. Colonial regimes should be judged not just by their 'idealism and enterprise' but by the speed with which they could be dismantled. According to Cordell Hull, FDR's Secretary of State, US rule in the Philippines provided 'the perfect example of how a nation should treat a colony or a dependency in co-operating with it in making all necessary preparations for freedom'. In short, the whole venture in the Philippines had been a mistake, 'a national aberration' from the start. Many had suspected as much at the time; they were right.

> [To] plunge into an inevitable war to conquer the Philippines [is] contrary to every profession or so called principle of our lives and history [wrote Henry Adams in 1898]. I turn green in bed at midnight if I think of the horror of a year's warfare . . . where we must slaughter a million or two

foolish Malays [that is, Filipinos] in order to give them the comforts of flannel petticoats and electric railways.

If, in the words of the historian Nicholas Tarling, 'the French had ambitions in south east Asia [and] the British had interests', then the Americans had misgivings. To a country, once a colony, whose self-belief as 'the land of the free' derived from its successful revolution against colonialism, the idea of itself acquiring overseas possessions and subject peoples should have been anathema. The principle of 'government with the consent of the governed' was enshrined in the US constitution. Along with the individual's inalienable right to 'life, liberty and the pursuit of happiness' it appeared to preclude any form of colonial rule except that 'of the people, by the people, for the people'.

Such sentiments were impossible to reconcile with the forcible occupation of an extensive, populous and disaffected archipelago in the South China Sea – let alone with the later massive military inter-vention in the political affairs of large chunks of the Asian mainland. They taxed the rhetorical ingenuity of American policy-makers and they strained domestic commitment. US rule in the Philippines eventually proved acceptable only to the extent that it appeared liberal, beneficial to the Filipinos, and short. Since latterly it did broadly conform to these criteria, the US is often credited with being a 'reluctant colonialist'. If undeniably an imperialist, then at least its was a 'benign imperialism', a 'sentimental imperialism', even an 'anti-colonial imperialism'.

On the other hand the fact remains that for nearly half a century the Philippines were as much a US colony as, say, the Indies were Dutch. In acquiring them the US would become the first colonial power in the East to suppress a nationalist uprising ('rescue' a people from rebellion in McNutt's choice phrasing), and so deny their right to self-determination. The US, in other words, set a prece-dent for precisely the intransigent oppression which President Franklin D. Roosevelt would later find so reprehensible in other colonial powers.

Nor was US colonialism in practice always so much more benign than that of the European powers. Suppression of the Filipino upris-ing would inflict greater suffering, claim more lives, and prompt worse atrocities than any action sanctioned by the British during one and a half centuries of colonial rule in the Far East. Once reduced, the Philippines were subjected to a more pervasive American

acculturation and enticed into a closer political and economic dependence on the US than anything achieved by France's policies of
assimilation in Indo-China. These factors would continue to operate
in the post-colonial era, rendering Filipino independence suspect to
its neighbours, affording to the US a neo-colonial influence greater
than that exercised by any of the other erstwhile colonial powers, and
so, incidentally, confounding McNutt's anxieties about economic
disaster and the loss of a strategic salient.

In fact, in 1946 McNutt would happily return to Manila to preside
at the official hand-over of power and to become the United States'
first ambassador to the new Philippine Republic. In torrential rain he
would lower the American flag while above the boom of gun salutes
and the carillons of church bells, General Douglas MacArthur,
having duly 'returned' as liberator of the islands from Japanese rule,
saluted the new republic in terms as generous as those used by
McNutt of the colonial regime that preceded it.

MacArthur at least had no illusions about the one-sided character
of American rule in the Philippines. It was too much a part of his
family history. In 1902 General Arthur MacArthur, his father, had
been the man who commanded the US forces that overran Malolos,
capital of the first Philippine republic. To a multitude of jubilant
dripping Filipinos the son now proudly declared 'the end of mastery
over peoples by force alone'. Putting American rule firmly in the
context of other colonialisms, and so dashing the pieties of his friend
McNutt, he further announced 'the end of empire as the political
chain that binds the unwilling weak to the unyielding strong'.

Jumping the Gun

Had the General cast his steady gaze still further back, he might have
drawn other parallels with the despised empires of America's
European rivals. For US rule in the Philippines may be traced, like the
British acquisition of Hong Kong and the French of Indo-China,
back to the eighteenth century and the mouth of China's Pearl River.
That the Yale brothers, who from Madras pioneered the Canton
trade in 1689, were American-born was incidental. Not so, however,
the important role played by American shipping and traders a century
later by which time American-born meant an American citizen.

In 1784 the *Empress of China* sailed from New York to Canton via
the Cape of Good Hope. Returning with a cargo mainly of tea, she

became the first vessel to trade with the East under an American flag. The voyage had been a success and by the turn of the century American trade on the China coast was exceeded only by that of the English East India Company. About fifty sailings a year from America's east coast ports used the Atlantic route to reach Portuguese Macao and Spanish Manila. Thence, like other shipping beyond the East India Company's control, they traded opium, mostly of Turkish origin, for tea, silk and ceramics. American companies like Russell and Co. (one of whose partners in the 1870s would be a certain Warren Delano, grandfather of Franklin Delano Roosevelt) rivalled the British hongs of Dent's and Jardine Matheson in circumventing the Company's monopoly and eventually suborning it. When in the 1840s the British took the offensive in the Opium Wars, Americans eagerly awaited the outcome. They then made their own treaty with Peking by which all concessions awarded to the British or anyone else were also to be extended to US citizens and US trade. In the following decade Anglo-American roles were reversed in Japan. There Americans took the initiative in opening the country to foreign trade, the British being content to follow the American lead.

Imitating not only the commercial offensives of Great Britain but also the missionary programme sponsored by France, in 1845 Captain Percivall of the USS *Constitution*, while cruising off the Vietnamese coast, took the opportunity to demand the release of the imprisoned Monsignor Lefèvre, Vicar Apostolic of Annam. Failing to secure the said bishop, Captain Percivall vouchsafed the Vietnamese a taste of times to come. According to a report filed from Singapore, he 'fired upon the town [of Tourane, that is Da Nang] and destroyed several of the inhabitants'. Further south, American traders enjoyed a near monopoly in some of the north Sumatran pepper ports and, when the independence of these ports came under threat from the Dutch in the 1870s, Washington was duly favoured with overtures from their sultan in Aceh.

Meanwhile Americans had gained a new perspective on the East by heading west. Columbus's quest for a shorter passage to Asia had been resumed and in the early nineteenth century provided the inspiration for pushing out into the plains and then the deserts of the American continent. Lewis and Clark first crossed the continent in 1804–6. A 'manifest destiny' was found to underlie the expansion that followed. Texas was incorporated into the Union in 1845,

California joined in 1848, Alaska in 1867. Transcontinental railroads were promoted as new Asian trade routes. When Chinese labourers, shipped from Hong Kong to California to build them, met gold-crazed overlanders from the eastern states, east and west came face to face in the boom towns of the Sierra Nevada. 'Expansionism, even imperialism, was in the genes of American civilisation,' write the authors of a study of America's *Sentimental Imperialism*.

Having fulfilled its manifest destiny to engross all available territory from the Atlantic to the Pacific, dispossessing even native peoples in the process, the question for Washington was where next. By 1890 Hawaii's incorporation was a near certainty. Still further west lay much ocean until, eventually, there came the Philippines.

This Pacific route was that which Magellan had taken when in 1521 he 'discovered' the Philippines during the first circumnavigation of the world. Magellan claimed them for his patron King Carlos of Spain but was hacked to death by the natives while attempting to enforce the claim. Although the islands produced no spices, they swarmed with potential converts to Christianity, were conveniently near the spice-rich Moluccas where Portugal's monopoly might prove vulnerable, and were also well sited as a base for trade with China. Christening them after Crown Prince Felipe as the 'Felipinas', hence 'Philippines', the Spanish launched an expedition of conquest from Spanish Mexico in 1565. As the historian Stanley Karnow has noted, 'It was a uniquely American enterprise . . . [It was] comprised of men who lived in America travelling aboard ships built and equipped in America to bring the wealth of Asia back to America.' Subsequently the islands were administered not from Spain but from its New World surrogate in Mexico while their trade with China, the lifeblood of the colony, was financed by an annual fleet carrying Mexican silver. The Philippines, in short, had been an American colony for over 300 years before the United States saw fit to challenge this Hispanic hegemony.

Throughout this period it was no secret that Spanish Mexico's rule was vulnerable. During the Seven Years War a British expedition from Madras had experienced little difficulty in occupying Manila from 1762 to 1764. A second expedition during the Napoleonic Wars, assembled at Penang by Arthur Wellesley in 1797, would probably have enjoyed comparable success had it not been countermanded at the last moment. Such offensives were essentially diplomatic and strategic. The islands produced nothing of unique commercial potential and the British had no intention of retaining them. They were seen principally as useful bargaining counters in the eventual peace negotiations. By the turn of the century, however, Manila was gradually opening to international trade and several British and American companies had opened offices there. During the Opium Wars the port-city briefly served as a temporary base for the whole Canton trading community. By the 1850s a US consul was permanently stationed in Manila. When, forty years later, it was America's turn to intervene, intelligence about the Philippines was plentiful, while tacit British support could be expected.

There was also a new element, namely the likelihood of considerable Filipino support. In 1896 Dr José Rizal, the founding father of Filipino nationalism, was publicly executed by the Spanish authorities before a vast crowd on the Luneta, Manila's central park. A Spanish-speaking polymath and a highly readable novelist, Rizal had studied in Spain, France and Germany before returning to his homeland to preach social development and political reform. He had made no claim for independence and he decried the armed insurgency already advocated by some of the oppressed peasantry. Nevertheless his charismatic leadership posed a formidable challenge to Spain. The colony's governor had no hesitation in adopting the only negotiating expedient recognised by Spain's conquistadors, namely the firing squad.

An inquisitional crack-down on other supposed traitors and heretics ensued, but it was the death of Rizal, a martyr for Filipino justice, which turned what had previously been local anti-clerical risings into Asia's first popular nationalist revolt. 'Let us march under the Flag of Revolution,' exhorted Emilio Aguinaldo adding, by way of explanation to his less educated followers, 'whose watchwords are Liberty, Equality and Fraternity.' Aguinaldo, a dapper young *mestizo* (half Chinese, half Filipino) of good family, modest education and undoubted courage, had by 1897 emerged as *generalissimo* of the rapidly growing *insurrectos* and *presidente* of their government.

True, in the context of Asian nationalism, he did appear to have jumped the gun. In China 1898 found the Manchus still presiding over their fraying empire from Peking's Forbidden City while Dr Sun Yat-sen orchestrated ineffectual risings from abroad. Elsewhere M. K. Gandhi was already defending Indian rights but in South Africa, not India; Nehru and Ho Chi Minh were still schoolboys, Sukarno had yet to be born. Decidedly premature, Filipino nationalism also looked improbably precocious. The islands, all 7,000 of them, were home to many ethnic groups speaking a variety of Malayo-Polynesian languages. Unlike Java, Sumatra, Cambodia or even Laos they cherished no traditions of pre-colonial splendour; nor, like Vietnam, could they lay claim to any gritty history of resistance to foreign dominion. Observing the vacillations of the diminutive Filipino *generalissimo*, his posturing and his inconsistency, the colonial powers in the East found it hard to take Filipino nationalism seriously.

Seen, however, from an American perspective, it should have caused less surprise. Spanish rule in the Philippines had already lasted for 330 years, considerably longer than the period during which Dutch rule had been effective in Java, let alone in the rest of the Indies. It was indeed comparable only with the span of Spanish empire in Central and South America. Except in Muslim areas like Mindanao and Sulu, most Filipinos were now Catholics, deeply attached to the teachings of the Church although highly resentful of the archaic agrarian regime operated by the religious orders, especially the friars. Intermarriage had resulted in a numerous creole or *mestizo* élite who adopted the Spanish language and looked to Spain for cultural inspiration in everything from dress to dance and drama. Conditions, in other words, compared with those prevailing in most of the Americas when in the 1820s Spanish rule had succumbed to a succession of nationalist revolutions led by Simon Bolivar. Bolivar had in part been inspired by the example of Abraham Lincoln and George Washington. Just so Rizal and Aguinaldo drew inspiration from Bolivar. As the belated response of an Hispanic American colony to the collapse of Spain's colonial authority, Aguinaldo's Filipino revolution made decidedly more sense than as a harbinger of Asian nationalism.

Holed up in the mountains of Luzon, whence his troops harried the Spanish to within a few miles of Manila, Aguinaldo appeared capable of defying the ponderous colonial militia indefinitely. But his chances of taking Manila and decisively overthrowing colonial rule looked equally remote. What he needed were weapons, international recognition, even perhaps an ally.

Take up the White Man's Burden

Spain's impotence in the face of this Filipino challenge of the late 1890s stemmed from its preoccupation with an even more serious revolt then underway in Cuba. As a neighbour and an important trading partner, Cuba was also of considerably greater consequence to the United States. Powerful US business interests demanded intervention on behalf of the Cubans and they were supported by a growing lobby of frankly expansionist opinion headed by the likes of Theodore Roosevelt. America, it was argued, had a duty to promote and support the values it held most dear, like social equality and individual liberty. It could not stand indifferent when these freedoms were under threat on its doorstep. Thus the American revolution, far from precluding overseas adventures, could be invoked to endorse them. In effect, revolution must be exported; in its proven ability to transcend class and race (if not colour), it might even hold the key to a new and more equitable world order. Alternatively, if America continued to turn its back on the world, it was doomed to stagnate. The dynamic of its society required new challenges just as the pace of its industrial growth required new markets.

Either way, in the late nineteenth century expansion meant entering the fiercely competitive struggle in progress between the other colonial powers. This struggle covered the globe and was conducted principally through the deployment of naval power. Roosevelt, therefore, made it his business to re-equip the US Navy while President William McKinley, after much heart-searching and repeated attempts at arbitration, in April 1898 finally bowed to Congressional demands for war on Spain. The war was all over in three months, the main theatre being of course Cuba. By way of diversion Puerto Rico was also seized; and on a similar pretext the US Navy's eastern squadron was detailed to sail for Manila.

Commodore George Dewey was a recent Roosevelt appointee. His task had long been anticipated and his squadron was already assembled at Hong Kong. He sailed on 27 April, three days after receiving his orders.

PROCEED AT ONCE TO THE PHILIPPINES. COMMENCE OPERATIONS AGAINST THE SPANISH SQUADRON. YOU MUST CAPTURE OR DESTROY. USE UTMOST ENDEAVOURS.

Four days later, on 1 May, Dewey steamed into Manila Bay. For the Spanish fleet, sheltering under ineffectual shore batteries, it was indeed May Day. The American vessels opened fire at 5.41 a.m. and, although 'utmost endeavours' did not mean Dewey's men going without a mid-morning breakfast, by 12.30 the fighting was over.

Only one Spanish vessel out of a dozen remained afloat, and some 300 men had perished. On the American side not a single ship had been lost, and the solitary fatality was ascribed to heat-stroke. The shore batteries had been silenced, the white flag shown. Manila lay at Dewey's mercy. It was the most one-sided victory in naval history. Evening found Dewey's flagship cruising inshore to play troubadour as the ship's band serenaded the mossy ramparts of Manila's Intramuros with a medley of Spanish airs.

There is nothing like a victory to dispel an administration's policy doubts. Banner headlines announced the 'SURRENDER', and over-night Dewey became a national hero, an admiral, even a potential Presidential candidate. More sanguine now of his own chances of re-election, the incumbent McKinley basked in the glory while feigning a lofty disdain for its more gung-ho manifestations. He later claimed that at the time he 'could not have told where those darned islands were to within two thousand miles'. At least he knew they were islands. Most of his fellow countrymen, according to 'Mr Dooley', the syndicated creation of satirist Finley Peter Dunne, thought the Philippines were some kind of 'canned goods' (sardines, perhaps). Ignoring America's long cherished ambitions in the China trade, its established commercial presence in Manila, and the previous activities of its Asia squadron, ignoring, too, Roosevelt's rearmament and Dewey's preparations, all agreed that a glorious victory 4,000 miles away had to be at least a miracle and perhaps a portent. 'Blind is he who does not see the hand of God in events so vast, so harmonious, so benign,' intoned Senator Beveridge.

Whether divinely ordained or merely a sardine supper, it scarcely mattered. The main thing was that sleepless consciences be lulled before the next move. Already troopships were being chartered for the 10,000 volunteers and regulars who had been converging on a vast encampment outside San Francisco even before Dewey's triumph was known. Lest neither God, Dewey nor the Filipino revolutionaries were up to the task, the US Army was about to embark on its first term of active duty outside the Americas. The destruction of the Spanish fleet was, it seemed, not the only objective of US policy. Manila's Spanish garrison had to be winkled out, the city taken, and 'order and security [brought] to the islands' as McKinley vaguely put it.

For the next two months Dewey waited for the troopships. A small naval contingent was landed, but for the most part his men preferred to catch such breezes as rarely blew aboard ship. Their concern was less with taking Manila than with preventing anyone else from taking it. Before leaving Hong Kong Dewey had received visits from representatives of Aguinaldo's Filipino revolution. Independently Aguinaldo himself had held discussions with US representatives in both Hong Kong and Singapore. The Filipino revolutionaries, having accepted a Spanish offer of exile in return for a substantial cash payment, were using the opportunity to buy arms and find friends. News of Dewey's assignment could not have been more welcome. Here was a friend indeed. It remained only to secure US guarantees of Filipino independence in return for revolutionary support in smashing the Spanish. In due course Aguinaldo thought he had secured just such an understanding, Dewey that he had declined any such thing. Neither side seems to have put anything in writing.

Dewey did, however, summon Aguinaldo and his colleagues back to Manila as soon as the coast, quite literally, was clear. He had, it seemed, underestimated 'these little men' who kept 'taking a good deal of my time'. Their forces, numerous, well-disciplined and greatly encouraged by the sight of upturned Spanish hulls, already held the upper hand throughout the main island of Luzon and were now converging on Manila. Aguinaldo's arrival with several thousand rifles brought a new flood of recruits, many of them deserters from Spanish Filipino units, plus a closer investment of the city. They numbered about 30,000 to the city's 8,000 Spanish and Filipino defenders. The final assault, according to Aguinaldo, was imminent. Dewey urged patience and caution. Aguinaldo, alarmed by what appeared to be American equivocation, responded with a Declaration of Philippine Independence (18 June 1898) and proceeded to form the republic's first government.

Thanks to a last-minute amendment, the US resolution in favour of war with Spain had been qualified by an undertaking not to annex Cuba. This was as good as guaranteeing Cuban independence. But, whether fortuitous or intentional, no such undertaking had been made in respect of other Spanish territories. Compared to the Cubans, Dewey actually thought the Filipino patriots 'superior in intelligence and more capable of self-government'. But he boycotted their independence celebrations. (The only American present was an itinerant demonstrator of the new cinematography; to Hollywood if not to Washington Filipinos would ever be warm.) From Aguinaldo's new administration there immediately came a stream of proclamations, directives, appeals and overtures; from Washington came neither recognition nor acknowledgement, just an ominous silence and the promise of the now imminent reinforcements.

Meanwhile the apparent collapse of Spanish rule had brought other interested parties to Manila Bay. 'Five German, three British, one French, one Japanese men-of-war in port,' reported Dewey on 18 June. All had ostensibly come to protect their nationals in Manila. The Germans, though, made no secret of their willingness to mediate on behalf of the Spanish, thus laying prior claim to any concessions that might result, while British manoeuvres displayed a clear intention of supporting Dewey in order to frustrate the Germans. Whether they wished it or not, the Americans were being drawn into the great imperial board-game. Even as their troops finally disembarked on to Asian soil, the other players were dealing themselves a further round of concessions in China: 1898 was the year in which the Russians got Port Arthur, the Germans Kiaochow Bay, the French the Kwangchow peninsula, and the British Weihaiwei and Hong Kong's New Territories. Never had the disintegration of the whole Chinese empire looked so likely.

Once again it was as if some greater authority had ordained that at this critical juncture the US be uniquely placed to bring its beneficent influence to bear. Another destiny was manifest. American business sensed vast new markets, American opinion sensed a new 'career as a great power'. It mattered not that Manila was eventually captured in a mock battle which had been ingloriously pre-arranged with the Spanish to avoid bloodshed and deny the Filipinos a share of the victory; nor that the capture of the city actually came a day after Spain had signed the armistice which was supposed to have put a stop to all hostilities. It was like a goal scored after the whistle and with the connivance of the keeper, but it was not disallowed.

On the contrary, Manila, it now seemed, was to be retained as a base and entrepôt in the Orient, a US Singapore. The rest of Luzon and all the other islands were also desirable, like Malaya, as sources of tropical produce and fields for US investment. The only question was how to manage this acquisition without alienating US domestic opinion, infringing the constitution (which included no provision for subordinate territories), and incurring a war of attrition with the Filipino people. Withdrawal was no longer considered a serious option. If the Spanish were allowed back, they would have to reconquer the islands first, taking untold lives in the process which would lie heavily on American consciences; but if they were not allowed back, Germany, France or Japan would surely move in. As for Filipino independence, it was a possibility only if US guarantees of international protection were forthcoming. This was never seriously explored. Somewhat naïvely considering the success of British protectorates in Borneo and French in Indo-China, the US insisted on 'no responsibility without control'. That left outright annexation as the only possibility.

Throughout the peace negotiations which had now opened in Paris, with greater intensity as the resultant treaty came before Congress for ratification, and with much wringing of hands as the terrible cost of the ensuing war became apparent, the great debate about America's world role dominated the national agenda. Quickly into the fray with an exhortation to the expansionists came the arch-imperialist himself, Rudyard Kipling.

> Take up the White Man's burden –
>   Send forth the best ye breed –
> Go, bind your sons to exile
>   To serve your captives' need;
> To wait in heavy harness
>   On fluttered folk and wild –
> Your new-caught, sullen peoples,
> Half devil and half child . . .

Kipling, lately a US resident and married to an American, was well-intentioned and his view anything but roseate.

> Take up the White Man's burden –
>   And reap his old reward;
> The blame of those ye better,
>   The hate of those ye guard.

It may nevertheless have misfired. The racism was a little too explicit for American tastes, the Anglocentrism a little too patronising. It also invited parodies which probably became more popular than the original.

> Pile on the brown man's burden
>   To gratify your greed;

Go, clear away the 'niggers'
Who progress would impede;
Be very stern, for truly
'Tis useless to be mild
With new-caught sullen peoples,
Half devil and half child.

Such lines, emanating from the ranks of the Anti-Imperialist League, failed to dissuade McKinley and his negotiators from demanding anything less than the outright cession of the entire archipelago. They also failed, though by only two votes, to dissuade Congress from ratification. With the US claim to sovereignty finally recognised, it remained only to 'go clear away the niggers'.

Manila, now occupied by the Americans, was still surrounded by Aguinaldo's cohorts. But, increasingly 'fluttered' if not downright 'wild', the Filipinos were now defending the land that lay behind them rather than menacing the metropolis that lay before them. Their government at Malolos counted on the peace treaty not being ratified, then on McKinley's Republicans losing the 1900 elections. It might even have waited for the outcome of those votes. But US troops were still arriving (the original 8,500 had now become 24,000) and, with the Filipinos refusing to give ground, a mere nudge could have started the fighting. When it did erupt in February 1899, the blame was hard to apportion; it was more a case of spontaneous combustion.

Hopelessly outgunned, the Filipinos fell back on the farming provinces, then the hills and the forests. Militarily the Americans seemed to be having it all their own way. But they were never safe. A pacified village became a 'rebel' refuge the moment they moved on. The 'insurrection' would be put down in three months, six months at most, said the generals; and so it was in terms of conventional warfare. Instead there were three years of equally costly guerrilla attacks and increasingly vicious reprisals. Any doubts about the support enjoyed by Aguinaldo were soon dispelled. Civilians were hard to tell from combatants and just as hostile. Only the climate was more lethal; about a quarter of the US troops were either sick, wounded or malingering at any one time. By the end of 1899 the original commitment of 8,500 US troops had risen in leaps and bounds to 70,000, and this at a time when the total strength of the regular US infantry was only 100,000.

Many were volunteers. Of the regulars a few had served in the

American Civil War; for most the only previous taste of action had come courtesy of native Americans. The inglorious 1890 massacre at Wounded Knee Creek was probably the most recent addition to the US battle roll. Major-General Henry W. Lawton, commanding the First Division in the Philippines, was the man who had tracked down Geronimo. He would have liked to add Aguinaldo's scalp but in December 1899 he became the most senior casualty of the war when killed by sharp-shooters near San Mateo. (They were commanded, ironically, by a General Licerio Geronimo.) To most Americans the Indios, as the Spanish called native Filipinos, were just brown, rather than red, Indians. They called them 'gugus', 'niggers' and worse. Enemy wounded were routinely shot; if the 'Indians' took prisoners only as hostages, the Americans took them only as informants. In both cases torture was deemed salutary. Karnow calls it 'as cruel as any conflict in the annals of colonialism' and does not exclude Vietnam. When peace was prematurely announced in 1902 the death toll ran to over 4,000 Americans and at least 20,000 Filipinos. A further 200,000, mostly civilians, are thought to have died of starvation, exposure, torture and disease.

The bane of war is imperfectly assessed in lives lost. Just as relevant is the cause thus served or the evil thus averted. In 1900 the anti-imperialists found a champion to challenge Kipling when Mark Twain returned to America. As a flag for 'the Philippine Province' Twain suggested the Stars and Stripes – but with skulls and crossbones for the stars, and the white stripes painted black.

> There have been lies, yes, but they were told in a good cause. We have been treacherous, but that was only that real good might come out of apparent evil. True, we have crushed a deceived and confiding people; we have turned against the weak and the friendless who trusted us . . . debauched America's honour and blackened her face before the world; but each detail was for the best . . .

Attraction

To balance the equation, any 'real good' to come out of such a catalogue of crime would have to be just that, *real* good. But what exactly was good for the Filipinos? As the strength of their nationalist feeling became clearer, and as the cost of suppressing it escalated, even expansionists were having second thoughts. MacArthur senior, as Commanding Officer in the Philippines, became converted to the idea of a rapid transition to independence. It was what the people wanted and, like Dewey, he thought they could handle it. Yet Commissioners dispatched from Washington reported more favourably on the possibility of Americanisation. The benefits, though perhaps novel to Filipinos, would prove incalculably greater than a fragile and impoverished independence; through policies of 'benevolent assimilation' or 'attraction', the Filipinos themselves would soon come to realise this even if, at first, they dismissed all such ideas as intended merely to detach Aguinaldo's support and soothe US consciences.

'Attraction' was the brainchild of William Howard Taft, leader of a second presidential commission to the Philippines in 1900 who in the same year succeeded MacArthur as head of the island's first civilian administration. A federal judge and a future President, Taft was chiefly remarkable for a stature which rivalled that of most Filipino homes and a 325lb bulk which exceeded that of entire Filipino families. Beaming benignly down on what he called our 'little brown brothers', he resolved to 'attract' them with a package of opportunities and privileges undreamt of in the annals of colonialism. So transparently beneficial would this package prove that Filipinos would, he anticipated, voluntarily forgo ideas of independence in favour of a close and enduring relationship with their bigger, whiter brethren.

Under Taft and his immediate successors the Philippines were therefore reinvaded, this time by an army of teachers, agriculturalists, engineers, doctors, health workers, evangelists, statisticians and surveyors. Thousands of miles of road were built, hundreds of railway; ports were improved, inter-island shipping extended, docks and wharves constructed. New crops were tried, the processing of existing staples like sugar and hemp were mechanised. The currency and legal system were overhauled; the influence of the Church was drastically curtailed; elections were held; local and municipal autonomy introduced, and Filipino participation in all levels of government encouraged. Above all primary and vocational education were extended even into the remotest areas.

It was indeed a monumental achievement even if the monument was sadly flawed. Taft had declared his policy as ensuring 'the Philippines for the Filipinos', but it was to be an American Philippines for American Filipinos. 'American efforts at reform and development became retentive political acts, amounting to a policy of nation-building without regard to nationality,' according to P. W. Stanley, a Harvard authority on US-Filipino relations. The infrastructure was designed to serve development, not national cohesion. US tariff preferences aimed at safeguarding the islands' exports resulted in dependency on US markets and exposure to their fluctuations; reciprocal Filipino preferences in favour of US imports and investment had a similar effect and were additionally much resented by the Filipinos themselves. Most telling of all, the new schools not only taught English, they taught *in* English, thus marginalising the prospects of Tagalog, Luzon's principal tongue, ever becoming a national language.

For those Filipinos who could afford it, the ultimate goal became attendance at a US college. Karnow quotes Virginia Licuanan, one such beneficiary, who though her husband was also a Filipino, admitted that we 'never made love in Tagalog'. Presumably it would have debased the experience; for any activity other than dressing down inferiors, English was the language. Baseball became the national game, cornflakes the national breakfast, Hollywood the ultimate dream. Filipino culture, less than robust after three centuries of Hispanic 'attraction', was simply overwhelmed.

In 1901 the elusive Aguinaldo had finally been 'brought in'. When MacArthur pardoned him in return for an oath of allegiance and a proclamation to his followers to lay down their arms, Taft was appalled. He should at least have been deported; clemency to conspirators and 'fools', thought Taft, would undermine the US policy of attracting moderate opinion. Already some representatives of the so-called *ilustrados*, the Filipino élite, had formed a Federalist Party whose ultimate aims included American statehood and incorporation into the Union. Collaboration with such a narrow clique foundered when the *federalistas* deemed their privileged position as conduits of US favour prejudiced by tax reforms, but in 1907 the first elections to a National Assembly threw up a new breed of potential allies. Winning votes in the name of independence, these new *nacionalistas* showed themselves willing to qualify their demands once in power. Autonomy and office evidently eased the pangs of injustice while, for the Americans, collaboration with *nacionalistas* like Osmena and Quezon helped reconcile the opposing positions originally represented by MacArthur and Taft. With independence acknowledged as a welcome but long-term goal, it became a useful element in the policy of attraction. Seen in this context the passage in 1916 of the Jones Bill promising the Filipinos immediate autonomy and eventual independence once 'stable government' had been established was not quite the milestone it appeared to be.

After a short visit in 1920 the novelist Stella Benson rated US rule in the Philippines as '50 per cent liberty, 49 per cent equality and 1 per cent fraternity'. She might have cited Bishop Brent, the Episcopal Church's bishop for the Philippines, who in explaining for the benefit of those back home that the natives had long since awoken from the slumber of ages, felt obliged to add that 'what the Americans have done is to get the Filipinos out of bed. They are now instructing them how to dress themselves.' With whites-only clubs, a hill station at Baguio, and much ill-disguised contempt for their 'little brown brothers', Americans in the Philippines reminded Benson of the British in India. Only here they pretended that things were otherwise. 'Politically a great deal is said about brotherhood, personally almost nothing.'

This gap between rhetoric and reality applied as much to Filipino tactics as to American attitudes. 'Damn the Americans – why don't they tyrannise us more?' complained Manuel Quezon, leader of the *nacionalistas*. Here was a colony where even nationalism was being debased by the backing of the colonial power. Quezon and his supporters, though loud in their public demands for immediate and outright independence, invariably followed them with a private apology whispered in the ear of the nearest American official. Unequivocal US acknowledgement of the right to independence, a schedule of how it might be implemented and a time-table of when, were always somehow preferable to the thing itself. The younger MacArthur, already on his third tour of duty in the islands, was appalled by the racial hostility and, like his father, disposed to accept the feasibility of independence. But when he left in 1930 little had changed. It would take economic turmoil in the decade ahead and world war in the next to end the era of make-believe.

PART TWO

At Half Mast

1930–1945

6

Intervention and Recession

Seven Days to Singapore

'One of the best ways of keeping an empire is by neglect; and one of the surest ways of losing it is by deepening intervention.' So wrote Dr Anil Seal in the introduction to John Gallagher's provocative analysis of *The Decline, Revival and Fall of the British Empire*. The 'revival' of British imperialism, though short-lived and principally expressed in the wartime rhetoric of Winston Churchill, dated from the inter-war years. In the East Clementi's attempts at consolidation in respect of Hong Kong's New Territories, and his subsequent schemes in respect of what is now Malaysia, may be seen as typical of this assertion of imperial authority. They were also good examples of the deepening intervention which hastened empire's end.

The same was true of the Philippines where, if Spain's indifference had been a classic case of neglect prolonging empire, America's hands-on approach certainly hastened Filipino independence. Neglect, however, was not now a serious option. Though the norm in the eighteenth century, and still evident in parts of Africa in the late nineteenth century, it was becoming increasingly impractical in Asia. Only Sarawak bucked the trend, the Brooke rajahs having concluded that a minimum of intervention was as well suited to the undemanding nature of their subjects as to their own easy-going inclinations.

Elsewhere it was a different story. 'Ethical' policies as in the Netherlands East Indies necessitated intervention; evangelising missions, especially in China, the Philippines and New Guinea, demanded it; so did industrialists anxious to expand their markets, and commercial conglomerates avid for more primary produce. The climate of international competition now meant that any occupation of overseas territory had to be made effective if it was not to be challenged; meanwhile public opinion increasingly sought reassurance that such occupation was proving of some benefit to the subject peoples. Above all, advances in the speed and capacity of global communications removed the usual excuse for neglect and provided both colonial administrators and their metropolitan masters with channels for direct action. Indeed, such was the novelty and convenience of these facilities that the question of whether intervention was actually advisable could get ignored.

For the British public the first week of October 1930 nicely illustrated the priority now being accorded to communications. On Wednesday 1st, from a Royal Naval cutter off the coast of Shantung, Sir Reginald Johnston and his staff were casting last landward glances over their beloved Weihaiwei while the drone of the bagpipes still lingered on the soft seaside air. Yet such was the excitement on the other side of the world over an imminent British breakthrough in mass transportation that this first imperial retraction went almost unnoticed. All eyes were on the Shropshire village of Cardington rather than Weihaiwei.

Four days later, at exactly 0210 hours on the morning of 5 October, a band of more chastened imperialists withdrew from an inferno some thirty miles north of Paris. As they bolted through dank woods, a series of mighty explosions showered the darkness with blazing debris and shattered Sunday morning slumbers. Of the 54 crew and passengers aboard the R101's maiden flight, including the Secretary of State for Air and many of aviation's top brass, there were only four survivors. Directed and funded by government, constructed within the largest buildings in the empire, powered by no less than five of the new diesel engines, and equipped with the latest of everything in the way of gadgetry and comfort, the biggest and most expensive airship ever built in Britain, six years in the making, had been flying east from Cardington when, off course, buffeted by headwinds, in thick cloud, and far too low, she gently grounded near Beauvais. The friction was just sufficient to ignite her 5.5 million cubic feet of sensationally inflammable hydrogen. In the conflagration that followed perished the hopes of a whole incipient industry.

It also ended all prospects of a dirigible empire. Karachi had been the airship's destination. This was the maiden flight of the first leg on what was to have become an imperial network of airship lanes connecting the furthest outposts from Hong Kong to Cape Town. Unlike conventional aircraft, airships required no expensive out-of-town runways; they could load while floating in the heart of a city, needing only roof-top moorings and an elevated access. Their payload was far in excess of anything then possible between fixed wings, and running costs promised to be lower. With space, as on the R101, for a dance floor and dining tables, a smoking room, a promenade deck and Pullman-style cabins for a hundred passengers, the airships were to be the liners of the skies, serenely cruising the clouds and cutting voyage times from so many weeks to as many days.

But it was not to be. Instead, Britannia's hopes of ruling the skies as well as the waves were quickly transferred to what appeared to be a more natural compromise, flying boats. During the 1930s Imperial Airways, following the lead set by KLM, at last began to live up to its name with regular services to the East. Flying boats even enabled the airline to offer some of the vaunted comforts of airship travel.

The convenience of a through flight was not one of them. To reach Singapore passengers had to change planes six times and spend ten nights on the ground, some in the doubtful comfort of a desert pipeline station, others in the sleeping compartments of connecting trains. Only cloudless skies and negligible wind speeds constituted acceptable flying conditions. The capacity of the bi-planes serving the overland links was limited to a dozen passengers while the safety record of flying boats left much to be desired. 'One collided with an Italian submarine,' writes James Morris, 'one dived into Lake Habbaniyah, one sank in the Hooghly river, one was blown up by an exploding fuel barge at Southampton and one was permanently stuck in the mud in a lake near Tonk.'

Not surprisingly, of the privileged few who were rich enough to afford a ticket and robust enough to face aviation's uncertainties, many preferred to travel east on KLM's well-established service to Batavia via Singapore. In the early 1930s Air France inaugurated its Saigon service and by 1936 the first Pacific flights had opened a route from California to Manila and on to China. A more developed network of short-haul flights, often in the smaller sea-planes, linked most destinations within the East. By the end of the decade even Imperial Airways had pared down its ten-day flying boat service to Singapore. It meant having to sacrifice passenger numbers to fuel capacity in the new 'Empire' class flying boats; but according to

Sjovald Cunyngham-Brown, who made the trip in 1938, standards of comfort were unaffected.

> One went down from London in reserved first-class accommodation, boarding the great swan-like craft, redolent of Chanel No. 5, at the decent hour of ten-thirty in the morning as she lay at her moorings in Southampton Water . . . We had twenty-six passengers on board for whom there was ample room on her two great decks; a sitting room on the upper one and a splendid club-room or foyer complete with bar down below.

Cruising at 120 knots and barely 3,000 feet above the ground, they averted their eyes, no doubt, over Beauvais, then circled the Eiffel Tower 'just for fun', and made Lake Marignan in time for tea.

> Here one spent the night at Aix-en-Provence – transported in Rolls Royces to the Hotel Princess, whose first floor was permanently booked for Winston Churchill. And so on – luncheon the next day at Fort Augusta in Sicily; and down on the Nile that evening for a two-day stop at the Heliopolis Hotel in Cairo to ride camels and enjoy the pyramids. Thence over Arabia . . . and on, after lunching at Bahrain, to one night in Karachi. A lake in the middle of India; frightful Calcutta; Rangoon, Bangkok – night-stops at each place – it took seven extremely happy days to reach Singapore.

Though what Cunyngham-Brown calls 'the best of all means of travel', such exclusive transport was more a novelty than a service; for most, until well after the Second World War, intercontinental air travel remained, like its champagne breakfasts, the stuff of screen-time fantasy.

Where air transport did make a major difference in the 1930s, and why the heavily subsidised routes of Imperial Airways, Air France, KLM and Pan Am were all accorded a high priority, was in the carriage of mail. The revolution in communications, begun with the construction of the overland telegraph in 1871 and now being hastened by the introduction of the radio telephone, played a vital part in the consolidation of Western imperialism. Nowhere was this more true than in the trading empires of the East. Commercial decisions affecting the fate of companies and the livelihoods of whole communities no longer rested in the hands of a delirious agent poised between his gin *pahit* and his quinine bottle in some god-forsaken outpost five days up-river. The latest fluctuations of the London and New York commodity markets now became common knowledge in

Singapore and Shanghai within hours. Cash transactions, legal authorisations and personnel changes could be effected within days. The East had been integrated into a new world trading system where markets could be instantly manipulated; commercial intelligence had become the most valuable commodity of all.

By 1937 so dependent had big business become on this new technology that when, for security reasons, the Chinese authorities in Shanghai banned the use of the radio telegraph, desperate dealers in Jardine Matheson's office suddenly became avid pigeon fanciers. John Keswick's recollection of the arrangement was recorded by his daughter Maggie in her *The Thistle and the Jade*.

> Our ships [sailing up the Yangtze] took out the pigeons, and the birds then flew the eighty or so miles back to head office with messages addressed to Ewo [that is, Jardine's] attached to their legs. For some weeks our competitors were astonished by our knowledge of what cargoes were on offer. Alas, an inexperienced young pigeon came down for a drink in a Chinese tea house. He was caught and so were we.

When Somerset Maugham had made his two brief visits to the Far East in the 1920s, the gramophone had been all the rage. In the heat of the day from an adjacent hotel balcony a splutter of music, 'ragtime of course', invariably came wafting through the open windows. As portrayed in those crisply written short stories, Maugham's Malaya itself partakes of the urgency and inconsequence of a short-play gramophone record. The humdrum routine of an apparently immutable society is abruptly shattered by some breathless liaison, some tragic injustice; the affair swiftly mounts to its climax with a suicide, a furtive departure; then the music abruptly dies and everything is back to normal as tea-cups clink reassuringly and a new hand is dealt at the bridge table.

A decade later the novelty of the repetitious record-player was wearing thin. Gramophones had become bazaar fare; every Singapore tea-stall had one. 'Now radio was conquering even the jungle,' wrote R. H. Bruce Lockhart in 1936. He was referring not to the two-way radio sets operated by the likes of Jardine Matheson but to the ubiquitous bakelite receivers with their calibrated wave-band selectors. In remote up-country rest-houses the illuminated glow of a dial was as much a marvel as the sounds that came from the speaker. From Singapore to Shanghai, Manila and Batavia, radio stations proliferated. Come war and revolution their influence would be formidable. With uncanny prescience a Javanese cab-driver invited Lockhart to speculate on the consequences of a world informed by wireless. 'For sure, Tuan,' said the driver, supplying the answer himself, 'the Dutch will be driven out.'

Meanwhile instant communications heightened the frenzy of inter-war diplomacy. Civil servants struggled to assimilate the deluge of reports and recommendations from around the world which every policy initiative prompted. Government ministers accustomed themselves to the novelty of international conferences; now personal chemistry compounded global complexities. Though calculated to reduce tensions, this intercourse, like that at the League of Nations, tended to be counter-productive. So did that scope afforded to home governments for more frequent and direct interference in the regulation of their dependencies. Returning to Malaya after an absence of twenty-five years Lockhart rued the dearth of enterprising colonial servants like those who had so impressed Colonel Lyautey; but their passing he thought inevitable.

> To-day, the speeding up of communications by air and by wireless has enabled Whitehall to spread its tentacles over the local administration in almost every corner of our Colonial Empire. Ministers, too, descend out of the sky by air-plane, spend a feverish week in touring the country, and return home with a little dangerous learning, and the local Governor is . . . little more than a human post-box for receiving the instructions of the home government.

Lockhart fancied he detected shades of imperial Rome's decline in the lack of initiative and enterprise now required of the men on the spot. The home government must learn 'to leave well alone'.

Crash Landing

It was not that simple. Returning to Malaya in 1933 after a spell in India, Cunyngham-Brown had noted the effects on the peninsula's rubber plantations of an economic system now capable of responding instantly to the vagaries of demand in the industrialised West. 'A neglected allure hung over everything – empty clubs, silent roads, abandoned bungalows with weed-grown paths and broken shutters creaking in the evening breeze.'

There had been hiccups in demand before the First World War and there had been slumps in the 1920s, but the Wall Street crash of late 1929 and the Great Depression that followed were infinitely

more serious. They bore especially heavily on an economy dependent on rubber and tin exports, most of which went to the United
States. In 1936, as Lockhart revisited old haunts in Negri Sembilan,
he too found deserted bungalows amongst the gloomy ranks of the
rubber trees, the erstwhile homes of European plantation assistants.
'They will never be reoccupied.' Worse still was the fate of Malaya's
contract labourers, mostly recruited in India. Between 1929 and 1932
their number declined from 258,000 to 145,000. Repatriated to
Madras, they spread the curse of unemployment from Malaya to
south India in a ripple effect typical of the Depression.

In 1910, Lockhart's last year as a planter in Malaya, rubber had
been selling at thirteen shillings (that is, 156 pennies) a pound. By
1932 it had plummeted to under two and a half pennies a pound.
Plantation owners had been forced to sell their properties while their
redundant assistants were obliged to seek menial work in Singapore
and then beg or borrow their passage money home. Whole families
had been ruined, not least Lockhart's own. An uncle, one of the first
to plant rubber, had rewarded his grandmother's £25,000 investment
by making her the 'Rubber Queen' of Edinburgh, worth over half a
million. But such was their faith in rubber that, like others,
Lockhart's relations refused to sell out until obliged to do so by the
catastrophic collapse. As a result the family's fortune was lost.
Rubber estates privately owned and run by European planters now
became a rarity. Nearly all were bought out by major companies,
some British like Guthrie's or Harrisons & Crosfield, others French,
German and, especially down the east coast of Malaya, Japanese.

Venturing on to Batavia by KLM ('less than six hours whereas the
journey by steamer wastes the best part of two days') Lockhart
relayed news of a Japanese consortium's acquisition of estates in the
Riau islands, Dutch possessions but within sight of Singapore's
harbour. Oddly these acquisitions, though much frequented by their
new owners, had yet to attract any obvious investment. Were the
Japanese waiting for an improvement in the economic climate, won-
dered Lockhart; or did they have other interests in such a strategically sensitive location?

In the Dutch archipelago, as in the British peninsula, the
Depression had been disastrous. The plantations of Sumatra, where
rubber had largely replaced tobacco as the boom crop of the Medan
area, were run by some of the same companies as in Malaya –
Harrisons & Crosfield, Guthrie's and the Franco-Belgian Société

Financière des Caoutchouc. The Dutch welcomed such international investment partly because the level of their own investment failed to match the potential of the Indies and partly because international involvement was seen as underwriting their rule in the Indies. Other international investors in Sumatra's rubber now included the American Goodyear Tyre Company and Italy's Pirelli.

However, this diversification of ownership proved no protection against falling prices. The Sumatran planters' plight was much the same as that of those in Malaya, while their Chinese and Javanese labourers fared even worse. In Java itself, the still vast sugar industry had been equally devastated. Out of two hundred cane mills, barely thirty were operating. Lockhart found Surabaya's refineries idle and the price of sugar down by 95 per cent. Four hundred thousand Javanese had lost their jobs. For the big-spending sugar kings of old 'the spate of champagne had ceased'. 'Europeans were drinking whisky and soda or Bols gin'; the Hungarian whores at the 'Tutti-Frutti' had been obliged to change their clientele. 'Today they sleep only with the Arabs and the Chinese who, slump or no slump, are always rich.'

Here, as in Malaya, to offset falling government revenues from primary produce, taxation had been increased to what de Jonge, the hard-line Governor-General, he who anticipated another 300 years of Dutch rule, admitted was its utmost limit. Even some of his own officials were becoming highly critical, none more so than Hubertus Johannes van Mook. A shy and shambling giant of a man, van Mook, born in Java of Dutch parents, was then a member of the Volksrad, the largely advisory assembly of the Indies, and had taken it upon himself to champion the cause of, amongst others, the unemployed sugar workers. Against 'the dismal romanticism of a business age in which lack of efficiency [is] deemed identical with deficient humanity' van Mook inveighed so successfully that Governor de Jonge appointed him to the ministry of economic affairs. 'He must be made to work a full 24 hours,' advised de Jonge; only thus could he be stopped from 'filling all the daily and weekly newspapers with articles showing that the government knows nothing . . . and acts in a totally mistaken fashion'.

Similar criticisms were appearing in the Philippines where distress and unrest were also on the increase. There, however, preferential access to the US market for Filipino sugar worked in the colony's favour. It was the exception. On the Moi plateau of Cochin-China,

France's incipient rubber industry was saved only by massive government intervention. No crop was unaffected and, *pace* the Philippines, no colony immune. This, however, made the introduction of restrictions and quota systems easier. British, Dutch and French found common ground for collaborating to reduce supply and so shore up prices. Production of tin, sugar and rubber were all restricted. The speed of modern communications which, like a well-laid powder trail, had so disastrously ignited the Depression, now served to damp it down. In an unprecedented example of fine-tuning, quotas were revised quarterly and new rubber plantings carefully regulated.

But to many planters the quota system seemed an even worse evil, its main effect being to prolong the agony and postpone recovery. As Deputy-Controller of Rubber in Kuala Lumpur, capital of the Federated Malay States, Sjovald Cunyngham-Brown found himself responsible for issuing the requisite credits.

> The difficulty was not simplified by the fact that a quarter of the country's rubber was owned . . . by the small-holding community of Malays and Chinese to all of whom coupons were given at the rate of a certain number per acre . . . Ingenious – but it had many loopholes. Coupons became no less than another form of currency.

Compared to the big corporate plantations, these native small-holdings were under-assessed and were further penalised by the various limitations on new plantings. In both Malaya and Indonesia, Chinese, Malay and Javanese small-holders bitterly resented the restriction scheme as an unwarranted and discriminatory interference.

Van Mook, who as the last Governor of the Netherlands East Indies would one day come to epitomise the intransigence of Dutch rule, remained highly critical. As he later recalled, his now crippling work-load, as much as his official position, was typical of the times.

> Direction from above and from without penetrated everywhere; every year saw some new Western initiative, some additional adaptation of native customs and institutions to Western standards. In practically every phase of life this trend appeared, introducing new conceptions, erasing traditions, letting light and air into dark, stuffy chambers, but nearly always hurting someone in his interests or feelings. It could happen that a modern system of taxation, while alleviating the burden on the peasants, destroyed a whole class of feudal nobles and petty officials. It could also happen that a foolish speculation in pepper by a firm of London brokers could reduce

an entire district to poverty for years. And every time the origin of these evils lay wholly outside the perception of the people concerned.

A Hate that Seemed Deep-rooted

Just as war would soon betray the political fallibility of colonialism, so the Great Depression seemed to have laid bare its economic fallibility. If the markets could so easily and suddenly plunge colonies on the other side of the world into the deepest depression, it stood to reason that governments must be willing to act with equal dispatch. Whether or not disposed to intervene, they were being obliged to do so. The consequences for empire were dire but not immediately disastrous. More alarming was the effect that the crisis was having on their subjects, both at home and overseas.

In 1930 General Douglas MacArthur, having been appointed US Army Chief of Staff by President Hoover, returned from the Philippines to an American winter of bank failures, bread lines and soup kitchens. Behind the lengthening dole queues, the hunger marches and the occasional riots, many detected the revolutionary designs of international Communism. MacArthur shared the administration's growing alarm. When, in 1932, veterans of the First World War converged on Washington to demand payment of a promised bonus to see them through these workless times, he showed no sympathy for his erstwhile comrades-in-arms. It was MacArthur who took the initiative in dispersing the protesters with riot squads and tear gas, then burning their pitiful encampment to the ground. Casualties were mercifully few although, to men so desperate and destitute, even the loss of spare boots or a battered forage cap was a disaster.

Despite overwhelming evidence to the contrary, MacArthur insisted that the 'Bonus Expeditionary Force' was a mob of revolutionaries out to take over the government. He had, as he put it, 'released in my day more than one community which had been held in the grip of a foreign nation' – a reference presumably to his war record rather than to his service in the Philippines – and he was glad now to have been able to do the same for the government of the United States. Regardless of his personal motives for such controversial statements, the inference here was that the jobless, even veterans, were not only revolutionaries but anti-American revolutionaries backed, presumably, by Moscow.

Throughout the 1920s and 1930s similar hardships provoked similar protests right across the industrialised world. These in turn prompted similarly alarmist conclusions. To relieve the distress, to pre-empt the security threat and, incidentally of course, to stand any chance of re-election, governments found themselves obliged to increase spending on social welfare. There could be no question of reducing their imperial responsibilities to pay for it since recovery depended on the raw materials and the markets which the colonies furnished. But the resources available for administering and defending those colonies could be cut. The sinews of empire were being stretched to their limits. In Singapore a new naval base and dockyard, deemed essential ever since the end of the First World War, were repeatedly delayed. On the other side of the world MacArthur railed against what he called 'the skeletonisation' of the army under Roosevelt's 'New Deal'. In 1936 the worsening international situation did at last spur on the Singapore installations and lead to some reinstatement of US military spending. But in that year MacArthur returned in disgust to the Philippines. 'A bellicose swashbuckler' out of favour in Washington, he would look to Manila for a more appreciative public.

And all this at a time when colonial subjects were also unusually restless. Faced with hardships not of their own making, subject to the sort of interference noted by Lockhart and van Mook, seeing the flow of Western investment suddenly reversed, and encountering impoverished Europeans whose lifestyle no longer inspired envy, many Asians began to question the whole system into which they had been co-opted. The West's industrial capitalism was failing them; alternatives were therefore worth considering. Organised labour began to make its voice heard with strikes in Singapore, Java and Vietnam. The 1930 peasant revolt in north Annam, which resulted in those 'Xo-Viets' for which 'Nguyen the Patriot' was sought by the Sûreté, presaged more radical solutions.

During his few, very full days revisiting Singapore in 1936, R. H. Bruce Lockhart found time for an excursion to the city gaol to inspect its Communist inmates. As the public well knew from his highly successful *Memoirs of a Secret Agent*, Communism and gaols were subjects of which Lockhart had some experience. In 1918 he had seen the inside of both the Lubyanka and the Kremlin. Arrested by the Bolsheviks as a spy, he would have been executed but for one of the first East-West exchanges of agents. Now something of a celebrity, he was travelling on behalf of a London newspaper whose readers would no doubt relish his reflections from outside the prison bars.

The Singapore Communists, all Chinese, were held in their own cell. Most had been convicted for circulating seditious material amongst disaffected fellow Chinese in the tin and rubber industries. To this agricultural and industrial proletariat, the Party directed calls for unity and revolution, citing pay cuts and the restriction quotas used to justify them. Lockhart, unable to speak Chinese, let the prison governor conduct his interviews.

> While the governor talked in quiet, matter-of-fact tones to these yellow disciples of Moscow, I made a careful scrutiny of their faces. I was struck by their impassive composure. Some of the men looked intelligent. They made no complaints. Only a certain dignified surliness revealed a hate which seemed deep-rooted.

With China itself currently divided between warring Communists and Nationalists, both of whom looked to the overseas Chinese communities for recruits and financial support, it was not surprising that Singapore's predominantly Chinese population found itself taking sides. What was surprising was that neither the Kuomintang Nationalists nor the Communists were content simply to rally support and pursue mutual vendettas. Both demanded political rights, condemned colonial rule and were intent on overthrowing it.

British administrators in Malaya who insisted, like Sjovald Cunyngham-Brown, that there were 'no movements toward democracy and/or independence' in pre-war Malaya may have had a distorted view of the matter. As Malay-speakers, governing in the name of Malay sultans, and naturally inclined to identify with this native aristocracy, the British were wont to discount Malayans of Chinese origin as immigrants. The smaller community of Malayan Indians, fired by the political freedoms being won in India, were also discounted. That 'hate which seemed deep-rooted' could therefore be ascribed to the machinations of extraneous forces, like the Moscow-backed Communist International, the Shanghai-based Chinese Communist Party or India's Congress Party, operating on the sympathies of a displaced and alien element.

Yet in the Straits Settlements and the Federated Malay States (though not the Unfederated) these alien elements now constituted a majority of the population; and in Malaya as a whole they now represented nearly 40 per cent. It was to adjust relations with this mainly Chinese component, and so defuse worsening labour relations, that in 1930 the Colonial Office had appointed Sir Cecil Clementi, its outstanding Sinologist, to the governorship of the Straits Settlements, a post which meant that he also became High Commissioner for the Malay States.

The Buffalo of Integration

For a patrician scholar who found relaxation in little-known Latin poets and Mandarin love-songs, the prospect of five years in Malaya must have been daunting. The British community reciprocated this caution. Its rugby-minded rubber-planters and Malayanised martinets looked on the new governor with as much suspicion as had Hong Kong's stuff-shirted race-goers. According to Cunyngham-Brown, 'Chinese and Indian-speaking members of the Service were still regarded as "Specialists" – "Cranks" – probably driven lunatic by their labours in learning such uncouth tongues and therefore not to be taken too much notice of.'

Clementi, whose lofty stature and zealous reach more than matched his formidable reputation, soon commanded their notice. To combat Chinese agitation, he introduced a system of screening for all future immigrants. He also clamped down on Communist propaganda and proscribed the Malayan branch of the Nationalist Kuomintang. On a more positive note, he increased the opportunities for both Chinese and Malays to join the colonial civil service, made access to primary and secondary education cheaper, and encouraged even Chinese schools to adopt Malay as the language of instruction. At the federal level, although the idea of a customs union embracing all the Malay states had to be abandoned, some progress was made in standardising the different administrative structures by devolving the powers of the Federation back to the state councils (and their sultans) of the individual federated states.

All these measures were greeted with howls of protest from old Malaya hands. In what they considered 'a Tory Eden in which each man is contented with his station and does not wish for change', such tinkering seemed a classic example of superfluous interference. Old rivalries between sultan and sultan would be aroused, so would those between Malay and Chinese, and between the Straits Settlements and the Malay States. Worse still, more alert critics rightly suspected that behind such measures there lurked a more sinister design, namely to undermine the region's complex structure of colonies, federations and protectorates, and to create the basis for some future amalgamation of all Britain's peninsular dependencies.

Devolving powers to the Federated Malay States, for instance, was rightly seen as a means of returning them to a status similar to that of the Unfederated Malay States (UMS); thus in any future scheme of union or federation the UMS's fears of being absorbed into the existing Federation, an institution for which they had nothing but contempt, would be allayed. The various social and educational reforms would have a similar levelling effect, in this case as between Chinese and Malays. And what was talk of a customs union if not a step towards economic union? Clementi, in short, was daring to take by the horns the notoriously intransigent buffalo of Malayan integration.

If Clementi's inclinations corresponded to those of his old friend Reginald Johnston, his pursuit of Malayan integration deserves recognition as being the first step on the road to eventual self-government. Alternatively, integration could be seen as an imperial adjustment in which the old system of colonial rule based on collaboration with the sultans was to be replaced by a new system based on collaboration with a broader and more representative élite. Probably Clementi would have subscribed to both views. That inter-war 'revival' of British imperialism identified by Gallagher was not incompatible with the empire's gradual democratisation.

Either way, Clementi's immediate objectives of rationalisation and integration, first evident in his proposals for Hong Kong's New Territories and then in his tinkering with the Malay states, finally came into the open in respect of the constitutional anomalies which comprised Britain's responsibilities in the north, or non-Dutch area, of the neighbouring island of Borneo.

As Governor of the Straits Settlements Clementi was responsible not only for the colonies of Singapore, Penang and Malacca which punctuated the Malayan coastline, but also for that eminently forgettable island-colony of Labuan off the coast of north-west Borneo. Additionally, as High Commissioner of the Malay States, he was responsible for Brunei, the much diminished Malay sultanate in north Borneo. And finally, as the senior British administrator in south-east Asia, he also acted as the British government's agent in dealings with the Brooke family's 'White Raj' in Sarawak and the

British North Borneo Company's corporate rule in neighbouring Sabah. If only to relieve a severe case of administrative schizophrenia, some rationalisation of these responsibilities was desirable.

Labuan and Brunei, territorial specks even on a map of Borneo, were largely irrelevant; their concurrence in any new scheme was not essential but could probably be taken for granted. Sarawak and Sabah, quite as big as England and Scotland and both exceedingly jealous of their autonomous status, were a different proposition. In 1930 Clementi had visited both, holding talks with British North Borneo's Governor and with Rajah Vyner Brooke's brother, the *tuan muda* Bertram.

Neither, it soon became clear, viewed the prospect of a Borneo federation with enthusiasm. The British North Borneo Company was worried about its shareholders and particularly about how their support and expectations would be affected if its authority became subject to direction by some new federal authority. The Brookes were more worried about their subjects whose unquestioning loyalty to their White Rajah was, according to Bertram, of such a peculiar and personal nature that the raj would prove unworkable if the Rajah's authority were diluted in any way.

Tuan muda Bertram, a correct and conscientious stand-in, chose his words with care but could not, of course, speak for his brother, Rajah Vyner. The third Brooke rajah, a Noël Coward look-alike with retiring habits, was, as usual, in England, extremely difficult to meet, and impossible to tie down. Nor could Bertram speak for the various other members of the family who, since Rajah Vyner had no male heir, were interested parties. They included the *rani* Margaret, Vyner's forthright mother, and the *rani muda* Sylvia, Vyner's wife. Sylvia was about to head for Hollywood in connection with a forthcoming film on Sarawak, but this would in no way distract her from lobbying for a change in the succession so that one of her three daughters might have a claim to it. Then there was the *dayang muda* Gladys, Bertram's wife and Sylvia's deadly enemy. Gladys and Bertram had a son, Anthony Brooke (otherwise known as 'Peter') who, as the Rajah's nephew, was the obvious successor; but he had yet to be acknowledged by Vyner as *rajah muda*, or 'crown prince'. Additionally there were several other, mostly illegitimate, contenders plus a mercurial Irishman called MacBryan who appeared to enjoy a unique place in the Rajah's affections and to have his own agenda for Sarawak's future.

Whether Clementi appreciated all these complications is not clear. The Brookes were anomalous enough without their repeated succession crises. Obsessed with preserving 'the most absolute monarchy in the world' and opposed to even the most innocent forms of commercial exploitation within their 'anthropological garden', they epitomised a paternalism that many now thought more perverse than romantic. Yet their sovereignty had been conceded, their rule was apparently popular, and their connections in London were powerful. If they were opposed to any kind of federation there was little that Clementi or the Colonial Office could do about it. Perhaps the raj's centenary, due in 1941, would present a better opportunity for reform and integration; perhaps Vyner himself would eventually come round to the idea.

The chances of this happening might be improved if the other components of British Borneo had already endorsed integration. Although the British North Borneo Company baulked at the idea of federation, its directors were apparently open to the possibility of a straight take-over in which the government would buy out the Company and its shareholders. Clementi explored this idea with grim determination. At one point he was all for making Sabah, Brunei and Labuan a separate Bornean colony, at another for incorporating them into the Straits Settlements as an overspill for Chinese immigration, and at yet another for 'linking' them with 'a scheme – now under discussion – for a federation of the whole Malay peninsula . . .'

This last option, though probably one that he would have preferred not to have let slip, prefigured the modern concept of Malaysia in that it united all the Malay states with those of north Borneo. Quite possibly the early 1930s were also the ideal moment for anticipating it. As Clementi observed, the rubber slump was 'very seriously affecting the finances of British North Borneo' and would therefore influence the terms under which a take-over would be acceptable to the Company. Unfortunately the slump was also very seriously affecting any government's willingness to fund such schemes. The Directors were reportedly ready to settle for £1 million; additional expenditure would be needed to upgrade Sabah's skeletal services. It was out of the question, retorted the Colonial Office. No imperial funding whatsoever was available. Clementi was being carried away by his own enthusiasm. 'If ever there was a more inopportune time to make a suggestion of this kind, I don't believe he could have found it . . .' minuted the under-secretary.

Malayan integration would have to wait for better times. Clementi's only contribution to the rationalisation of the region's political geography came when, just before retirement, he promoted the retrocession to Perak of that forgotten entity known as the Dindings. Effected in 1935, it was technically a 'decolonisation' and so grounds, maybe, for some consolation in fireside reminiscences with his old friend Reggie Johnston.

Bustling through the Malay states a year later, Bruce Lockhart never mentions Clementi. Swettenham, Clifford and the other demigods of British Malaya come in for fulsome praise; Clementi's existence is merely hinted at in a reference to 'an unprecedented example of British interference'. This referred to the scheme to reduce the powers of the Federal government and enhance those of the states. Lockhart thought it typical of the meddlesome attitudes that now prevailed and which, in his opinion, would prove the empire's undoing. This and the 'vast strides in education' made by all the subject peoples constituted 'the real danger to colonial empires in the East'. It might take twenty-five years, probably longer, but the end was in sight. 'Most experts, including the British, held the view that the French would go from Asia first, the British second, and the Dutch last.' Lockhart disagreed. He knew nothing about the French but he thought the British would outlast the Dutch; nationalists in the Indies were as assertive as in India but their counterparts in Malaya were as yet barely audible. He also noted a more obvious threat to empire.

> In the Dutch East Indies and even in Malaya I had found most thinking Europeans obsessed with the danger of Japan . . . There was the incontrovertible fact that Japan is today the most powerful nation in Asia and that her word, and not the word of the League of Nations or any other combination of powers, is law to half the world . . . It would be foolish to ignore the Japanese problem . . .

Yet the real danger, he thought, would come from within, from a combination of that 'deepening intervention' by government with a growing resentment amongst its native subjects. Although in the long run he was probably right, in the darkening days that lay immediately ahead, Lockhart, like Clementi, seemed to have hopelessly miscalculated.

7

Shanghai Express

Worlds Apart

If, for the British, India was the work-place of empire and Africa its great outdoors, then the Far East was its evening off. For cocktails, it was said, one could do no better than the Malay states. A planters' club in Negri Sembilan boasted the second longest bar in the world; and in Maugham's Malayan stories the endless gin *pahits*, *stengahs*, slings and whisky airs become after-hours clichés. Dinner, according to Bruce Lockhart, would be better with the Dutch whose *rijstaffel* he rated the most gargantuan meal on the imperial menu; including every fish, fowl, flesh and fruit known to Indies' appetites, it was usually eaten from a receptacle the size of a soup tureen. Then on, humoured and replete, to fairer fare. For a *tuan*-about-town celebrating the mid-1930s recovery of rubber prices, there was nowhere to rival the 'Worlds'.

Singapore had several, including a Great World and a Gay World. All were basically dance-halls with highly rated bands and bevies of slender hostesses. The latter were known as 'taxi-girls' because a ticket, purchased from their minder, bought only a dance; it ran out with the music. Longer assignations, though not impossible to arrange, took many dances to negotiate.

'Worlds' were found in all the major cities of the Far East but differed in ambience. Saigon's Grand Monde was reckoned the East's biggest gambling den. In 1950 it became the object of a private war which would have a fateful bearing on French rule in Indo-China; subsequently it was transformed into what Graham Greene adjudged the world's largest brothel. All 'Worlds' were Chinese-run. No one understood a man's fancies like the Chinese and, for variety and wild exuberance, no establishment could touch the quintessential Great World in Shanghai. To a film-maker like Josef von Sternberg, director of the 1932 *Shanghai Express* starring Marlene Dietrich, it was an irresistible location.

When I had entered the hot stream of humanity there was no turning back even had I wanted to. On the first floor were gambling tables, singsong girls, magicians, pickpockets, slot machines, fireworks, bird-cages, fans, stick incense, acrobats, and ginger. One flight up were the restaurants . . . actors, crickets in cages, pimps, midwives, barbers, and earwax extractors. The third floor had jugglers, herb medicines, ice cream parlours, photographers, [and] a new bevy of girls, their high-collared gowns slit to reveal their hips in case one had passed up the more modest ones below who merely flashed their thighs . . . The fourth floor was crowded with shooting galleries, fan-tan tables, revolving wheels, massage benches . . . dried fish and intestines, and dance platforms serviced by a horde of music makers competing with each other to see who could drown out the others. The fifth floor featured girls whose dresses were slit to the armpits, a stuffed whale, story-tellers, balloons, peep-shows, masks, a mirror maze, two love-letter booths whose scribes guaranteed results, rubber goods, and a temple filled with ferocious gods and joss sticks.

Such was Shanghai's Great World. It stood at one of the city's major intersections where the retail bustle of Thibet Road met the stately façades of Avenue Foch/Avenue Edouard VII. The latter was the dividing line between the French Concession, still a distinct entity with its *képi*-ed gendarmes and well-wooded boulevards, and the much larger, mainly British, International Settlement. At the Great World, all worlds met. This high-rise 'house of multiple joys' epitomised the cosmopolitan riot of energy, style and greed that was Shanghai in the 1930s. Its fevered activity mirrored that of the metropolis outside; and just so, its imminent fate would foreshadow that of the imperial presence in its midst.

As the West's most valuable asset in the East, Shanghai had always rested on an outrageous presumption. Here, and in a minor way at the other treaty ports, there flourished that commercial ideal to which the China traders had originally aspired – empire without imperial responsibilities, traffic and trade without the sort of entanglements which Clementi had been trying to unravel. The treaty ports were bits of Asia in which the white man, relieved of his civilising burden, could ride roughshod.

With three-quarters of Britain's China investments located in Shanghai, its 6,000 Britons considered the place their own creation.

Malaya might boast the world's second longest bar but the longest was that in their Shanghai Club. The Settlement's government, their self-appointed Municipal Council, acted in their interests and was answerable to none but themselves. Unsurprisingly they acquired the reputation of being 'the most reactionary Englishmen abroad' and 'the spoiled children of Empire'. But like the pitch-pine pilings which, driven thirty feet into the one-time swamp along the Whangpoo River, still failed to prevent the monstrous skyline of the city's corniche from gradual sinkage, so Shanghai's soaring reputation rested on bluff; and the bluff was about to be called.

Making Whoopee

One of the five original treaty ports at which the British had gained commercial and extraterritorial rights in 1842, Shanghai had grown so prodigiously thanks to its pivotal location. Not only was it both the fulcrum of China's coastal trade and the nearest Chinese port to Japan but, much more important, it commanded access to the mighty Yangtze. This river, navigable for two thousand miles, was the principal means of communication with a vast area more populous and more productive even than the Nile or Ganges basins. Rising in the Kun Lun mountains north of Tibet, the Yangtze first assumed commercial importance near Chungking (Chonqing) in the highlands of Szechwan (Sichuan). Thence, posing a navigational challenge second to none, it plunged down spectacular gorges to Ichang (Yichang). In the maze of lakes and waterways of the middle river it almost lost itself. Finally it rolled royally past the ancient cities of Wuhu and Nanking. Its last tributary, a few miles from the open sea, was the Whangpoo where, just above the confluence, Shanghai's skyline commanded the estuarial waters. In all, a tenth of the world's population lived on land drained by the Yangtze. Arguably it offered the most exciting commercial potential in the world. If there was a single solution to the crisis of confidence that had precipitated the Great Depression, it lay, thought many, in the still barely developed markets up the Yangtze.

When, in the late nineteenth century, additional treaty ports had been added to the original five – at one time there were about forty – more than half those so designated were not sea-ports at all but Yangtze river-ports. The river became as much a highway of Western empire as the Malacca Strait; Shanghai was its Singapore. The foreigners who set up home in the new concessions up-river found themselves in the heartland of China, dangerously exposed in turbulent times and totally dependent on the renowned steamer services down to Shanghai. Some of these were operated by the French or the Americans but mostly they were British. Latterly Japanese vessels also joined in; and if all else failed, there were native junks which, when travelling upstream, relied on gangs of coolies towing from the bank.

A similar division of responsibilities existed in Shanghai itself. But there, while the prestige-minded consuls of France had jealously guarded their own Concession, the Americans had evaded the embarrassing imputation of imperialism by submerging their sector in that of the British. In 1863 these two had thus become the International Settlement. Other nations, most notably the Japanese, had subsequently acquired extraterritorial and commercial rights within the International Settlement; but it remained dominated by the British and run, with minimal interference, by the Municipal Council on which the British retained their majority until 1930.

By then the nineteenth-century port had hatched, like a cuckoo's egg, into the monstrous twentieth-century metropolis. Outgrowing its nest, the insatiable prodigy made ever heavier demands on its bemused and exhausted Chinese fosterers. Together, the International Settlement and the French Concession now accounted for an area of over 12 square miles while those sectors of the city under Chinese rule amounted to only 8. Except in times of disturbance the divisions were not immediately apparent to the unobservant visitor. No Berlin Wall cleft the city, no check-points differentiated the different sectors. Though unrepresented and often treated as of little consequence, far more Chinese ('Shanghainese') resided in the foreign settlements than did foreigners ('Shanghailanders'). Similarly many Shanghailanders opted to live in the Chinese sector where were located some foreign-owned businesses and nearly all foreign-owned industries.

Unfortified, the two foreign settlements still felt safe enough. Both fronted the Whangpoo River where the gunboats and warships of the European powers continued to afford protection. Additionally their approaches could be sealed by road-blocks manned by the Shanghai Volunteer Corps whose improbable composition exposed the uniquely international character of the whole city. Commanded by a British regular, the Corps comprised American and British units (including kilted Scots and turbanned Pathans), plus separate companies of Chinese, Danish, Eurasian, German, Filipino, Italian, Japanese, Jewish, Portuguese and White Russian troops. Additionally the French Concession had, of course, its own contingent. Not until the United Nations dreamt up peace-keeping forces would such a multinational force be constituted.

Access to Shanghai was open to all; it was, in effect, a Free City. The currency was chiefly Mexican dollars (a legacy of the Spanish trade in Mexican silver via the Philippines) and the police force partly Sikh (recruited by the British in India). Amongst those who originally came as refugees were some immensely influential Iraqi Jews, many thousands of White Russians who had escaped across Siberia from the Bolsheviks, and numerous Chinese revolutionaries availing themselves of the settlements' sanctuary. Of the dozen or so foreign newspapers four were British, one American, two Russian, one German and one French. 'Forty-eight distinct nationalities are represented in Shanghai,' reported a 1934 guide-book, 'and there are over 100 radio stations.'

The same source gave the city's total population as just under 3.5 million but rising so fast that, by the time the guide-book was published, it would have overhauled Chicago and possibly Berlin. Only London, New York and Tokyo would then surpass it. Like them, and unlike any other city under colonial rule, Shanghai was not just a trading port with financial facilities but a major industrial centre. Singapore, when arguing against Clementi's idea of a Malayan customs union, had stressed that its ancient entrepôt trade with India, the archipelago, Borneo and China still far exceeded its trade with Malaya, and this in spite of its monopoly in the smelting of Malaya's tin. Shanghai, on the other hand, powered the whole Chinese economy. It was the Japanese who, gaining concessions after the Russo-Japanese War of 1904–5, first began setting up industrial plants to exploit China's cheap labour. Their example was quickly followed by other foreign companies. From trade and transport Jardine Matheson had moved into brewing, food-processing and textile mills. The pall from a thousand smokestacks engulfed the city and made the breeze along the riverside Bund even more desirable.

Here, in the world's fourth largest port, moored the ships of all nations, dazzling cruise liners lying alongside rusty tramp steamers, sleek grey destroyers nosing past antediluvian junks. To sailors the world over Shanghai was a port like no other. Though the Club was far too exclusive for Jack Tar, and the Great World somewhat overwhelming, the dives off Soochow Creek employed temptresses so importunate that no man had ever, it was said, run the gauntlet of Blood Alley. It was while reeling from the squalor and shame of Soochow Creek that Hickman Powell, hankering after an Arcadian antidote, had sailed for Buleleng in the Dutch Indies to discover that 'last paradise' in Bali.

The authors of the city's standard guide-book found less to censure. They did, though, object to Shanghai being called the 'Paris of the East'; Paris could call itself 'the Shanghai of the Occident' if it wished, but Shanghai was demeaned by comparison with anywhere else.

Whoopee!
 High hats and low necks; long tails and short knickers; inebriates and slumming puritans.
 Wine, women and song
 Whoopee!
 Let's go places and do things! . . .
 When the sun goes in and the lights come out, Shanghai becomes another city, the city of Blazing Night, a night life Haroun-al-Raschid never knew, with tales Scheherezade never told . . .

Having the most exotic *demi-monde* on record, Shanghai naturally included some of the most ravishing and accomplished prostitutes; the blondes, mostly White Russians, claimed to be princesses; some actually were. Amongst their *madames*, Victoria Litvanoff, clairvoyante and blackmailer as well as brothel-keeper, brought to her business an unrivalled flair with specially designed beds and chairs to challenge the fantasies of her jaded customers. She also advertised a stable of gigolos for respectable but frustrated matrons.

Opium, like the joss-sticks and fan-tan tables of the Great World, was a cliché of the Shanghai experience; heroin was said to be included in the price of a hotel room. Other cities had occasionally added an adjective to the English language – Manila was an envelope, Madras a cotton – but only Shanghai ever furnished a verb. To be 'Shanghaied' was the lot of more than just sailors. Seduced, intoxicated and abducted, it nicely summed up the mixture of madness and menace which was Shanghai.

Here then was a new and unique colonial phenomenon, quintessentially imperialist and aggressively capitalist yet technically under

Chinese sovereignty and regarded by the British, its major participants, not as a colony but as an expatriate settlement. Its relations
were handled, if at all, by the cold and calculating brains at the
Foreign Office rather than by the paternalistic interventionists at the
Colonial Office.

This should have made letting go that much easier. Always the
most disposable of imperial assets (since technically not part of anyone's empire), the treaty ports could theoretically be abandoned
without making elaborate transitional arrangements and without the
embarrassment of 'surrender' or 'rendition'. Some had so little trade
that they had become liabilities. Withdrawal could be represented
simply as a rationalisation or as a gesture of goodwill. Others, though
desirable, were scarcely essential. Only Shanghai was in a class of its
own. The question about to be posed was whether it was worth
fighting for.

In that the International Settlement epitomised the increasingly
collaborative approach of the imperial powers to eastern empire, the
answer was yes. Once locked in competition for trade and prestige,
the British, French, Dutch and Americans now acknowledged a
shared concern for the maintenance of Western dominance. Joint
action to combat first German imperialism, and then the effects of
recession and the menace of international Communism entrenched
this attitude. In 1927 Shanghai was so eminently worth fighting for
that 20,000 troops from Britain, France, America and Japan were
sent to the aid of its polyglot Volunteers. But ten years later no such
consensus would exist about the new threat emanating from Tokyo.
Was Japan merely protecting its China interests as the British seemed
to think? Or was this new threat, as the Americans feared, the
prelude to a bid for Asian supremacy? And either way, what sort of
response would prove most effective?

Flogging the Jelly-fish

Had the Second World War preceded the First, the latter might never
have counted as a world war. In 1914–18 less than half the world had
taken sides. Actual fighting was largely restricted to Europe and Asia
Minor; civilian casualties were comparatively few. In the East, where
hostilities scarcely impinged at all, the colonial powers had gone
about their business as usual. There was always a chance that a
second 'world' war would prove equally irrelevant.

In the first, Indo-China had supplied France with labour, and Malaya raised a war fund which paid for a battleship; given the wartime demand for rubber and other tropical produce, both could afford to be generous. Holland for once had stayed neutral; neither the flow of Indies' produce nor that of Indonesian students heading for Dutch universities was interrupted. In 1915 a mutiny in Singapore briefly caused panic amongst the depleted British community who welcomed French, Japanese and Russian naval assistance in suppressing it. The mutineers were part of an Indian regiment and seem to have been largely responding to the calls of Indian nationalism. The affair had little to do with the British regimes in the Far East.

Penang, on the other hand, 'had if anything, enjoyed the first World War'. According to its biographer Raymond Flower, this was because this normally somnolent outpost of the Straits Settlements saw some of the action. Very early one morning in October 1914 the *Emden*, a German raider, had slipped into harbour flying the Royal Navy's ensign. To make her look still more like HMS *Yarmouth*, whose arrival was awaited, she also sported a false fourth funnel. Coming alongside a Russian cruiser, she changed her colours to those of the Kaiser's Germany and blew the cruiser out of the water. She then headed back to sea, sank a returning French destroyer, and disappeared over the horizon.

Nothing so exciting happened in the Philippines where war on the other side of the world had gone almost unnoticed except for an exceptionally buoyant demand for coconut oil, then used in the manufacture of explosives. Japan, Britain's faithful ally at the time, did even better. She had accepted the surrender of Germany's scattered outposts in the west Pacific, including her China concession around Shantung's Kiaochow Bay. Taking her role as one of the allied powers seriously, she had also significantly augmented her naval strength. Both these moves would have far-reaching consequences. While the other powers emerged from the battlefield debilitated, indebted and so shell-shocked that they thought the war had ended all wars, the Japanese found themselves with a booming economy, a new fleet, an incipient empire, and a strong feeling of having come of age as a world power.

The Anglo-Japanese alliance, which had served them so well, dated from the turn of the century. Detecting a pleasing symmetry in their geographical situations, both signatories had seen themselves as stable offshore powers anxious, like book-ends at the extremities of an unsteady Eurasian shelf, to contain their wobbly continental neighbours. In so far as the Russo-Japanese War had curbed Tsarist ambitions at one end, and the First World War Germany's ambitions at the other, it had worked. The signatories also appeared to have much else in common. Island groups, they were both thought to be over-populated and therefore entitled to seek outlets for settlement and enterprise elsewhere. Similarly, since they were heavily dependent on importing primary produce and exporting manufactured goods, they both required open markets and a strong navy to protect them. The alliance identified these shared interests and was supposed to eliminate the costly arms race that might result from the lack of any such understanding.

All these arguments still applied, some with even greater force, after the First World War. Had the Anglo-Japanese alliance been maintained, the Pacific War just might have been avoided and the leisurely pace of colonial tutelage maintained. The British might have been successful, as they fancied they already were, in influencing Tokyo to moderate its expansionist tendencies. Tokyo, cold-shouldering its militarists, might have continued to bask in the fellowship and approbation of the great powers and not have felt itself being isolated and victimised by a Caucasian cabal of racist imperialists.

Such, more or less, had been the thinking of Lord Curzon, the British Foreign Secretary, when arguing for a renewal of the alliance at the Imperial Conference of 1921. The Prime Minister Lloyd George agreed: 'two years after the war, when this gallant little people in the East backed us through thick and thin, now to drop them – we cannot do it'.

But it was admitted that other considerations, like US hostility to the alliance and Anglo-American undertakings to uphold China's integrity, made this an exceptionally complex problem. Action was therefore deferred until the Washington Conference later in the same year. There US suspicions not just of Japanese militarism and European colonialism but of bilateral alliances and imperial aggregations in general won the day. Instead of a precarious world order constructed, like a Meccano mechanism, of enmeshed reciprocities and balanced polarities, American policy-makers envisaged something much more idealistic, organic rather than mechanical, in which interdependent political economies, like cells, would automatically expand given only a congenial environment of peaceful co-operation.

This meant adding demilitarisation to the agenda and replacing alliances with a series of multinational treaties. One such treaty declared a 'naval holiday' or moratorium on the building of battle-ships; the navies of the US, Britain and Japan would be pegged at the existing ratio of 5:5:3 respectively. Japan agreed to withdraw from the erstwhile German concession in Shantung and Britain to start nego-tiations for the surrender of Weihaiwei. All agreed not to develop military facilities in the South China Sea (principally at Hong Kong and in Formosa). China's integrity was guaranteed; and the principle of equal commercial access to all foreign concessions in China, the so-called 'Open Door' policy, was affirmed.

This framework, endorsed by the League of Nations, survived for ten years while China succumbed to revolutionary turmoil. It was the decade in which the Chinese Communist Party, founded in Shanghai in 1921, appeared to be spearheading the Nationalist revival. Skilfully organised by Moscow's agents, it recruited amongst the industrial proletariat of Shanghai and Canton, organised the strikes and pro-tests of 1925 which brought even Hong Kong to a standstill, and then led the military thrust to reunite the country under the new republic with an advance north from Canton to the Yangtze.

In early 1927 left-wing Nationalists attacked the British Concession in the treaty port of Hankow (part of Wuhan) on the middle Yangtze. Casualties were avoided only by the British pulling out. Eight weeks later the Nationalists reached Nanking, sacked its foreign consulates, killed three British citizens and disrobed a number of foreign ladies 'including Mrs Giles, the wife of His Majesty's consul-general'. British and American vessels responded in time-honoured fashion with a bombardment of the city. It put a stop to further outrages but not to the Nationalist advance. 'Punishing China is like flogging a jelly-fish,' noted Winston Churchill, then Chancellor of the Exchequer.

To pre-empt similar chaos when the Nationalists entered Shanghai those 20,000 multinational troops were drafted into the city. Half were British, the largest contingent yet sent to the Far East. Shanghai, in 1927, was definitely worth fighting for. The Settlement and the Concession were wrapped around with barbed wire and the river jammed with warships. Hordes of servicemen surged amongst the booths of the Great World; business was brisk down Blood Alley. In the end the troops saw little other action; they would depart with only VD by way of a souvenir, for instead of invading the city,

Generalissimo Chiang Kai-shek engineered the hand-over of its Chinese sectors with the help of their organised crime bosses. He then used the reassuring proximity of the foreign troops to purge his forces of their Bolshevik elements.

This fateful split between China's Nationalists and its Communists changed the international perception of Chiang Kai-shek. From being the 'Red General', he suddenly became the great white hope for China's future. His timely conversion to Christianity and marriage to Soong Mei-ling, Dr Sun Yat-sen's sister-in-law and the darling of American missionary interests, conferred further legitimacy. Moscow's interference was now being condemned. Borodin and other Russian agents were sent packing; Shanghai's Chinese Communists were simply massacred.

Their comrades still clung on in the middle Yangtze. Communism in China was far from being a spent force. Though they were much on the move, their discipline commanded respect and their redistribution of property won hearts. European skippers on the Yangtze, like Graham Torrible commanding one of Butterfield and Swire's steamers, respected their dedication more than their menace.

> Foreign shipping was anathema to them, carrying our Red Ensign on their own waters. They used to fire on ships; they put up huge placards and sometimes they'd have a publicity man banging away with a stick as you went by to make the passengers take notice. But they knew nothing about ships at all. They used to fire at the funnel . . . There was no doubt that Communism was well and truly in control over a vast area.

Meanwhile Chiang Kai-shek's purged Kuomintang forces pressed on to Peking. They entered that city in 1928. In the same year the Generalissimo set up his first national government with its capital at Nanking. On the lower Yangtze, 300 miles up-river from Shanghai, Nanking was both more secure and more central than Peking.

The split with the Communists had not, of course, heralded any abatement in Nationalist demands for an end to foreign interference and exploitation. It did, however, influence Anglo-American attitudes towards these demands. Commercial activity depended on a modicum of security and stability. Any effective government, the foreign powers reasoned, was better than none, and the fortunes of one that renounced Communism were definitely to be encouraged. Conciliatory moves to strengthen the new government in its struggle against the Communists and to secure its goodwill were therefore desirable. Hence it was at this point that Weihaiwei was finally handed back.

Further negotiations focused on what the Nationalists called the 'unequal treaties' of the nineteenth century and particularly on the system of treaty ports which they enshrined. Hankow, the place illegally seized by leftist Nationalists in 1927, provided a test case; but it was the implications of any agreement for the other treaty ports, and especially Shanghai, which dominated the talks. In mind-boggling detail these explored all the ramifications of extraterritorial jurisdiction; it could have been extraterrestrial jurisdiction for all the layman could make of it. Thus the talks dragged on until 1931 when a draft treaty was overtaken by events.

Important concessions had, nevertheless, been made. The five British members of Shanghai's Municipal Council were to be matched by five new Chinese members; and Hankow plus two other, admittedly minor, Yangtze ports were to cease being treaty ports. In giving an inch on the middle Yangtze, the British empire had kept a mile, or rather 12 square miles, on the heavily built-up banks of the Whangpoo. Shanghai could breathe again. Although there had been talk of a ten-year timetable for the surrender of all extraterritorial rights, no treaty to that effect had been signed when talks were abruptly interrupted.

Tokyo Intervenes

The events which overtook these negotiations soon plunged Shanghai into a scare comparable with that of 1927 when the Nationalists had arrived. This time the trouble originated far away in Manchuria, China's most northerly province bounded today by Mongolia, Russia and Korea. Korea had long been under a degree of Japanese influence and, following the 1904–5 Russo-Japanese War, Japan had obtained extensive commercial rights in Manchuria itself. These rights included control of the Russian-built railways which had provoked Japan into declaring war in the first place. Now in her hands, they became handy highways for promoting Japanese trade, industry and settlement inside Manchuria. What the Yangtze was to the British in central China, the railways were to the Japanese in the north.

When extended down to Peking, the railway system attracted to Manchuria waves of Chinese settlers. Cities like Mukden (now

Shenyang) grew rapidly and acquired an importance comparable with Shanghai in its early days. Like the Shanghailanders, the Japanese in Mukden saw the city's growing prosperity as their own creation. Tension arose when the Chinese began construction of a rival railway alongside the Japanese-run line to the south. Cut-throat competition, at a time when the worst effects of the Great Depression were just beginning to be felt, provoked an affray. This in turn provoked the Japanese occupation of Mukden and other key points in September 1931. No declaration of war was made. Tokyo claimed simply to be protecting its nationals and their investments. But Manchuria was in effect taken over, a situation obliquely acknowledged by Tokyo when Henry Pu-yi, Reginald Johnson's former pupil and the last of the Manchu emperors, was installed as a puppet head of state in what the Japanese now called 'Manchoukuo'.

The Chinese responded to what Japan still insisted was just a 'Manchurian incident' with a nation-wide boycott of Japanese goods and services. This bore especially heavily on the 30,000 Japanese living in Shanghai. They were subjected to vilification and assaults which soon escalated. In January 1932 the first fatalities occurred. Reprisals followed. The Japanese appealed to their navy for reinforcements and by February 20,000 Japanese troops were engaged in a full-scale war with Chinese forces throughout the northern sector of the city adjacent to the International Settlement.

From their roof-tops and verandas members of the international community, with cigar in one hand and camera in the other, watched the fires raging and the shells whizzing overhead. Where else in the world could one observe from perfect security a war going on at the end of the street? In black tie and high heels, or 'long tails and short knickers', the *beau monde* strolled from the Club to inspect the front line, then adjourned to the city's latest cabaret. Whoopee! Another place to go, another thing to see! On the whole they favoured the Japanese. As accepted members of the international community 'the Japs' were doing everyone a good turn in reminding the Chinese that foreigners could look after themselves.

The Chinese forces put up an unexpectedly spirited resistance but were nevertheless driven out of the city. When in May a truce was at last arranged through the intercession of the British Minister in China, the body count had reached 14,000. The Japanese had made their point. A demilitarised zone round the city was established.

There was no more talk of returning the International Settlement to the Chinese.

If press coverage of events in distant Manchuria had been sketchy, the corps of correspondents in Shanghai had more than made up for it. Vivid accounts of the fighting outraged American opinion, which took a rather different view of matters to that current in the Settlement. Japan's aggressive designs were self-evident. These contravened both the League of Nations' Covenant and the agreements made at the Washington Conference. Japan should therefore be required to repudiate them on pain of sanctions or even the threat of armed coercion.

Britain, however, prevaricated, torn between its past sympathy for the Japanese and its current loyalties to the League and the US. It was unclear to the Foreign Office, for instance, whether the Manchurian affair had not been provoked by the Chinese; moreover the Japanese response seemed to have been prosecuted by the military authorities on the spot without Tokyo's knowledge. Tacit sympathy might encourage moderate opinion in Japan; condemnation and pressure would merely provoke Tokyo's militarists.

To the extent that this attitude made British arbitration in Shanghai acceptable, it worked. But when it permeated the League of Nations' report on the Manchurian affair, and so ended all chance of a firm condemnation and possible sanctions, it alienated the United States and China. British conciliation looked uncommonly like appeasement – to everyone, that is, except the Japanese who found it nowhere near appeasing enough. The League, claimed Tokyo, had no more right to pontificate in Manchuria than it did in India. Japan accordingly withdrew from membership in 1933. In the following year, flouting the Washington agreements, it began rebuilding its navy.

Meanwhile Japanese troops from Manchuria and Tientsin began to infiltrate Hopei (Hebei) province near Peking. To face this threat Chiang Kai-shek was reluctantly persuaded to form a united front with his Communist rivals. With Japan having just joined Germany in the Anti-Comintern Pact, ideology added a new dimension to the simmering antagonisms. In July 1937 Chinese and Japanese troops again clashed, this time at the Marco Polo bridge outside Peking. As at Mukden, it was not clear who was the aggressor, although the Japanese quickly took advantage of the situation. Again no declaration of war was made. The Sino-Japanese struggle, which would last eight years and account for nearly as many deaths as the Pacific War, seemed to have flared spontaneously. To the Japanese it remained just the 'China incident'. In retrospect it was the beginning of the war in the East.

As the Japanese navy began sealing China's ports, Shanghai awaited its fate with a mixture of bravado and foreboding. Wives and children were evacuated to Hong Kong, the Volunteers mobilised. When a Chinese army crossed the demilitarised zone into the Chinese sectors of the city, thousands of refugees poured from the Chinese sectors into the International Settlement. As before, they thought they would be safe there.

Calling the Imperial Bluff

In August 1937 the 13th of the month fell on a Friday. Since to the Chinese this conjunction is of no significance, it went largely unnoticed in Shanghai. By late afternoon that day, although the factories, like the dance-halls, cinemas and cabarets, never really closed, the offices along the city's corniche-like Bund were emptying. From a riverside frontage of grey corporate buildings, more City of London than 'city of blazing night', bank clerks and stenographers poured out into the sticky sunlight. They flowed along the corniche with weekend purpose, then eddied in the turgid tide of shoppers, prostitutes, touts and beggars that clogged adjacent streets. A ruckle of rickshaws, all spokes and shafts and boney limbs, wheeled about to converge on office steps like a stampede of stick insects. Black limousines nudged bundles of begging children from the roadway. Girls in *cheongsams*, their side-slits revealing upper thighs of porcelain pallor, teetered into doorways on slender high heels. Overhead roared a small formation of aircraft. Those who looked up actually saw the bombs falling; they appeared as small black dots jettisoned in the slipstream.

One landed on the Palace Hotel, which stood at the junction of Nanking Road and the Bund. A crowd of the rich and the idle had early gathered on the roof to watch the fun as the same planes had made passes over the Japanese flagship anchored in the river. They felt safe enough. The Chinese and Japanese were fighting again; it was like 1932; that they might turn on the glitzy International Settlement never occurred to anyone.

Another bomb just missed the Cathay Hotel, which stood across the road from the Palace and was the pride of Sassoon and Co., one of Jardine Matheson's rivals. It landed in the crowded street outside. Both exploded on impact. The first smashed through the upper floors of the Palace ('suites by arrangement'); the second gouged a massive crater in both pavement and pedestrians.

Yet a third fell, a quarter of an hour later and ten blocks away, on the Great World. On 13 August the 'house of multiple joys' was being evacuated to accommodate refugees. The bomb only partially demolished it. Yet such was the press of humanity that in the choking aftermath of dust, dangling cables and burning timbers, the ratio of flesh to rubble was probably unprecedented. Limbs littered the street, blood gushed from the masonry. In this one explosion a thousand people were thought to have died; a thousand more, their moans staying with the rescuers for weeks afterwards, were badly mutilated. No longer could the International Settlement be considered a safe haven in Shanghai's tumultuous affairs. As Harriet Sergeant writes in her exemplary biography of the city,

> The bombing presaged the future, made a break with the past and unified the city. This battle proved different from any other in Shanghai's history . . . The foreigners in particular suffered from shock. Nothing, they told me, not even the Second World War, was to seem as bad as that afternoon in August. It caught them completely unprepared. They had nothing to compare it with. They could not believe that the mayhem and suffering . . . could touch them.

Not until more than four years later would the Second World War engulf the East and plunge its alien empires into total eclipse; but that they would indeed now soon be challenged was a certainty. On Friday, 13 August 1937, the spell of imperial inviolability had been broken.

The dead were mostly Chinese; the planes were also Chinese; so were the bombs. No one quite knew why they had been dropped. The Nationalist government claimed it was a mistake. Cynics thought it was more likely a plot to get the imperial powers to intervene in the undeclared Sino-Japanese War. 'Whatever the truth, the foreign governments failed to react,' continues Harriet Sergeant. 'It was finally admitted. No one was going to save Shanghai.'

In 1932 the fighting had killed under a hundred civilians from the International Settlement. In 1937, at the Great World and on the Bund, two thousand died on the first day. With the Chinese ensconced to the south and the Japanese to the north, the foreign settlements became a no man's land across which flares and shells passed in a nightly fireworks display. Thanks to the poor marksmanship of the Chinese bombers another tragedy occurred on the 23rd when a department store on Nanking Road was hit.

Again the British endeavoured to get negotiations started; but this time there was no chance of an honourable truce. By October the Chinese forces were facing defeat. Rather than surrender to the Japanese they either fled inland or crossed into the foreign settlements. In the French Concession Robert Guillain, a news agency reporter, watched several hundred surrender to the French rather than the Japanese. 'They threw down their German guns and their helmets marked with the blue sun of the Kuomintang. Their faces shone with tears. Some shook with emotion. Others made strange cries like wounded animals.'

Though the International Settlement would linger on in name for another six years it would no longer be part of empire. Powerless to do anything other than appeal to Japan's long support of its 'treaty' status, both the French and the British had to acquiesce in a Japanese victory parade through their midst. Thereafter, with its population more than doubled by the influx of refugees, and with the Japanese detaching half the Settlement and demanding an ever greater say in the administration of what remained, Shanghai lost both its panache and its trade. Crime, terrorism and rampant inflation took over.

An imperial anomaly that was always more about business than dominion, empire ended for Shanghai when business confidence collapsed. Those diehards who stayed on after 1937 laboured against prodigious odds only to be rewarded, four years later, with internment in Japanese camps. In 1943, during the darkest days of the war, the British finally agreed to surrender all treaty port rights in a bid to strengthen Chiang Kai-shek's stand against the Japanese and his Communist rivals-cum-allies. Some foreign companies did, nevertheless, return to Shanghai after the war. It was not the same; and they were ousted again after another four years, this time by the Communists.

The city had declined so fast because, as the Japanese moved inland in late 1937, it lost its greatest asset, the trade of the Yangtze basin. Heading up-river to secure this prize, Japanese bombers prepared the way with repeated strikes at Nanking, Wuhu, Hankow and

Changsha. At Wuhu two British vessels, one belonging to Jardine's, the other to Swire's, were hit; so were two gunboats, the USS *Panay* and HMS *Ladybird*. The Japanese apologised but by now the Chinese had effectively blocked the lower river at several points by sinking barrages of vessels. Undeterred, Japanese forces worked their way steadily inland. In December 1937 they entered Chiang Kai-shek's capital of Nanking and there perpetrated a massacre of Chinese civilians in which the bayonet and the bullet claimed as many victims as would the atom bomb on Hiroshima.

Before this onslaught Chinese troops and civilians fled, heading first for Hankow and then for the hills and the safety of Chungking on the upper river. There Chiang Kai-shek had finally established his new headquarters. Chungking was also the highest point to which the Yangtze steamers plied. A voyage to sanctuary meant navigating the famous gorges whose passage was only possible when the river was in spate. Even then, according to Butterfield and Swire's Captain Torrible, the ships that undertook this run required three rudders and extremely powerful engines.

> I was sent up to relieve a captain called De Freitas when all this trouble was going on, getting people up to unoccupied China, getting the whole of China up through the Gorges. The Gorges were just like that picture of the Klondike. Those men toiling up. Well that was us trying to get the whole of China up through the Gorges.

Like a run of salmon, the steamers had to wriggle through the rapids, dodging rocks, avoiding the main current, exploiting slack water where they could find it, and giving a wide berth to the dreaded whirlpools.

In the summer of '38 the stampede of refugees swamped the ships, swarming aboard them 'like cockroaches'. Captain Torrible made an incredible forty-six round trips, 'which means to say that we never stopped'. Junks, long since laid up as unserviceable, were also commandeered by the fugitives. Overloaded and manned by people with little knowledge of the treacherous waters, they were soon in difficulties. Along the 180 miles of river through the gorges, Torrible counted ninety wrecks. And that did not include those which simply disappeared. One, forced back into the swollen river by soldiers on the bank, was carried downstream into a whirlpool.

> the junk went round and round, and got nearer and nearer the centre, and then down. Gone . . . I think this tragedy was the most impressive sight

I've ever seen, sort of man's inhumanity to man. It was getting dark, and whether any of them would ever be saved was very doubtful.

The gorges, so dramatic and so deadly, stopped even the Japanese advance. Chiang Kai-shek would retain Chungking throughout the war, aided and armed principally by the US. Initially arms and supplies could be sent in from Hong Kong and Canton. After 1938 they came via Hanoi and François Garnier's back door into China, and after 1940 by the infamous Burma Road. When Burma itself fell, there would be just the hazardous 'Hump', the air bridge from India across the eastern Himalayas.

China's seaboard had been effectively sealed in the north by Japan's reacquisition in 1938 of Kiachow Bay, the erstwhile German concession in Shantung, and in the south by her seizure of Canton later that year. Other treaty ports like Swatow (Shantou) were mopped up in 1939. For the Western powers who for just on a century had lorded it on the China coast, it was indeed 'getting dark'. Western empire in China, like that junk on the Yangtze, was simply being sucked under. Only Hong Kong remained; and by 1939 its days, along with those of all the West's other imperial holdings in the East, were numbered.

8

Countdown

The Rising Sun

The supremacy of the Western powers had been successfully challenged in China, but in 1938 there was little evidence to suggest that Japan had territorial designs anywhere else in Asia. Tokyo's anodyne pronouncements still emphasised the limited nature of its objectives. From Manchuria to Canton aggression was justified in terms of commercial priorities and strategic safeguards. The language was in fact much the same as that employed by the European colonial powers when elbowing their own way into China a hundred years earlier, a parallel which Japanese spokesmen were eager to emphasise. They also made mention of the need to oppose international Communism, but this occurred more often with respect to Stalinist Russia's supposed designs in the north of China than to republican China's opposition in the south. It was, anyway, a concern shared by the Western powers.

But of anti-Western sentiment, of anti-imperialism, of Asian solidarity, or of colonial emancipation, little was yet heard. Such rhetoric was more usually invoked by Tokyo's deadly enemies in Chungking. To Japan, itself an empire, imperialism seemed a not illogical ambition. Likewise Westernisation. It was by emulating the West that the country had transformed itself into a modern industrial state. The US was still its major trading partner, and so not a power it wished to alienate. Great Britain, on the other hand, though no longer its ally, was also no longer a serious rival. In the crude terms of the Washington ratios for capital ships, Japan's fleet was only three-fifths that of the British; but Japan's three-fifths were in the East with all the advantages of home bases; Britain's five-fifths, an adequate deterrent in the Atlantic or the East but not both ('the one-ocean standard'), yet presumed to police the world. If seldom seen east of Suez, the fleet was said always to be within 48 days' sailing of Singapore. This estimate had a way of increasing. When war in Europe broke out, it grew to 70 days, then 180.

To the Japanese their new naval supremacy was desirable because it safeguarded supply lines to China and enhanced their status as a Pacific power. It could also result, as it had for the Western powers, in opportunities for expansion and the opening of new sources of raw materials. But as yet the Western empires were not in Japan's sights. Unlike Russia they posed no threat to her security, and unlike China they were not in such disarray as to invite interference.

For their part Western governments were wary but far from panic-stricken. They continued to observe the Washington undertaking not to upgrade naval facilities in the South China Sea, principally at Hong Kong and in the Philippines. Instead, the Americans extended their vast naval complex at Pearl Harbor in Hawaii; the French were considering a naval base at Cam Ranh Bay in Cochin-China; and the British were finally completing their vital naval dockyard at Singapore.

To Singapore the Dutch also looked for their security. Straws in the wind made the Dutch in Indonesia more anxious about Japan's ultimate intentions than any of their Western colleagues. This was understandable. They lacked any defensive capability; their empire was anyway of an indefensible configuration; and yet its resources, its strategic position, and its development potential were the most invit-ing of all. Much of the Indies' production of tin, rubber and oil already went to Japan and as early as 1934 Tokyo had opened nego-tiations with Batavia to obtain guarantees of supply. The tireless van Mook represented the Indies government.

> [The negotiations] were conducted by the Japanese in a way that barely veiled [either] their conviction that they ought to supersede the Netherlands as the paramount power [or] their impatience at finding such a dense incomprehension of this necessity.

Two years later van Mook went to Tokyo to continue the discus-sions and was reassured. In the course of 'long-drawn and slightly alcoholic' exchanges he discovered that Russia was 'the only enemy that they feared'. Although the 1937 attack on China was 'brewing', no Japanese adventures further south were being contemplated.

When the assault on China finally got underway, the likelihood of an adventure in south-east Asia receded still further. Japan's military appeared to have bitten off more than they could chew. British diplomats, not without glee, recalled the fate of Napoleon's invasion of Russia; winters could be hard even in the Yangtze basin, and the Chinese, though obliged to retreat, showed no signs of throwing in the towel. Meanwhile the Japanese, overstretched and internationally isolated, were having trouble finding Chinese collaborators and were barely able to hold what they had won.

What no one could foresee was that, as a result of this impasse, some radical rethinking was going on within Japan. Wounded pride welcomed new counsels and indulged radical solutions. The Japanese armed forces had, it seemed, badly miscalculated. They had expected the Kuomintang (KMT) to offer little resistance. In return for Japanese support against its Communist rivals, they had assumed that the KMT would speedily make terms and that, if not, it would be speedily forced to do so by the Japanese blockade. In fact, thanks to American support, the KMT stood firm, the Communists soon began to strike back against the Japanese in the north, and the blockade was circumvented. Instead of a limited operation to secure Japanese commercial objectives, Tokyo seemed by late 1937 to have become unwittingly embroiled in an attempt to conquer China. Such an undertaking, given China's size and population, was probably impossible. Moreover, the sacrifices involved made no sense without some loftier and more inspiring rationale than narrow commercial objectives.

Hence, in 1938, alternative designs were formulated and unfamiliar phrases began to characterise Japanese statements. Ideas then current about economic regionalism were seemingly being grafted on to older ideas of pan-Asian solidarity to introduce the then novel concept of an indigenous and self-sufficient East Asian order. This would take concrete, if wordy, shape in the ideal of a 'Greater East Asia Co-Prosperity Sphere', Japan's grand design for Asian regeneration. According to Akira Iriye, a Harvard-based Japanese academic who has explored the development of this concept, the war in China could now be more convincingly presented as the first stage in the creation of this new Asian order. 'It was actually an *ex post facto* rationalisation of Japan's policy of close supervision of economic affairs in Manchuria and north China, calculated to meet the nation's [that is, Japan's] needs as much as possible within the area.'

But what, precisely, was 'the area'? 'East Asia' could mean the whole of the Far East. Initially only China was being invited to participate in this venture, but further invitations could not be discounted.

The bare bones of this hastily improvised economic programme were meanwhile being fleshed out with cultural features and political muscle by a succession of official reports and academic treatises. Obviously the emphasis on Asian solidarity necessitated the exclusion of extraneous rivals, notably the Western imperialisms (which included Soviet Russia). Their presence was now seen as destabilising and their ideologies as corrupting.

> Asian unity was the antithesis of nationalism, individualism, liberalism, materialism, selfishness, imperialism and all the other traits that characterized the bankrupt western tradition. Instead pan-Asianists stressed themes such as regional co-operation, harmony, selflessness, and the subordination of the individual to the community.

These values now have a familiar ring. At the time Western observers saw them as a smokescreen for totalitarianism and militarism. Later, when evoked by Asian nationalists like Sukarno, they would be interpreted as a feeble pretext for autocratic and unrepresentative dictatorship. Only in the 1990s, as the Far East crawled with 'tigers' flexing their economic muscles, did they begin to be hailed as the enviable 'Asian values' responsible for the enviable 'Asian miracle' of double-digit growth.

The Japanese of an earlier generation preferred to emphasise their traditional nature. Japan prided itself on having resisted Western domination for longer than China or anywhere else. East India Companies had been sent packing in the seventeenth century; nineteenth-century treaty ports had been swiftly reclaimed. Japan was therefore the only true repository of Asian values. Latent resentment of the racist attitudes of the imperial powers, particularly over the denial of emigration rights to America and Australia, fuelled such self-belief. Western imperialism had relied on a combination of prestige and power. But the British, like the French, seemed now to rely far more heavily on the prestige than on the power. In short, the failure of the West's imperialist and capitalist systems was laying bare their more objectionable features. With a propaganda fanfare to regeneration, renaissance, reawakening and resurgence, the peoples of Asia were bidden to arise and greet the warmth of the Rising Sun.

Easing into Tonkin

As if to illustrate Japan's contention about the bankruptcy of Western values, in September 1939 the European powers went to war. Not until more than two years later would hostilities in the East make it a world war, but the danger for the West and the opportunity for Japan were immediately self-evident. Appeasement in Europe had been accompanied by an unaccommodating policy towards Japanese encroachments in China; financial credits had been granted to Chungking, its lifeline via the Burma Road was completed, and those Japanese overtures to Batavia had been largely resisted. By avoiding war in Europe, the European powers had aimed to reassert their authority in the East. But the failure of this policy necessitated an about-turn. Now war in Europe meant a more appeasing policy in the East. In 1940 the British agreed to a temporary closure of the Burma Road and the Dutch agreed to further negotiations over Japanese access to the raw materials of the Indies. More crucially, the French would be obliged to make concessions to Tokyo in Tonkin. Japan's attention was still focused on China. There is little evidence to suggest that this first move into Vietnam was seen as the beginning of an advance into south-east Asia. It would, though, show that Tokyo was not averse to taking advantage of the European war.

Ever since 1937 Japan had been demanding that the French authorities in Indo-China ban the use of their ports for supplies and armaments destined for Chiang Kai-shek's forces in Chungking. Now served by a railway, one of Garnier's back doors into inland China had at last come into its own. From Haiphong, the main port in Tonkin, to Hanoi and on up to Lang Son on the Chinese border went the gasoline and guns on which the Kuomintang depended. Back down came KMT missions, Yangtze steamer skippers going on leave and Imperial Maritime Customs officials shuffling between postings. Stella Benson, the elfin novelist, had married a Customs man. It was while availing herself of this route that, long prone to a mysterious and incapacitating disease, she had died near Haiphong.

The French resisted Tokyo's demands even while the war in Europe obliged them to denude their empire of the ships and aircraft required to defend it. When German troops swept into France in the spring of 1940, the Japanese saw their chance. Renewed demands were backed up with air raids on the Tonkin railway and a massing of troops on the frontier. On 19 June the Japanese issued a two-day ultimatum. General Catroux, Indo-China's Governor-General, had no option but to accept it. France itself was falling. The Japanese ultimatum ran out on the day that France accepted the Nazi armistice.

Initially the Japanese demanded only closure of the frontier to specified items like arms, and the installation of a Japanese mission to monitor the arrangement. Catroux claimed that in accepting these terms he was buying time to seek support from the British in Singapore and organise his forces within Indo-China. The puppet Vichy government in France declined to accept this explanation and appointed Admiral Decoux, commander of the French naval forces in the East, to take over the Governor-Generalship. Catroux went off to join de Gaulle's Free French, a decision with which many of Indo-China's 40,000 French residents may have sympathised; but at this stage it was not clear that Marshal Pétain's Vichy government would be other than a staunch supporter of the 'Pearl of Empire'. Tokyo had not yet aligned itself with Berlin other than through the Anti-Comintern Pact, a largely worthless rodomontade; and there was every chance that Vichy France's German patrons would appreciate Indo-China's raw materials, especially its rubber, and so stand firm against Japanese interference.

In August the Japanese made further demands, this time for the use of Tonkin's airports and sea-ports and for transit rights up to the Chinese border. Still Chungking was the target and again the French were obliged to give way, although not without securing a Japanese recognition of French sovereignty in Indo-China. This concession was respected until 1945 and enabled the French to preserve and even strengthen their colonial authority during the war years. It would have important repercussions for Vietnam's nationalists and especially for the Communists. Re-emerging from China, in 1941 'Nguyen the Patriot' rededicated his cadres to a broad-based independence movement, dubbed the Vietminh, which opposed both the French and the Japanese. He in turn adopted his final incarnation as 'Uncle' Ho Chi Minh.

For the French authorities, on the other hand, the preservation of their sovereignty would encourage illusions of an immutable and intransigent continuity. Other colonial regimes might be discredited by defeat and undermined by occupation but French rule in Indo-China would, if not exactly stand its ground, at least decline to be dislodged. The *tricolore* continued to fly over Decoux's headquarters in Hanoi; no emaciated Frenchmen were seen begging from behind barbed wire or crumpling beneath Japanese rifle-butts. Not until 1945, by which time France itself had been liberated and the Vichy government toppled, would Decoux's Vichy-backed administration in Indo-China be overthrown. Having survived a world war more or less intact, France's colonial prestige was not thereafter going to kow-tow to niggling nationalists, whatever their ideology.

Despite their generous concession to French pride, the Japanese soon found Decoux even less amenable than his predecessor. In September 1940 Japanese forces took the law into their own hands, staging landings on the Tonkin coast, bombing raids over Haiphong and an invasion across the border from China. The latter lasted only a few days, just long enough to secure the railhead at Lang Son and shatter any illusions about the superiority of French firepower. As Decoux reluctantly complied with the new directives, Japan entered into formal alliance with Germany and Italy in the Tripartite Pact. War in the East was still a year away, but as of late 1940 the possibility of a Japanese strike into south-east Asia began to look increasingly probable.

This impression grew throughout 1941 as attention swivelled from China west and south towards Thailand (Siam). The Thais, under a strong military government and with some encouragement from Tokyo, also sought to take advantage of France's plight. With Indo-China isolated from the *metropole*, it seemed the ideal moment to revive claims to those parts of Cambodia and Laos of which the French had deprived them in the late nineteenth century. Demands for restitution were followed by border clashes in December 1940 and a French defeat in January 1941. French naval units responded with an attack in the Gulf of Siam which put paid to Thailand's marine. In what he identified as 'the only pitched battle fought by the French navy in two world wars', Admiral Decoux hailed a rare victory. It scarcely offset the losses on land. Arbitration seemed the only way of avoiding the ignominy of defeat and, on German insistence, the Vichy government invited the Japanese to effect a Franco-Thai settlement. Negotiations took place in Tokyo in April 1941 with the intermediary emerging as one of the main beneficiaries. Thailand got three Cambodian provinces plus a bit of Laos while Japan obtained vital diplomatic and intelligence representation in various parts of Thailand, including the isthmus stretching south to Malaya.

France's only achievement was a cessation of hostilities. Defeat and humiliation in Europe in 1940 had been followed by compromise and concessions in Asia in 1941. However gratifying to French pride, the preservation at all costs of French rule in Indo-China did not impress their Vietnamese subjects. In failing to defend the interests of the peoples of Indo-China against Japanese demands, France stood accused of having forfeited any claim to their loyalty.

The Squeeze

For the British in Singapore and Malaya the defining moment came two months after the Franco-Thai accord in Tokyo when in July 1941 Japanese troops were first stationed in Saigon and elsewhere in Cochin-China. A move so far south could have nothing to do with the war in China. Nor was any credence given to Japanese claims that it was a necessary defensive precaution in the face of encirclement from an alphabetical combine known as the 'ABCD' powers (that is, Americans, British, Chinese and Dutch). All save China, already reluctantly involved, were desperately trying to avoid war in the East. The only conceivable reason for the new deployment was to menace Malaya.

The threat, therefore, to the empires of Britain and the Netherlands was obvious four months before the invasion materialised. Whether it would, indeed, materialise depended on how the Western powers responded and how Japan read the course of the war elsewhere in the world. Thus far the German pact had served her well. Occupied Holland and defeated France could no longer afford their eastern colonies any effective protection while the British, their cities in ruins and their direct sea route to the East cut in the Mediterranean, looked to be headed for a comparable impotence.

Then in June 1941, without any prior consultation with Tokyo, German troops invaded Russia. Suddenly another welcome if unexpected opportunity had presented itself. The only power that had ever really threatened Japanese security was not A, B, C or D but R. Following clashes on the Manchurian frontier in which the Japanese had fared badly, a non-aggression pact with Moscow had been signed in April. It could now safely be broken and advantage taken of the sensational German advance in European Russia to acquire large tracts of Asiatic Russia. Any move into south-east Asia could come later.

Such, at least, was the argument advanced by the Japanese Foreign

Minister; and it had much to recommend it. Siberia would be a worthy addition to the Greater East Asia Co-Prosperity Sphere. It had vast resources and, above all, it had oil. So, though, did the south-east Asian archipelago.

In the 1880s A. J. S. Ziljker, a Dutch planter, noting viscous seepages amongst his tobacco fields north of Medan in Sumatra, had started drilling. He sold out in the 1890s to a Netherlands consortium calling itself the Royal Dutch Company for the Exploitation of Petroleum. Other concessions in Java and south Sumatra were acquired, rivals bought out, storage tanks built and tankers operated. By 1903 the Royal Dutch Company's only serious rival in the East was the London-based Shell Trading and Transport Company. Founded in 1897 and so named because its chief backer had previously specialised in the import of painted cowries, Shell's eastern interests were largely in Borneo – at Tarakan on the east coast and later at Miri in Sarawak territory south-west of Brunei.

Between 1903 and 1907 the two companies slowly amalgamated to emerge as Royal Dutch Shell whose numerous subsidiaries included the Asiatic Petroleum Company with a distribution network that covered most of China. Helped by a subsidiary of Standard Oil of New Jersey (Esso), by 1940 the company had boosted production in the Indies to 8 million tons per annum. There were seven refineries, the most important in Sumatra; and the export value of petroleum was now second only to rubber. From providing Mr Ziljker with a novel kind of illumination, oil had become the world's most valued energy source, vital alike to industry, automobiles, aviation and the diesel marine engines which now powered the world's shipping. Wars could not be fought without it, and Japan had none.

Most of Japan's oil, and nearly all of its aviation fuel, came in fact from the United States. So did the iron, steel and scrap for its manufacturing industries as well as all manner of finished goods. For all the talk of Asian co-prosperity, the Japanese economy remained tied to that of the West. This, though cause for resentment in Tokyo, was a source of congratulation in Washington. The US was quietly confident that, since Japan could not manage without it, it would be mad to risk war with it.

Washington's response to Japanese aggression (and to the pleas for ever greater support coming from Chungking) was therefore both more robust and more risky than that of the battered British and the powerless Dutch. During 1940 US embargoes were imposed on the export to Japan of aviation fuel, scrap iron, and then all iron and steel. There followed in July 1941 the freezing of all Japanese assets in America; and in August, in response to the Japanese advance into Cochin-China, the ultimate sanction of a complete oil embargo. Stocks on hand in Japan were thought sufficient for two years; in effect Tokyo must now talk or fight.

She did both. Talks aimed at lifting the embargoes were never formally broken off while preparations at last went ahead for the move south. The alternative of a Russian campaign was abandoned; the German advance from the west had run into difficulties and the US sanctions had to be confronted. Malaya, therefore, would be the route, Singapore the hurdle, and the oil of the Indies the prize. As with any linear advance, the danger would come from the flanks and especially from the Pacific. Washington's application of embargoes, as well as precipitating Japan's move, also convinced Tokyo that the US, with its sanctions' armoury now exhausted, must respond with a declaration of war. It was therefore imperative to stage simultaneously a Pacific offensive to neutralise the Philippines and a long-range strike to incapacitate the US Pacific fleet in Pearl Harbor.

Dancing in the Twilight

Between the two invasion routes, one through Malaya and the other through the Philippines, nestled Borneo, like a nut in the jaws of a cracker. In September 1941, while across the South China Sea Japanese agents were infiltrating the Malay isthmus, while Japanese units were massing in Cochin-China, and while the Japanese invasion fleet was gathering at Hainan, the White Raj of Sarawak was celebrating its centenary. It was a hundred years since James Brooke had been created rajah by the *tuan muda* of Brunei. To mark the occasion special stamps had been printed and a centenary medal struck. Rajah Vyner and Rani Sylvia were attending in person; important announcements were expected. Across the Kuching River in front of the *istana*, state barges paddled by liveried retainers shuttled purposefully. From up and down the Sarawak coast Sea Dayaks and Land Dayaks, Malay patriarchs and Chinese entrepreneurs converged on a Kuching bedecked with flags.

Had anyone outside Sarawak had leisure to observe this colourful occasion they might have felt that, with Rommel rampant in north

Africa, Moscow being evacuated and London in ruins, celebrations were inappropriate. The Brookes' sense of timing had evidently deserted them. But then the Brookes had always been a law unto themselves. In fact, they were the law. Absolutism was the essence of their mystique and the reason given to Clementi for their being unable to fall in with his schemes of federation.

Curious indeed, then, was the news not only that the Sarawak Raj was fêting a century of colonialism just as the empire itself entered its darkest hour but also that the same administration was contemplating a radical constitutional change aimed at establishing a representative legislature. Self-government was being mentioned as a long-term objective; so too was direct colonial rule by the British government. Either way, the last days of the White Raj appeared imminent. After a century of heading the most autocratic and conservative colonial regime in the East, the Brookes had evidently seen the light.

But appearances were deceptive. As usual the affairs of the Raj had little to do with political principle and everything to do with family intrigue and the personal exigencies of the Rajah. Although age now offered some excuse for Rajah Vyner's chronic lethargy and diffidence the Rani Sylvia more than compensated; and from her injudicious statements to the popular press it was clear that both Brookes were bored of their fief. He preferred the amenities of Malaya and London and she (*Sylvia of Sarawak, Queen of the Headhunters*, according to the titles of her books) those of New York and Hollywood. Maintaining a royal estate in the twentieth century was expensive, especially for a couple not wedded to economy and blessed with fun-loving offspring. The latters' failed marriages to, respectively, a band leader and a Puerto Rican wrestler had left Elizabeth ('Princess Pearl') and Valerie ('Princess Baba') straining the Rajah's patience as well as his purse. Only Leonora had made an acceptable marriage, to the heir of a shipping magnate. They had a son, Simon Brooke Mackay, who had just turned 7 when the Raj celebrated its centenary.

Young Simon's claim as Vyner's successor was championed by his parents and by the Rani Sylvia in association with Gerald MacBryan, the Rajah's Machiavellian confidant who, after converting to Islam, marrying a Malay, and making a pilgrimage to Mecca, had returned to the Rajah's side in 1940, his plausibility seemingly undented. He was, however, regarded with deep suspicion by the righteous

Bertram, Vyner's brother (otherwise the *tuan muda*), and by Bertram's bookish wife, Gladys. Author of a memoir aptly entitled *Relations and Complications*, Gladys, forsaking Christian Science, then Roman Catholicism, had also just converted to Islam. This shared experience failed to endear her to MacBryan or vice versa, since it was her and Bertram's son, Anthony, whose claims were threatened by those of young Simon Brooke Mackay.

Anthony, 29 years old in 1941, had hitherto looked a safe bet for the succession. In 1939, at the Rajah's behest, he had engineered a purge of senior Kuching bureaucrats. It was felt that they had been abrogating to themselves supervisory powers of which the usually absent Brookes had seldom taken advantage, and that their constant interference in the paternalistic methods of the District Officers was causing resentment. Anthony thereby became the hero of the Administrative Service and was named as *rajah muda* ('crown prince') by his uncle. Within a year, however, he had fallen from favour, was declared 'as yet unfit to rule' and was temporarily banished. This unexpected rejection threw the succession wide open. According to the Rajah, it was now brother Bertram who had always been the legitimate claimant and remained so. Bertram, though, had suffered a stroke, and could never be more than a stop-gap.

The Rajah, no doubt prompted by MacBryan, had thus in effect confounded all those, both officials and family, who might have opposed his next move – namely the sale of his royal prerogatives. This involved a cash payment to the Rajah of $2 million (£200,000) from state funds in consideration of his agreeing to the appointment of a Supreme Council whose advice and consent would be essential to all executive measures. The Council was designed to contain some Sarawak representatives as well as its administrative, and so British, majority; and in the accompanying preamble to the new constitution lip service was indeed paid to the 'goal of self-government'.

Such then was the constitutional bombshell, more a squib, let off by the Rajah when, fortified by several brandies, he eventually made his reluctant appearance at the centenary celebrations. Of those who took exception to the change, Anthony was predictably the most outspoken since, if he ever did succeed, it would now be as a constitutional monarch. To Anthony's outbursts, the Rajah replied by citing them as further evidence of his unsuitability. The succession was still undecided when in November 1941 the Rajah left the East for a holiday in Australia.

The British government, deeming Sarawak's affairs increasingly unseemly and its administration unsatisfactory, had taken advantage of the constitutional change to install a Representative. His authority, however, was limited to external affairs and his appointment may have been prompted by a recent oversight. Due to the continued uncertainty over Sarawak's international status, it was found that, despite the British government's declaration of war on Germany and Italy, Sarawak remained neutral. As a sovereign state, it would have to make its own declaration of war. Regrettably, K. H. Digby, the Raj's legal adviser, failed to rise to this challenge. 'We firmly decided to leave Germany and Italy alone. In our opinion Sarawak was enough of a joke in the eyes of the world already without our going out of our way to provide further fodder for the war-time music halls.'

Thanks to its protected status, Sarawak could nevertheless expect some support against the threat of invasion. In early 1941 a regiment of Punjabis arrived from Singapore. They were detailed to defend Kuching's recently completed, but plane-less, airport. 'There have been too many retreats,' declared General Percival. 'You in Kuching must stand and fight.' Considering that in Malaya Percival's 80,000 troops would merely add to the catalogue of defeats, this was expecting a lot of the 600 deployed in Sarawak. They might merely invite attack.

When in December 1941 the attack came, they were barely sufficient for destroying strategic installations. The oil wells at Miri were imperfectly sabotaged although the Kuching airstrip was successfully flooded by blowing up its drainage system. This feat was achieved using sticks of gelignite inserted into contraceptives to keep them dry. R. H. W. Reece, author of the most incisive account of the last days of the White Raj, notes that it may have been the first time condoms were used in warfare. The Punjabis, accompanied by most of Sarawak's senior administration, then withdrew to Dutch Borneo and thence to Australia. That ancient promise of British protection on which successive Rajahs had prided themselves was found to apply, like so much else, not to the people of Sarawak but only to its White Raj.

The Lights Go Out

While Sarawak had been celebrating its centenary, Singapore had sweated. Visitors were in the habit of noting what a magnificent setting Raffles had chosen for his city. Promontories and islands ringed the main anchorage, all of them top heavy with a profusion of exotic vegetation well capable of concealing formidable shore batteries.

> No outsider knows the actual extent of Singapore's military fortifications or just how many units there are of the big land batteries with their 18-inch guns. All this is kept very secret – as it should be.

Mona Gardner, a visiting American writer, saw no reason to doubt that, though invisible, garrisons of engineers and lesser artillery also abounded. The 20 square miles of new naval base and dockyard, plus the island's three air bases, were evidence of a reassuring intent. 'These grimly expensive units are not gestures,' noted Gardner, 'they all mean business. They very definitely and explicitly say that Great Britain is not retiring from Asia.'

As for the port-city itself, though its society was not as exciting as Shanghai's, it was almost as cosmopolitan and, though not as rigid as Hong Kong's, it was still reassuringly British. Rubicund gentlemen, sublimely oblivious above limp shorts, gartered stockings and highly polished brogues, twitched their moustaches and talked incomprehensibly of rubber. To Mona Gardner it seemed that the entire city was 'dependent on the American motoring public'.

> If you can't talk rubber – and by that I mean quotas, surplus stocks, market prices, cover crops, the doings of the 'rubber pool', and 'the Colonial Secretary better be careful, by gad, sticking his finger in the crew-hiring question' – then take along a book to read when you go to dinner parties, because conversation in Singapore begins, runs eight-course circles, and ends with rubber.

There were other drawbacks, like the island's excessive humidity which so taxed Anglo-Saxon toiletry. This, and the leaden skies which for days on end turned the water to a gunmetal gloom, sent men scurrying north to the Cameron Highlands where Clementi had championed a sylvan hill-station; amongst its palatial 'cottages' was one which served as the summer palace of the Brooke Rajah. Only the leisured few and the administrative élite could take advantage of such retreats. For most Singapore, even before the Japanese invasion, offered little chance of escape. In the soft evening light a Somerset Maugham character in *The Casuarina Tree* detected a hint of mystery, even menace, hanging over the closely packed harbour.

'You felt that all those vessels, their activity for the moment suspended, waited for some event of a peculiar significance.'

By late 1941 the waiting was almost over. Churchill, now Prime Minister, still insisted that the Japanese would not attack and that, even if they did, 'fortress Singapore' was impregnable. It was what everyone wanted to hear. It was also what he wanted the Japanese High Command to think; public statements in troubled times may not reflect strategic realities. The London *Times* faithfully followed suit. In February it had announced that the arrival of reinforcements from India had rendered Singapore 'well-prepared for any eventuality'. They were soon joined by Australian detachments and Royal Air Force squadrons. Tanks were deemed inappropriate to jungle terrain and the planes were antiquated; there were also far too few to provide air cover for a whole peninsula. Nevertheless 'the balance of air power in the Far Eastern area is now swinging in favour of Great Britain', declared a *Times* leader. By October 'the fortress of Singapore' had become 'one of the great strong points of the world'. Over 80,000 troops, half of them Indian, now guarded its Malayan approaches. Additionally, two capital ships, one a First World War battle-cruiser (*Repulse*) and the other a new battleship (*Prince of Wales*), plus accompanying cruisers and destroyers, were on their way east round Africa. Even if the Japanese, shunning Singapore's seaward defences, were mad enough to attack down the peninsula, they would first have to effect a landing somewhere. The presence of this Royal Navy 'Z Force' was seen to be an ample deterrent.

These and countless other assurances were swallowed all too readily. The habits of 150 years of virtually unchallenged supremacy could not easily be discarded. 'Life in the East', observed Ronald Mackie, 'satisfies a latent instinct in us all, the desire to dominate.' A laconic Australian journalist with a Philip Marlowe prose style, Mackie had just left Singapore after a three-year assignment. Rented rooms and a ramshackle office amid the noise of Chinatown had provided insights denied to the knobbly-kneed *tuan* 'sure of his privileges behind a high fence of three-ply'. For such buffoons Mackie had nothing but contempt.

> For once stupidity or lack of education is not a barrier, for once position is so assured that it becomes one of the certainties of existence. The Tuan, with no more intelligence than a hen, with a public school education and a first class record as a football player, does not only feel, but knows, that

he is superior to the Indian barrister, the Chinese doctor with three degrees, the Eurasian engineer who graduated head of his year at Oxford.

To this list of Asian stereotypes the British *tuans* would cheerfully have added the Japanese fighter-pilot whose well-known myopia made him an aviational liability, or the Japanese guardsmen in gym shoes, the Jap cavalry on bicycles, and the deadly Japanese 'APR' ('the armour-plated rickshaw'). Their inferiority was self-evident. To the Englishman behind his fence Asiatics were 'just a lot of smelly bounders . . . the sort of people you do not know socially and cannot possibly recognise as having any place in existence'. He dismissed them all, supremely confident in his own Rafflesian estimation.

> He exists on the credit of tradition. He lives a pleasant, artificial, indolent, unprogressive sort of life. He need not struggle for existence like the man in the big city because the mechanism of competition turns at half speed and efficiency has not much place except in a dictionary.

Mackie's strictures made no allowance for cherished English traits like self-caricature, sang-froid and understatement. Some of those he ridiculed were quietly organising the defence of the colony. Air-raid drills were being held, volunteers enlisted, intelligence collected. In Europe the 1939 declaration of war had been succeeded by months of 'phoney war' in which nothing much happened. A similar interlude in the East might have dispelled accusations of complacency.

As it happened, war erupted ahead of its declaration, Malaya receiving only a few hours' more warning of attack than Pearl Harbor. Anglo-Saxon complacency had always been affectation as well as habit. As of 0200 hours on 8 December 1941 it could also pass for fortitude.

It was no substitute, however, for strike power, decisive leadership, reliable intelligence, elementary strategy, effective communications and inter-service collaboration, all of which proved woefully lacking. The Japanese landings were made on the east coast of the peninsula in both Malay and Thai territory. A pre-arranged plan to forestall the Thai landings was never activated, leaving the invaders free to push quickly south across the frontier towards Penang. The landing on Malay soil at Kota Bahru in the extreme north was vigorously opposed and might have been repulsed had not a misunderstanding led to a precipitate retreat. The first of many misunderstandings, it was the first of many retreats.

Neither of these initial reverses constituted a disaster. Nor did the simultaneous bombing raid on Singapore, although many thought it curious that no warning siren was heard, that the city remained a blaze of light throughout, and that not a single fighter was scrambled to engage the attackers. Such oversights were later seen as symptomatic; at the time, with everyone 'pulling together', they were soon forgotten. News reports of the attack on Pearl Harbor were actually greeted with relief; America was now in the war and, since the reports said little about the scale of the Hawaiian tragedy, its Pacific fleet was presumably speeding into Asian waters. Churchill, who knew better, reckoned the now possible loss of Singapore a tragic but acceptable price for US support.

As for the initial setbacks in the north of Malaya, the British were thought to have better defensive options further south. Anyway 'Z Force', that Royal Naval squadron with its two battleships, was already heading up the coast of the peninsula. Its mere presence should pre-empt any further landings and so cut off the invaders.

Early on the 10th the squadron was sighted by a Japanese submarine. Bombers and torpedo bombers flying from Cochin-China attacked in late morning. They came in wave upon wave and by early afternoon both battleships were at the bottom of the South China Sea. With the war just two days old, British troops were in retreat, Singapore had been bombed, its vast naval dockyard was redundant, and Japan now ruled the waves. For Churchill the loss of the battleships was the worst shock of the whole war; 'as I turned over and twisted in bed the full horror of the news sank in upon me'. For the empires of the East it was as if the lights had finally gone out.

When the grim tidings of the loss of 'Z Force' reached Singapore, dusk was indeed falling. The tennis courts were emptying, the bars filling. Then the music stopped. An expressionless radio announcer read the news flash. In clubs and cafés, in the 'Worlds' and the cabarets, a stunned silence ensued. 'It's the beginning of the end,' said a small anonymous voice enunciating the horror of an empire. 'It was unbelievable,' recalled John Davis. The man who had joined the Malayan Civil Service because he liked the tigers on the postage stamps was stunned.

> I've never been hit so hard in my life. The whole thing suddenly for the first time became terrifying, because if the Japanese could sink our fleet like that, they could do anything. I think this broke my morale and I think it broke the morale of a tremendous number of people during the campaign, from which we never properly recovered.

'The certainties of existence' had been shattered. There remained only 'the credit of tradition'. Next day Penang was heavily bombed. The immediate evacuation of European residents, and the consequent betrayal of the Malayan population, set another pattern. Whatever credit tradition might have afforded was thereby forfeited. Although officially withheld, news of Penang's fall after 155 years of uninterrupted British rule soon leaked out. More shivers coursed down Singapore's ramrod spines.

Across the causeway from Singapore Island, Sjovald Cunyngham-Brown, connoisseur of flying-boat travel and administrator of rubber quotas, was now working for the Johore government. Below his garden a stream of jalopies, overflowing with pets, prams and anxious planters, queued to cross to the supposed safety of the 'fortress'. He had never met so many of his up-country friends all at once; it was 'like a macabre and everlastingly prolonged cocktail party'. All had harrowing tales to tell, and as distant acquaintances from the north were succeeded by colleagues from Pahang and then near neighbours from Negri Sembilan, the horrifying speed of the Japanese advance became apparent.

Hospital trains chugging across the causeway laden with casualties confirmed the worst suspicions. On 11 January Kuala Lumpur, the Federated States' capital, was abandoned. Three weeks later the last troops trailed wearily across the causeway. Argyll and Sutherland Highlanders, specialists in the business of imperial retraction ever since Weihaiwei, piped them off the peninsula. Then the causeway was blown. It was like raising the drawbridge of the fortress. Yet even this seemingly simple operation miscarried. The breach was wide enough but it was in the wrong place; the water beneath proved wadeable. Equally misconceived were the island's shore batteries, all trained on its seaward approaches; so would be the deployment of its still formidable garrison. A siege of six months had been confidently anticipated; the Japanese were now short of ammunition, numerically inferior (as they had been throughout), and exhausted; even one month's resistance would have allowed for the reinforcement of Singapore and the evacuation of non-combatants. In fact, the island held out for just over a week until 8 February, the city for just under another week until 15 February.

Churchill had exhorted the defenders to contest 'every inch of ground' and destroy 'every scrap of material or defences' that might be used by the enemy. It was to be a struggle to the last man and the last bullet. 'No question of surrender is to be entertained until after protracted fighting among the ruins of Singapore city.' In the Philippines combined US and Filipino units were staunchly defying the Japanese; in Hong Kong the surrender of the city had brought only reprisals and atrocities. Shamed by the first and forewarned of their fate by the second, Singapore's 80,000 defenders might yet have redeemed the reputation of British empire in the East. Immortality lay within their grasp. To men schooled on the do-or-die sieges of Delhi and Lucknow, a prolonged rearguard action should have held no horrors. London had just weathered the worst of the Blitz with honour; after Dunkirk, even defeat and evacuation contained possibilities of glory.

Had 'Z Force' included, as planned, an aircraft carrier, it might have survived the Japanese bombardment and severed the invaders' supply lines. In Malaya more planes and some tanks might have slowed the Japanese advance. Better planning and communications might have delayed the Japanese landing on Singapore Island. But, in the final analysis, retreat and surrender stemmed from the fragile and ambiguous nature of British authority in the East. Informal empire, indirect rule, minimal intervention and administrative flexibility – all those pragmatic solutions on which the British had rightly prided themselves – were revealed for what they were, *ad hoc* expedients designed to minimise costs and mask the absence of real power. They were totally inadequate for the mobilisation of men and resources required to deny an invader; hence the inadequate defences, the lamentable intelligence and the minimal civil defence. In the staunchly British mind of Sjovald Cunyngham-Brown they even provoked serious doubts about the propriety of such resistance.

> The Malays were not taking any great interest, and can you blame them? It was their country that was being rolled over by two vast overseas giants, who were fighting their disgusting battles in Malaya's own garden, smashing and destroying everything. The Malays had benefited by joining Western civilisation and now they realised with horror that they were about to pay for it; this was what happened if you joined the West – so they stood by.

Indian plantation workers were equally indifferent. Only Chinese Malayans had good cause to fight Japan and many did so. But that was mostly after the fall of Singapore; before it, little was done to enlist their involvement. In fact it was the fate of the city's mainly

Chinese population which weighed most heavily in the decision to surrender. With air-raid shelters almost non-existent, thousands of civilians were dying in the relentless bombing and strafing of the city. Whole streets were ablaze; a pall of black smoke obscured the sun; discipline amongst the demoralised troops was crumbling. In the opinion of the Governor and his advisers it was unthinkable to expose the city and its much swollen population to any further punishment. When the cease-fire was signed and the indignity of surrender agreed, he is reported to have muttered: 'It doesn't matter about us. It's the people I'm sorry for. It's *their* country – and somehow we've let them down.'

Presumably he was reflecting on the wretched series of retreats which had now culminated in the greatest reverse ever suffered by the British empire. He could equally have been thinking of the failings of British rule in the East, among which none was more obvious than the reluctance to promote an identity of interests between rulers and ruled or to create anything resembling national cohesion.

9
Eclipse

Snakes and Rabbits

In territorial terms the advance of the Japanese in 1941–2 remains the most successful offensive ever staged. Barely ninety days (8 December – 8 March) sufficed to engross south-east Asia and overrun the eastern empires of Great Britain, the Netherlands and the United States. Both the western Pacific and the eastern Indian Ocean were brought under Japanese naval control. As well as devastating Pearl Harbor, by the end of the ninety days Japan's airforce was flying out of Bali to bomb Darwin in Australia while its warships were threatening Colombo in Ceylon (Sri Lanka) and its infantry was entering Rangoon in Burma.

Churchill, when discounting the feasibility of any such assault, had declared the distance from Tokyo to Singapore as being the same as that from London to New York; a more geospherically appropriate comparison might have been New York to Lima, or London to Lagos. The instantaneous deployment of ground forces, including tanks and support aircraft, over such vast distances astounded mid-century strategists and beggared popular comprehension. In retrospect the Japanese onslaught was characterised as a 'typhoon', a 'locust swarm', a 'lava flow', unpredictable and completely irresistible. Against such natural disasters even empires were powerless. If the ninety days of 1941–2 failed to signify the demise of the Western imperialisms, it was because no one, neither erstwhile sovereign nor subject, could view such sudden and improbable events as other than a freak occurrence. They marked not the end of empire, merely its 'eclipse', an awesome and possibly ominous experience, yet finite and even perhaps inconsequential.

This disbelief echoed the incomprehension and complacency

evinced by many at the time. The British in particular, though seldom sanguine of victory, had viewed the prospect of ejection from their colonies as frankly incredible. When informed that, unlike Sarawak, no troops whatsoever could be spared for the defence of the British North Borneo Company's territory of Sabah, its Governor failed even to order the evacuation of women and children. 'Indifferently the rabbit gazed at the snake and knew not that it was a rabbit,' writes K. G. Tregonning, the colony's historian. As a result, at the east Sabah port-capital of Sandakan virtually the entire European community was consigned to the horrors of a long internment. Amongst them was Harry Keith, the colony's Conservator of Forests, his American wife Agnes and their 1-year-old son George. Agnes Keith's restrained but heart-rending account, later filmed, of survival in Japanese detention would typify a popular and influential post-war genre. The 'typhoon' itself would be speedily forgotten but its aftermath of humiliation and deprivation would stay to haunt a whole generation.

'If war is forced on Hong Kong,' its Governor had declared in July 1941, 'it can resist, it is ready to resist, and it will resist.' *The Times* approved; here was another 'fortress, ready to give blow for blow if attacked'. Such pronouncements, flying in the face of all received wisdom, made no more impression on Britain's phlegmatic pro-consuls than did those of the Jeremiahs who had fled Shanghai. Even the ever upbeat Churchill had already conceded that there was 'not the slightest chance of holding Hong Kong'; that did not stop him sending, in November 1941, two Canadian regiments to augment the colony's British and Indian garrison, thereby consigning them to the near-certainty of either detention or death – in many cases, both.

The theory was that resistance, however hopeless, might slow the pace of the Japanese advance and allow for the arrival of reinforcements. Once 'Z Force' had been consigned to the deep on 10 December 1941 the chance of any British reinforcements reaching such a distant outpost as Hong Kong could be discounted. There remained, though, the possibility of Chinese Nationalists staging a diversion behind Japanese lines. In this faint hope the colony's now six regiments went dutifully about the formalities of defence. As in Singapore the biggest guns were all trained out to sea, air cover was inadequate, and Japanese bombers soon operated at will.

An elaborate system of trenches and bunkers stretching across the New Territories, their dug-out entrances waggishly named after fashionable London thoroughfares, was supposed to guard the landward approaches, so denying to an attacker the command of the harbour; that, after all, had been the reason for acquiring the New Territories in the first place. As it happened, 'Oxford Street', 'Shaftesbury Avenue' and the like held out for just forty-eight hours. The Japanese dropped grenades down the air vents. 'There was little resistance,' wrote Compton Mackenzie when visiting the ruins in 1947, 'the garrison was chased around like rabbits in a burrow by active ferrets.' With the loss of this 'Maginot Line', Kowloon and the rest of the mainland were abandoned.

The defenders withdrew to Hong Kong Island. Being on the far side of deep water was always an Englishman's preference; that, after all, was why the island had been chosen in the first place. But to an amphibious war machine which had already effected massive landings as far away as Thailand, Malaya, Borneo and the Philippines, the few hundred yards of Hong Kong harbour were no more than an inconvenience. As at Singapore so at Hong Kong, the Japanese were across the water in a week.

By 21 December, less than two weeks into the war, the Governor was asking for the unthinkable, authority to surrender. Little of the island still remained in British hands and the population was being needlessly exposed. Singapore, with its 80,000 defenders and its regional responsibilities was meant to hold out; Hong Kong with its 6,000-man garrison and its now hopeless isolation, was not. Churchill, however, turned Churchillian. 'The eyes of the world are upon you. We expect you to resist to the end. The honour of the Empire is in your hands.' There was no mention of relief and no sign of the hoped-for Nationalist diversion. How many of Hong Kong's overwhelmingly Chinese citizens must die to redeem the honour of the empire? He did not say. The men on the spot made their own appraisal and opted for surrender. Hostilities ceased on Christmas Day, the New Year being ushered in with reprisals, atrocities and internment. Give or take a few days, it was 101 years since Captain Belcher had first raised the Union Jack on the rocky foreshore below the then virgin slopes of the Peak.

A Week in Java

'Hong Kong fell. That was all right. We'd made up our minds to that.' On the opposite side of the South China Sea, Agnes Keith bought up

British North Borneo's supply of baby milk for 1-year-old George while husband Harry built a family hide-out in the jungle. 'The Malay peninsula sweated and trembled. That wasn't so good. We hadn't made up our minds to that. Singapore itself couldn't fall.'

Yet January 1942 saw Malaya succumb along with most of the Philippines. North Borneo was also occupied. The Keith family had already been herded into camps when in February Singapore did fall.

The way was now clear for Japan to lay hands on the ultimate prize of the Indies. In a many-pronged advance, landings had already been effected in Sumatra (to secure the precious oil installations) and in the islands of the eastern archipelago. The latter witnessed a rare instance of do-or-die defiance when a force of Australians in the spice islands' capital of Ambon held out for twenty-four hours; of 1,200 men only 121 survived. The action, although it epitomised what Churchill meant by 'resisting to the end', did little to inspire Dutch confidence in being able to offer an effective resistance elsewhere.

This became clear when in mid-February the Japanese navy invaded Bali. If the testimony of an unlikely observer can be believed, the island fell 'without a shot being fired in its defence'; K'tut Tantri recalled watching

> all the Dutch businessmen and the agents from the shipping company and even the Dutch military running for their lives as the news spread that the Japanese had landed . . . They threw away their uniforms or whatever else they wore, and donned native clothing and stained their faces brown. The panic grew as the Dutch set fire to all the military installations . . . My beloved Bali was in flames.

To the only survivor of that international set inspired by André Roosevelt and Hickman Powell, 'the last paradise' became paradise lost. 'K'tut Tantri', the Balinese title used by a Scots-born American called Vaneen Walker, had opened the first hotel on Bali's Kuta beach in 1934. Thanks to celebrity visits to the island by the likes of Charlie Chaplin and Noël Coward ('As I said this morning to Charlie/ There is *far* too much music in Bali . . .'), tourism had boomed. On the other hand the island's select community of residential aesthetes had gradually dwindled. Some had returned to fight for their countries; others were purged by the Dutch as undesirable aliens or homosexuals. Walter Spies, André Roosevelt's successor as the island's ultra-cultivated impresario, was arraigned on both counts. Emerging from imprisonment for 'unnatural practices' in 1940, he was promptly interned for being German. Even as Bali was being overrun by the Japanese, the ship that was removing him to India was sunk off Ceylon.

The mysterious K'tut Tantri had her own reasons for staying on. Moreover her hotel, adjacent to the island's airport, had remained in business. Kuta's five-mile beach, the island's later Waikiki, might be swathed in barbed wire, but allied aircrews operating out of Bali had comprised a valued clientele. Searchlights and anti-aircraft guns had been erected and a spirited defence of this strategically crucial installation was expected. Instead, the place was deserted after the first bombing raids. The Japanese navy landed a few days later and took over the entire island. Under naval administration, generally less intrusive than that of the Japanese army, Balinese society was again spared the worst horrors of foreign oppression. Meanwhile K'tut Tantri went underground to emerge, four years later, in a still more controversial guise. For the Japanese there now remained only the conquest of Java, the richest and most populous island in the East.

As the nucleus of Dutch empire for 300 years, Java merited a last-ditch defence. From Surabaya, its eastern capital and main naval base, a hastily assembled Allied squadron put to sea in late February to oppose the first wave of the Japanese assault on the north coast. Command went to the Dutch of whom it was soon being said that they had not fought a naval battle since the eighteenth century. With British, Dutch, Australian and American vessels, the squadron typified the disparate and often uncoordinated nature of the Western response to Japan's aggression. The ships also lacked air cover and were hopelessly outgunned. Giving, nevertheless, a better account of themselves than 'Z Force', they were eventually scattered in what became known as the Battle of the Java Sea (27 February). This was quickly followed by that of the Sunda Strait (1 March) when two surviving cruisers, one Australian and the other American, ran into a second Japanese invasion force which was heading for west Java. Again the Allied ships inflicted heavy casualties. Yet both were finally sunk within yards of the Sunda Strait between Java and Sumatra through which lay their escape into the Indian Ocean.

Survivors of these ships were washed up on islands in and around the Strait. There they encountered stranded evacuees from Singapore whose overcrowded ships were being remorselessly bombed as soon as they put to sea. Some of these castaways eventually reached

Sumatra and Java only to find the Japanese already in control. No last-ditch defence had been offered. The official surrender of all forces in the Dutch East Indies had come on 8 March barely a week after the first landings. Plans for a concentration of forces in the hills of west Java and a protracted resistance had been made, then aborted. British, US and Australian units dispatched to Java to assist the Dutch had valiantly opposed the enemy advance but had not even been consulted over the surrender. Now faced with indefinite detention and unspeakable hardship, they felt utterly betrayed. So did the Allies' High Command which had counted on the Dutch tying down large sections of the Japanese army for at least a few precious weeks. So too did many of the perhaps 100,000 Dutch and Eurasian civilians who were now interned.

Lieutenant-General Ter Poorten, the Dutch Commander-in-Chief, also felt betrayed. Singapore was supposed to guarantee the security of the Indies; it had failed. Van Mook had spent January in the US desperately seeking more aircraft and munitions; he too had been disappointed. Under the circumstances, and given that any resistance in such a populous island as Java must be attended by appalling fatalities, Ter Poorten saw no alternative to capitulation.

Van Mook supported him, though for different reasons. Now Lieutenant-Governor of the Indies, the indefatigable van Mook was more concerned about the collapse of civil power. That raw authoritarianism on which Dutch rule had so long depended was crumbling before his eyes.

> [The deterioration] proceeded by numerous little steps: a hotel servant who left for the comforting surroundings of his village; a shop that no longer filled orders; a cab that did not stop; a gradually emptying street. Until all of a sudden, we realised that the social texture had frayed and that authority hung in rags. It was like some experience of the unreal . . . an almost volcanic convulsion . . . Gone overnight was a structure that had seemed solid and trustworthy and immovable as granite.

Instead, during the last chaotic days of Dutch rule, Indonesians turned openly to alternative loyalties like religion and, more especially, nationalism.

Van Mook was not unsympathetic. Though of Dutch parents he had, uniquely for a Lieutenant-Governor, been born and largely educated in Java. Massive, scruffy and ungainly, he could scarcely pass for an Indonesian, yet he considered the Indies, rather than the

Netherlands, as his country and, whilst attending Leiden University during his first visit to the Netherlands, he had been closely associated with Indies' patriots. Back in Java, he had sat in the Indies Assembly (the Volksrad) in the 1930s and had championed the cause of the Indonesian peasantry. When Holland fell to the Nazis in May 1940, he welcomed the opportunity for the Indies to manage their own affairs without interference from The Hague. 'There was a feeling of standing on one's own feet,' he wrote, 'there was elbow-room and there was room for initiative.' He sincerely believed that an accommodation with Indonesian nationalism was possible and, after the war, he would play a crucial role in exploring this possibility.

By then, however, it would be too late. Those Indonesians who had once thronged the rallies of nationalist leaders like Sukarno viewed the advent of the Japanese with less than horror. A cherished Javanese prophecy told of national redemption courtesy of a race of small men from the north. Additionally Tokyo's co-prosperity propaganda about 'Asia for the Asians' and 'liberation from the colonial yoke' neatly echoed Sukarno's rhetoric. Behind Ter Poorten's calculations of the military situation and van Mook's of the political, there lay a real fear that Javanese elements might prove embarrassingly eager to support the Japanese invader.

It was another good reason for capitulating. In the nick of time van Mook escaped to Australia and then London, thus losing touch with what would prove to be the decisive phase in the development of Indonesian nationalism.

'*I Came Through*'

Given a free hand, the status which van Mook would seek for the Indies was that of a 'commonwealth'. The term, readily understood by the British in the context of 'white settler' territories like Canada and Australia, now had international connotations as a transitional stage in the process of decolonisation. It also had an Asian connotation in that, as of 1935, the Indies' neighbouring archipelago, now also under Japanese attack, had been designated the Commonwealth of the Philippines.

Affording full autonomy with the promise of ultimate independence, this new status was seen to have defused relations between the US authorities and Filipino nationalists, to have strengthened America's international credentials as an advocate of colonial self-determination, and to have successfully engaged the Filipino nation in supporting US resistance to the Japanese invasion. As President Roosevelt saw it, it was the failure of the other colonial powers to implement similar reforms that undermined their defensive efforts in 1941–2. Had, say, Malayans or Indonesians felt as involved in the political process as Filipinos, they would willingly have mobilised to repel the invader.

Of course, neither the Malay states nor Indonesia had experienced a national revolution like that of the Philippines when rejecting Spanish rule. In Malaya, as also in much of Indonesia outside Java, there was no nationalist movement, no consensus about who actually constituted the nation, and no tradition of centralised government. To most of their colonial masters autonomy, let alone independence, still seemed a far distant goal. Opinion canvassed by R. H. Bruce Lockhart in 1938 had suggested twenty-five to fifty years as a realistic timetable for imperial disengagement.

Nor was it self-evident that Filipino loyalty to the US represented a spontaneous expression of national gratitude. It could be seen simply as the considered response of a particular class anxious to retain its control of the country's wealth. Additionally it would increasingly appear to stem from a recognition not just of America's sincerity but of the personal commitment of a single American citizen, namely Douglas MacArthur.

Nevertheless, a new and more equal relationship between Washington and Manila was undeniable. Other colonised peoples noted with envy how Manila had successfully negotiated the imminent restoration of Filipino sovereignty; other colonial powers noted with interest how Washington yet retained its strategic and economic pre-eminence. The Filipino example, like the fitful but parallel progress underway in India, rightly commanded attention throughout the East.

A US commitment to eventual Filipino independence had been official ever since the Jones Act of 1916 guaranteed recognition of Filipino sovereignty 'as soon as a stable government can be established therein'. But what constituted 'stable government', the extent to which it should be underwritten by the US, and the actual timetable had remained uncertain for another twenty years. Under the Republican administrations of the 1920s there had been some dragging of feet in Washington. This suited Manuel Quezon and Sergio Osmena, the *nacionalista* leaders, who capitalised on US intransigence to increase their support. Then came the recession of the early 1930s which highlighted the extent to which the Filipino economy depended on favourable access to US markets. To cushion the effect of losing its US import preferences, as well as to safeguard the interests of the landed oligarchy within the *nacionalista* party, a long run-up to complete independence was deemed desirable.

With this in mind, in 1933 the US Congress had passed a further act promising independence after ten years, during which interval the colony would enjoy the status of a self-governing commonwealth. The act, passed in spite of President Hoover's opposition, was unexpectedly rejected by the Filipinos. Secretly Quezon had earlier floated the idea of a twenty-year run-up. In a power struggle with Osmena who had negotiated the new arrangement, Quezon now denounced the ten-year run-up as too long and persuaded the Filipino assembly to withhold ratification. Flamboyant as well as wily, Quezon ('Casey' as he was known in America) then headed for Washington where he secured a new arrangement – the Tydings-MacDuffie Act of 1934. Its terms were almost identical to those of the earlier act but now Quezon instead of Osmena could pose as the father of Filipino independence. Defeating the still sprightly Emilio Aguinaldo, president and generalissimo of the first Philippines republic back in 1898, Quezon was duly elected President of the new Commonwealth in 1935. Delays for these elections and the ratification of the new constitution meant that Filipino independence would actually come into effect in 1946.

Still there were uncertainties. In 1935 the *sakdalista* agrarian revolt in central Luzon revealed the fragility of the *nacionalistas'* power base and their dependence on US support. It also presaged decades of similar unrest amongst landless peasants and plantation workers to which Communist ideology would soon give a sharper edge. American willingness to collaborate with and, through trade preferences, to appease and entrench the archipelago's landed and educated élite, the *ilustrados*, fatally perpetuated inequalities of wealth and opportunity within Filipino society. Unlike in China, Indo-China and Indonesia, social justice played little part in the nationalist struggle, and no social revolution resulted from it.

There were flaws, too, in the international pretensions of the new Commonwealth. At the inaugural ceremonies Quezon demanded the 21-gun salute due to the head of a sovereign state. President Roosevelt demurred and would authorise only 19 guns; a sulking

Quezon had to acquiesce. The country was still subject to what Roosevelt called America's 'benediction'. In fact with Japanese activity in the region causing ever more alarm, the Philippines were assuming a higher US priority as a commonwealth than they had as a colony. Similarly the Commonwealth's dependence on US military support was becoming even greater than its dependence on US trade. Having unintentionally hijacked Filipino nationalism, Washington was now piloting it towards a vitiated independence. Instead of a parting of the ways, decolonisation seemed to be ushering in an era of still closer clientage.

As well as the retention for the foreseeable future of US military protection, both Washington and Manila were agreed on the urgent necessity of raising a national Filipino defence force. Happily for both parties, to create it Quezon secured as Military Adviser the services of the one American whose commitment to the Philippines and to Quezon personally was as much a matter of record as his devotion to right-wing Republicanism. Indeed, though the scourge of US liberals, he had also been the one American who supported the Filipino President's demand for a full 21-gun salute. Not just bridging but bestriding the new US-Filipino relationship, General Douglas MacArthur was back in Manila for the fourth time.

MacArthur's reputation as one of the century's outstanding commanders is unassailable. For his wide circle of admirers, including 17 million Filipinos, even the General's irritating sense of mission, his penchant for high-flown phrases and his extravagant posing held an irresistible appeal. Others, not looking for an endearing leader, acknowledged that beneath the controversial public persona there lay courage, dedication, purpose and humanity plus the mental machinery of a tactical genius. He had proved it in the First World War in Europe and he would do so again in the Second in the Pacific.

Not so, however, in the Philippines. Although there his stature still borders on the messianic, it owes less to his military record in the country and more to his devotion to the Filipino people and their cause. Quezon became his 'brother', the islands his 'second country'. During his previous posting as commander of US forces in the Philippines he had conceived a passion for Isabel Rosario Cooper, otherwise known as 'Dimples', a sugary Filipino starlet. She later accompanied him back to a Washington love-nest within a lunch break's saunter of his office. When the relationship eventually soured, Dimples' silence cost the Chief of Staff 'the equivalent of three years salary and allowances'. Secrecy was necessary to protect him not from the strictures of public opinion but from those of his mother. A demanding octogenarian, she now accompanied him back to Manila but died within the first six weeks. Romance promptly reinvaded his life. Miss Jean Faircloth, twenty years his junior, became the second Mrs MacArthur and in Manila was duly born Arthur MacArthur (otherwise 'Sergeant'). To 'the General', as even his wife called him, the Philippines represented a lush and gratifying indulgence in a life otherwise dedicated to the heavy demands of an imperious destiny.

As Military Adviser to the new Commonwealth MacArthur commanded a far higher salary than as US Chief of Staff. In keeping with it, he gazetted himself a Field Marshal (the only US officer ever to hold that rank), adopted a Ruritanian uniform of black trousers and white filigreed tunic, and installed himself and family in the penthouse suite of the de luxe Manila Hotel. Opting for a large, decentralised citizens' army of partially trained conscripts rather than a smaller force of highly trained professionals, he promised Quezon that he was 'forging . . . a weapon which will spell the safety of your nation from brutal aggression until the end of time'. Though over-budget and under-equipped, he continued to portray his army as ahead of schedule and exceeding all expectations even as the Japanese moved into China.

In July 1941 the further Japanese move into Cochin-China prompted the creation of a US Army Far East Command to include both US forces and the new Filipino army. To it MacArthur was inducted as Commanding General. Quezon, who had in secret been proposing to Tokyo a guarantee of Filipino neutrality, promptly changed tack and welcomed both the appointment and its evidence of US determination to stand by his country. Aircraft, munitions and reinforcements were at last becoming available; and, instead of writing off the Philippines, as proposed by the Pentagon, or attempting merely to hold out from previously fortified positions around Manila Bay ('Plan Orange'), MacArthur suddenly opted for an ambitious scheme to defend the whole archipelago.

Redeployment for this purpose was still underway when in the early hours of 8 December word reached the Manila Hotel of the raid on Pearl Harbor. Unaccountably no action was taken until nine hours later. By then wave upon wave of Japanese aircraft had surprised the main airbases on Luzon and in the space of ninety minutes had destroyed half the US bomber fleet and most of its fighters. For this cardinal error and for thus handing to the enemy the decisive advantage of air supremacy, MacArthur declined any responsibility. Admissions of failure did not accord with a self-image of invincible resolve. It was likewise with the collapse of his plan to engage the Japanese wherever they might land on the islands' interminable coastlines. The shore defences were incomplete while the much vaunted Filipino army, supposedly 200,000 strong but still hopelessly ill-equipped and under-trained, dwindled alarmingly. Casualties and desertions accounted for some; as many simply got detached and lost. Less than forty-eight hours after the main Japanese landing, MacArthur ordered a reversion to Plan Orange, the long-matured scheme to withdraw all forces to the Bataan peninsula and the neighbouring island of Corregidor at the mouth of Manila Bay.

Manila itself was declared an open city on Boxing Day. It was thus in effect abandoned without a struggle only a day after the fall of Hong Kong. In its re-taking three years later it would suffer as badly as had Nanking or Warsaw. By comparison, the 1942 inferno, the result of continued Japanese bombing plus American scorched-earth tactics, was almost innocuous. It yet reminded Albert Klestadt, a pipe-smoking back-packer with a taste for intelligence, of the sack of Rome. Ensconced in the YMCA, Klestadt listened to the city's main radio station signing off with 'God Save America, Keep 'em Flying'. 'Rather pathetic,' he noted in his diary under 2 January.

> The looting is terrible, the disarmed police powerless. The Japanese are expected in the city this afternoon or evening. Wish to get it over with quickly now. Saw mobs breaking into the Chinese groceries in the fashionable Ermita district. Fires are everywhere. Saw bedlam near the Post Office where the mob looted a small ship which was already half ablaze. People snatched goods from the burning hold – a fiendish sight . . .
>
> While having a shower at the Y, at seven pm in the fading daylight, lorries full of Japanese soldiers drive through our street. There are no people in the streets, no cheers, no jeers. They are here, and the curtain of lead comes down.

Next day Klestadt was rounded up and, like other stranded foreigners, detained for questioning. Some fluency in Japanese, the result of a long and dubious residence there, plus his German birth, secured his release. He headed south, travelling by car and boat.

Improbably he had set his sights on Australia. Though twice recaptured, he continued to disguise his lack of a passport, his ambiguous past and his staunchly pro-British sympathies. A first attempt to sail single-handed through enemy waters for 2,000 miles ended in the Sulu archipelago. There followed a long delay in a hideout in Mindanao. Eventually, pooling his sea-faring expertise with a Filipino lieutenant and a cut-throat crew of Suluese buccaneers, he made a second attempt and at last reached the Australian coast east of Darwin. It was two years since his escape from Manila; and MacArthur was already plotting its liberation.

In early 1942, having abandoned the city, 'MacArthur's Men' (as his press releases invariably called the US/Filipino forces in Luzon) had begun their heroic stand with a fraught withdrawal into the Bataan peninsula. The staged retreat from different parts of the island of 50,000 men, subject to frequent aerial attack and in constant danger of being cut off by a more mobile and effective enemy, taxed MacArthur's tactical skills to the limit. 'A more difficult operation . . . or one beset by more disastrous contingencies had seldom been attempted in military history,' according to MacArthur's biographer, D. Clayton James. Thanks to the steadiness of his commanders and the caution of the Japanese, as well as the General's brilliant planning, it was effected with minimal loss and was immediately hailed as a feat of quite exceptional genius. Allied feats of any sort were rare in the early weeks of 1942. Once in Bataan, the gallant force dug in deep amongst the crags and swamps of Luzon's primeval rain forest. Along with MacArthur, now holed up with his staff and family in the rock galleries of neighbouring Corregidor, they became the focus of a nation's fragile hopes.

Unfortunately, the careful planning devoted to withdrawal had not been replicated in the supply arrangements for Bataan. Partly because he had previously sneered at the idea of allowing himself to be besieged there, but mainly out of deference to Quezon's objections to the commandeering of Filipino supplies, MacArthur had failed to stock the peninsula with either adequate food or medical supplies. Bataan's 80,000 defenders found themselves on half rations from the start and were soon having to survive on considerably less. Additionally, every disease in the dictionary of tropical medicine quickly made its presence known; yet of MacArthur, though much was heard, particularly his frequent assertions that 'help is on the way', little was seen.

Corregidor, like Bataan, was sporadically subject to heavy bombardment. But the cavernous tunnels of its Gibraltar-like Rock afforded ample protection, and it was much better stocked, a fact not long unnoticed by the hungry hordes on Bataan. In between munching on roots, berries and monkey meat they vented their feelings in new lyrics for the 'Battle Hymn of the Republic'.

> Dugout Doug MacArthur lies a shaking on the Rock
> Safe from all the bombs and from any sudden shock
> Dugout Doug is eating of the best food on Bataan
> And his troops go marching on.
>
> *Chorus*
> Dugout Doug come out of hiding
> Dugout Doug come out of hiding
> Send to Franklin [Roosevelt] the glad tidings
> That his troops go starving on.

As the weeks drifted by, the nation's idol found increasingly fewer admirers in Bataan. By March, according to Lieutenant-General Jonathan 'Skinny' Wainwright who commanded there, 'at least 75% of the command was incapacitated to some extent'; and there was still no sign of the promised reinforcements. Indeed there was still no sign that they had ever been promised – except, that is, by MacArthur who was by now aware that relief was impossible.

Naturally, considerations of morale dictated an up-beat prognosis. To the Filipinos in particular, both civilians and recruits, it was vital to appear to be keeping faith. In February Quezon, also on Corregidor, revived the idea of neutrality. If Roosevelt would authorise immediate independence, he (Quezon) would declare the Philippines neutral, disband the Filipino army, and insist on a mutual withdrawal by both Japanese and American forces. MacArthur appeared to agree, noting that 'in spite of my great prestige amongst them' the temper of the Filipinos had 'become one of violent resentment against the United States'. Many Filipinos were already collaborating with the new Japanese administration in Manila; nearly all felt betrayed by the US which, while sending troops to Europe in support of a colonial power like the British, withheld reinforcements from freedom-respecting allies like the Filipinos. MacArthur could not but sympathise. Granting immediate independence would, he thought, undercut support for Japanese promises of independence within the

Greater East Asia Co-Prosperity Sphere. And if the Bataan men were doomed anyway, nothing would be lost by a mutual withdrawal.

Roosevelt disagreed. Resisting Japanese aggression was what the war was about and this, he insisted, transcended any obligations in the Philippines. Yet MacArthur still seemed to miss the point; arguably he never did accept it. If there could be no deal on neutrality, he replied, he would evacuate Quezon but must himself stay on, 'fighting my present battle position in Bataan to destruction and then holding Corregidor in a similar fashion'. He would go down with his men; just as important, he would go down for the Philippines. Again Roosevelt remonstrated. The Philippines were not the priority. MacArthur's charisma and genius were needed elsewhere. He was to head a new command in the south-west Pacific. He should on no account risk capture. In fact he must depart immediately.

He did so on 11 March, but only after seriously debating disobedience 'even to the extent of resigning my commission and joining the Bataan force as a simple volunteer'. Still apparently in two minds, he was secretly whisked away from Corregidor at night along with his staff and family, taken to Mindanao by high-speed patrol boat, then by air to Alice Springs in Australia and on by train to Adelaide and Melbourne. When cornered by reporters in Adelaide, he explained that he had been ordered out by Roosevelt to organise the American offensive against Japan, 'a primary object of which is the relief of the Philippines'. 'I came through,' he added, 'and I shall return.'

'I Shall Return'

Bataan and Corregidor held out heroically for another two months, but without MacArthur they failed to hold the world's attention. Unlike in Malaya, there were long lulls in the fighting. For the Japanese as for the Americans, Bataan was not a strategic priority in the overall Pacific context and never had been. Though its defence had proved a triumph of the spirit, its loss, the worst disaster hitherto suffered by US forces, was dismissed as inevitable. Nothing was known of the subsequent 'Death March' during which, to the already horrific fatalities from disease and combat, were added 10,000 more before the survivors reached their prison camps in central Luzon. There, facing three years of starvation and oblivion, they had occasion for further reflection on the inspirational leadership of 'Dugout Doug'.

The headline heroes of March had become the back numbers of May because, additionally, their surrender coincided exactly with the Battle of the Coral Sea. This novel engagement, fought not in the Coral Sea and between ships which never sighted one another, frustrated the Japanese assault on Port Moresby in Papua New Guinea. That, and the fact that the Japanese lost slightly more of their carrier-borne aircraft than the Americans, made it a victory which, however inconclusive, was welcome. It also presaged the more decisive naval triumph a month later at Midway. Thereafter a steady stream of victories and landings confirmed the turning of the tide.

Many of the victories were MacArthur's. Given command of US army forces in the south-west Pacific and based in Australia, his primary task had been that of containing the Japanese advance and defending Australian territory. This involved operations in New Guinea and adjacent islands, but such was the General's standing and disposition that he was soon spearheading the advance beyond. By September 1944 he had leap-frogged along the north coast of Irian Jaya (West Irian, Netherlands New Guinea) and snatched Morotai in the northern Moluccas. With the Marianas Islands also secured, the next move, according to the Navy, should be north to Taiwan and Okinawa. But that meant leap-frogging the Philippines. MacArthur would have none of it. He had no objection to sidestepping the Dutch East Indies but the liberation of the Philippines could not be postponed. America owed it to the Filipinos; he owed it to the Filipinos; he owed everything to the Filipinos.

Entering Corregidor a hero, he had left it a legend. To the 'Lion of Luzon' Congress had voted its Medal of Honor and the nation had followed suit, smothering him with awards and naming buildings, babies and boulevards in his honour. For a time 'MacArthur-for-President' had looked a serious proposition. Yet, as he later hinted, the 1941–2 campaign in the Philippines had left the deepest of scars. Personal honour was at stake. He had pledged to return, so return he would, whatever the cost and whatever the strategic demands of the Pacific war. 'The return to the Philippines', writes Clayton James, 'became his obsession – and his redemption.'

He had also endeavoured to make it a national obsession, bombarding the Philippines with 'I will return' propaganda and assiduously promoting the Bataan/Corregidor legend. The Filipino straw hat and the corn-cob pipe which he now invariably sported were intended as cogent reminders; so was the 'BATAAN' emblazoned on the fuselage of his personal B-17 aircraft. At a meeting with Roosevelt in Hawaii in July 1944 he backed up his commitment with a good strategic argument for securing, prior to the attack on Taiwan, at least a staging post in the Philippines. The island of Leyte was so designated and approval given for an October 1944 assault on this basis. The rest was up to MacArthur.

An initial invasion force of 700 vessels, 200,000 men, a ton of ammunition for each man, and 235,000 tons of combat vehicles ensured overwhelming superiority. Superiority bred success and on this he capitalised to make the Leyte landings the prelude to a laborious, immensely costly and largely irrelevant crusade to liberate every island in the archipelago. From whence he derived the authority to employ US forces in this task has never been discovered. The troops in question were badly needed at Okinawa and elsewhere, and the campaign was still incomplete when Japan's surrender obviated its purpose. American casualties were heavy, those of the Japanese ten times worse, and those of the Filipinos astronomical. In Manila alone 200,000 Filipinos are said to have died during its bombardment and capture in February 1945. Unlike the Spanish in 1898, the Japanese declined a face-saving surrender and held out to the last. The walled city, the Intramuros, had to be taken street by street, house by house, room by room. As MacArthur explained in a speech so moving that he was unable to complete it, 'My country has kept the faith!'

> Its soldiers come here as an army of free men dedicated, with your people, to the cause of human liberty . . . an army of free men that has brought your people once again under democracy's banner . . . Your capital city, cruelly punished though it be, has regained its rightful place – Citadel of Democracy in the East . . .

At Leyte MacArthur, dressed for the wardroom rather than the beach, had been obliged to wade through the shallows, an act in which the camera captured him, high-stepping and disapproving. The image appeared worldwide, and the look of disapproval was hailed as one of determination. MacArthur thereupon endorsed it, adopting the same procedure at Luzon and other islands. Like the papal kiss on sundry airport aprons or that of the Jew newly arrived in Zion, it signified both benediction and home-coming. Signing photos of the occasion, the General would add a suitably redemptionist quote from another speech. 'I have returned. By the Grace of

Almighty God, our force stands again on Philippine soil, soil conserved in the blood of our two people.'

Quezon had died during his wartime exile in America. Osmena, his colleague and rival, waded ashore with MacArthur at Leyte and was duly installed as President of the restored Commonwealth as soon as the 'Citadel of Democracy' had been secured. MacArthur had favoured an immediate grant of full independence but the military situation precluded this. The 1946 deadline must, nonetheless, be met and in the meantime he was most anxious that his military authority should not be exercised in an 'imperialistic' manner.

Besides the release of all prisoners, the mopping up of pockets of enemy resistance, and the colossal demands of relief and rehabilitation, he was faced with the delicate question of reprisals. Generals Homma, the victor of Bataan, and Yamashita, the conqueror of Singapore and subsequent commander in the Philippines, were tried in Manila, convicted of war crimes and executed. More problematical was the question of Filipino collaborators. The Japanese had installed a puppet regime in which, willingly or otherwise, numerous members of Quezon's government had served. Osmena, given to understand that US aid in the rehabilitation of his country depended on his prosecuting such quislings, instituted the first proceedings. But among those under suspicion was Manuel Roxas, Quezon's protégé, previously Speaker of the Assembly, and subsequently the patron of an ambitious young Ferdinand Marcos. Roxas was also a close friend of MacArthur. Finding Osmena less than pliant, MacArthur saw in Roxas a more dynamic and amenable leader whose rehabilitation would ensure the primacy of America's interests.

To assist Roxas' advance, MacArthur publicly exculpated him and then recalled the National Assembly. Since many of its members had also collaborated, they noted MacArthur's preference and happily rallied round the clemency policies of Roxas. In a presidential campaign Roxas, aided by US endorsement and heavily funded by Filipino cronies with doubtful war records, duly ousted Osmena in April 1946. The way was now clear for a moratorium on war trials and a favourable outcome to the final negotiations for independence.

These included defence arrangements whereby Manila agreed to the exclusive use by US personnel of twenty-two military bases in the Philippines. Some, like Clark Field and Subic Bay, were of vast extent and embraced adjacent townships which were transformed into leisure-dromes of fast food, cheap sex and duty-free liquor. Within these concessions, even Filipinos were subject to US law. With their extraterritorial jurisdiction and their 99-year leases, they were in effect as much an infringement of national sovereignty as British concessions in China like Weihaiwei or the New Territories, and rather more so than the pre-war treaty ports. Major sources of employment and massive contributors to the Filipino exchequer, they came to occupy a no less influential place in the national economy.

For the vast investment required to rebuild Manila and reinstate a war-ravaged countryside, a further price was paid in financial and commercial concessions. The peso was pegged to the dollar to encourage and protect US investors who, under a controversial parity bill, were given a free hand in exploiting the country's resources. Tariffs continued to protect US exports to the Philippines from cheaper foreign competition, thus flooding the country with American brand names; US imports from the Philippines were tariff-free provided they did not compete with American products, an arrangement which discouraged the Filipino manufacturing industry. The cumulative effect was to leave the economy of the Republic of the Philippines, if anything, more dependent on that of the US than it had been as a commonwealth or a colony.

Yet although, arguably, nowhere in the East paid a higher price for its independence, nowhere did the ex-colonial power enjoy greater popularity. MacArthur, flying in from Tokyo for the independence celebrations, was still the most respected figure in the country. Few would have quarrelled with his, and America's, 'having kept the faith'. The country desperately needed American reparation and investment, however insidious they were; it also accepted the necessity of sheltering under the US military umbrella, however humbling that might be. The US had taken no more liberties with the Philippines than their government was willing, and sometimes eager, to concede. Manila had not won independence; Washington had conceded it. Like the junk-food outlets and the car lots which characterised the rebuilt city, sovereignty was a US concession, a branded franchise. America had defined the independence of the Philippines just as she had their tutelage. And no one was complaining.

As if to emphasise the point, the official proclamation was made on 4 July 1946. Independence Day in the Philippines would be the same as in America; hence it could be celebrated without hurting US feelings. Roxas received the full 21-gun salute. The Stars and Stripes came down. On the same cord was hoisted the Sun and Stripes of the Filipino flag; in the rain, from a distance, it was hard to tell the difference. MacArthur hailed 'the end of empire as the political chain that binds the unwilling weak to the unyielding strong'. Observers confirmed the first voluntary cession of sovereignty by an imperial power.

It was not, though, the end of US imperialism. The Philippines' military bases were links in a new chain binding the willing weak to the super-strong in the containment of Communism. Far from withdrawing from the East, America was discovering a new imperative, defining a new imperialism. Nor was it the first proclamation of independence by a colonial people. That had been Aguinaldo's, the one quashed when Americans first took up the white man's burden. It was not even the first such proclamation of the twentieth century. In the post-war baby boom of independent Asian states, Manila had been forestalled by both Jakarta (Batavia) and Hanoi.

10

Heavy Cloud

Waving and Cheering

In mid-1945, with victory in sight, the European colonial powers imagined themselves returning to their eastern empires flushed with success just like the Americans in the Philippines. The shame of 1941–2 would be forgotten; the price had been paid. They too had 'kept the faith'. Riding the crest of a wave of victories, they would stoop to deliver the East from the brutality and chaos of Japanese rule. This would earn them the gratitude and compliance of their Asian subjects. It would also vindicate Western colonialism. The war indeed, far from signalling the end of imperialism, could be a golden opportunity for its reassertion. Edging out of eclipse, empire would shine again.

It was a most gratifying prospect; and for Richard Broome, a member of the British Malayan Civil Service, it would all come true. In the post-colonial era the memory of Malaya's liberation would be something worth clinging to.

> There's been a great deal of criticism about colonialism but I wish that the critics had been able to be present when the British returned to Malaya after the Japanese surrender . . . It was totally rapturous from all sections of the population, Malays, Chinese, Indians and anybody you can think of . . . I had to drive upcountry in the car and they were coming out of their houses by the roadside waving and cheering. The obvious relief on their faces was something terrific to see.

Had this enthusiasm been shared, as anticipated, by all the peoples of south-east Asia, the reinstatement of colonial rule would have been a mere formality. It would also have provided the perfect opportunity to push through such modifications as seemed desirable. General de Gaulle, while maintaining Indo-China's indissoluble link with France, was hinting at some form of autonomy for France's colonies; in the Indies the Dutch – or at least Hubertus van Mook – appeared to favour a looser relationship with the Netherlands along the lines of the pre-war Philippines' Commonwealth; and in their disparate Malayan territories the British had new plans for that integration and nation-building first attempted by Clementi.

All these schemes either mentioned, or were taken to imply, eventual self-government for the colonies. Whether or not this concession was sincere, it was intended to meet international, and especially American, objections both to colonialism in principle and to the restoration of a world order based on the rivalry and protectionism of different imperialisms. By the end of the war, the US alone possessed the armaments and shipping on which the European powers must depend for the reoccupation of their colonies. American wishes would therefore have to be respected. Following a Japanese retreat, this looked to the Europeans to be the main threat to a successful return.

In the 1941 Atlantic Charter, both Roosevelt and Churchill had upheld the inalienable right of all peoples to determine their own form of government. Churchill, though, had taken this to refer only to the peoples of Europe and was horrified by the idea that it might be applied to colonial subjects. Even suggestions that Hong Kong, now revealed as a strategic liability, might be restored to Nationalist China, a staunch ally and potentially a post-war power-broker, were totally unacceptable. 'I have not become the King's First Minister in order to preside over the liquidation of the British Empire,' he had snorted in November 1942. He was equally opposed to American proposals for the international (or United Nations) trusteeship of erstwhile colonies. Like de Gaulle, Churchill saw trusteeship as a cloak for American expansion.

Roosevelt stuck to his guns. The disastrous collapse of the European empires in the East in 1941–2 demonstrated how little support they commanded and how vulnerable must be any world system based on such fragile constituents. Then in 1943, with intercontinental air travel still involving many stops, the President spent a night in the Gambia *en route* to Morocco for the Casablanca conference. This chance to witness colonialism in practice confirmed his worst suspicions. The Gambian's average daily wage, he was told, was just 50 cents, his life expectancy twenty-six years; 'their cattle live longer.' French rule in Morocco appeared no more enlightened, and the arrogance of the French colonialists was insupportable. In any post-war settlement, European exploitation must make way for some system of international supervision under which better public health, higher standards of living, genuine development and political self-determination would have priority.

The British pointed out that Malaya was not the Gambia and that its impressive development into the world's major producer of rubber would have been impossible without the security and investment which colonial protection had afforded. If Malayan self-government was a distant prospect, it was because Malayan society was so hopelessly divided, not because the British were being obdurate. Witness the massive concessions already made to nationalism in India. But Roosevelt remained unconvinced. London, now home also to the Free French and the Dutch government-in-exile, continued to be apprehensive of Washington's disapproval and anticipated further objections.

In the end, the Europeans would be pleasantly surprised. American opposition even to a French presence in Indo-China, Roosevelt's particular *bête noir*, slowly evaporated as the war drew to its end. Instead, the European colonial powers would find their triumphant return to the East unexpectedly forestalled by Japan's precipitate surrender, and then opposed by forces far more formidable than US opinion. Although the eclipse was over, 'the clouds are rolling up in the Far East' warned Esler Dening, Mountbatten's political adviser in 1945. It could be some time before clear skies brought a glimpse of the sun; for, as Dening foretold, 'there is a very real danger of the West being regarded as aligning itself against the East, with incalculable consequences for the future'.

In parts of the Netherlands East Indies Dutch rule would never be reimposed; where it was, it would last only five fraught years. In Indo-China the French would hang on for nine years but at the cost of incessant hostilities in the south and a major war in the north. The British in Malaya and Borneo fared better, surviving insurgency and restoring prosperity. Yet had Richard Broome postponed his drive up-country for only a few weeks he would have met with a rather less rapturous reception; and within twelve years of the war's end Malaya too would be independent.

Why US attitudes changed and how it came about that the restoration of European colonialism, although unimpeded by the US and actually aided by the Japanese, proved anything but straightforward defy simple explanation. Many factors conspired to frustrate the process. Local conditions and grievances were often paramount. Certain crucial facts are unascertainable, and extraneous events would exert an unexpected influence. One such was the 1944 US capture of Saipan, a small island in a remote Pacific archipelago.

Second Thoughts from Saipan

For the Japanese mid-1944 had marked the turning-point in the war. In some of the heaviest fighting yet encountered, their advance through Burma to India was finally halted just inside the Indian frontier at Imphal and Kohima. At the same time in the Pacific the US Navy overtook MacArthur's leap-frogging along the coast of New Guinea to strike deep into Japanese-controlled waters and overwhelm, after equally fierce fighting, the Marianas Islands including Saipan. Of these two reverses, the latter was strategically the more serious for Japan. Suddenly it dawned on the Japanese that in spite of their dazzling initial successes and their heroic sacrifices, Nippon would probably not after all win the war. In Java, where a young officer-cadet called Sadao Oba had just been posted to Japan's 16th Army, the strategic implications meant a complete about-turn,

> The loss of Saipan Island in June 1944 forced the 16th Army to restructure its strategy to defend Java. Until Saipan, the assumption was that the enemy would land on the southern coasts of Java. Defence fortresses had been built along the southern shore of Java in order to counter possible landings by allied forces based in Australia. The new situation, however, obliged us to think that the enemy would come from the north and the construction of defence fortresses had to be undertaken instead along the northern coast of Java.

The Japanese in south-east Asia had, in other words, been outflanked, this being precisely the danger which they had tried to anticipate by knocking out the US Pacific fleet at Pearl Harbor. Worse still, the loss of the Marianas was a telling psychological blow in that, though remote from Japanese home territory, the islands were the next best thing. They had been under Tokyo's control for a quarter of a century and were home to perhaps 20,000 Japanese citizens.

Due east of the Philippines, 500 to 1,500 miles out into the western Pacific, the Marianas (or Ladrones) and the adjacent Caroline Islands are not really island groups, more scatters. The

Marianas lie roughly north-south, Guam near the southern extremity being the largest. Below them, the even more disjointed Carolines sprawl east and west, Palau at the Asian end being about 1,000 miles from Ponape at the eastern end. Many of the individual islands are uninhabited and none is possessed of inviting resources other than those associated with any coral and coconut paradise. Only Guam and Palau had previously impinged on colonial history, the former having been occupied by the Spanish and then acquired by the US when the Philippines changed hands, and the latter having briefly welcomed to its Elysian shores an appreciative shipload of English East India Company castaways who there hoisted the Union Jack over what they called Fort Abercromby.

In 1898, having lost the Philippines, the Spanish disposed of their doubtful claim to all the Marianas excluding Guam by selling out to the Germans for $4 million. Desperate for any other trifles in an already overcolonised world, the Germans also snapped up the Carolines and the Marshall Islands to the east of them. During the First World War these German colonies, like the German concession at Kiaochow Bay in China, were taken over by Japan with the agreement of her British allies. After the First World War, though relieved of Kiaochow Bay, Japan retained the islands under a League of Nations mandate. They thus became the Japanese Mandated Islands (JMI); and Japan thus became a Pacific power a long time before Pearl Harbor. Attempts to develop the islands eventually established their suitability for sugar-cane, and considerable emigration resulted. This Japanese expansion, accompanied by further economic migration to Mindanao in the Philippines, attracted the attention of the Dutch in Indonesia. Well before the outbreak of the Pacific war, van Mook and others suspected the Japanese of eyeing up the settlement potential of their easternmost islands.

Under its League of Nations mandate Japan had no right to fortify the JMI or employ them for military purposes. But when in 1933 Tokyo pulled out of the League, she was immediately suspected of flaunting this condition. The disposition of the islands, whether seen as a barricade across the western Pacific or as a Japanese salient prodding at eastern Indonesia and Australasia, suddenly looked ominous. Air power, still limited in its range to about 1,000 miles, had transformed perceptions of many oceanic islands. Instead of remote liabilities, the JMI were now seen as a potentially formidable fleet of static but unsinkable aircraft carriers. According to one

American analyst, they 'largely control the Pacific Ocean between Hawaii and the Philippines'. Guam, the only US foothold in the islands, was just fifty miles from adjacent Japanese islands and was reckoned quite untenable in the event of war.

So it turned out. Guam fell within days of Pearl Harbor and the islands duly proved crucial to Japanese air-sea strategy in the Pacific. Under any post-war settlement it was therefore deemed essential that they be detached from Japan. Moreover if, as US planners proposed, American security demanded that the Pacific become 'our lake' and America become the post-war policeman of east Asia, then the US retention of the JMI was as vital as that of bases in the Philippines. Civil aviation experts confirmed their importance as stop-over points on the long haul across the Pacific; the palmgroves-turned-cemeteries where 7,000 Americans had lost their lives, half of them on Saipan, added powerful sentimental reasons for retention.

Against such an assertion of US authority over what would now become 'Micronesia' the only objection lay in the interpretation that others, especially the European colonial powers, might put on it. In defending their own colonial regimes, the British and the French were not above making impertinent enquiries as to the status of Puerto Rico, or the political rights enjoyed by black Americans, or the applicability of international trusteeship to native Americans. It was no coincidence that the Malay press, when warning its readers of the dangers of becoming submerged by aggressive immigrants (that is, the Chinese), invariably cited the plight of America's indigenous peoples. So were the Micronesians, it was asked, going to be invited to determine for themselves whether they wanted US administration? And why was international trusteeship so desirable for cultivated and progressive peoples like the Vietnamese and the Javanese but not for vulnerable Pacific islanders like the Micronesians?

Roosevelt's sincerity about self-determination and international trusteeship are not disputed, but the times were changing. As noted by W. R. Louis in a study of wartime imperialism, 'his enthusiasm for trusteeship reached its peak in the winter and spring of 1944, after which time he began to retreat. His large ideas began to crack on the necessity for precise solutions.'

Saipan's capture demanded just such a precise solution and may be seen as the test case. Within nine months even Indo-China, hitherto the prime candidate for international trusteeship, was adjudged a legitimate sphere for a reassertion of colonial rule; or as Roosevelt preferred, France could become the trustee. Apart from the problem raised by US requirements in Micronesia, it was not at this time obvious that anyone could stop the French from re-establishing their authority. Of the Vietminh little was known other than its existence. In Indo-China as elsewhere the post-eclipse forecast was still for clear skies and excellent visibility.

Roosevelt died soon after this concession, yet his commitment to self-determination lingered on into the Truman years and was enshrined in the United Nations charter. No less enduring was the American presence in Micronesia. In effect the islands became a US colony. Although the occupation was eventually sanctioned under a UN mandate, it served only to confirm suspicions that trusteeship was indeed being used as a cloak, or in this case a grass skirt, for US imperialism.

Merdeka

In Tokyo the loss of Saipan, plus the discovery that from its bases US Super Fortresses could bomb Japan itself, had a more immediate impact. The cabinet of the war-mongering Tojo Hideki was quickly toppled and that of Koiso Kuniaki, no dove, sworn in. With the new ministry and the new strategic situation came new policies towards the occupied territories. On Sadao Oba, the young Japanese cadet who had correctly surmised that switching Java's defences from the south coast to the north augured ill for the strategic situation, these developments made an even greater impression.

> On 7 September 1944 Premier Koiso announced that Japan would permit the 'East Indies' (he did not say 'Indonesia') to become independent in the future. I heard this news when I was making a tour [in west Java] and it came as a considerable surprise. I immediately thought that the war was going so unfavourably for Japan that she had to allow Indonesians their independence.

Besides shattering Sadao's illusions, the effects of this new policy would, in retrospect, prove decisive for the future of empire in Indonesia and not without implications for Indo-China and Malaya. To reinstate their colonial presence, the British, Dutch and French, though as yet unaware of it, would now have to reckon with indigenous populations familiar with anti-imperialist propaganda, alerted to the prospect of independence, and confident of being able to handle it. Moreover, as soon became apparent, a whiff of self-government was both intoxicating and addictive, too stimulating to be relinquished without a struggle and not easily assuaged with less exciting substitutes.

In the early months of Japanese occupation, military priorities had been paramount throughout south-east Asia. The jubilant demonstrations which had sometimes greeted the invaders slowly gave way to disillusionment in the face of heavy-handed efforts to mobilise the resources of the Greater East Asia Co-Prosperity Sphere for the war effort. In Java the flag and the anthem of Indonesian nationalism were again banned, crops and transport commandeered, and forced labour exacted. It was much like old times. On the other hand the internment of practically the entire Dutch administration presented their Indonesian juniors with opportunities for career advancement. To ensure their loyalty and to win support for the sacrifices being asked of the rest of the population, the Japanese military authorities released from detention Sukarno and other leading nationalists, including Mohammed Hatta and Sutan Sjahrir, the Sumatran duo who would largely orchestrate the independence struggle.

Whether the subsequent collaboration of Sukarno and Hatta with the Japanese was afforded zealously or reluctantly is disputed. In that some nationalist leaders, most notably the committed socialists Sjahrir and Amir Sjarifuddin, the fourth member of the nationalist quadrumvirate, withheld their co-operation and went into hiding or exile, there was clearly some doubt about how to respond to the new situation. It was later claimed that this parting of the ways amongst Indonesia's nationalists was the result of a private understanding whereby they might retain a foot in both camps; Sukarno and Hatta would garner whatever concessions to nationalism the Japanese might make and Sjahrir and Sjarifuddin would snap up whatever promises the Allies might make.

Insofar as Indonesians had not been consulted about resisting the Japanese, had been given no opportunity to do so, and had been deserted by their Dutch protectors, their collaboration scarcely amounted to betrayal. Sukarno and Hatta had just spent ten years in Dutch detention. Only the most perverted logic could portray their association with their liberators as treason. The support subsequently given, especially by Sukarno, to Tokyo's propaganda and to local Japanese demands for forced deliveries and forced labour gangs (*romusha*) would indeed be resented. Of the estimated 150,000 Javanese labourers packed off to the outer islands and to Malaya, many died and few returned. But without his support for such distasteful measures it seems unlikely that as of June 1943 Sukarno would have been allowed to set up and lead a nationalist umbrella organisation. This was the Centre of People's Power (*Putera*), which soon acquired an advisory role and was seen as a first step towards self-government.

Other opportunities for participation in government followed. A volunteer defence force (PETA) was recruited and trained as what Sadao Oba soon recognised as 'the core of the future Indonesian army'. Youth groups, women's groups, Islamic groups and a pioneer corps added to the atmosphere of mass politicisation. All instilled Asian values and anti-Western propaganda. The Japanese language was taught and Japanese ideas of discipline promoted. Every village acquired its 'singing tree', a loudspeaker wired to a radio set. From a nationalist's standpoint, any mobilisation was preferable to Dutch disparagement and, through the radio in particular, Sukarno lost no opportunity to rouse the people with allusive rhetoric in which the patriotic content usually swamped the official propaganda. When, post-Saipan, the Koiso government conceded that independence was indeed on the way, Sukarno's willingness to work with the Japanese appeared to have been vindicated.

> The announcement [wrote Sadao Oba] was naturally welcomed by the Indonesians. The red and white national flags were hoisted on many buildings and places. Newspapers reported that Mrs Sukarno was sewing red and white flags. *Merdeka* (independence) which had been the national goal for many years was coming nearer. In Jakarta the city authorities celebrated by allowing the public to ride free on the trams. It was reported than many Indonesians, therefore, thought *Merdeka* meant a free tram service.

No date was yet set for *merdeka* and, 'curiously enough' according to Sadao, 'the hoisting of the national flag and the singing of the national anthem were only allowed on Japanese national holidays'. Even Sukarno was under no illusions as to what independence within Japan's new Asian order actually meant. In Manchuria, now Manchoukuo, 'the last emperor' Henry Pu-yi was a mere cipher with no more authority than he had enjoyed as a child-prisoner within Peking's Forbidden City. More recently Tokyo had authorised independence for Burma and the Philippines. In the case of the latter, independence within the Greater East Asia Co-Prosperity Sphere meant less autonomy than had commonwealth or even colonial status under US rule. Japan's strategic and economic requirements took precedence regardless of constitutional niceties. As General Yamamoto, Supreme Commander in Java, put it, the idea of independence was to establish 'a country that would co-operate with Japan to win the war'. Concessions to nationalism were designed not to lessen the burden of co-operation but to galvanise the nation into greater co-operative effort.

On the other hand, should Japan fail to win the war, Yamamoto anticipated the residual satisfaction of having presided over a constitutional insemination whence would result 'the birth of a country that was, at least, not anti-Japanese'. 'Asia for the Asians' and the reawakening of nationalism had always been Tokyo's policy. Many Japanese argued with complete sincerity that, whatever the fate of Japan, the struggle would not have been in vain if countries like Indonesia, Burma and the Philippines had thus acquired the courage and confidence to defy colonialism. MacArthur, when making his last stand at Corregidor, had been given to expressing similar sentiments about America's role; in principle Tokyo's blueprint for a post-war order of self-governing states bore an eerie similarity to Washington's.

Yet by 1945 Java, hitherto a paradise posting for Japanese servicemen and widely regarded as the most successful of their military administrations, was crippled by shortages and seething with discontent. Supplies were being stockpiled, allegedly for a prolonged defence against the expected Allied invasion. Allied bombing had already destroyed Japan's mercantile marine, thus cutting the island off from essential imports. Textiles were virtually unobtainable and near famine conditions prevailed in some areas. In Blitar, east Java, PETA units mutinied, killing their Japanese NCOs, prompting a succession of other outbreaks and raising serious doubts about the militia's loyalty in the event of invasion. Attempts to disarm the militias merely increased their hostility. Some deserted to swell the ranks of partisan bands wedded as much to revolution as to nationalism. Others bided their time. 'Japanese get the girls, *Tiong Hua* (the Chinese community in Java) get the money, Indonesians get the misery' went a popular adage.

Meanwhile an investigative body for the preparation of Indonesian independence had been set up, before which in May 1945 Sukarno enunciated the five principles, or *pancasila*, which would become the pillars of Indonesian nationhood. All things to all men, they endeavoured to weave together the many strands of dissent that comprised Indonesian nationalism from the green shades of Islamic revivalism and the liberal yellows of social democracy to the blood-red of Trotskyite Communism.

Again, though, it was events elsewhere which nudged independence a step nearer. Until 1945 the Japanese navy, responsible for the administration of all Indonesia east of Java, had strongly opposed concessions to the nationalists because of the strategic importance it attached to places like Ambon and Makassar. Defeats in October–November 1944 in the Philippines, especially in Leyte Gulf, changed all that. Now so crippled that in 1945 it rarely ventured out of home waters, the Japanese navy lost its interest in Indonesia. The main opposition to independence for the Indies was thus swept away. By July 1945, with Tokyo still expecting the war to last many more months and painfully aware that any defence of Java would require Indonesian support, independence was suddenly accorded top priority.

The correlation in Japanese planning between military setbacks and political concessions became still more obvious during the final frantic hours of the war. On 7 August, the day after the first atomic bomb was dropped on Hiroshima, Japan's Supreme Commander for south-east Asia authorised the formation of a Preparatory Committee for Indonesian Independence. Next day Sukarno and Hatta were summoned to his headquarters, which were located in south Vietnam. Arriving on the 11th, two days after the Nagasaki bomb, they learnt that independence would be granted on the 24th. Even this accelerated timetable proved too slow. On the 14th, the day Sukarno and Hatta arrived back in Jakarta, Tokyo announced the surrender of all Japanese forces. It looked as if Indonesia had missed its independence by just ten days.

Cheated by events beyond their control, the Indonesian leaders were uncertain how to proceed. Sukarno, well-built, devastatingly handsome and an impulsive extrovert, instinctively played to the people; Hatta, diminutive, bespectacled and incisive, played foil and strategist to Sukarno. Like a music-hall duo, they now weighed the options. Expectations amongst their supporters were at such a pitch that their leadership would be utterly discredited if they failed to deliver. Sutan Sjahrir and the various underground groups which had withheld support from the Japanese were even more adamant. Their independence proclamations were already circulating and students were taking to the streets. Yet under the terms of the armistice, political life was frozen, the Japanese forces being under orders to maintain law, order and the status quo until relieved by the Allies. Independence could, therefore, be achieved only through an act of revolution. In Sukarno's expansive estimation, if not in Hatta's legalistic mind, that would actually enhance its validity. But, a compassionate leader in spite of his fiery rhetoric, Sukarno was much concerned about the consequences for public order. The Japanese would be obliged to oppose any grab for power, while large sections of the population wanted nothing better than a chance to avenge themselves on their now cowed conquerors. There was every prospect of a bloodbath.

The deadlock was broken with the kidnapping of both men in the early hours of 16 August. Setting a dangerous precedent which would be much followed in the forthcoming months, heavily politicised youth groups (*pemuda*) comprising radical students, maverick militias and underground leaders had resolved to force the pace of revolution. Driven to a house outside Jakarta, Sukarno and Hatta were confronted with an ultimatum to declare independence or stand aside. Reluctantly the two men agreed to make a declaration but with Hatta's proviso that it should carry the pan-Indonesian authority of the Preparatory Committee. This body was summoned to the house of Admiral Maeda, a Japanese sympathiser, and after more all-night discussion, a proclamation was issued. A few hours later, at 10 o'clock on 17 August 1945 Sukarno, flanked by Hatta, read the document to a handful of well-wishers outside the former's residence.

> We, the people of Indonesia, hereby declare Indonesia's independence. Matters concerning the transfer of power and other matters will be executed in an orderly manner and in the shortest possible time.

One of Mrs Sukarno's home-made red and white flags was then hauled up an improvised flagpole. All present sang 'Indonesia Raya', the nationalist anthem. Then they dispersed.

It was the simplest independence ceremony ever staged; though scarcely intentional, no greater snub to the 300 years of Dutch rule could have been devised. The peremptory, not to say presumptious,

1. Destined to 'die like flies'.
Bonded labourers in Surabaya,
east Java, await shipment to the
plantations of north Sumatra
during boom years in the
Netherlands East Indies at the
turn of the century

2. 'Three cadets' in Weihaiwei,
c. 1910. James Stewart Lockhart
(*centre*), a Confucianist, and
Reginald Johnston (*left*), a
Buddhist, would ensure that
this remotest of British colonies
remained 'more Chinese than
China'. Cecil Clementi (*right*),
also a notable Chinese scholar,
would become the reform-
minded Governor of
Hong Kong and then of
Singapore and the Malay
peninsula

3. A day at the races in Hanoi. 'It is better not to scratch beneath the surface,' wrote sceptical Hubert Lyautey, later Marshal of France: 'Everything would collapse.'

4. 'Britain's first cession of territory to a nationalist government since the American War of Independence.' Sir Reginald Johnston (*second left*) departs Weihaiwei, 1 October 1930. The territory, like Hong Kong, was to become a Special Administrative Area within the Republic of China with Commissioner Hsu (*far right*) as Johnston's successor

5. Ladies' Day at the Penang Swimming Club, *c.* 1910. 'A good lunch is served, and there is a bar and a good supply of comfortable long chairs in which members can lounge after their exertions.' In December 1941 their fair-skinned successors would be speedily evacuated following Japan's entry into the war. No such arrangements were made for Penang's Malayan population

Sir Vyner Brooke, otherwise the third and last of the White Rajahs of Sarawak, and Lady Brooke, otherwise Rani Sylvia, 'Queen of the Headhunters'. Both preferred England and were reluctant participants in the last days of the White Raj

7. and 8. A Japanese cruiser (*above*) overawes Shanghai in February 1932. Some 20,000 Japanese troops stormed through Asia's largest metropolis but spared the British-run International Settlement barricaded in its midst (*below*). Five years later the return of Japan's navy would signal the end of Shanghai's prominence as the flagship of empire in the East

9. and 10. Japanese troops
celebrating the capture of the
Bataan peninsula in the
Philippines (*above*) in May
1942. A desperate defence, plus
the defiant rhetoric of General
MacArthur, helped obscure 'the
worst disaster hitherto suffered
by US forces'. No such heroics
spared British blushes when in
less than two months the
Japanese overran Malaya and
were approaching the causeway
to Singapore (*below*).
Singapore island, 'one of the
world's great strong points',
held out for just two weeks

11. Dr H. J. van Mook (*right*), Lieutenant-Governor of the Netherlands East Indies, with Rear Admiral K. B. F. Doorman shortly before the Japanese assault on Java in March 1942. Three hundred years of Dutch rule were overthrown in a matter of days. Van Mook escaped and would later head Dutch negotiations with the Indonesian Republic. Doorman went down with his flagship in the Battle of the Java Sea

12. and 13. Major Jean Sainteny accompanied by his wife (*above*) arriving at Orly airport from Hanoi in 1947. Sainteny had brokered a pact with Ho Chi Minh (*below*) for the return of French forces to north Vietnam. His excellent relations with 'the old fox' held out real hopes of a negotiated devolution of power. They were dashed by 'parochial politicking' in Paris and hawkish manoeuvres in Saigon

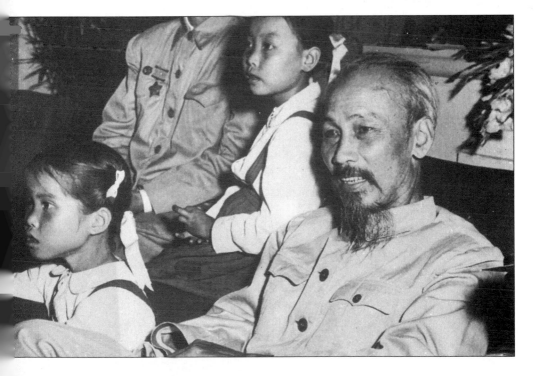

14. The end of a nightmare. Inmates of Stanley Camp in Hong Kong salute the flag in August 1945 after 42 months of captivity. Their efforts, plus the timely arrival of Royal Navy squadron, frustrated Chinese and American plans to pre-empt the post-war restoration of British rule to Hong Kong

15. and 16. 'I will return.' General Douglas MacArthur, accompanied by President Sergio Osmena, stands again on Philippines' soil (*above*) during the assault on Leyte in August 1944. The General's obsession with keeping his pledge to the Filipinos would cost them dear. Manila (*below*) was almost obliterated by US bombardment, Osmena was ousted, and the Filipino economy was rendered more dependent than ever on the US

17. Comrades in arms. Admiral Lord Louis Mountbatten congratulates Chin Peng of the Malayan Peoples' Anti-Japanese Army during victory celebrations in Singapore in September 1945. Two years later Chin Peng, as leader of the Malayan Communist Party, would return to jungle warfare in command of the Malayan Peoples' Anti-British Army during the protracted 'Emergency'

18. President as prisoner. Sukarno, under arrest by Dutch troops, awaits deportation following capture of the Indonesian Republic's capital during the second Dutch 'police action' in January 1949. US and international condemnation quickly secured Sukarno's release. A year later, in another Dakota, he would return to Jakarta in triumph

19. Into the jaws of hell. In November 1953 the seizure by French airborne troops of the remote Vietminh stronghold of Dien Bien Phu was hailed as a triumph. Six months and 15,000 lives later, the obliteration of the French forces at Dien Bien Phu virtually ended French rule in Indo-China

20. 'Not how empire was supposed to end.' A. S. Taylor, a rubber planter in Malaya, relaxes within reach of his bren gun during the Communist 'Emergency'. Planters, by reason of their isolation, were frequently targeted and were loud in their demands for protection. Yet fatalities amongst Malaya's Chinese community far exceeded British fatalities

21. Lee Kuan Yew addresses supporters of Singapore's People's Action Party. In the 1950s Lee combined populist appeal with a shrewd exploitation of British, and then Malayan, security concerns. Once regarded as a crypto-Communist, he outwitted rivals to turn his followers into disciples of free enterprise and his state into a bastion of the free world

22. Tunku Abdul Rahman, here with British Commonwealth Secretary Duncan Sandys in 1961 possessed neither Lee's guile nor his rhetorical skills. Yet, trusted implicitly by the British and by his own United Malay National Organisation, he enjoyed a comparable ascendancy as Malaya's, and then Malaysia's, first Prime Minister

23. 'Onward Malaysia'. In 1963 British rule in south-east Asia officially ended when Singapore, plus the north Borneo colonies of Sabah and Sarawak, joined Malaya to form the new state of Malaysia. The four constituents, as represented in a larger-than-life poster at the Singapore celebrations, did not link arms for long. By 1965 the young man in shirt and trousers had been painted out of the picture as Singapore opted to go it alone

24. 'He was just someone you didn't notice.' Edward G. Lansdale (*centre*), aka 'the Ragtime Kid' and 'the Quiet American', sits in on an in-flight briefing of Air Vice Marshal Ky (*right*) in 1966. Ky was then Prime Minister of South Vietnam, Hubert Humphrey (*left*) Vice President of the US, and Lansdale a Major-General. He was also back at the US embassy in Saigon, still masterminding the 'running of someone else's country'

vague and deeply uninspiring wording of the proclamation read more like a policy directive. From Sukarno, a demagogue capable of holding spellbound for hours an audience of a quarter of a million, it must have sounded like a confidential aside. Not surprisingly the world, when eventually news of it leaked out, failed to take it seriously. Like Aguinaldo and his Filipino revolutionaries of 1898, the Indonesians appeared to have jumped the gun. Dutchmen like de Jonge had foretold another 300 years of colonial rule and they should know. Straddling two continents, with 14,000 islands, several hundred languages, innumerable ethnic groups and a kaleidoscope of religions, Indonesia appeared to lack even the basic building blocks of a nation state.

Predictably, the proclamation of independence soon appeared to be wishful thinking. 'Matters concerning the transfer of power' were not executed 'in an orderly manner' nor 'in a short time'. Indonesian independence, first disputed by the Japanese in their new role as post-war peace-keepers, then engaged by the British, and finally assaulted by the Dutch, was in for a rough ride. So were its leaders, compromised by their wartime collaboration and increasingly divided as to their ideologies. Ahead lay five years of revolution, intermittent war and tortuous negotiation. Half a dozen nationalist ministries would prove unequal to the task; a succession of regional and ideological revolts would add to the confusion. Yet amazingly the new republic would survive.

Initially this owed much to the fact that for some weeks the Indonesians had only the defeated and sometimes sympathetic Japanese to contend with. It was not until 4 September that Mountbatten, the Allies' Supreme Commander for South East Asia, became aware of 'a local resistance movement in Java'. 'Known as the Indonesian Republic', it 'will require careful handling,' Mountbatten noted in his diary. Four days later a small fact-finding party was parachuted into Jakarta and a week later a British cruiser arrived on the scene. To these envoys of his victorious but invisible enemy, Yamamoto emphasised the explosive nature of the situation, an appraisal that was supported by Colonel Laurens van der Post to whom the Japanese command in Bandung had surrendered. According to van der Post, a British officer who had been captured while organising a guerrilla resistance in 1942, the independence movement had 'started to spread like a grass fire which could inflame the whole of Indonesia'. Already Japanese weapons were finding their way into Indonesian hands and then being used against Dutch internees as they emerged from their prison camps.

With further prompting from van Mook, now desperate to get back to Java, Mountbatten began to appreciate the seriousness of the situation. But not until October would Allied forces at last converge on Java. By then the Sukarno government had had two months in which to take over the administration and substantiate its claim to independence. In van der Post's opinion, it more than proved itself and enjoyed almost universal support. The best chance of any compromise with the returning Dutch had therefore been lost before they arrived. Instead of 'a local resistance movement', Mountbatten found himself confronted with a people's revolution. It was not the only revolutionary situation into which the largely British forces of South East Asia Command had blundered and, though ultimately the most demanding, it was still not accorded top priority.

Simply Not Cricket

Given the ferocity of the US bombing of Japan in 1945, it is probably true that the use of atomic weapons to secure Tokyo's prompt surrender saved more Japanese lives than were lost at Hiroshima and Nagasaki. It also saved Allied lives. Van der Post, three years a prisoner in west Java yet a most understanding victim of Japanese brutality who would later refuse to testify against his captors, insisted that the Japanese military authorities had planned to execute all Allied prisoners-of-war before themselves fighting to the death. This was confirmed by reports like that from Sjovald Cunyngham-Brown. Escaping from Malaya just before the fall of Singapore, the irrepressible Cunyngham-Brown had been captured in Sumatra and put to work on the Sumatran equivalent of the notorious Burma-Siam railway. Then, one day in July 1945, 'matters once more took a serious turn'.

> Reinforcements of Japanese arrived and we were all suddenly ordered to dig pits thirty feet long, seven feet wide and six feet deep, a work which was undertaken under the strict guard of an exceptionally unpleasant squad of Korean soldiers. When we saw the machine-gun positions being arranged, we realised what these pits were for. They were our graves.

Only Tokyo's sudden and wholly unexpected surrender three weeks later spared Cunyngham-Brown and his fellow prisoners.

Beneficiaries of a nuclear dividend, they did not condemn Hiroshima. Instead of a sentence of death, out of the blue there came an angel of mercy. A small plane landed on the camp's improvised airstrip and disgorged a trim female figure in a British uniform. This apparition caused some embarrassment since Cunyngham-Brown and friends possessed only the scantiest of loincloths. He nevertheless shook hands, introduced himself, accepted a cigarette and then enquired who she was. She said 'I'm Lady Mountbatten.' 'Gosh!' said Cunyngham-Brown.

In camps scattered throughout Greater East Asia's now far from co-prosperous sphere, prisoners and internees were dying in their thousands of malnutrition and disease. The Emperor's sudden capitulation, followed by mercy missions like that of Edwina Mountbatten, probably saved as many lives from starvation as from execution.

Yet the atomic bombardment was not an undisguised blessing for the Allies. By provoking Japan's precipitate surrender it robbed the European powers of their cherished hour of triumph. With the exception of Burma and the Philippines, the erstwhile colonies were never retaken, simply reoccupied. The Dutch, British and French were thus cheated of that splendid spectacle, deemed so essential to the restoration of colonial prestige, in which white supremacy triumphed, Asian armies took to their heels, and a string of Allied victories cemented the bond between the *tuan* and his grateful subjects.

As if to make up for this deficiency, much fuss was made by the British of the handful of undercover agents who had infiltrated Malaya during the Japanese occupation. The rapport established with the Malayan – mainly Chinese Malayan – guerrilla resistance by ex-philatelist John Davis, the rapturously received Richard Broome and others was taken to demonstrate the continuity of British efforts on behalf of Malaya and the strength of Anglo-Malayan loyalties. Introducing *The Jungle is Neutral*, an exceedingly popular account of their work by F. Spencer Chapman, Lord Wavell likened the 1941–2 campaign to the first leg of a cricket match. Japan's sudden submission on the eve of the second leg, however, simply 'wasn't cricket'.

> The Japanese surrender made the return match a walk-over; had it been played the result would have been an innings defeat for the Japanese, in which the guerrilla forces organised within the Peninsula would have played a large part.

Wavell had been Supreme Commander of Allied Forces in South East Asia during the disasters of the first match. Mountbatten, captain of the team for the return match, had the keen eye for kudos and camera of MacArthur. Since 'Operation Zipper', the code name for the reinvasion of Malaya, was past the planning stage when Japan surrendered, and 'since', as Mountbatten put it, 'I had no atomic bomb to take its place', he decided to invade anyway. Returning with a bang was vital. The Malayan landings, because uncontested, would not exactly be another D-Day, but they could at least serve as the grand overture to the surrender proceedings he was planning in Singapore.

MacArthur, equally preoccupied by ceremonial, insisted that no operations of any sort be mounted until he had taken the imperial Japanese surrender in Tokyo Bay. This meant a two-week delay while he assembled his entourage, plus the world's press and a massive display of naval strength, then a further week for area commanders throughout the Japanese territories to signify compliance with the imperial order. Nationalists in both Indonesia and Indo-China took full advantage of the delay. Meanwhile Mountbatten's 'Zipper' armada had to heave-to off Penang, 'waiting for the covers to come off' as Wavell would have put it. On 9 September the all-clear came through and the 100,000 men of 'Zipper' duly swept ashore unopposed on to the tranquil beaches of Port Dickson and Port Swettenham.

Two days later Mountbatten staged his surrender ritual in Singapore. It included the hoisting of a crumpled Union Jack which, forty-three months earlier, had flown over Government House. Pocketed by Mervyn Sheppard, a scholar-administrator, just as the Japanese entered the city, it had remained in his possession throughout his captivity. 'I put it inside my pillow. I wrapped a towel around it and there it remained for the rest of the Japanese occupation.' The flag symbolised continuity. A cherished if crumpled talisman throughout the years of eclipse, it bespoke the resurgence of an empire upon which, though the sun never set, the head often rested.

Mountbatten's speech took up Wavell's theme of 'an innings defeat'. His invasion armada was for real. He 'wanted to make it plain'; this was not a negotiated surrender; the Japanese were 'submitting to the superior force now massed here'. Like MacArthur's return to the Philippines, the manner of Mountbatten's to Singapore had to match the magnitude of the occasion.

To receive the unconditional surrender of half a million enemy soldiers, sailors and airmen must be an event which happens to few people in the world [he noted in his diary]. I was very conscious that this was the greatest day of my life . . .

Later he crossed out the 'half a million' and wrote '2/3 million actually'. The precise figure was uncertain because, as a further consequence of Japan's sudden surrender, his South East Asia Command (SEAC) had just been dramatically extended. So that MacArthur could concentrate on new responsibilities in Japan itself and in China, Korea and Taiwan, SEAC's remit had been extended to include (as well as Burma, Thailand, Malaya and Sumatra), post-war responsibility for Java, Sulawesi, all Borneo, and French Indo-China south of the 16th parallel (that is Cochin-China and the southern half of Annam).

'Few people realise the immense scale of the enlarged SEAC,' noted its delighted commander; 'a million and a half square miles . . . a population of 128 millions . . . half a million Japs and over 200,000 prisoners of war and internees to be repatriated'. Equally few people, Mountbatten not being one of them, realised the immense scale of the difficulties thus incurred. Apart from Hong Kong, where a Royal Navy task force had arrived as early as 29 August in order to pre-empt any possibility of the Americans or the Chinese taking the colony's surrender, Mountbatten's intelligence about these new acquisitions was as inadequate as the mainly Indian troops at his disposal. Ignoring, therefore, rumours of 'local resistance forces' (like the Republics of Indonesia and Vietnam) he made his priority the headquarters of Japan's South East Asia Command, namely Saigon.

War and Peace and War

As already noted, after France fell in 1940 the colonial administration in Indo-China had opted to acknowledge the German-sponsored Vichy government. Faced with a stark choice between a compromised French sovereignty and none at all, Admiral Decoux had acted in what he believed to be the best interests of France. As a naval officer, he may also have been influenced by the legacy of Lagrée, Garnier and the other pioneers of French empire in the East. The navy had opened up Indo-China and it continued to regard France's imperial role in Asia as its own affair.

Although obliged to concede to a succession of humiliating Japanese ultimatums for military facilities, raw materials and financial contributions, Decoux stood firm on sovereignty, preserved the French administration, and maintained Indo-China's neutrality in the Pacific war. Had this situation lasted until the Japanese surrender, in the opinion of Georges Gautier, head of the civil administration in Tonkin, Decoux's 'collaboration' would have been vindicated. '*L'expérience Decoux [était] un incroyable pari*,' wrote Gautier. '*Ce pari pouvait être gagné.*' ('The Decoux approach was an incredible gamble. The gamble could have paid off.')

In fact it very nearly did pay off and, according to Gautier, it would have but for the bungling of the de Gaulle government and the unreasonable behaviour of the Americans. In France these criticisms of de Gaulle are disputed; not so those of American mishandling of Indo-China.

As late as March 1945, with France already liberated and Japan staring defeat in the face, Decoux's *pari* looked safe. Japan's military achievements and its anti-Western propaganda had made little impact on the Vietnamese; 'Asia for the Asians' was heavily compromised by Tokyo's recognition of French sovereignty; the mobilisation of nationalist opinion through youth groups and militias, as in Indonesia, was impossible while French rule lasted; and the nationalist Vietminh relied far too much on its Communist components to consider seeking endorsement from the Japanese. On the contrary, it was the Vietminh who, like the Chinese and Malayan Communist Parties, spearheaded opposition to the Japanese presence. Although not particularly effective in destabilising the Japanese military, this *maquis* (as the French sarcastically called it) did infiltrate large areas along the always unstable Chinese frontier in the north. It also re-established contact with revolutionary groups in the south and engaged in those detailed and doctrinaire projections so dear to ideologues.

Decoux's anxieties, such as they were, stemmed less from the presence of the Vietminh and more from that of other Frenchmen. In Paris de Gaulle's newly installed provisional government was anxious to stake an early claim to the colony and had enlisted mainly British support to smuggle into Indo-China the nucleus of both a guerrilla resistance and a parallel administration. The former relayed intelligence about the military disposition of Japanese forces; the latter endeavoured to enlist the loyalties of Decoux's troops and officials while waiting to take over as soon as the war in the East ended.

Decoux and Gautier duly acknowledged the de Gaulle government and showed their willingness to co-operate with its representatives, but they could scarcely make way for them without panicking the Japanese military authorities. They also made no secret of the fact that they would have preferred Paris to have left them alone. The portraits of de Gaulle which had begun to appear in government offices did not reassure the Japanese. Nor were the latter unaware that American bombing of such vital arteries as the north-south railway relied on information about troop movements provided by the resistance. To Gautier's mind, such destruction of a neutral nation's infrastructure merely provoked the Japanese. It also condemned to famine those Vietnamese who lived in rice-deficit areas and were dependent on supplies by rail. The Communists had exploited rural distress in the 1930s. They now did so again, at the same time stepping up their organisational efforts in response to the evidence of an imminent reassertion of Paris' authority.

To the Japanese all this renewed activity by a resurgent France and a radicalised Vietnam was indeed provocative. Probably, too, they suspected Decoux of complicity; and they were particularly irritated by his reluctance to meet their demands for a massive new transfer to Tokyo of Indo-Chinese funds. Yet this scarcely justified their draconian response. On 9 March 1945, out of the blue, Decoux was presented with another ultimatum. In view of a likely Allied invasion, he was to surrender administrative control of the country plus the command of all French troops and police. He had two hours to respond. When the two hours elapsed without a satisfactory response, the overthrow of French rule was announced and Japanese troops moved out of their barracks.

In Saigon Decoux was placed under house arrest and in Hanoi Gautier was thrown into detention. Thousands of lesser functionaries were imprisoned, some tortured, some killed. Troops of France's colonial army suffered even heavier casualties, although in the north, in a French equivalent of Dunkirk or Bataan, Generals Sabattieri and Alessandri fought an epic rearguard action as they withdrew across appalling terrain into Nationalist China. It was small consolation for having jeopardised French empire in the Far East. Decoux's gamble had failed; his fate was sealed. A few months later he would be exchanging Japanese detention for a prison in France.

That the situation within Indo-China was solely responsible for the Japanese coup seems unlikely. Tokyo had higher strategic and political objectives. By 1945 Indo-China had served its purpose as a staging post to China, Burma and Malaya, and was about to become a front-line state. The priority now was to deny it to the enemy. If it were to be invaded the Japanese needed a clear field of fire, uncluttered by an administration of doubtful loyalty; and should it be lost, it was infinitely preferable that it be lost to the Vietnamese rather than the French. As in Indonesia, the idea was to substantiate, albeit retrospectively, that objective of liberating Asians from Western imperialism, and to leave 'a country that was, at least, not anti-Japanese'.

That this was indeed the idea became apparent when, the day after the coup, Japanese officials confirmed that Indo-China had been released from colonial rule and might resume its sovereignty. Bao Dai, the last Nguyen Emperor of Annam, was encouraged to declare the independence of all Vietnam and to renounce all treaties with France. His example was followed by King Norodom Sihanouk in Cambodia and Sisavang Vong in Laos. But Bao Dai, a playboy prince who had spent most of his life in France, commanded few followers in Annam and almost none at all in Tonkin. His government, compromised in Vietnamese eyes by its Japanese support, proved unequal to the task of relieving the famine that now ravaged the north and was unable to gain a footing in the south, where the Japanese set up their own administration. The first nationalist government was therefore already tottering when in August the Vietminh moved on Hanoi.

Ho Chi Minh would later claim that, technically, the Vietminh did not seize power because, as he saw it, there was no power to seize. Fragmented both by the rapid succession of administrations (two French, one Vietnamese and, in all but name, one Japanese) and by the proliferation of insurgents (French and nationalist resistance groups, tribal warlords, sectarian, ideological and plain criminal militias), authority within the country had completely collapsed. It awaited not a new government but a new ideal, not another commissar but a messiah.

Timing their arrival to coincide with Japan's surrender, the jungle-hardened forces of the Vietminh arrogated to themselves the credit for victory and marched into Hanoi much as Mountbatten would have liked to have done in Singapore. Their Communist cadres proclaimed novel ideas of revolution and equality; and in the now lined and scantily whiskered face of their leader, people recognised the reincarnation of the legendary 'Nguyen the Patriot'. To the vast crowds who hailed his reappearance, even to Bao Dai who now abdicated in favour of the newcomers, 'Uncle' Ho and the Vietminh represented a heaven-sent chance of peace and unity.

Paradox or Presentiment?

Across the Vietnamese frontier at Kunming in Nationalist-controlled China, the de Gaulle government had previously established a military mission to direct its agents within Vietnam. For Major Jean Sainteny, the leader of this mission, premonitions of the Vietminh's 'August Revolution' in Hanoi had overshadowed the news of the Japanese capitulation. As victory was toasted in whatever liquor the mission could lay its hands on, Sainteny sat alone brooding. When pressed for his views, the dashing Major, a Bogart look-alike and a hero of the Resistance in France, shrugged despondently.

> Indeed I did not share unreservedly in the general euphoria. So I replied as follows.
> 'For those of us whose job it is to lead France back into Indo-China the hardest part is yet to come.'
> Was this a paradox or a presentiment? I don't know, *mais, hélas, si bien dire* . . .

Two days later in distant Jakarta Indonesia was proclaiming its independence beneath Mrs Sukarno's home-made flag; a fortnight later, on the very day when MacArthur was taking the official Japanese surrender in Tokyo Bay, Hanoi celebrated its own 'Fête de l'Indépendance'. A greater contrast with the almost clandestine affair in Jakarta could hardly be imagined. Sainteny, who had by then just arrived in Hanoi as France's first post-war emissary, observed the occasion from behind the railings of the Governor-General's palace. Although installing himself there was supposed to signify the re-establishment of French authority, he was in fact a prisoner in the palace. No fan of the Vietminh, he nevertheless watched in amazement.

> I estimated the number of demonstrators at this celebration as several hundred thousand . . . The provinces were represented, their delegations filing past in national costume. Numerous Catholic priests also took part. One of the most remarkable features was the order that prevailed and in particular the absence of seditious or hostile shouting . . . even when they passed in front of the palace.

Amongst the speakers, all of whom solemnly proclaimed Vietnam's independence, were Ho Chi Minh and Vo Nguyen Giap. The latter, according to Sainteny, was 'one of the most brilliant products of our [that is, France's] culture, a distinguished graduate and doctor of law'. Of boyish demeanour in a crumpled suit, tie and trilby, he was not immediately recognisable as a military mastermind capable of engaging both the French and the American war machines. Nor did it seem likely that America would ever fall foul of the unassuming General Giap. On the contrary, Roosevelt was well known to have been as contemptuous of French rule in Indo-China as were the Vietminh. Indeed in their role as anti-Japanese partisans, members of the Vietminh had been recipients of both arms and intelligence from the United States via its Office of Strategic Services (OSS) in Nationalist China.

Reciprocating this friendship, the Vietminh leaders now prefaced their proclamation of independence with an extract from the American Declaration of Independence. That they enjoyed the support of the Americans was one of their proudest boasts. Indeed an unofficial American delegation headed by Archimedes Patti, a big-talking major in the OSS, was prominent at the independence celebrations. Sainteny, whose mission to re-establish French authority was being frustrated as much by the 'unspeakable' Patti as by the stony-faced Vietminh, could hardly mention his name without a Gallic expletive. Worse still, in the midst of the celebration, two US Lightnings staged a low-level fly-past, apparently paying their respects to the new government.

Of France's so-called Allies, only the British were showing any favours. Nine days after the 'Fête de l'Indépendance' in Hanoi, and so on the very day (11 September) that Mountbatten was staging his surrender ceremonial in Singapore, the first SEAC forces began landing in Saigon. Conditions there differed from those in the Vietminh-controlled north, and General Gracey, the SEAC commander, would be mainly concerned with rounding up the staff and troops of the Japanese High Command. Nevertheless Hanoi's newly declared Democratic Republic of Vietnam claimed the allegiance of the whole country. It took particular exception to Gracey's interventions on behalf of the frightened French citizenry of Saigon and, not without reason, it suspected the British of clearing the way for the return of French rule. One of the first measures taken by the new Hanoi government was therefore a declaration of war. Sainteny, still in detention in his palace, saw it as another example of the Vietminh's passion for mass mobilisation.

> The high point of the [Vietminh's] brainwashing came with the demonstration of 14 September 1945 which marked Vietnam's declaration of war on the British empire. Throughout this memorable day Vietnamese youths marched through the streets of Hanoi, waving, shouting and carrying banners which informed the British empire that, Vietnam having declared war, if the empire did not want to become involved in the direst catastrophes, it had no alternative but to withdraw the troops which General Gracey had just landed at Saigon!

Although never officially acknowledged, this unexpected challenge meant that for the British empire peace had lasted just twelve days. Happily for Mountbatten, the empire's involvement in Indo-China would last only slightly longer, the French being willing and able to prosecute the war themselves. It was, though, a warning. As Sainteny had feared, for the empires of the East the hardest part was yet to come. In Indonesia the British, then the Dutch, would be involved in another war which, though never declared, would last longer and be considerably more compromising. And in Malaya Communist insurgents would eventually engage the British in yet a third war of attrition which, though also undeclared, would rumble on for all of twelve years.

PART THREE

Lowering the Flag

1945–1976

11

Definition

Sunday in Batu Pahat

Not the least of the problems facing the nationalist governments which proclaimed their independence in Jakarta and Hanoi in August 1945 was that of defining the nations they represented. Observers emphasised that though the new governments appeared to enjoy overwhelming support within and around their respective capitals, their claims to represent less politicised rural, feudal and tribal populations in distant provinces were highly questionable. Except in Java, much of Tonkin and parts of Cochin-China and Sumatra, revolutionary fervour was essentially an urban phenomenon.

Creating potentially cohesive nation states had not been a prime consideration for the colonial powers. Responding to the imperatives of the moment, they had acquired territories piecemeal and then shuffled them into administratively convenient and politically manageable units. The classic example was Malaya with its four-state Federation, its five Unfederated States and its several crown colonies (the Straits Settlements). But clearly, what made a particular unit of territory, like North Borneo, administratively convenient as a source of forest produce did not necessarily make it a defensible dependency let alone a viable nation state. It was to rectify this situation that in the 1930s Clementi had explored the idea of integration. Postwar the British resumed the quest, this time with a vengeance.

The other colonial powers looked on with amazement. Perhaps the British were indeed in earnest about preparing their colonies for self-rule. Why else were they playing into the hands of nationalism? In Indo-China, after the war as before, the French were doing exactly the opposite: they were endeavouring to prolong the existence of political entities like Tonkin and Cochin-China as a way of undermining the nationalist challenge. The Dutch would go even further, creating within the Indies a jigsaw of mini-states which could not possibly survive without continued Dutch patronage.

Such policies of fragmentation were intended to counter the ambitious and all-engrossing territorial claims being advanced by Hanoi and Jakarta. For the nationalist leaderships in both cities, the freedom struggle was not just about asserting their independence or even, as in Indo-China, their ideology; it was also about asserting their territorial integrity. In the Indies this posed a particularly acute problem. Consisting of several thousand islands with a wondrous variety of peoples, the Netherlands East Indies seemed to have nothing in common with one another except their 300 years of Dutch rule. Without the 'Netherlands', in other words, the 'East Indies' became pure geography, like the 'West Indies'.

Before proclaiming a national identity, it had therefore been necessary to identify a new concept, something other than the shared experience of Dutch rule, which would define the nation and its territory. Also a new word had to be found to express it. In the nineteenth century liberal Dutch writers, while seeking some neutral term for the 'Netherlands East Indies', had come up with 'Insulinde' or 'Insulinda'. A Latin derivative meaning 'Indies Islands', it would have served the nationalists well if only it had not been a Dutch invention. Instead they preferred 'Indonesia' which means exactly the same (though from Greek rather than Latin). According to one authority the word had been coined by 'a Mr Logan in the 1840s', but this was not a widely known fact and the word's origins were therefore sufficiently uncertain to make it acceptable to nationalist opinion.

Crucially it first entered nationalist dialogue as a term used to denote the Malay language as spoken in most of the ports of the archipelago. *Bahasa Indonesia* ('the Indonesian tongue'), as it was now called, was actually the first language of very few Indonesians. But, long used as a lingua franca by the trading fraternity of south-east Asia, it did have an impressive distribution which to some extent transcended both the chaotic geography of the archipelago and its bewildering diversity of ethnic groups and religions. Here then was the new concept, the shared culture, on which a nation state could be founded. The use of *bahasa Indonesia* and its promotion throughout the Indies became a crusade in itself. From denoting an emotive language, the word was readily adopted by political activists in the 1920s to denote the country. It remained only for the Dutch to ban its use for 'Indonesia' to become the rallying cry of the new nation.

'Vietnam' seems to have had a similar provenance. Meaning the 'Free South' it appears to have enjoyed little, if any, currency until adopted by nationalist groups in the 1920s to denote the region, occasionally ruled by the emperors of Hue, in which a common language, now called Vietnamese, prevailed. The French, of course, preferred 'Indo-China', a word which like the vast territory it designated was their own grandiloquent invention. As with the Dutch term 'Netherlands East Indies', the French 'Indo-China' implied that, without the colonial strapping, the whole edifice would disintegrate into petty principalities; and by making Cochin-China a colony, Annam a protectorate and Tonkin something in between, they perpetuated this idea of fragmentation. An indigenous label, like 'Vietnam', which implied that these three units actually shared some common pre-French heritage was frowned on. The French declined to countenance the new term and thus they too obligingly endowed it with talismanic qualities for the nationalists.

No such semantic sniping occurred in British south-east Asia. This was perhaps unfortunate, since much confusion might have been avoided if only someone had coined a new term for the Malay peninsula. Instead the ethnic root word ('Malay') became so grossly overworked that 'Malay', 'Malaya(n)', and 'Malaysia(n)' came to denote different and often contradictory concepts.

The origins of the Malay language and of the peoples who speak it, the 'Malay race', lie in neighbouring Sumatra. They had much intrigued Thomas Stamford Raffles who dreamt of creating a Malay empire which would embrace all those regions where the Muslim Malays were established, from Sumatra to Malaya, Borneo and the ports of Java, Sulawesi and the Moluccas. Singapore, his island foundation, could have made the ideal port-capital for this aqueous empire. But instead of a steady influx of Malay gentleman-traders, the new city attracted a deluge of industrious Chinese immigrants – entrepreneurs, artisans, labourers. Hailing from different parts of southern China and from existing Chinese communities in south-east Asia, the Chinese who colonised Singapore and spread deep into the peninsula spoke different languages and formed numerous distinct communities. So did the Indians who, with British encouragement, also flocked to the peninsula. Both were, however, readily distinguishable from the native Malay-speaking, Allah-worshipping *bumi-putras* or 'sons of the soil', that is the Malays.

On a visit to Johore state in March 1947, the novelist Compton Mackenzie was ushered into an unprepossessing house beside the main road through Batu Pahat. As he recalled in his subsequent travelogue *All Over the Place*, it was a Sunday; the village was resting.

> Inside I was astonished to see a number of [Malay] men, mostly elderly, with notebooks in front of them squatting all round a large room with their backs to the walls. In the middle was the teacher, seated in a wicker chair at a small circular table, for this was a sort of Sunday-school class for grown-ups . . . On the other side of the road a Chinese school was having a music lesson to the accompaniment of a gramophone; and the contrast between the young voices and these elderly men taking notes on the Koran was piquant.

Both schools were privately financed by voluntary taxation of their own communities. The desire for education was impressive but not calculated to encourage integration.

As one whose *Whisky Galore* had just been published, Mackenzie was being paraded round the state as a visiting celebrity. His host was Sjovald Cunyngham-Brown, the man who had witnessed that sorry exodus of up-country planters in the dark days of January 1942 and who had since narrowly escaped execution in Sumatra. He was now installed as Johore's Deputy Resident.

> C-B addressed the elderly scholars and told them I had written over sixty books, which evidently made a profound impression. After he had finished our host asked where Cunyngham-Brown was nowadays, and on hearing that C-B was himself, almost embraced him. He pleaded his failing eyesight as an excuse for not having recognised him.

Old Malaya hands of the British colonial administration, like Cunyngham-Brown, had always tended to identify more closely with the traditional Malay hierarchies than with the clamorous immigrant communities. It was, after all, as allies and upholders of the Malay sultanates that the British had forced themselves on Malaya in the first place. Yet by 1947 Chinese and Indians accounted for nearly half the population of the four-state Malay Federation. In the Unfederated Malay States Chinese and Indian 'Malayans' (as they were known so as to distinguish them from Malays) were less well represented. Consequently in Malaya as a whole there were less 'Malayans' than Malays. But if to the peninsula were added the considerable populations of the islands of Singapore and Penang (which area was then known in its totality as 'Malaysia'), the Chinese and Indian 'Malayans' were slightly more numerous than the native Malays.

In short, the elderly Malay gentlemen at their Sunday school were in danger of being drowned out by the youthful Chinese chorus across the road. From a British point of view the ethnic tension which resulted had possibilities. According to cynics it was why, for instance, they could cheerfully buck the trend and pursue that goal of political integration. In a country with such an obvious religio-ethnic fault-line the chances of any nationalist movement stabilising the tectonic action long enough to win the support of both native Malays and immigrant Malayans looked impossibly remote. With a clear conscience and utter conviction the British could advocate self-rule and work conscientiously towards it while, in the words of the historian Nicholas Tarling, 'contemplating the joyously long time it would take, the constructive employment it would offer, or the influence it would confer'.

A Disgusting Concept

Not even the Japanese had been able to fan the flames of nationalism in Malaya. As described by one writer, it was more like 'trying to start a fire with damp wood'. The dampest sticks, given that Japan was at war with China, were of course the Chinese Malayans. As generous contributors to both the Nationalist and the Communist war effort in China, they were clearly beyond the reach of Japanese propaganda. Throughout the occupation of Malaya they were treated with extreme hostility. Many thousands were killed and not surprisingly it was Malayan Chinese who composed the Malayan Peoples' Anti-Japanese Army (MPAJA), the main guerrilla resistance to Japanese rule.

The Malays, on the other hand, had less to fear from the invaders. The Malay sultans and their governing hierarchies were co-opted into the Japanese administration and collaborated with their Japanese Governors much as they had previously with their British Residents and Advisers. As in Java, the Japanese saw mobilisation of the masses as essential to their war effort and were soon organising study groups, Co-Prosperity demonstrations, slogan-writing competitions and Japanese language courses. Religious councils were set up to emphasise Japanese respect for Islam, and there was also recruitment for an armed militia or PETA. Malays, a people whom the British had usually written off as far too easy-going even for civic activities, began to acquire a taste for politics. Amongst those who responded to the new propaganda was Dato Onn bin Ja'afar, the man who would soon emerge as the Malays' first political leader. 'Under the Japanese I learnt that an Asian is just as good as a European . . . [The Japanese] were brutal, true, but they inspired us with a new idea of what Asia might become.'

Unlike in Java, however, the Japanese made no mention of independence. With its vast production of rubber and tin, plus iron and bauxite of which the Japanese economy was in direst need, Malaya was considered economically too important to be other than a directly ruled Japanese colony. It was the same with Sumatra, whence came also oil. In fact these two areas were so crucial to the Japanese war effort that Sumatra was detached from what had been the Netherlands East Indies and combined with Malaya under the military administration based in 'Shonan' (as Singapore was now called). In 1943 a reverse adjustment was made in the north of Malaya when four of the poorer erstwhile Malay states were transferred back to Thai sovereignty whence they had been wrenched by the British in the previous century.

This redrawing of the colonial boundaries had interesting repercussions. By negating the territorial carve-up of the region between the British and the Dutch, the Japanese had, perhaps inadvertently, restored the ancient links between Malaya and Sumatra and so gone some way towards creating the Malay empire of which Raffles had dreamt. The new Sumatra-Malaya entity particularly delighted the Union of Young Malays (KMM), a small group of radical intellectuals which had been formed in Perak in 1938. Suspicious alike of Western colonialism and of its Asian protégés, the immigrant Indians and Chinese, the KMM had been advocating pan-Malay unity under the banner of *Indonesia Raya*, or 'Greater Indonesia'. More a slogan than a geographical description, *Indonesia Raya* demonstrated the elasticity of the concept of 'Indonesia' and would come to haunt the politics of the peninsula for the next decade. For if 'Indonesia' embraced all those who spoke *bahasa Indonesia*, which was the same as the Malay language, then it could indeed include Malaya, and also Sarawak and North Borneo. Sukarno in particular was alert to the possibilities thus opened, and he would bear them in mind.

Indonesia Raya was not, however, a catch-phrase that won any prizes in those Japanese-sponsored slogan-writing competitions. The Japanese administration rewarded the KMM's support by disbanding it as potentially subversive of East Asian Co-Prosperity; and in 1944 they actually restored Sumatra to the Indies in line with their just avowed sponsorship of Indonesian independence.

The preparations for Indonesian independence could not but attract interest, even envy, amongst Malays in Malaya. But towards the end of the war they had more immediate concerns. Acute shortages of rice and most other foodstuffs led to fierce, indeed cut-throat, competition for land holdings as ethnic tension between Malays and Chinese Malayans degenerated into ethnic massacres.

In July 1945, in a last-minute bid to stimulate opposition to any Allied invasion of Malaya, the Japanese administration abruptly reversed its opposition to Malay independence and endorsed the idea of Malay autonomy within 'Greater Indonesia'. Ibrahim Yacoob, an ex-KMM activist, was authorised to meet with the Indonesian leaders Sukarno and Hatta, and to form KRIS, a pro-Indonesian revolutionary group. As in Indonesia, the plan was to enlist the support of the paramilitary PETA, join forces with the MPAJA guerrillas, and take advantage of Japanese stocks of military hardware to defy the Allies in the name of *Indonesia Raya*. With weeks to prepare it might have worked. But Japan's sudden surrender after the bombing of Hiroshima and Nagasaki found KRIS hopelessly disorganised and isolated. It also brought the Chinese guerrillas of the MPAJA out of their jungle hide-outs to pose as the victors. Instead of making common cause with Malay nationalists, the guerrillas were more intent on settling old scores with the Japanese-sponsored PETA and the mainly Malay police. Ibrahim Yacoob fled the scene in frustration; KRIS, like a sacred heirloom, went underground for safe-keeping.

Improbably it was the British, usually adept at letting sleeping dogs lie, who brought Malay paranoia back to life. During the war, with three and a half years in which to reflect on its rule in Malaya, the Colonial Office had come up with a new blueprint for the whole of British south-east Asia. The lessons of 1942 had been learnt. Both Malays and Malayans must now be given a greater and, crucially, an equal stake in the country. A common citizenship would be introduced for both. The proliferation of administrations must be rationalised and centralised. This meant that the sultans, while retaining their personal authority, must surrender their sovereignty, and that their states, while retaining their identity, must surrender their autonomy. Instead of the FMS and the UMS and the Straits Settlements, there would be a single unitary state, the Malayan Union, to which in due course Sarawak, North Borneo and Brunei could also belong. The Union would have a central government and would prepare the country for self-rule under British auspices. Only Singapore was excluded, a move partly dictated by its military importance and partly designed to reassure Malays by excluding its predominantly Chinese population, thus preserving the Malays' majority status within the Union.

A masterplan on this scale, etched on tablets of stone in Whitehall and then implemented with what would appear unseemly haste, was devastatingly un-British. What of that famous pragmatism? What about consultation, flexibility, gradualism? Edward Gent, the official mainly responsible for the scheme, evidently felt that the opportunity for a clean sweep was too good to miss. The British would be returning victorious. Arriving in strength amongst a chastened populace, they could organise the new set-up while the country was still under military administration. Restoring the dollar-earning Malayan economy, an imperial priority second to none, also demanded speedy implementation of the plan.

Yet even the Colonial Office may have had qualms, for it kept the whole plan secret. When, a month after Mountbatten had staged the uncontested 'Zipper' invasion, Sir Harold MacMichael set off for Malaya to visit each of its sultans as a special emissary of the British government, his mission was still a mystery.

Back in Britain the men who had won a world war were being demobilised. As a reward they received whatever pittance was their due by way of back-pay, plus a 'demob suit' in which to launch themselves back into civilian life. The suit, a dark two-piece outfit, came in half a dozen sizes but was negotiable neither as to colour nor cut. It was thus as recognisably a uniform as that which it replaced, although it often fitted worse. In much the same spirit, MacMichael confronted each of the Malay sultans with an identical piece of constitutional tailoring designed to end their sovereign status. No variation was possible and refusal was not an option.

Some sultans, anxious about their wartime record of collaboration with the Japanese, donned their new outfits with a sign of relief. Others, who had succeeded to their thrones during the Japanese occupation, saw its uniform cut as welcome evidence of British recognition. Very few consulted their state councils, partly because they were given no time. 'The technique adopted by His Majesty's Government appeared to be not unlike the familiar Japanese technique of bullying,' recalled the Sultan of Kedah. He did insist on consultation but, like others, eventually signed on the dotted line 'because no other course was open to me'. In under two months, having kitted out all nine sultans, MacMichael was back in London with a bag full of signatures.

The government issued its White Paper a few days later on 22 January 1946. In both London and Malaya the outcry was instantaneous. Probably no colonial directive has ever been greeted with such universal condemnation. Bristling with indignation, a home-based caucus of ex-governors rushed into print with damning letters and articles in the British press. Sir Frank Swettenham, Sir Richard Winstedt, Sir George Maxwell, Sir Cecil Clementi, men who had often found themselves bitterly opposing one another in the past, united in decrying both the Union as a flagrant betrayal of Britain's original commitments to the sultans, and the method of enforcing it as tantamount to blackmail. Objections from these 'white knights' of the past were not unexpected. Nor was the disquiet of old Malay hands like Cunyngham-Brown. He was then in up-state Johore doing the rounds of his subordinates.

> The District Officer was an acquaintance of mine, a very friendly acquaintance. Nothing can indicate the burning anger of the Malays, rightly so, against this disgusting Malayan Union concept. He didn't get up when I came in. He asked me what I wanted. I said 'I've come to see if there is anything I can do.' He said 'Yes, you may leave.' Well, I mean, imagine, an officer, a superior officer [being treated] in that manner. And yet I could not dislike him because that is exactly what I felt myself.

Yet even the disgust of the Malayan Civil Service was as nothing to the instant protest launched by the supposedly dozy Malay masses. Two days after the issue of the White Paper, Dato Onn bin Ja'afar proposed a Malay congress in Kuala Lumpur to organise nation-wide opposition. The congress met on 1 March. Two hundred representatives attended from all over the peninsula and duly formed the United Malay National Organisation (UMNO) to oppose the new constitution. Dato Onn, the spindly and bespectacled scion of a family which had regularly supplied Johore state with its chief ministers, was elected President. He thus became what the popular press called 'the Malay Gandhi' while UMNO, with its broad and lasting appeal, became the would-be equivalent of India's Congress Party.

UMNO's first move was to address the British government, declaring in no uncertain terms that the MacMichael treaties were invalid and demanding the repeal of the Union. The new constitution was due to be inaugurated – and Edward Gent, its instigator, sworn in as High Commissioner – on 1 April. UMNO made sure that it was indeed April Fools' Day by successfully organising a total boycott of the ceremony. Lesser boycotts throughout the country threatened the vital work of economic recovery. The Malay press was now calling the Union 'a kick in the pants', and likening the plight of the Malays, forced to acknowledge the equal citizenship of non-Malays, to that of other endangered indigenous peoples. Sideways glances were again being cast across the Java Sea to Indonesia. Unwittingly, the most docile and profitable piece of imperial real estate in the East had been turned into a hotbed of political ferment.

Six months earlier the British, alone amongst the European colonial powers, had been received back with enthusiasm; 'they were coming out of their houses waving and cheering'; it was 'like a bridegroom entering the bridal chamber'. Yet scarcely had the groom bounded over the threshold than he behaved, in Richard Winstedt's words, 'as if it was an Augean stable'. Unsurprisingly the incensed bride withdrew her favours and threatened divorce.

Amazed by this display of pique and alarmed at the prospect of an Indonesian-style independence struggle, by May even Gent was arguing for adjustments to the new constitution. Whitehall was not amused. The High Commissioner was, however, supported by his superior, the Governor-General in Singapore. Both argued that the Union was not actually essential; a new rationalised Federation could serve the same centralising purpose. To this end negotiations with UMNO were opened in August and would drag on until the end of the year. The Union was indeed jettisoned, and a new Federation of Malay States came into being a year later in January 1948.

Malay objections had focused on the transfer of sovereignty implicit in the MacMichael treaties, and on the provisions for equal citizenship. According to Dato Onn, by signing away their sovereignty to the Union the sultans had unwittingly made Malaya, instead of a collection of protected states, a 'colony with no rights'. This was

not quite correct. The status of the Union was still that of a protectorate. He was right, though, in seeing the centralised Union as
tightening the bonds of empire rather than loosening them.
Moreover, under Malay customary law sovereignty was revealed as
something that the sultans were not entitled to discard without con-
sulting their subjects. Therefore the treaties were invalid and their
replacements involved an acknowledgement of something close to
popular sovereignty.

The British also gave ground over the issue of citizenship. Under
the Union a common citizenship was available both to native Malays
and to Chinese and Indian Malayans subject to a minimal residential
requirement. Although the principle of common citizenship was
now retained, the residential requirement was considerably tightened
up. Instead of practically all non-Malays qualifying, only a few could
immediately enjoy citizenship, although provision was made for a
gradual increase.

On both counts the new Federation therefore satisfied most
Malays and restored a modified, because more broadly based, Anglo-
Malay consensus which would last until independence. But at a
considerable cost. Chinese Malayans, who had supported the Union
and especially its citizenship proposals, were bitterly disillusioned.
Their guerrilla fighters, the MPAJA, despite their Communist sympathies, had recently been fêted as war heroes and paraded in
London. Chin Peng, one of their leaders, had actually been congrat-
ulated by Mountbatten and awarded the OBE. Now, it seemed,
Chinese Malayans were again being treated as immigrants and
second-class subjects. The Malayan Communist Party (MCP), of
which Chin Peng was about to be elected Secretary-General, would
find a ready audience for its anti-colonial rhetoric.

At the other end of the political spectrum, the new Federation
also failed to satisfy radical Malay opinion. The left-wing Malay
Nationalist Party (MNP), a descendant of the pre-war KMM and
likewise wedded to the idea of *Indonesia Raya*, had been steering an
erratic course, first welcoming the Union as a step towards independence, then opposing it as anti-Malay, then opposing the new
Federation as collaborationist. Hopelessly upstaged by UMNO, the
party was being steadily marginalised. Yet it continued to pursue the
dream of a pan-Malay state and it was not alone. 'Most young Malay
liberals hope for an ultimate union with Indonesia,' reported the
American writer James Michener as late as 1951. He quoted in

particular the words of Dato Onn: 'What I would really like to see would be the establishment of a great Pan-Malay Union consisting of Malaya, Indonesia, Borneo, and perhaps the Philippines.'

But the moment had passed. The real significance of the Malayan Union crisis is that the British had been forced to choose. Alienating their Malay subjects meant risking a pan-Malay backlash; alienating their Malayan subjects meant risking a Communist backlash. They chose the latter, thus remaindering *Indonesia Raya* to the shelves of Rafflesian fantasy and of Jakartan demagoguery while promoting Malayan Communism to the forefront of international struggle. Within six months of the new Federation being inaugurated the country would be plunged into a war which the British, obsessed with understatement and with sustaining business confidence, insisted on calling an 'emergency'.

The Last Days of the White Raj

While visiting Singapore in 1951, James Michener met other opponents of the Malayan Union, one of them being 'a young Englishman . . . witty and wise in many things . . . [with] a cleft chin, a rounded face and the gentle half-stumbling accent of a P. G. Wodehouse hero'. This was Anthony Brooke, the nephew of Sarawak's Rajah Vyner Brooke and the man long regarded as his most likely successor. Anthony, no longer that young (he was 39), still considered himself *rajah muda* (crown prince) of Sarawak, and he arrived for dinner with Michener in a car from which still flew the yellow flag with the red and blue cross of Sarawak. It was its last outing. 'A pity really,' he told Michener, but 'I've gone and done it.'

> No recriminations. Never a second chance on this one. This morning I surrendered all claims to be the white Rajah of Sarawak. A ruling family came to an end today. By voluntary action I gave up substantial claims to land larger than England . . . Today marks the end of a kingdom.

According to Brooke, the trouble had all begun after the war when his uncle had sold out to the British government for £1 million. More money had changed hands to secure a majority in the State Council in favour of becoming a British colony. It was at the time of the Malayan Union proposal and was all part of the same policy. Yet the peoples of Sarawak had not been properly consulted. Indeed they had been protesting ever since, and Anthony had every sympathy for them.

> I am morally convinced that Britain played me a foul trick. They tried the same thing here in Malaya, but the natives made them back down. No colonial status for Malays. I was the one on whom the trick worked.

Whether this version of events aroused Michener's suspicions is not recorded. He surely had his reservations. Michener, after all, was the author whose monumental researches so gutted his subjects and so overwhelmed his readers that the 'blockbuster' became an accepted literary genre. He must also have known that, amidst the Byzantine complexities of Brooke rule, nothing had ever been that simple. Nor was it in the last days of the White Raj.

It will be recalled that in 1941, just before the Japanese invasion, the Raj had celebrated its centenary. The reclusive Rajah Vyner, roused from his habitual indolence by several brandies and the importuning of the Rani Sylvia, had attended in person and had taken advantage of the occasion to alter the constitution. By derogating his personal prerogatives to a Supreme Council and by accepting the presence of a permanent British 'Representative', he had apparently demoted himself to the role of a constitutional monarch. This served a number of purposes. It gave the Raj a veneer of liberal respectability; it frustrated the ambitions of the tiresome Anthony, his presumed successor; and, most important of all, it relieved the Rajah's pressing financial obligations by securing to him as a *quid pro quo* £200,000 from state funds.

As usual the negotiations had been largely handled by the Rajah's plausible but decidedly devious 'secretary', Gerald MacBryan. Indeed MacBryan, to whose Bornean lifestyle intrigue was as natural as perspiration, probably dreamt up the whole scheme. He had his own agenda, much of it involving romantic alliances with ladies of the Brooke and Brunei royal families and all aimed at securing the highest office, if not the Raj itself, for Gerald MacBryan. Even war had barely interrupted his ambitions. He had been 'holidaying' with the Rajah in Australia when Japan struck. For a variety of reasons, not least that of securing the state treasury, he had quickly tried to regain Kuching only to be arrested in Dutch Borneo on suspicion of trying to arrange for Sarawak's collaboration with the Japanese. After a spell in Singapore's Changi gaol, he was released shortly before the city's fall and, on the Rajah's surety, readmitted to Australia.

What part MacBryan played in the wartime negotiations between the Rajah and the Colonial Office is unclear. The 1945 decision to cede Sarawak to the British government seems to have been Vyner's. Although under the 1941 constitution it was not technically his to make, he could justly claim that ceding Sarawak to the British crown had been the ambition of both his predecessors. More to the point, the cost of the post-war rehabilitation of the country would clearly be beyond the means of the Raj. With the North Borneo Company agreeing to a similar cession of Sabah for precisely this reason, and with a Labour government in London clearly determined to remove what it chose to regard as feudal anachronisms, the time had come to call it a day.

Additionally there were excellent reasons of a more personal nature for 'ending the kingdom'. The Rajah's chronic lassitude scarcely concealed the fact that he was horribly bored with the place and perfectly indifferent to the burdens of office. Naming King George VI as the next ruler of Sarawak solved the invidious issue of his succession and nicely spited the ambitious Anthony. And finally there was every prospect of another juicy cash settlement.

The story of Judas and his thirty pieces of silver is said to have leapt to the mission-educated minds of Sarawak's Christian community. But before the pay-out, and before the British crown could lay claim to its last belated colony, some indication of Sarawak's concurrence in these arrangements was considered essential. The State Council, which included a few hand-picked representatives of the local Malay, Chinese and Dayak communities, would have to approve. And since this approval could not be taken for granted, the Rajah appointed an agent to organise matters in Sarawak much as the British had dispatched MacMichael to Malaya. Primed with £55,000 in cash to distribute by way of inducements, and despite the grave misgivings of the Colonial Office, the man chosen for this delicate task was Gerald MacBryan.

While MacMichael did the rounds of Malaya's sultans, MacBryan corralled the leading figures in Sarawak. Adopting a variety of dubious expedients, he duly secured the requisite signatures and, hard on MacMichael's heels, returned to London in January 1946. News of Sarawak's cession was then published and occasioned a reaction scarcely more favourable than that shown by Clementi and his fellow 'white knights' to the Malayan Union. 'BRITAIN BUYS SARAWAK' read the headline in the *Standard*. A £1 million trust fund set up for the Rajah and his dependents was widely seen as a pay-off and was welcomed as such by the tactless Rani; to celebrate this 'compensation' she threw one of her always extravagant parties in a London nightspot. Meanwhile Bertram Brooke, the Rajah's ailing brother, and Anthony, Bertram's son, mustered opposition. When MacBryan's methods came in for critical scrutiny in Parliament, the British government felt obliged to admit that from a legal point of view the cession was less than satisfactory. The £1 million trust fund was shelved; instead, the Rajah would get a not inconsiderable £200,000. And another attempt was made to establish that cession to the British crown met with the approval of Sarawak's people.

This time both the Rajah and his brother were to visit Kuching. So were various observers including two Members of Parliament and a Colonial Office official. The MPs baulked at too arduous an exploration of local opinion and the supposedly impartial man from the CO was under no illusions as to the outcome desired by the British government. All were, however, impressed by the strength of anti-cession feeling. 'No Cession', 'Hands Off Sarawak', 'We Want Brooke Rule' proclaimed the banners. In the 1941 constitution there had been specific mention of eventual self-rule for Sarawak. Colonial status was seen as distancing this prospect, while the probable incorporation of the country into a Malayan Union or Federation seemed to preclude all possibility of an independent Sarawak. Nationalists as well as monarchists therefore opposed cession.

Yet their banners of protest were as nothing to the flags and the crowds which welcomed the returning Vyner. The mystique of the White Rajah was undeniable. His authority still counted and his support for cession, however lackadaisical, carried the day. By a slender margin, and not without some distinctly eighteenth-century 'management', the State Council approved the Rajah's transfer of Sarawak sovereignty from himself to the British government. Sensitive Whitehall consciences were mollified. Anti-cessionists had to content themselves with boycotts, resignations and more protests.

'The Sarawak Nineteen'

'The die is cast,' wrote Duncan Stewart exactly three years later when he accepted the Governorship of Sarawak. After postings in Palestine and Bermuda, Stewart had serious misgivings about asking his wife and young family to share the hardships of the Empire's last and least known acquisition. But for a 45-year-old colonial servant a governorship was decidedly flattering and, as his ship nosed up the Kuching River, he was pleasantly surprised to find the place 'much less flat and uninviting than I had expected'. The sun shone, the police band played in front of the fort, and the royal sampan was waiting to whisk Stewart from the steamer to the *istana*. As he confided to his diary, 14 November 1949 'was a day of unreality'. It was also a day of ill omen.

> Before this, and until I had finally disembarked at the *[i]stana*, the most noticeable feature was the parade of anti-cession boats and the display of placards along the bank of the river. Apparently rather more than had been expected . . . These notices usually said 'We don't want Governor. We want Rajah of our choice.'

It must also have been somewhat galling to be making his grand entry into Kuching aboard a ship called the SS *Rajah Brooke*. In Malaya, where Stewart had stopped for briefings and consultations, he had noted the presence of various Brookes, including Anthony. They were holidaying in a governor's residence. As Anthony was still encouraging the anti-cessionists and so was banned from visiting Sarawak, Stewart had made no attempt to contact him.

Ensconced in the Rajah's *istana*, the new Governor spent his first two weeks exploring Kuching and getting to know his staff. A meeting of the new colony's Supreme Council reminded him of Alice in Wonderland. Sarawak's yellow flag had now been replaced by the Union Jack but, when he attended the sounding of the retreat (that is, the Last Post) at the police barracks, a tropical storm sent the bandsmen scattering for cover with the rendition still incomplete and the flag at half-mast. Much more successful was the St Andrew's Night dinner-dance to which Stewart's kilt and Argyll ancestry lent unwonted authenticity. On the whole it had been a successful beginning. Well pleased with matters, he left for Sibu, the colony's second city, on 2 December.

Next day, having sailed up the Rejang River, he had just inspected the guard of honour at Sibu's landing-stage when he was confronted by a smiling young man. Apparently a press photographer, the young man produced a *kris*, the long Malay dagger, and plunged it into the Governor. Stewart was rushed to Sibu's Residency but died a few days later. He had been in office barely three weeks. A more innocent victim of the Brooke family's machinations, of Sarawak's confused loyalties, and of the British government's post-war mishandling of Malay affairs could scarcely have been found.

The assassin, a 19-year-old Malay called Rosli bin Dhoby, was found to belong to a radical anti-cessionist splinter group against which the government now moved with vindictive intent. Nineteen Malays were convicted, Rosli and three others being hanged while the rest received long gaol sentences. Although the sentences were harsh, moderate opinion throughout Sarawak was genuinely outraged by the assassination and there was widespread support for the subsequent clamp-down on nationalist and anti-cessionist activity.

Even Anthony Brooke began to have second thoughts about his continued support of the anti-cessionists. Disclaiming any responsibility and blaming the whole affair on Rosli's supposed Communist sympathies, plus the government's refusal to take Sarawak separatism seriously, he was nevertheless appalled by the assassination. Hence, as he explained to Michener in 1951, the time had come 'to close ranks'. As Brooke saw it, if the choice was now 'between a Communist Sarawak and a free British colony I must in honour choose the latter'. That was why, on his way to dine with the American writer, he had stopped by the Governor-General's office to inform the British authorities that he was 'throwing in the sponge'.

More obviously, Stewart's death seemed finally to have discredited the vestigial romance of the White Raj. Yet twenty years later, the affair was given a new gloss when the actions of Rosli and his companions were re-examined in a Malaysian context. 'Malaysia' was now the term used to designate the territories of Malaya, Sarawak and Sabah which had at last been united. A new nation needed a new and, preferably, an anti-colonial pedigree. With martyrs for the cause of Malayan, let alone Malaysian, freedom noticeably lacking, the 'Sarawak Nineteen' were resurrected. Their loyalty to the most extreme form of white paternalism was forgotten, and their dedication to Sarawak separatism travestied. Instead, Tunku Abdul Rahman, the first Prime Minister of Malaysia, hailed them as heroes of Malaysia's fictitious freedom struggle.

> These nineteen men were the first Malay patriots to suffer in the cause of independence . . . The Imperialist government was determined to make an example of them, but their action, instead of quenching the flame of patriotism in the hearts of the Malay people, produced quite the opposite

effect. It kindled afresh a new spirit of Independence, and this was how many young Malays began to change their attitude towards their British 'rulers'.

All Over the Place

Attitudes were certainly changing, but in Britain's eastern colonies the change was as much amongst the rulers as the ruled. Arguably the main difference between the British empire in the East and that of France or the Netherlands had been not its commercial character, nor its strategic supremacy, nor even the Royal Navy's vaunted capacity to uphold it. The main difference was, and in 1946 remained (though not for much longer), India. It was India's eastern trade which first made the Far East attractive, India's opium which then made it so immensely profitable, and India's manpower which made its retention so cheap.

Under the aegis of empire, India's vast service industry – Parsee entrepreneurs, Gujerati shopkeepers, Bengali servants – spread throughout the East. Indentured Tamil labourers in their hundreds of thousands tapped the rubber trees for the empire's most valuable export. Turbanned Sikhs policed Singapore and Shanghai, and drove the locomotives on Malaya's railways; conspicuously they also manned the doors of every up-market hotel from Penang's exclusive Eastern and Oriental to the Hong Kong Hilton. More crucially, Indian troops comprised the bulk of the garrison wherever there was a barracks to house them. The Rajput Horse clattered over the cobbles of Shanghai in the 1930s; Gurkhas were still manning the hill-top outposts along Hong Kong's frontier with China in the 1990s. When striking miners occupied Malaya's single coal mine in 1936 it was a Punjabi regiment which shot their way in and overcame the strikers. In the First World War the only major scare in the East had come when a Sikh regiment mutinied in Singapore. In the Second World War the only British troops that could be spared for Sarawak were those Punjabis who discovered a new use for condoms.

Commissioned in 1946 to chronicle the wartime exploits of the Indian army, Sir Compton Mackenzie had decided to visit every re-levant battlefield. It meant travelling from Tunisia to Java and it was while thus visiting Malaya that he happened to meet Cunyngham-Brown at the height of the Malayan Union crisis. Five years earlier, during the Japanese invasion of Malaya, Indian troops had out-numbered the British and Australians combined. Mackenzie's sympathies went out especially to the 45th Brigade. Comprised of Rajputs and Pathans trained for desert fighting, in December 1941 the brigade had been *en route* to north Africa when their ship was suddenly ordered to turn around. 'Although most of the troops had never seen a tree', they were deployed against the Japanese in the deepest jungle warfare ever fought.

The title of Mackenzie's subsequent book, *All Over the Place: Fifty Thousand Miles by Sea, Air, Road and Rail,* said it all. Nowhere east of Gibraltar had Indian troops not been involved. It had been the same in the First World War when the Mesopotamian campaign had relied almost exclusively on Indian forces. Ever since India had been British it had supplied the one necessity of empire which the British Isles were neither able nor willing to contribute, a vast land army. It is no exaggeration to say that on India's apparently unlimited capacity to supply loyal and disciplined troops at no expense to the United Kingdom depended the empire in the East.

In the course of his battlefield tour Mackenzie found Indian troops still at their posts; at dusk in Kuala Lumpur, for instance, it was a Gurkha bugler who sounded the 'Retreat'. There were, however, less of them. For the year was now 1947. Mackenzie's work was by way of an epitaph. India was about to gain its independence; the 'Retreat' for the Indian army was being sounded all over the East. Thereafter only Nepalese Gurkhas would be available for British recruitment.

Without India, ever 'the jewel in the crown', there would be a gaping hole in the imperial conceit. It had never been the largest empire in the Far East nor the most senior; now it was no longer the most prestigious. In fact, since the King-Emperor was technically emperor only of India, it was arguably no longer an empire. There were still British colonies and, of course, a British Commonwealth; but of 'Empire' progressively less was heard. Within a decade, Empire Day had become Commonwealth Day and the Imperial Institute the Commonwealth Institute. Along with India went, it seemed, not only the Indian army but also the imperial appetite. Like one stricken with senile impotence, the British found that losing the means to perform coincided with losing the inclination. In Malaya and elsewhere their only option appeared to be ritual foreplay followed by an embarrassed withdrawal.

Yet it was not all bad news. Liberal being laudable in the post-war UN-led consensus, India's loss had a positive side: its independence could be portrayed as incontrovertible evidence of British good faith. Making necessity the mother of, in this case, intention, the British could portray themselves as having accommodated India's aspirations and selflessly surrendered its sovereignty. Who now could question the sincerity of their commitment to self-government and eventual independence for all their colonies? And who could deny that the British built well, leaving in south Asia not one but two strong, friendly and democratic nation states?

Losing the Indian army was undoubtedly a disaster; without his dogs, the imperial shepherd would be at a serious disadvantage. But perhaps he no longer needed them. A flock convinced that its interests were being well served might never stray. And if there were no strays, perhaps the wolves, north American as well as Russian, would keep their distance. It was an exciting challenge. It was also gratifying to be, for once, on the right side of the moral argument.

No such warming thoughts coursed through Dutch and French minds. India might slip beneath the horizon, but its shadow would still divide the British from the other European colonial powers. In 1944 the Brazzaville Conference presided over by de Gaulle had considered the future of the French colonies. Much was said about affording colonial subjects a greater say in their affairs; even Roosevelt was impressed. Yet amongst the conclusions of the Conference appeared two sentences of unambiguous intent which literally translate as follows.

> The objectives of the task of civilisation undertaken by France in the colonies exclude all idea of autonomy, all possibility of evolution outside the French block of the Empire. The eventual, even remote, creation of *self-gouvernements* in the colonies is excluded.

Overseas territories like Indo-China were regarded as part of France; their inhabitants could become French citizens, their deputies sat in the French parliament. *Self-gouvernement* would be tantamount to secession; it was therefore unthinkable. It tarnished the unique, all-embracing character of French civilisation and it struck at the *amour propre* of every Frenchman. For France the retention of empire was a matter of principle.

For the Netherlands it was more a question of necessity. In the nineteenth century, thanks to the wealth of the Indies, Holland had recovered from the Napoleonic excesses and transformed itself into a prosperous, integrated and enviable European power. To rise from the ashes of the Second World War and to avoid, as one Dutch statesman put it, 'becoming another Denmark', it desperately needed again to mobilise the resources and prestige of its eastern empire. Concessions to nationalism, if desirable, would only be considered after Dutch rule had been re-established and after *rust en ordre* were restored; as much 'peace and quiet' as 'law and order', this cherished condition was considered operative when the Indies economy was performing to expectations.

The only Dutch statement of post-war colonial intentions had come in a broadcast made by Queen Wilhelmina in 1942. Given in English, it was intended for an international audience, not for the Indonesians. It promised a conference to consider reorganising the Netherlands, the Indies, Surinam and Curaçao (the other Dutch colonies) into a commonwealth based on 'partnership' and 'self-reliance'. There was also to be greater native participation in government and no racial discrimination. President Roosevelt rated Dutch rule the least heinous of colonialisms; by this exceedingly vague pronouncement he was therefore reassured. When MacArthur's leap-frogging advance towards the Philippines brushed the corner of the Dutch Indies in what is now Irian Jaya and at Morotai in the Moluccas, van Mook secured agreement for Dutch civil administrators to ride along with the Americans and install themselves in their wake. In out-of-the-way places where the sparse population had scarcely heard of Indonesia, let alone its aspirations to independence, this arrangement worked well.

Whether it would have done so in Java is doubtful. Van Mook reportedly opposed the last-minute transfer of the island from MacArthur's South West Pacific Area Command to Mountbatten's South East Asia Command. Presumably he felt that the USA's prestige and overwhelming resources would make reoccupation easier. Yet the US commitment to self-determination could scarcely have ignored the claims of the new Republic of Indonesia. No one denied Dutch sovereignty over the Indies, but whilst for the Dutch the problem remained that of how to re-establish it, for everyone else it soon became a question of how quickly it could be dismantled.

Compton Mackenzie's determination to visit all the battle sites where Indian troops had lately been involved was frustrated only in respect of Java. Waiting in Singapore, he was told that transport was not available, then that the trip would have to be cancelled; it was 'because the Indonesians shoot at planes'. That there had been post-war battles in Java was no secret, but that the place was still 'unsafe' in early 1947 seems to have taken Mackenzie by surprise. At a cost of over 1,000 British and Indian lives, plus at least twenty times that number of Indonesians, the British had just left, their task supposedly completed. With immense relief Indonesia's disasters, after a year in the headlines, were being relegated to the news agencies, its unfathomable problems left to the Dutch. For the British and their Indian army, it had been an unhappy experience.

In this, its swan-song, the loyalty of the Indian army would be tested to the limit; so would that of the few British troops involved in Indonesia. The patience of a succession of negotiators would be exhausted. Ruffled feathers would be evident even in the impeccable plumage of Admiral Lord Louis Mountbatten. If he, at least, was not ungrateful it was because the lessons of Indonesia would serve him well in his new assignment as Viceroy-cum-liquidator of British India.

I 2

Mass Merdeka

Fair Deal in Bandung

Back in 1945, Mountbatten's South East Asia Command (SEAC) forces, though ill-briefed, inadequately manned and long delayed, had begun arriving in Jakarta on 29 September. Their role, as in Indo-China, was to disarm and repatriate the occupying Japanese, to assist in the release and, where necessary, repatriation of prisoners-of-war and civilian internees, and to re-establish peaceful conditions preparatory to handing over authority to the civil administration. It was assumed that the country was still controlled by the Japanese in accordance with the terms of their surrender, and that the incoming administration would be that of the Dutch. That being the case, it looked a simple enough operation.

Intelligence gathered by, especially, Laurens van der Post shattered this illusion. The Japanese High Command located at Bandung in west Java had picked out van der Post as the most acceptable prisoner in its numerous camps to whom to surrender. An idiosyncratic officer with mystical tendencies but decidedly progressive ideas, van der Post left little doubt as to where his sympathies would lie. Fluent in Japanese, Dutch and Malay, he was well-informed about events outside the barbed wire and he immediately extended his knowledge by touring the other camps in the area before travelling the 200 miles to Jakarta. There he made contact with the first SEAC reconnaissance parties and, as the most senior British officer (albeit one born in South Africa) with first-hand knowledge of the country, in mid-September he was whisked off to Ceylon, where were SEAC's headquarters. Mountbatten, greatly impressed by his insights, immediately sent him on to London.

His message was simple. The Japanese were no longer in control of Java. An effective nationalist government had been formed. It enjoyed popular support and a considerable defensive capability. The Dutch would have to negotiate with it, and SEAC would have to work with it even if this meant prejudicing the re-establishment of Dutch rule. As van der Post would recall in *A Walk with a White Bushman*, one of several later memoirs, the Dutch could expect no favours from the British.

> We cannot help the Dutch over this. We have just been through a world war and this is not the purpose for which we have been through it. We, the British, are dismantling our empire. How can we fight a colonial war on behalf of the Dutch?

From London, the Prime Minister Clement Attlee sent him on to Holland. Still short of laundry and little more than a walking skeleton after the starvation regime in Bandung, he collapsed with hiccups during dinner with the Dutch prime minister. Unlike Attlee, Dr Schermerhorn led a fragile and provisional government. Any lowering of Dutch expectations in the Indies was therefore out of the question. So were negotiations with the nationalists and their 'so-called' Republic. Wartime collaboration with the Germans being a burning issue in the Netherlands, no Dutch government could think of dealing with Indonesian 'quislings' like Sukarno and Hatta.

After a short recuperation van der Post returned to Java as Mountbatten's personal envoy. SEAC's British Indian troops were by then established in Jakarta (which now, briefly, reverted to the Dutch 'Batavia'). Van der Post could not help being reminded of the last time British Indian troops had served in 'Batavia'. This was during the occupation of the island in the Napoleonic Wars when Raffles had become what van der Post considered 'the most imaginative leader that Sumatra and Java ever had'. Raffles too had been trying to ward off the return of Dutch rule; then as now the Dutch owed their empire to the British. The parallels were everywhere. Not without panicking Dutch officials to whom the name of Raffles was as a red rag to a rampaging buffalo, van der Post saw himself as a reincarnation of the great empire builder. In Jakarta he would, as he put it, 'play a principal role in what was to be a repeat performance in contemporary dress of the piece of high history enacted at the beginning of the nineteenth century round Raffles'.

A better judge of the situation's potential as theatre saw it differently.

Every building was covered with patriotic graffiti screaming for 'Bloodshed or Freedom', and the blood flowed. Nightly the explosion of bombs planted by 'extremists' (as they were called) rocked the city. Machine-guns stuttered and chattered on the deserted suburban streets around the perimeter, fires drenched the starry nights with orange and crimson light, and the crump and crash of mortars and grenades was a familiar sound at any time of the day or night.

This was Jakarta in late 1945 as remembered by Captain Dirk Niven van der Bogaerde, another mildly eccentric British officer with a very Dutch name. Familiarly known as 'Pip' and professionally as plain Dirk Bogarde, he had just arrived with a tin trunk, a battered suitcase and a stolen typewriter. He was attached to the 23rd Indian Division and his speciality lay in the analysis of aerial photography. Reconnaissance of any sort being rudimentary in Java, Bogarde's unusual talents were directed elsewhere. He arranged a spectacular party, contributed to, and was soon editing, the Divisional newspaper, and read the English news on Radio Batavia. He also came to the attention of Major-General Hawthorn, the Divisions commander.

Sadao Oba, that young Japanese officer-cadet who was still at headquarters in Bandung, would remember Hawthorn as driving around in an open car accompanied by a large dog and a luscious blonde. To this entourage the dashing young 'Pip', himself soon possessed of a grinning Gurkha batman, 'a ravishingly beautiful' Eurasian secretary and a small panther called 'Ursula', was a welcome addition. He became the General's ADC. In search of suitable accommodation for his general, in early 1946 Bogarde was dispatched to Bandung.

Whatever SEAC's instructions about establishing peaceful conditions, there had never been any question of the British occupying the whole of Java. The single division of troops originally designated for the island would have been insufficient even if it had been unopposed. In the event, though the British were at first welcomed in Jakarta, the appearance of elements of the old Royal Netherlands Indies Army (KNIL) as reconstituted by the first Dutch officers to reach Java proved highly provocative. The KNIL's troops, mainly Christian Ambonese, went on the rampage, extreme nationalist groups fought back, and the SEAC troops were obliged to restore order. Hence the nightly fire-fight recorded by Bogarde. On the reasonable assumption that SEAC troops were being used as a shield for the KNIL and the eventual return of Dutch administration, the Republic's leadership protested. When SEAC's commander denied any such intention and expressed willingness to work with the Republic, the Dutch protested. Under the circumstances, and given the shortage of troops, it was decided to limit Allied occupation of the island to its two major port-cities, Jakarta at the western end and Surabaya at the eastern.

Bandung, a spacious modern metropolis 200 miles south-east of Jakarta up in the coffee-growing Priangan highlands, was the island's third city. It was where 15,000 Japanese troops and their High Command were based and, according to van der Post, it was also where some 50,000 of his fellow prisoners, many of them seriously ill, were still being held in camps guarded by the Japanese. This was for their own safety. Those, mainly Dutch, who had celebrated peace by venturing forth to savour the hard-won fruits of freedom and dominion had been rudely disillusioned. Instead of a rapturous welcome from their loyal subjects, they found hostile mobs and gun-toting militias. Many had been intimidated, kidnapped or murdered. When news of their plight reached Jakarta in October 1945, it was decided to extend SEAC's range and make Bandung its third 'safe haven' for the collection and evacuation of internees.

Heavily armed convoys began making weekly runs up into the hills. Although they moved only by day and by agreement with Sukarno's Republican government, they were invariably ambushed. In Bogarde's convoy a truck was hit, its driver killed and five passengers wounded. 'A quiet trip, with only minor incidents,' he reported. 'We had, in truth, been lucky.'

The situation which awaited them in Bandung was reflected all over Java. According to Sadao Oba, erstwhile members of PETA and other Japanese-sponsored paramilitary groups had openly espoused the nationalist cause as soon as the Japanese surrender was announced. Some of these militias acknowledged the Republican leadership in Jakarta and so constituted a loosely organised and regionally based national defence force. Others, known to Indonesians as *pemuda* ('youth'), to the British as 'extremists' and to the Dutch as 'terrorists', 'bandits', 'Nazis' or worse, espoused more radical aims and more impetuous tactics. Infused with Japanese militarism and intoxicated with the idea of *merdeka* ('independence', 'freedom'), they scorned authority, diplomacy and international opinion in favour of total revolution.

From both these groups Japanese troops had come under strong pressure to continue the anti-colonial struggle by joining their ranks, or at least handing over their weapons. 'A beautiful lady officer visited remote camps and asked the Japanese "Why don't you join us, I am yours."' Shattered by defeat and apprehensive of the fate that might await them in Allied hands, 277 Japanese succumbed to such blandishments in Bandung; more seriously a vast quantity of arms disappeared. Although some were recovered, Sadao Oba, well-placed in the Japanese Supply Department, gives an alarming inventory of what remained missing from the west Java arsenal.

> By force and sometimes through negotiation, Indonesians obtained rifles (51,698), machine guns (1,804), infantry guns (48), trench mortars (201), anti-tank guns (56), field guns (64), 100mm howitzers (27), cannons (31), AA weapons (437), and corresponding ammunition for the above weapons, plus tanks (50), armoured cars (159), cars and trucks (5,431), dynamite (7,624 kg), hand grenades (318,454), gun powder and materials for making gun powder.

'These weapons', he concludes with dazzling naïvety, 'must have helped the [Indonesians'] struggle against the British and Dutch armies.'

Although the Japanese were initially culpable, they did try to make amends. In Bandung they resisted a complete take-over of the city, mounted an offensive to recover arms and, under British orders, eventually drove the Indonesians south of the railway tracks which bisect the city. The British and their Japanese prisoners-turned-allies retained the downtown area north of the tracks plus the airport. From the encircling hills, shells and mortars rained down on them. They responded with bombardments, air-strikes and, in March 1946, a successful outwards thrust. Bogarde's skills as an interpreter of aerial photography at last came into their own as he identified enemy gun emplacements and road blocks. For Sadao Oba, fighting alongside his erstwhile enemies turned out to be a novel experience. 'Generally speaking the British army was gentle.' Someone, perhaps the Divisional Chief of Staff, actually wrote a letter of appreciation to Sadao's commanding officer.

> I was very surprised to read the letter. Where in the world would an occupation army write a letter to a surrendered commander praising him for his 'success' and thanking him for his co-operation? That was a model instance of a 'fair deal'.

All the while, prisoners and internees were being flown or convoyed out. The Japanese followed in June 1946, then the British. SEAC's work in Bandung was all over by August. Fierce though the fighting had been, it was mostly at long range. Bombing and mortars did the damage. The enemy kept their distance and melted into the forest. So, eventually, did Bogarde's 'Ursula'. Riding down with the last convoy, the panther made its escape during the inevitable ambush. 'So that is that. I mind very much.' He only hoped that no 'gun-happy Indo' ever got the cat in his sights.

The great advantage of fighting at arm's length was that the mettle of the participants had never been seriously tested. Bandung, though scarcely a resounding victory, counted as a SEAC success and features little in the national mythology of the Indonesian Republic. Elsewhere it was a different story. In central Java attempts to evacuate internees via the port of Semarang, a fourth 'safe haven', badly misfired. Japanese troops suffered heavy casualties, British officers were hacked to death, and Dutch internees were massacred.

This, however, was as nothing to the eruption in Surabaya. By comparison 'Bandung was an island of occupied tranquillity and central Java an armed and anxious fortress,' according to the Cornell historian Benedict Anderson. Surabaya, though, 'was a sea of fire'. To Indonesians it became 'the city of heroes'; 10 November, its finest hour, rates second only to Independence Day in the national calendar. During the four years of sporadic conflict known as the Indonesian independence struggle, Surabaya was much the largest and most serious engagement. For the British it may well have been the bloodiest battle ever fought in peace-time and for their Indian troops it was a last heavy test of their loyalty. To both it would demonstrate that, in all but name, they had walked into a war in Java. Above all, it brought home to them that there was no military solution to the problems of Indonesia. Sadly the Dutch failed to draw the same conclusion.

Surabaya, Sea of Fire

At the eastern end of Java's long north coast, Surabaya is and was the country's main naval base. Out of it in 1942 had sailed that ill-fated Allied squadron which encountered the Japanese invasion force in the Battle of the Java Sea. Behind the docks and dockyards the metropolis reaches deep inland, following the north-south axis of the Kali Mas ('River of Gold'). Marshalling yards, sugar refineries and oil depots give way to rambling bazaars and then an elongated commercial/financial centre whence greener suburbs mount into the hills. This linear alignment with all main roads running north-south was to prove crucial. The internment camps lay south of the city and the docks north. To evacuate the internees there was no alternative but to drive through the heart of the teeming metropolis.

The island's main manufacturing centre as well as its second city, Surabaya in 1945 had a volatile, industrialised and already politicised population of about three quarters of a million. August's news of the proclamation of Indonesian independence had been greeted by mass demonstrations of organised labour. As in Bandung, radical *pemuda* groups seized the initiative and began setting up *ad hoc* revolutionary committees.

On 19 September an incident at the Oranje Hotal, a plush watering-hole in the centre of the commercial district, triggered the first casualties. A group of just released internees, primed on patriotism and gin, had hoisted the red, white and blue stripes of the Dutch flag. When armed *pemuda* activists lowered it, snipped off the blue stripe, and re-hoisted it as the *merah putih* (red and white) of the Republic, scuffles broke out and a Mr Ploegman was mortally wounded. In this and subsequent clashes with both Dutch vigilantes and the Japanese military, the nationalists prevailed; but, as van Mook saw it, the mob ruled.

> In Surabaya all the succeeding phases of the French revolution from the first seizure of power to 'the terror' seemed to follow each other in a few weeks, ending with a gruesome 'people's' tribunal in the club.

The club was the hallowed Simpang Club to which sundry Dutchmen were hauled off, there to be interrogated in the billiard room, beaten senseless on the dance floor, and lynched on the lawn. Better regulated Republican units began pressurising the Japanese into surrendering arms and eventually secured their entire arsenal. As in Bandung it included tanks, transport, artillery and vast quantities of small arms. By early October the city was a bubbling cauldron of gun-slinging militias, agitated by the heat of their own rhetoric and stirred to delirium by the spirit of the times.

Units which acknowledged the authority of the Republic were under the command of a willowy ex-*peta* officer called Sudirman. In baggy suit and open shirt he no more conformed to the conventional idea of a general than did Vo Nguyen Giap; yet he would prove an able leader and become the first Commander-in-Chief of the Indonesian army. More representative of the *pemuda* mobsters was a wild-haired, pistol-packing firebrand in his early twenties known to the masses as Bung Tomo (Sutomo). An ex-journalist with messianic pretensions and a flair for anti-imperialist rhetoric, Tomo formed his own revolutionary corps and set up his own Revolution Radio (Radio Pemberontakan). Corps members, like their leader, swore neither to touch a woman nor cut their hair until Indonesian soil was untainted by Dutchmen. The radio, exploiting social grievances, Islamic loyalties and Javanese mysticism, poured forth a torrent of inflammatory invective.

Into this cauldron on 25 October sailed the 49th Brigade of General Hawthorn's 23rd Division under the command of Brigadier Aubertin Walter Southern Mallaby. A cerebral and respected, if unexciting, officer, Mallaby had spent most of his life in staff jobs. This was his first active command. In typically business-like fashion he quickly established his men between the docks and the city, then made contact with the Indonesian authorities. Next day he gave priority to the rescue of a Dutch reconnaissance party which had been detained by the Indonesians for the past month. Given the strength of anti-Dutch sentiment it was a provocative move, not helped when on the 27th Surabaya was showered with SEAC leaflets demanding the surrender of all weapons in Indonesian hands. The planes had come from Jakarta and Mallaby seems to have had no prior knowledge of their directive. Nevertheless, on the 28th his troops started commandeering transport, confiscating arms, and even removing the odd *merah putih* flag. Indonesian suspicions mounted. Perhaps the SEAC forces had not come simply to release internees and evacuate the Japanese.

> Everywhere one could sense uneasiness: in the people, in the cars roaring past along the streets, in the printing presses, and in the dogs. The dogs barked themselves hoarse till their ... bellies collapsed like flat bicycle tyres; no one remembered to feed them. Everywhere people were saying the same thing; 'Of course the Allies aren't our enemies, but still they're killing and kidnapping people in Jakarta.' And like a badly trained choir they shouted; 'We won't be treated like the people in Jakarta ... We'll fight.'

Idrus, a native Surabayan from whose account the above is extracted, subscribed to the simplistic affectations which permeated *pemuda* attitudes. Strung about with bandoliers and gunbelts, the youthful heroes saw themselves as the big-hearted cowboys of countless Westerns, defending their homesteads against marauding bandits. Other groups affected the samurai ethic with bandanas, swords and martial antics. To both it seemed that foreign bandits, 'black as locomotives' (nearly all the SEAC troops were from India), were taking over the town.

> Nothing was safe: cattle, girls, gold, not even the revolvers and knives of the cowboys. Along the streets the cowboys were stopped by the bandits and forced to surrender their weapons . . . The cowboys did not put up their hands, nor were they prepared to surrender their weapons. They shouted back 'Take our lives!' And as they shouted these words, they began to fire. The bandits too opened fire and a fierce fight ensued.

Quick on the draw, the Indonesian offensive began on the afternoon of the 28th and continued all night. Numerous British Indian detachments on guard duty were isolated and massacred. A convoy of 200 Dutch and Eurasian internees was waylaid while threading the city's streets *en route* to the docks; though its Indian escort put up a doughty resistance, men, women and children were hacked to death or taken into a custody from which they never reappeared. Against Mallaby's 4,000 Indian troops, mostly Marathas and Rajputs, an estimated 120,000 *pemuda* plus 20,000 regular troops were under arms in the city. Casualties on both sides were heavy, but whereas the Indonesians could afford them, Mallaby could not. To prevent the imminent extermination of his entire brigade, an urgent appeal was sent to Jakarta.

Next morning Sukarno and Hatta, now President and Vice-President of the Republic, flew in. Sukarno made a broadcast appealing for calm and a ceasefire; Mallaby and Sudirman toured the city sitting side by side on the bonnet of Sudirman's grey Lincoln. Next day General Hawthorn arrived and a conference was convened with the Republic's leaders plus Sudirman, Bung Tomo and other Surabayans. It was agreed that the SEAC troops would withdraw from forward positions in the city and cease confiscating arms; the nationalists would assist in the safe transit of internees. On the 30th the dignitaries returned to Jakarta leaving Mallaby to implement the new arrangement. By 6 p.m. on the same evening he was dead.

'MALLABY MURDERED' announced the main headline in the London *Times* of 1 November; 'ALMOST WAR IN EAST JAVA'. An entire division plus tanks and artillery – the 5th Indian which Mountbatten had requested as back-up in Jakarta – had been re-routed to Surabaya; it was due on the 4th. Sukarno, in another appeal for the fighting to stop, had virtually disowned the Surabayan *pemuda*.

> One incorrect action, even one incorrect action by one individual, can ruin the whole upbuilding of the nation ... Don't let us be forced to face alone the whole military power of England and all the Allies ... Once again I order all fighting with the Allies to stop. Carry out my orders. *Merdeka!*

Simultaneously General Christison, the SEAC Commander-in-Chief in Jakarta, demanded the surrender of all those involved in Mallaby's death. Failing this, continued Christison, 'I intend to bring the whole weight of my sea, land and air forces and all the weapons of modern war against them until they are crushed.'

But who were those involved in Mallaby's murder? To this day the verdict remains open. Wild discrepancies, even in eye-witness accounts of the affair, cannot be reconciled. Along with Sudirman and other Indonesian leaders, Mallaby and three of his officers had gone to a building in the downtown area where a small force of Marathas were being besieged by a *pemuda* mob. Persuaded that the Marathas would be withdrawn the next morning, most of the mob dispersed. Mallaby and his men got into a car and began to drive away. They were halted by a new mob a stone's throw from the building near the 'Red Bridge' over the Kali Mas. Suddenly bullets started to fly. Whether the Marathas in the building or the mob outside were responsible is disputed. In the confusion Mallaby was shot while still in the back seat of the car. He died almost immediately. His companions escaped after throwing a hand-grenade which burnt out the car. This led to suppositions that perhaps Mallaby had been killed in the blast. Whatever the truth, it was clearly impossible to identify the guilty party, let alone to surrender him.

A stunned quiet now descended on the city. It was interrupted only by the passage of convoys as the internees were brought down to the docks and by the ravings of Radio Revolution. At about this time the fire-breathing Bung Tomo introduced the novelty of English-language bulletins, the idea being to refute the soothing platitudes emanating from broadcasters like Bogarde on Radio Batavia. For this purpose Tomo secured the services of a 'Miss Daventry' who claimed to come from the Isle of Man. In the tradition of

'Tokyo Rose' and 'Shanghai Lil', to the troops of the 5th Division she became 'Surabaya Sue'. In fact she was none other than the Scots-American red-head Vaneen Walker, alias the Balinese 'princess' K'tut Tantri, she who had opened the first hotel on Bali's Kuta beach and then gone underground after the Japanese invasion.

K'tut Tantri's account of her wartime exploits as a gun-runner for the Indonesian resistance and then as a prisoner of the Japanese has strained the credulity of critical readers. No doubts, however, surround her presence in Surabaya. When, after a ten-day lull, Christison issued his second ultimatum, she was one of the first to sound the alarm. This time not only were the murderers of Mallaby to be handed over but also all hostages and prisoners, and all 'Indonesian leaders including the leaders of the youth movements (*pemuda*)'. Additionally all arms other than those of the regular forces were to be surrendered; and women and children were advised to leave the city immediately. Failing compliance with these directives within twenty-four hours, SEAC troops would enforce them.

The only omission in this ultimatum was a demand for the surrender of its fiercest critic, in other words 'Surabaya Sue'.

I was shocked to hear of this ultimatum and immediately broadcast a warning to the General that the British could make no greater mistake . . . 'The Indonesians will never accept your terms, even if you bomb Surabaya to the ground and kill every man, woman and child,' I blazed at him.

The General ignored the broadcast, and the Indonesians ignored the ultimatum. The outcome was the bombing of Surabaya by the British on three consecutive days and nights. Hundreds upon hundreds were killed. The streets ran with blood, women and children lay dead in the gutters. Kampongs were in flames and the people fled in panic to the comparative safety of the rice fields. But the Indonesians did not surrender.

The assault had begun on 10 November, henceforth 'Heroes' Day'. Encountering heavy casualties and fanatical resistance on the ground, the British command called in tanks and artillery, and ordered a naval bombardment from the ships in the harbour. Overhead Mosquitoes and Thunderbolts bombed and strafed. The shelling and bombing were not indiscriminate. Indonesian positions and strategic targets had been pre-identified; but all lay in and around a vast, densely populated and highly inflammable metropolis. Civilian casualties could not be other than horrific, the incendiary effect little short of an inferno.

To the troops of the 5th Indian Division, already battle-hardened in Burma, it may not have seemed out of order. This, after all, was war. And yet, of course, it was not war. There had been no declaration of hostilities. The SEAC forces were there simply to oversee the repatriation and keep the peace. Indonesia's revolution was none of their business. Neither the protection of internees nor retaliation for the death of Mallaby could possibly justify an all-out assault on one of south-east Asia's largest cities. As propagandists like K'tut Tantri were quick to point out, Indonesians demanded only those freedoms for which the Allies had just fought a world war. So how could their troops, least of all Indian troops, justify their action?

Fear that their Indian troops would indeed object to fighting fellow Asians engaged in a struggle for independence which was not unlike their own haunted the British High Command. Questions were already being asked in New Delhi and protests registered. Even if they were unaware of this, some of the Indian troops were clearly troubled. K'tut Tantri claims that Gurkha informants were feeding information to Radio Revolution and that others evaded orders. She also claims that one of the few all-British battalions refused orders.

> The most famous of these battalions was the British West Yorkshires. On their arrival in Surabaya they quickly learned the truth – and mutinied. They laid down their firearms and said they would not fight the Indonesians . . . A few days later the regiment was called back to England. The reason for its abrupt withdrawal was hushed up . . .

The battle of Surabaya lasted for nearly three weeks. A slow advance was necessary, it was claimed, to avoid incurring casualties. It was also less testing of doubtful loyalties. Before edging forward down a few more streets, it was safer to pulverise them with artillery. SEAC casualties were indeed limited to a few hundred; but such tactics were not designed to minimise the enemy's losses. Heads back and pistols blazing, the 'cowboys' stood their ground against Sherman tanks while the 'samurai' swiped at armoured cars. Sudirman's 20,000 regular troops of the Republic's incipient army extricated themselves early on, taking with them such transport and heavy weapons as remained. Bung Tomo slipped away to Malang whence Radio Revolution again took to the air; K'tut Tantri found her way to central Java where she continued to work for the Republican leadership. Only the tragically innocent and the fanatically uncompromising were left in the city to die for *merdeka*. How many such martyrs succumbed to 'all the weapons of modern war' is unknown. Ten thousand may be a realistic approximation.

David Wehl, a SEAC Intelligence Officer with pro-Dutch sympathies, described the battle of Surabaya as being, from an Indonesian point of view, 'a complete waste of time, of life, of ammunition and of property'.

> [It was] a tragedy of hysterical ferocity, fanaticism, self-sacrifice, and wasted effort . . . Had similar risings taken place all over Java millions would have died, and the Republic of Indonesia and the Netherlands East Indies would alike have been drowned in blood.

In fact no 'risings' comparable to Surabaya occurred either during the SEAC operations of 1945–6 or during the Dutch attempts to re-establish themselves from 1946 to 1949. Although technically an Indonesian defeat and certainly wasteful, Surabaya was also a massive psychological victory for Indonesian nationalism. For the Republican leadership it represented the consummation of their claims, hitherto untested, of total national commitment. To them and to the *pemuda* it became both a rallying cry and a turning-point. The Indonesian Republic, once dismissed as a test-tube product of Tokyo's experiments in constitutional insemination, was revealed as a lusty and viable infant state. To the world at large the strength of nationalist sentiment was now beyond dispute. In order to reduce the risk of further outbreaks on such a hideous scale, the British restricted their own intervention and redoubled their diplomatic pressure on the Dutch. It was Surabaya which triggered the diplomatic negotiations of 1946–7 between the Dutch and the Indonesians.

Back to the Basement

Throughout the upheaval in Surabaya, and despite the skirmishes in Jakarta, Bandung and elsewhere, relations between SEAC's British representatives and the Indonesian leadership remained cordial. The British had responded to Indonesian demands that Dutch KNIL troops be removed from Jakarta, and Sukarno had responded to British pleas that he mediate in Surabaya. While in east Java British and Indonesians were killing one another, in Jakarta the two sides met on the football pitch. The result was a 2-2 draw. No doubt the

Indonesian team wore red and white, and no doubt the Dutch, in line with their usual response to any direct British dealings with the Indonesians, protested at this further evidence of SEAC's *de facto* recognition of the 'rebel' Republic. Unimpressed the British, and especially go-betweens like Colonel van der Post, continued to explore political options with the Republican leadership and to urge van Mook, now returned to Jakarta, to do likewise.

As both Lieutenant-Governor of the Indies and the senior Dutch representative in Mountbatten's Allied command, van Mook's attitude was crucial. He could be highly critical of The Hague's intransigence and would ridicule the Dutch national character for 'its excess of caution and its deficiency of imagination'. The Hague reciprocated, never wholly trusting its ponderous if diligent Lieutenant-Governor but seeing in him one whose Indonesian birth and pre-war support of demands for greater autonomy should make him more acceptable to Indonesian opinion.

Yet van Mook was no colonial emancipator and could never accept the idea of an Indonesia in which the Dutch would play no part. He clung to the notion of Indonesian-Dutch partnership as something special, untainted by the racial prejudice which disgraced other colonialisms and uniquely productive. The two peoples had a basic affinity which, he believed, a modicum of peace and prosperity would quickly restore. Without the Dutch there was no such nation as Indonesia, just a lot of islands. He refused to deal with Sukarno and Hatta partly because they were 'quislings' and 'extremists' but also because their 'so-called republic of Indonesia' was frankly preposterous. Even after Surabaya, he refused to believe that the Republic enjoyed popular support. He would talk, he insisted, only to 'moderates'.

Just where these 'moderates' were to be found was something of a mystery until in November 1945 Sutan Sjahrir was appointed Prime Minister of the Republic's first government. Although detained along with Hatta in the pre-war years and subsequently associated with some of the more radical student groups, the 'handsome and slightly pot-bellied' Sjahrir was both a committed democrat and a socialist whose reformist ideas on education and social welfare were not unlike those of van Mook. James Michener, who met him in 1950, was reminded of Thomas Jefferson; Sir Archibald Clark Kerr, the British diplomat now appointed to mediate between the Dutch and the Indonesians, likened him to 'a spaniel whom one expects to jump on one's lap and lick one's face if petted'. Happily, Sjahrir had licked no Japanese faces. He had gone into hiding during the war and had since roundly condemned those who had collaborated, though without actually naming Sukarno or Hatta.

Here, then, was what the Dutch could regard as the acceptable face of Indonesian nationalism. Sjahrir's credentials as Prime Minister were further heightened when his President and Vice-President suddenly disappeared from Jakarta. Fearing attacks by extremist elements, in one of which Sjahrir himself had been lucky to escape with his life, Sukarno and Hatta had decided to relocate themselves 300 miles away at Jogjakarta. The move was rich in symbolism. To the country's Muslim majority Sukarno's flight recalled that of the Prophet from Mecca to Medina (*hijra*), while in Javanese eyes the choice of Jogjakarta as the Republic's new seat of government conferred additional legitimacy. An ancient capital, the fief of Java's most respected sultanate, it had also been the last redoubt of anti-colonial resistance in the nineteenth century.

With Sjahrir apparently in sole control of Republican policy in Jakarta, discussions with van Mook at last got underway. They lasted, on and off, throughout 1946. Van Mook expanded on Queen Wilhelmina's commonwealth proposals of 1942; Sjahrir smiled sweetly, said little, and declined even to make counter-proposals until the Dutch had recognised the *de facto* existence of the Republic. British intermediaries like Clark Kerr came and went; van Mook shuttled back and forth to the Netherlands; Sjahrir trundled up to Jogja. An election delayed consultations in Holland, a brief kidnapping of Sjahrir and an abortive coup by revolutionary leftists interrupted dealings with Jogja.

In April the agreement just reached by the French in Indo-China (whereby, as will be seen, the Vietminh government in Hanoi was recognised, but only as one of several members of an Indo-Chinese Federation within the French Union) suggested a promising new approach. However both principals soon found themselves in difficulty over selling the necessary concessions to their respective governments in Jogja and The Hague. Meanwhile the only real pressure was coming from the British who, largely in response to Indian demands, had agreed to have all their forces out of Indonesia by November 1946. Dutch troops were being quietly installed in their place, but this could only heighten the danger of war once the British had left.

On 15 November, just as the last British troops were embarking, draft proposals were agreed. Known as the Linggadjati agreement, they followed the Indo-China precedent to the extent that, instead of a commonwealth, there was to be a Netherlands Indonesian Union under the Dutch crown to which considerable if ill-defined powers were reserved. The Union was to consist of the Netherlands themselves plus the 'United States of Indonesia', to which further powers were reserved. Within the 'United States of Indonesia' there were to be three states, one of which was the Republic. The Republic, in other words, though its existence was recognised, was relegated to a third tier in the constitutional hierarchy. Criticisms which the astute Hatta had made of the commonwealth proposal a year earlier still applied.

> Why must Indonesia willy-nilly be made a partner of a commonwealth in which the Dutch tail will wag the Indonesian dog? . . . The Dutch are graciously permitting us entry into the basement when we have already climbed all the way to the top floor and up to the attic.

There followed four months of wrangling over the interpretation of the agreement's more contentious clauses. These were still in dispute when both governments, more in hope than expectation, ratified the agreement on 25 March 1947.

Since the new arrangements were not to come into effect until 1949 there was ample time for further clarification, also for further misunderstanding. Heated debate now focused on the interim arrangements. The Republic demanded the removal of Dutch troops within territory now acknowledged as coming under its own authority; the Dutch insisted that the Republic's failure to police its domain effectively made their presence essential. Jogja's misgivings about this and other aspects of the agreement forced the resignation of Sjahrir in June. Although his successor, Amir Sjarifuddin, proved no less able, the Dutch saw their chance. In July van Mook launched what was called a 'police action'. 'The clinical method had failed,' he later explained, 'a surgical operation was necessary to save the patient from the cancer of lawlessness and terrorism.'

Supposedly intended to enforce law and order, the 'police action' was in fact a large-scale military offensive. Heavily armed units, backed with air support, swept inland from SEAC's erstwhile 'safe havens', overrunning nearly all of west Java, most of east Java and all the more productive centres in Sumatra. Republican units fell back into the hills and countryside, thence to wage a protracted guerrilla campaign. From being responsible for a population and an area equivalent to that of France and Germany combined, the Jogja Republic was suddenly reduced to the land-locked circumference of a Javanese Switzerland.

The only compensation, a crucial one, came in the form of international condemnation of Dutch aggression. For every city lost, a United Nations vote was gained. Sjahrir had escaped to India where Jawaharlal Nehru now emerged as the international champion of the Republic's cause. Along with Australia, India raised the issue at the United Nations where the eloquent and likeable Sjahrir presented the Republic's case. From this resulted UN demands for a ceasefire and the appointment of a UN 'Good Offices Committee' to help the two sides reach a settlement.

Protracted negotiations brought a new agreement, signed in January 1948 aboard the USS *Renville*. The Dutch retained the military initiative in that they surrendered none of their just acquired territory; but politically the Indonesian Republic could console itself with continued UN support and involvement, plus the promise of a plebiscite to be held throughout Java and Sumatra.

Reclaiming the Attic

The belligerent stance adopted by the Dutch in 1947 had had a lot to do with events outside Java. To the west, the island of Sumatra had been the main bone of contention during the negotiations which led to the Linggadjati agreement. At first the Dutch had refused to acknowledge the Republic's authority there. To the extent that authority of any sort tended to be fragmented in an island 1,500 miles long, where the main centres of population were cut off from one another by almost impenetrable mountain and forest, they had a point. Moreover the island had not been exposed to the sort of politicisation experienced in Java during the Japanese occupation. As noted earlier, it had in fact been detached from the Indies and administered from Singapore as a colony until 1944.

On the other hand the island's important oil-producing centres of Medan and Palembang, once word reached them in September 1945, had enthusiastically hailed the Republic. On the opposite side of the island, the area now known as West Sumatra could even claim to be the Republic's birthplace. Hatta, Sjahrir and Sjarifuddin were all of

West Sumatran (that is, Minangkabau) origin. So were the Republic's Foreign Minister and a host of other notables, including the man who wrote the national anthem. The Dutch themselves admitted that, except for Sukarno, the Jogja government was really a West Sumatran government.

Yet the Dutch decision, embodied in the Linggadjati agreement, to concede Sumatra to the Republic took little account of these arguments. Rather, it stemmed from the chaos which followed the evacuation of SEAC troops from Sumatra in July 1946. Already Aceh, the north-western tip of the island, was churning with revolution as its land-and-trade-owning aristocracy were eliminated by Islamic *pemuda*. Suspicious alike of the Dutch, the British and even the Republic, the Acehnese were a law – or lack of it – unto themselves. Remote and incomprehensible, their affairs could be largely ignored; but in late 1946, in the vacuum left by SEAC's withdrawal, this revolutionary turmoil spread right down the north-east coast to engulf the immensely productive country around Medan. Fanatical mobs removed the local Malay sultans who had held sway under Dutch auspices, and then targeted the mostly foreign-owned plantations.

The scene of confusion which resulted corresponded well with the lawlessness and incompetence generally ascribed to Republican rule by the Dutch. Sumatra was therefore conceded to the Republic as an indictment of its ability to control its own followers. The self-same chaos was then advanced as a handy justification for the 1947 'police action' when Dutch troops at last retook most of the island's main population centres. Only to Aceh and parts of Republican west Sumatra did the Dutch never return.

East of Java, amidst the myriad islands between Borneo and New Guinea, exactly the opposite had been happening. Here, according to van Mook, was 'a brighter scene', unclouded by British interference because outside SEAC's area, and illuminated by the peace, prosperity and collaboration which he had in mind for the whole archipelago. Following the largely Australian recapture of the eastern islands, Dutch administration had been quickly and, for the most part, peacefully reinstated. In anticipation of a United States of Indonesia, representatives had been summoned to a conference at Malino in south Sulawesi and two incipient states had been formed, namely (Dutch) Borneo and the Great East (which was everywhere that was not Borneo). Such endorsement of federal tendencies led to further Balkanisation with, for instance, Borneo dividing into three states.

Yet the Dutch were immensely encouraged by these experiments. The peoples of the East, wary of exploitation by the more numerous and progressive Javanese, seemed to appreciate the guarantee of separate representation which the federal structure offered and found Dutch supervision an acceptable price to pay for it. Van Mook emphatically denied Republican accusations that the new creations were in any sense puppet states. The willingness of their federalist leaders to co-operate with the Dutch in no way prejudiced their nationalism.

> it was a revelation for the Dutch – at least for me [that is, van Mook] that those [federalists] who particularly wished the special relationship between Indonesia and the Netherlands to continue were keenest on a very early independence for Indonesia . . . only a self-respecting Indonesian nation would be able to accept Dutch assistance and turn it to the best and most enduring account.

Had the federal system been restricted to Borneo and the Great East, it might well have justified Dutch optimism. But when the Dutch repossessed themselves of most of Java and Sumatra in the 1947 'police action', the system was fatally extended. Areas like west Java and north Sumatra had been exposed to over two years of nationalist revolution and were never likely to settle for a Dutch-sponsored separatist identity. They nevertheless were consituted as separate states, the number of which, including Special Autonomous Areas, had risen to fifteen by 1948.

Clearly the idea was to negate the influence of the Republic which, as one of sixteen 'United States' within a Netherlands-Indonesian Union, would be hopelessly outvoted. Indeed so transparent was this ploy that the federal principle was thereby fatally discredited. Even van Mook was never able to deny the puppet status of these new states. Within them Republican sympathisers were imprisoned, Dutch collaborators were installed in office by a combination of nomination and rigged elections, and outside observers were excluded. For Dr Ide Anak Agung Gde Agung, the Balinese Raja who now emerged as Chief Minister of the Great East, it was a tragedy. If ever there was a nation that would have been better served by a federal rather than a unitary constitution, it was the spawling multi-ethnic archipelago. But thanks to crass Dutch management, it could never be.

That is the reason why even now federalism remains a dirty word in Indonesia, because it was misused by the Dutch at that time. You see they used it as a political weapon against the Republic and against our revolution. I am a federalist, yes, still a federalist. But not a separatist.

Meanwhile the guerrilla resistance of Republican sympathisers stiffened. Even in the supposedly more settled islands of the Great East, like Sulawesi and Bali, draconian measures became necessary. In the densely populated and determinedly Islamic coastal regions of south Sulawesi Captain Paul ('Turk') Westerling pioneered new methods in counter-insurgency. Whole villages were held responsible for Republican activities in their areas, their inhabitants being lined up and shot one after another until an informant spoke out. Westerling's reign of terror is reliably estimated to have cost as many lives as the battle of Surabaya.

Meanwhile in Bali a typically flamboyant resistance held out until 1948. Then, in time-honoured Balinese fashion, its leader Ngurah Rai and his hounded followers made the ultimate sacrifice. They marched out to certain death in that hallowed ritual of *puputan*. It was another 'unbelievable expression of defending one's honour'. And just as the *puputan* of forty years earlier had been turned, in Balinese eyes, into a triumph for the values of the old order, so that of 1948 rendered sacrosanct the revolution and the new Republic.

The Dutch saw it differently. Fortified by the apparent success of such repression in the outer islands, they revived the idea of repressive tactics in Java. A new administration in The Hague had tired of the patient paternalism of van Mook; replaced by a man of less ambiguous loyalties, van Mook eventually settled in France. The plebiscite, which under the *Renville* agreement was supposed to be held in the areas occupied by the Dutch in the 1947 'police action', looked like being an embarrassment. Moreover guerrilla resistance continued throughout the island. The time was ripe for sterner measures.

For nearly a year the embattled Republic had held out in Jogja. An airlift of medicines, arms and personnel occasionally operated from Bangkok via Bukittinggi, a Republican outpost in west Sumatra; otherwise the Dutch blockade totally isolated the Republic. Cut off, desperately short of almost everything, and lulled by the UN cease-fire and the UN-sponsored *Renville* agreement, the Republic's leadership was ill-equipped to meet an offensive. It was thus taken completely by surprise when in December 1948 the Dutch launched their second 'police action'.

Just hours before Sukarno was due to depart on a visit to New Delhi, Jogja's only airport was bombed, then captured by Dutch paratroopers. The Republican forces fell back on the rural areas. Their capital and the entire Republican leadership were in Dutch custody before nightfall. Sukarno, Hatta, Sjahrir and the rest began another spell in Dutch detention. The 'so-called republic' was erased from the map during the land offensive which followed. It lingered on only in the shape of a provisional government-in-exile in the little Sumatran enclave of Bukittinggi.

Once again, though, the Dutch had seriously, indeed disastrously, miscalculated. Territorial gains were no substitute for international indulgence. Nor was armed intervention much reassurance to Indonesia's fledgling federalists. The Hague, assailed from in front by world censure and from behind by its supposed collaborators in the sixteen new states, was about to be forced to bow to the inevitable. Exactly a year after the capture of Jogja, the 350 years of Dutch empire in the Indies would come to an end.

Ever since, with a sigh of relief, the British had withdrawn from Indonesia, both the Republic and the Netherlands had looked to the United States for encouragement. Sukarno still drew comfort from the words of the Atlantic Charter, van Mook from Roosevelt's apparent soft spot for Dutch rule. Though technically neutral, the US State Department had usually been prepared to give the Dutch the benefit of the doubt. Under the Truman doctrine of containing Communism, Europe's post-war recovery was the top US priority; if this meant enabling the Netherlands to mobilise the wealth of the Indies, then so be it. Additionally, Dutch rule in the Indies had looked to offer the best guarantee against the spread of Communism in offshore south-east Asia.

Doubts about this latter argument had surfaced in 1948 when the Republic ruthlessly crushed a Communist revolt within its own territory. Those, like Nehru, who supported the Republic were quick to point out that if Communism did take a hold in Indonesia, it would be because Dutch counter-insurgency measures and the Dutch blockade had driven Sukarno into Moscow's camp. US opinion took note.

Although the US remained perturbed by the strength and stamina of the Republican resistance to Dutch rule, it had seen fit to issue a stern warning against a further Dutch recourse to arms. The second 'police action' therefore constituted an outright rebuttal of American advice. It was also, of course, a flagrant breach of the *Renville* agreement in which the US had played a major part, as well as a flaunting of UN resolutions, a direct challenge to that body's authority, and an outrage to world opinion.

The Hague, as in 1947, anticipated such condemnation. UN resolutions demanding a ceasefire, the release of the Republican leadership, the withdrawal of Dutch troops and the resumption of negotiations were to be expected. It would, as usual, comply as and when it suited. Not so, warned Washington. Compliance must this time be unequivocal. US patience was exhausted. US opinion, ever the decisive factor in overseas policy, had changed. An argument, long since deployed by Hatta, Nehru and others, that it was actually the US which had enabled Holland to flaunt the UN and deploy its troops in Java, was at last grasped by the American press and then aired in the US Senate. Dutch troops had been using US equipment, supplied under lend-lease and other favourable arrangements, to suppress the Republic. More significantly, it was US aid in the form of the Marshall Plan programme for European recovery which had left the Netherlands free to divert other resources to the recovery of its colonial empire.

The Dutch, of course, denied this; it was difficult to prove one way or the other. But when given to understand that the flow of aid to Holland, indeed to the whole European recovery programme, would be halted unless the UN resolutions were respected, the Dutch government finally capitulated.

In 1949, with the Republic reinstated and its leaders released, a Round Table Conference got underway in The Hague. The structure under consideration was still that outlined in the Linggadjati agreement for a Netherlands-Indonesian Union comprising the United States of Indonesia and the Netherlands; the United States of Indonesia was still to consist of the Republic plus the new Dutch-sponsored states. There were thus three delegations – from the Netherlands, the Republic and the states. It was the last named who now administered the *coup de grâce*. The US had pulled the rug from under Holland's feet, but it was the states who gave the push which ended any prospect of the Dutch retaining a clog in the door of Indonesian independence.

Van Mook's earlier surprise over his protégé states being so wedded to nationalism should have served as a warning. The consultative assembly of the sixteen states had in fact begun making its peace with the Republic in 1948. In the course of these negotiations, the states undertook to support the Republican position on outright independence. In return the Republic would accept the federal principle and recognise the autonomy of those states, like the Great East, which wished to preserve their identity; it would also ensure their generous representation in the institutions of central government. This, then, was the deal which, by depriving the Dutch of their fig-leaf of federal support, obliged them to beat a speedy retreat.

The final settlement hammered out in The Hague, while relegating the concept of a Netherlands-Indonesian Union to international irrelevance, constituted the erstwhile Netherland East Indies as a sovereign state to be known as the Republic of the United States of Indonesia (RUSI); the title represented a wordy compromise of federal and centrist interests. On 27 December 1949 Queen Juliana solemnly gave her assent while in Jakarta vast crowds observed the lowering of the Dutch flag and the hoisting of the *merah putih*. Next day Sukarno, now President of the RUSI, flew in from Jogja in a plane painted red and white for the occasion. Even greater crowds lined the route from the airport. In the city's central park, now designated Medan Merdeka, an estimated 200,000 awaited him. The celebrations made rich recompense for that almost clandestine proclamation outside Sukarno's house fifty-two months earlier.

Yet the struggle was not quite over. Empire in the Indies survived in three enclaves. The Portuguese still retained their half of the island of Timor, the British were still ensconced in Sarawak and Sabah in the northern corner of Borneo, and the Dutch had managed to exclude from Indonesian sovereignty their half of the island of New Guinea, now Irian Jaya.

To these anomalies the new government in Jakarta would eventually turn, addressing them in reverse order. But there was no hurry. Sukarno had more pressing concerns within the vast and fragmented construct that was already Indonesia; and what he called 'NEFOS', the 'Newly Emergent Forces' of Asia, faced more momentous challenges elsewhere. The fate of places like Irian Jaya and East Timor fell within the scope of mopping-up operations. Larger, grimmer struggles against imperialism had first to be waged on the Asian mainland. One was already underway, in Indo-China.

13

Mission Impossible

Of Jeeps and Dakotas

On the last day of June 1950 eight twin-engined transports swung low over the ricefields of the Mekong delta to touch down in quick succession at Tan Son Nhut airport on the outskirts of Saigon. Their crews, US military personnel, were received by a like number of French pilots. The hand-over was completed in a matter of minutes. Lucien Bodard, a French journalist, witnessed the proceedings.

> No ceremonies, no speeches. Standing opposite one another the pilots of the two countries saluted; then soldiers appeared, carrying pots of paint, and they painted the red, white and blue rings of France over the white star of the American Air Force.

Some weeks later a Liberty ship, escorted by French minesweepers, patrol boats and covering aircraft, steamed slowly round the loops of the Saigon River. Although it docked under the tightest security, Bodard was again in attendance and somehow got aboard. The ship's cargo, he ascertained, was all military hardware; and its crew was American.

> I gazed at all these big tattooed uncaring men and I realized that America had really swung into action and that she was backing the [French] Expeditionary Force for good and all. The change was plain to see and it was unbelievable.

What, one wonders, would the Dutch in Java not have given for such support? It was less than a year since Washington had propelled The Hague's reluctant but, in Rooseveltian terms, conscientious colonialists to the negotiators' Round Table; now the same US government was supporting and arming those veritable pariahs of European colonialism, the intransigent French.

In that these were the first military deliveries direct from the USA to France's hard-pressed forces in Indo-China, they did indeed mark a turn-around in US policy which would have profound consequences. There was, however, nothing new about the equipment involved. The planes were C-47s, and the Liberty ship's cargo was mainly jeeps; the ubiquitous Liberty ship was itself symbolic of the US economy's dominating role as manufacturer to the world. In Asia as elsewhere it was American hardware which had won the Second World War; and it was with American hardware that the European colonial powers had been endeavouring to reclaim their empires ever since.

The Dutch in Indonesia, like the British in Malaya, had been dependent on American transport supplied under wartime lend-lease agreements. Some of the trucks had born insignia which the Dutch seem to have been less expert than the French at painting out. The Indonesian Republic duly noted their US provenance. Though not supplied direct from the US, nor intended for use in the suppression of nationalist governments, this transport pool represented an operational asset of incalculable value.

It could be argued that the transportation requirements of a war on the scale of that in the Pacific had made a more lasting impact on the region than the war itself. Distances had telescoped as bombers were upgraded, with the B-17, B-26 and B-29 steadily extending operational ranges and payloads. Such technology would be readily transferred to civil aviation. At sea the armadas of transport and landing craft deployed by MacArthur and Admiral Nimitz littered a thousand beaches and soon found post-war employment as inter-island ferries, displacing the native *prahu* on the most out-of-the-way routes.

Landward communications owed more to the Japanese. Under their direction prisoners-of-war and Javanese labourers had dug and died to push new roads and railways across hitherto impenetrable terrain, most notoriously in Sumatra and from Siam to Burma via, amongst others, the bridge over the River Kwai. In Hong Kong the most conspicuous legacy of Japanese rule was the extension along the Kowloon shoreline of Kai Tak, still in the 1990s its international airport. Similarly throughout Indonesia, New Guinea and the west Pacific, airstrips were laid, again by Allied prisoners-of-war and the equally maltreated Javanese, on islands which even now scarcely justify an air service. The ease of travel and contact which resulted was vital to the Dutch creation of entities like the Great East. It also played no small part in the Republic's subsequent success in realising the territorial ambitions implicit in the term 'Indonesia'.

For theatres of the war where roads were presumed to be rudimentary and transport non-existent, the US Army had specified a new General Purpose Vehicle (GPV). It was to be square enough to be packed in a crate, small enough to be dropped by parachute, and manoeuvrable enough to follow a mule track. The resultant GPV entered service, and found a place in the world's dictionaries, as the 'GP' or 'Jeep'. Produced in staggering quantities, the first all-terrain vehicle became the most ubiquitous transport wherever Allied forces deployed. For MacArthur the jeep, always without canopy so as not to disappoint the camera, was as much a part of his image as the corn-cob pipe and the straw hat. Mounted with bren guns, jeeps became the escorts of every convoy, be it bound for Bataan or Bandung. From them men fought, and beside them they slept, like horses. And when the war was over, they were mostly left behind. Whole economies came back to life thanks to the jeep. In Malaya the planter's jeep would soon be clad all over in steel plate to deflect the sniper's bullet, the driver navigating through a letter-box aperture left in the blanked-out windscreen. In the Philippines local body-builders stretched the chassis to produce bus-size 'jeepneys', or squashed the superstructure to make jeep-type dragsters. Fanciful customising of this most minimalist of automobiles became a Filipino art-form in which connoisseurs of comparative cultures invariably detected symbolic evidence of the 'special' US-Filipino relationship.

Recalling those first deliveries direct to Indo-China, the only vehicles which created a more dramatic change than the jeeps coming ashore in Saigon's docks were the transports that stood parked on the apron of the city's airport. The military C-47, also known as the Douglas DC-3 or 'Dakota', was produced in greater quantities than any other transport before or since. Introduced in the late 1930s, more than 10,000 had rolled off the production lines by the end of the war. When taxi-ing on some Jap-built jungle airstrip, nose in the air, tail tight to the ground, the Dakota's stubby profile seemed almost bird-like. To the starving inmates of many a Japanese prison camp they became the doves of peace, throbbing symbols of all that was reassuring and once again possible. In a death camp in Kuching, Agnes Keith, the American wife of British North Borneo's Conservator of Forests, and her now four-year-old son refused to believe reports that the three years of hell were over. Then a DC-3 swept low over the camp with Australian troops leaning out of the big side doors, cheering, blowing kisses and showering the bedraggled inmates with luxuries – soap, quinine, vitamins, chocolate. Then she believed; then she wept.

General Percival, the ill-fated commander of Allied troops in Malaya in 1942, was plucked by Dakota from his place of imprisonment in Manchuria to stand, cadaverous but unbowed, beside a triumphant MacArthur at the Japanese surrender in Tokyo Bay. A week later Mountbatten, from another Dakota, watched the exercise that should have been the full-scale 'Zipper' invasion of Malaya while *en route* to the surrender ceremonies in Singapore. By Dakota from Tokyo Manuel Roxas returned to the Philippines to be exculpated by MacArthur and then to wrest the Presidency from Osmena. And by Dakota from Kunming those rival Majors, Jean Sainteny and Archimedes Patti, ventured into Vietminh-controlled Hanoi at the height of the 'August Revolution'. Two months later it was a British Dakota which showered Surabaya with leaflets demanding the surrender of arms which triggered Mallaby's death and the 'sea of fire'. After the first 'police action', privately owned Dakotas operated the air-bridge from Bangkok via Bukittinggi that enabled the Jogja Republic to circumvent the Dutch blockade; and it was aboard one of these Dakotas, painted all over in red and white for the occasion, that Sukarno had eventually returned in triumph to Jakarta in December 1949.

By then many US military C-47s had been sold off to enter civilian service. Superseding the motley collection of bi-planes, sea-planes and flying boats of pre-war days, they became the backbone of an at last reliable network of scheduled air services. In the opening up of the East, if the jeep was the horse, the Dakota was the stage-coach. Available for charter and with capacity for 20–30 passengers, it enabled well-staffed political missions to shuttle between capitals. Before the war a man like Sukarno had never been outside Indonesia; he knew of other independence struggles and their leaders only from the press and radio. After the war his emissaries, like Sjahrir, could pop up in Delhi, The Hague or New York at a few days' notice. By 1955 Sukarno himself bestrode the world scene, hosting in Bandung the biggest gathering of 'third world' luminaries ever staged. Air transport made this Asia-Africa Conference possible, and thereafter Sukarno became an indefatigable traveller.

Perhaps the post-war internationalisation of the anti-colonial struggle owed as much to aviation as it did to ideology. Perhaps, too, empire as a mechanism of control was ending because ease of communication was making it obsolete. No longer did the ability to influence and intervene principally depend on the maintenance of elaborate administrative structures and far-flung military establishments. If a long-range capacity could afford equally effective control, empire's days were numbered. Imperialism, of course, was a different matter.

Nothing if not versatile, the Dakotas in Indo-China served as both civilian and military transports. You could tell there was a major operation on, it was said, by the sudden cancellation of scheduled services. By 1954 the French could deploy about a hundred Dakotas, more than any other type of aircraft in their command. On their drops of supplies and ammunition countless beleaguered jungle garrisons would utterly depend. When the struggle duly climaxed in the débâcle of Dien Bien Phu, Dakota pilots would fly round the clock, each plane making up to twelve passes through the Vietminh's lethal anti-aircraft flak to unload its 2.5-ton load through those awkward side doors. To a considerable extent the availability of air transport, coupled with the enemy's total lack of any airborne counter-capacity, would dictate the character of France's Indo-China war and fatally encourage the delusions of its high command.

Six months before that first delivery of American C-47s, while approaching Tan Son Nhut airport on a scheduled flight, the English novelist and travel writer Norman Lewis had noticed a puff of smoke rising from a small village below. A fellow passenger, a colonel in the Foreign Legion, also saw it. 'Assuming', writes Lewis, 'the easy expression of good fellowship of a man devoted to the service of violence', the colonel announced '*Une Operation*'.

> Somehow, as he spoke, he seemed linked psychically to what was going on below. Authority flowed back into the travel-weary figure ... Beneath our eyes violence was being done, but we were as detached from it almost as from history. Space, like time, anaesthetizes the imagination. One could understand what an aid to untroubled killing the bombing plane must be.

Who Would Strike First?

Not unlike an air-lift, the first Indo-China war bridged two of the twentieth century's most titanic struggles. It took off amidst the certainties of the Second World War and terminated, nine years later, on the front line of the Cold War. An obscure theatre of the Allied confrontation with Japanese hegemonism in 1945, Indo-China would become, by 1954, the principal venue in the global confrontation of late twentieth-century ideologies.

An overview of world history could simply present the story of its war as one of transition and escalation in the global power game, without so much as mentioning that it was also, and principally, a colonial war. Yet Vietnam's history, both before and since, provides ample testimony that independence rather than ideology was indeed the lodestar of the Vietnamese people. The flag of the Democratic Republic might be red but its only emblem is the single yellow star of a united Vietnam. Ho Chi Minh, however dedicated a Communist, was a nationalist first and last. His 'true and sole objective' according to Jean Sainteny, one of the few Westerners who would get to know him well, was the independence of Vietnam.

For France, too, the Indo-China war fitted into an all too familiar pattern of colonial authority under challenge from a subversive minority backed by predatory foreigners. Additionally it was seen by many, and in particular by de Gaulle, as a test of empire. Humiliated by the Germans in Europe, the glorious ideals of the motherland had survived the war, most notably in Africa, thanks to the wider *collectivité française* of the empire. This world-wide French 'community', a hundred million strong, whose good fortune it was to share in the enlightened republicanism and cultural supremacy that epitomised France, also held the key to the restoration of France as a world power. Reclaiming parts of the empire lost during the war was as essential to the process of rehabilitating its world-power status as reclaiming metropolitan France. In fact it was a continuation of the same process; the future of the empire was no more negotiable than that of the *metropole*; France could not be said to have been restored until it was completed.

A logical extension of this outlook was the Fourth Republic's emphasis on the concept of a French Union. Like the British Commonwealth, this was supposed to subsume both the *metropole* and the empire in an institutional framework founded on equality, mutual respect and shared values. But the powers reserved to the French Union, unlike the Commonwealth, would transcend those of its parts while its constitution, when eventually agreed, would ensure a built-in majority for the mother country. Hence talk of autonomy, freedom or even independence when, as was invariably the case, qualified by the phrase 'within the French Union', meant no such thing. Universal, indissoluble and spectacularly gratifying, the French Union became yet another device for frustrating nationalist aspirations.

This scheme for an over-arching French Union was what furnished the inspiration for the 1946 Linggadjati agreement between the Dutch and the Indonesian Republic. Parallels between the postwar experience of Java and that of southern Indo-China are legion. Responsibility for both places, it will be recalled, had been transferred to Mountbatten's South East Asia Command just as the war ended. Although intelligence about either was scarce, both had apparently acquired nationalist governments. To the French as to the Dutch, these were 'puppet', 'so-called' or 'self-styled' republics, heavily compromised by their association with the Japanese. The Americans, however, saw them in a different light; Washington, after all, was about to recognise the Republic of the Philippines. And for similar reasons many of SEAC's British personnel, like Major Charles Blascheck of the Gurkhas, doubted the logic of restoring rival empires.

> We had no antagonism towards the Viet Minh on our arrival. We knew that independence was coming for India, and thought that the Vietnamese should also have their independence – and we were all largely sympathetic to them.

In both Java and southern Vietnam SEAC's role was almost identical – disarm and evacuate the Japanese, facilitate the rehabilitation programme for prisoners-of-war, and maintain law and order. In neither case were the areas to be occupied, or the degree of intervention that this last requirement might entail, made crystal clear. There was also anxiety about the Japanese. Could they be trusted to observe the terms of the surrender? Could they be used to enforce law and order? To what extent were they sponsoring, assisting and arming the nationalists?

In Indo-China as in Indonesia, the Allied troops at Mountbatten's disposal were almost entirely Indian. What of their loyalty? Should they be deployed against Asian nationalists? Only one division, the Indian 20th under Major-General Douglas Gracey, was earmarked for Indo-China. Fortunately it was largely comprised of Nepalese Gurkhas and Muslims from the Punjab and Hyderabad. Vietminh appeals to 'the sons of Gandhi' were therefore badly miscalculated. Islamic sympathies went untested, there being no Muslims in Vietnam, while to the bloodthirsty Gurkhas the 'Vitamins', as they insisted on calling the Vietminh, became but a dietary supplement.

Gracey arrived in Saigon by the inevitable Dakota on 13 September 1945, two weeks ahead of Christison, his opposite number in Jakarta. In Vietnam, unlike in Java, no Colonel van der Post was on hand to brief the new arrivals about the strength of nationalist sentiment; nor was it evident that the Vietminh were running an effective government. Whilst Indonesian nationalists, under Japanese tutelage, had acquired several years' experience of administering the country, Vietnam had remained under French administration until the previous March when the Japanese had overthrown Decoux's regime. Even then the Japanese, while encouraging the Emperor Bao Dai to declare Vietnam's independence, had retained control of Cochin-China (including Saigon). This region, which with southern Annam comprised SEAC's area of operation, was only turned over to the nationalists on the eve of the Japanese surrender in August. Rent by factionalism, various nationalist groups had, nevertheless, formed a common front and in late August acknowledged the authority of the Vietminh government in Hanoi. A subordinate administration was set up in Saigon, mass demonstrations were organised, and public buildings commandeered.

This provisional government in Saigon hoped to collaborate with SEAC and so win international recognition before the French could eject it. A Vietminh deputation therefore presented itself at the airport to welcome Gracey. He ignored them. 'We didn't know who they were – they were just a little group which turned out to be the Viet Minh,' recalled the General's Chief of Staff somewhat ingenuously. Seemingly Gracey, unlike Christison in Java, had no intention of gratifying the nationalists.

Two weeks earlier, the 2 September 'Fête de l'Indépendance', though celebrated in Hanoi with a discipline that had impressed even Jean Sainteny, had gone badly wrong in Saigon. Outside the gloomy brick cathedral a Catholic priest had been mysteriously shot. This was the signal for more shooting, both French onlookers and Vietnamese demonstrators falling victim. The rally broke up in chaos, French residences were pillaged, and numerous French civilians disappeared into custody. Although soon released on the orders of the provisional government, their experience plus the ill-disguised hostility of the demonstrators had made a profound impact on French opinion. It also predisposed Gracey to shun the Vietminh and doubt their utility in his pacification programme.

Instead he worked closely with the French. On 21 September he issued a proclamation designed to restore law and order. A curfew was imposed, all arms were to be surrendered, and meetings and demonstrations were banned; additional curbs were imposed on the press and radio. In effect the nationalist government was being shut down. Although strikes and curfew-breaking followed, Gracey, a fine if guileless soldier whose nickname was 'Bruiser', went doggedly on his way, taking over police stations, banks and other buildings held by the nationalists and handing them to the French. The crackdown climaxed two days later when he authorised the French to stage an almost bloodless coup. A description of this bizarre episode by Emory Pierce, evidently a participant, is quoted in Peter Dunn's *The First Vietnam War*.

> As clocks chimed 0300 a ragtime, grim silent army of 300 men, armed to the teeth, padded silently along the deserted streets. The Coup d'Etat was beginning and Saigon was about to become French again. This was the culmination of an incredible week of turbulent rumours and imminent uprisings. Who would strike first? Would it be the Annamese, angry, confident, truculent? Or the French? 'Three o'clock Sunday morning', the word went round; and 300 tough men went out to take a city.

To those who hold France responsible for the subsequent war, this was when it began. For if the coup was bloodless, the immediate aftermath was not. Saigon's French community, plus troops belonging to France's colonial army who had just been released from Japanese camps, went berserk. They saw the coup as giving them the freedom of the city. Vietnamese were insulted and assaulted, their homes ransacked, old scores settled. Gracey berated the French High Commissioner and demanded he disarm his miscreants, but it was too late.

For those who hold the Vietnamese responsible, the war began two days later. In response to the French coup, armed nationalist groups, many of them apparently beyond the control of the now ousted provisional government, began to fire indiscriminately on French and SEAC forces. A general strike plunged the city into darkness, fires raged out of control because the nationalists had seized the fire engines, and in the midst of this black inferno a mob of

Vietnamese attacked an up-market residential quarter of the city. About 150 French men, women and children were mutilated or raped, then massacred; a like number were abducted for more leisurely disposal.

Gracey, still blaming the French colonial forces and the civilian *colons* as much as the Vietminh, urged Franco-Vietnamese talks while he waited for the arrival of the remainder of his Division. The talks got nowhere, neither the French nor the Vietnamese in Saigon being empowered to make the concessions on sovereignty which each demanded. A fragile and far from effective truce lasted until the second week in October, when nationalist forces ambushed a party of engineers *en route* to Tan Son Nhut, then very nearly took the airport itself. Mountbatten, whose support of 'Bruiser' Gracey's interventionism had thus far been less than whole-hearted, now authorised a significant extension of SEAC's responsibilities.

As it seemed clear that the Viet Minh spokesmen were incapable of ensuring that the agreements into which they had entered would be honoured, I [that is, Mountbatten] ordered that strong action should be taken by the British/Indian forces to secure further key points, and to widen and consolidate the perimeter of these areas.

Gracey's Division was at last approaching full strength and General Jacques Philippe Leclerc, the liberator of Paris in 1944, had just arrived to complete his work of liberation as Commander-in-Chief of French forces in Indo-China. Although the bulk of these last had yet to materialise, their shipment from France was now given the highest priority. In the meantime Gracey and Leclerc pushed outwards from Saigon, 'widening' their ever wider 'perimeter' and using Japanese troops to 'consolidate' it. Cambodia was reclaimed with scarcely a shot being fired; Anglo-French forces pushed far to the north-east to retake Dalat and Nha Trang, and further areas were cleared in the Mekong delta to the south-west. The nationalists usually melted away only to regroup, re-infiltrate and, under cover of night, retaliate. No road was ever 'safe', no 'cleared' area remained so for long. The 'war without fronts' had begun.

SEAC, however, was far from despondent. The French, and Leclerc in particular, were increasingly confident of being able to handle the situation for themselves. The Japanese were at last collaborating, both operationally and in their disarmament and repatriation. Above all, the alarming situation in Java now revealed events in

Indo-China in a much more favourable light. Saigon was safer than Jakarta and, as Leclerc observed, there had been nothing that could remotely compare with the recent 'sea of fire' in Surabaya.

In the light of these Indonesian difficulties, as 1945 came to an end the British priority in Indo-China was to disengage. The first troops had in fact just left and, with the arrival of a new French Division, most of the remainder would do so by the end of January 1946. As against fourteen months in Java, the British were in Indo-China for only four. It was still a controversial interlude. Gracey, in particular, would be much criticised for taking it upon himself to reimpose French rule. Leclerc's insistence that Gracey 'had saved Indo-China' seemed to bear this out; so did Saigon's generosity in making him a Freeman of the city. Whether he had exceeded his orders is still debated, but his initiatives were all subsequently approved. They may have averted a worse war and certainly left open the door to negotiations. Perhaps a more telling legacy of the Allied occupation was SEAC's disposal to the French of all arms collected from the Japanese and much of its own military hardware including transport, aircraft and artillery.

Equipped by the Allies and still acting as one of the Allies, the French were not going to be denied their foremost colony in Asia. Internationally their sovereignty was not in dispute and it was sanctioned by a domestic consensus which would survive even the frantic musical chairs of the Fourth Republic's administrations. On the other hand Saigon's short-lived Vietminh administration could scarcely claim even *de facto* status. It lacked the military and international credentials of its Jakarta counterpart and it lacked the discipline and leadership of its Hanoi sponsor. With or without British interference, it could never have withstood French determination to reclaim Cochin-China.

Tonkin Overture

The pattern of the French return to Indo-China resembles that of its conquest in the nineteenth century: first the toehold in Saigon, then the outward thrusts into Cochin-China and Cambodia, and finally the sea-borne assault on Tonkin. By February 1946 the time had come to address the last. The object, as before, was to gain a foothold whence to reoccupy the Red River delta and Hanoi, then push again up towards the treacherous Chinese frontier. But, as in

François Garnier's day, an amphibious assault on the Tonkin coast was not relished. Far preferable would be a gradual intervention which would secure French interests without precipitating war in the north and so jeopardising its considerable French population.

A legitimate opportunity for such intervention was provided by the Chinese. When the post-war liberation of Indo-China south of the 16th parallel had been awarded to Mountbatten and his South East Asia Command, the area north of the 16th parallel, that is all Tonkin and much of Annam, had been retained within the US sphere of operations; but to oblige an ally of whom much was expected in the post-war era, Washington delegated its role in Indo-China to the Chinese Nationalists. It was thus that Ho Chi Minh's just established Democratic Republic of Vietnam had first to contend not with the French or the British but with General Lu Han and his 200,000 Kuomintang troops and camp-followers. As one of the Allies, the General claimed, like Gracey, to be neutral in the war of words between the Vietminh government and the French. Yet as a Nationalist, he felt no sympathy for French ambitions to reclaim the country, while as a Kuomintang general he was highly suspicious of a Vietminh government dominated by Ho, Giap and other avowed Communists.

Aware of these Chinese reservations, the Hanoi government accommodated some of its nationalist rivals and assumed a less doctrinaire stance. According to Sainteny, the Chinese presence may also have saved the lives of the 20,000 French prisoners who had been in captivity ever since the Japanese coup in March 1945. Additionally the Chinese provided a much needed breathing space for the Hanoi government to introduce a wide range of social measures, including an impressive programme to tackle the appalling famine which now ravaged large parts of Tonkin. On the other hand, the famine was being exacerbated by the presence of the vast and none too disciplined Chinese army. Vietminh strongholds on the northern frontier were being taken over by the Chinese, and Vietnamese fears of being dominated by their ancient enemy across the frontier resurfaced. In the need to get rid of the Chinese as soon as possible, the Hanoi government and the French at last discovered common ground.

During February 1946 French and Chinese negotiators thrashed out an agreement in Chungking. In return for France abandoning all her treaty rights and treaty ports in China and conceding commercial privileges in Tonkin, the Chinese would withdraw from Indo-China.

Meanwhile in Hanoi, Jean Sainteny was engaged in prolonged talks with Ho Chi Minh. Apart from a short absence to be briefed as the new French Commissioner for Tonkin and to collect his beloved Irish setter, Sainteny had been in Hanoi continuously since the previous August. His lot remained unenviable. The Chinese were openly hostile while the small American contingent continued to be ambivalent. Vietminh propaganda roundly denounced him, Paris seemed deaf to his endless entreaties for assistance and direction, and his own compatriots in Hanoi scoffed at his impotence. The latter wanted to see the French flag flying once more from public buildings, but when Sainteny, to assuage their criticisms, ventured to tie a small *tricolore* on his jeep, the vehicle was mobbed and the French Commissioner hauled off for interrogation. Worse still, he had his American rivals to thank for his release.

During January 1946, an average month, Sainteny logged 145 crimes against Hanoi's French population including 6 assassinations and 12 attempted poisonings. They lived in fear, as did Sainteny himself; it was, he wrote, like walking a tight-rope. The only satisfaction came, improbably, from his almost daily meetings with Ho Chi Minh. To the dashing young Sainteny 'Uncle' Ho, now in his mid-fifties, was always 'the old revolutionary', 'the old fighter', 'the old fox'. They made an odd pair, the tall chain-smoking, dog-loving Commissioner with his white linen suits and his youthful looks beside the frail Annamite mandarin in whose wizened features the eyes so blazed as to threaten the kindling of the world's sparsest beard. Yet their respect was mutual and, though Frenchmen and Vietminh were already killing one another in Cochin-China, they forged a vital friendship. In 'the old fox' Sainteny saw the real possibility of a settlement.

> His wide knowledge, his intelligence, his unbelievable energy, his abstemiousness and his total dedication had earned him incomparable prestige and popularity in the eyes of the people. It is undeniably tragic that France had minimised this man and not known how to understand his strength and the power which he commanded . . . His words, his conduct, his attitude, his personality all led to the conviction that he was opposed to the use of force. Throughout this period it is beyond question that he aspired to becoming the Gandhi of Indo-China.

Max André, a French parliamentarian who had been sent to assist Sainteny, was also impressed by Ho's moderation. With the Vietminh government disappointed in its earlier expectations of US support and disillusioned by the Chinese, Ho seemed now to be pinning his hopes on the good faith of Sainteny and on the widespread expectation that France itself would soon have a left-wing government sympathetic to nationalist demands. Thus, even as 15,000 French troops from Cochin-China anchored off the coast of Tonkin, the almost unthinkable came to pass. On 6 March 1946 Sainteny and Ho signed an accord under which the French might peacefully return to Hanoi.

Next morning Sainteny raised the French colours in front of his Commissariat and for the first time in a year the French population surged out into the streets and decked their homes in hastily made *tricolores*. Sainteny was reminded of August 1944 when Paris had erupted with red, white and blue under the noses of the occupying forces. French troops began landing at Haiphong almost immediately. Ten days later Leclerc, the liberator of Paris, entered Hanoi to a rapturous reception from his compatriots. Sainteny's *pari*, unlike that of Decoux, seemed to have paid off.

> The enthusiasm of the French population was at its peak. Mobbed by the crowd which crammed Rue Richaud, Leclerc had to appear on the balcony of my office, where he simply announced 'Hanoi, the last stage of the liberation!'

In an atmosphere of goodwill and genuine respect, Leclerc and Ho Chi Minh raised their glasses to Franco-Vietnamese friendship. Giap, still dressed in flapping suit and floppy trilby, accompanied the ramrod Leclerc, uniformed and beribboned, to inspect the guard of honour. As Vietnam's *premier résistant*, it was, Giap confided to Leclerc, a real honour to salute *le Grand Résistant Français*. Leclerc, according to Sainteny, smiled; there had been little to smile about in Cochin-China and the General was already convinced that a similar war in the north would be disastrous. But now the Vietminh had ordered a ceasefire which was supposed to include Cochin-China while France had recognised the Republic of Vietnam as a 'free state having its own government, parliament, army, and finances'. There were grounds for optimism.

The inevitable qualification that this 'free state' formed 'part of the Indo-Chinese Federation and the French Union' meant little at the time. Neither entity had yet been defined. If belonging to the Union was, in the words of the historian Anthony Short, 'like taking up the tenancy of a building which had not yet been constructed',

Ho was confident of being able to influence the plans and, given a left-wing government in Paris, of working with a sympathetic architect. The stationing of French troops in Tonkin was supposed to be only temporary. The unification of Tonkin, Annam and Cochin-China was to be the subject of a referendum which Ho was confident of winning. And though, as all were painfully aware, the 6 March agreement left many crucial issues undecided, government-to-government negotiations were to get underway immediately.

They did so not just immediately but in two places at once. The Vietminh insisted they be held in France where Communist support within the French parliament could be advantageous; the French insisted on Dalat in Cochin-China where no such complication would arise. The Dalat Conference, though it met first, was still sitting when Ho left for France and the Fontainebleau Conference.

Neither location advanced the cause of peace. In Dalat the major stumbling block proved to be the status of Cochin-China on whose incorporation into a united Vietnam Vo Nguyen Giap was adamant. The proposed referendum he saw merely as a process of ratification. But the French, and in particular Admiral Georges Thierry d'Argenlieu, the High Commissioner for all Indo-China, still regarded Cochin-China as a distinct and immensely valuable colony in that it was both the rice-bowl and the rubber-bucket of Vietnam. To prove d'Argenlieu's point, the Saigon authorities had just installed an advisory council which dutifully proclaimed Cochin-China's separate status. The referendum was therefore unnecessary and certainly could not be contemplated until all the country's warring nationalist factions, many of them beyond the control of the Vietminh, had laid down their arms.

The same problem nearly scuppered the Fontainebleau talks before they had begun. After a long delay while Paris cobbled together another coalition government, the Conference opened to news that d'Argenlieu had just taken a further step towards confrontation by officially recognising Cochin-China as a separate 'free republic' with its own provisional government. To call this new creation a puppet state would be to flatter its credentials. So transparent a ruse to frustrate Hanoi's integrationist ambitions found no sanction in the 6 March agreement and was duly denounced by the Vietnamese delegates. They stayed at the talks only in the hopes of influencing the form of the still undefined French Union and of exploiting left-wing support within the French parliament. On both counts they were disappointed. A Union of sovereign states along the lines of the British Commonwealth, as suggested by the Vietnamese, found no favour with the French; and the support of the French Communist Party, though willingly given so long as the party remained in opposition, proved counter-productive. Right-wing delegates as a matter of course now opposed all Vietnamese demands simply because they were supported by the left; Vietnam became a casualty of the *metropole*'s chaotic party politics.

With France, like Holland, still trying to decide on its own constitution, colonial policy was bedevilled as much by confusion as by intransigence. Fifty years earlier the great Lyautey had blamed the wretched state of colonial rule in Tonkin on 'the anarchy of our government' and its 'muddled enterprises'. Nothing had changed. The provisional governments in Paris lacked the mandates to lay down policy, let alone make concessions. With 'no principles and as many methods as persons', Indo-China policy was left to officials like Sainteny and d'Argenlieu to make of it what they would. Thus the Fontainebleau Conference ended as disastrously as it had begun – with word of another Dalat conference. This time not only was Cochin-China to be represented as a separate state but d'Argenlieu, imitating van Mook's policy in regard to Borneo and the Great East, was floating the idea of yet another 'free state' in the southern half of Annam. The one Indo-Chinese republic not represented at Dalat was that of Hanoi, arguably the only properly constituted and democratically elected government (there had been elections to its National Assembly in 1945) within the still provisional French Union.

In disgust the Vietnamese delegation at Fontainebleau finally clambered back aboard their Dakota. Ho Chi Minh stayed on in Paris, as did Sainteny. 'The Gandhi of Indo-China' had gambled everything on winning concessions. Rebuffs at the conference tables had only discredited his moderation and strengthened his hard-line rivals in Hanoi; even his personal authority had been undermined. Yet still he hoped for some crumb of comfort to take back to Hanoi. 'Don't let me leave like this,' he begged Sainteny. 'Give me something with which to confront those who seek to sideline me. You will not regret it.' But all the French government could manage was a weak-worded *modus vivendi* which kept the negotiating door ajar. Adding his signature to this document, Ho was reported to have muttered that he was signing his own death warrant. A peace, already bogged down in indecision and acrimony, now threatened to drag its sponsors with it.

Enlisement, 'bogging down', would be a word much used to characterise the forthcoming war. In the last of their interviews Ho Chi Minh left Sainteny in no doubt as to what to expect.

'If we must fight, we will fight,' he declared with a look of resignation. 'You will kill ten of our men for every one of yours we kill, and it is you who will end up wearing yourselves out.'

The killing began in Tonkin – it had never really ceased in Cochin-China – less than a month after Ho regained Vietnamese soil. On 20 November a French attempt to levy customs dues in the port of Haiphong led to a scuffle, the taking of French hostages, and the loss of French lives. Although both parties in Hanoi seemingly accepted a settlement of the affair, orders came from the hawkish d'Argenlieu for retaliatory action. Two days later Haiphong became the Vietnamese Surabaya as artillery, naval guns and aircraft bombarded the city. The population, less perhaps 6,000 dead, streamed out into the countryside and the French took possession of Tonkin's major port.

Lang Son on the Chinese border and Tourane (Da Nang), the port for the Annamite capital of Hue, also saw fighting and were then occupied by the French. Their compatriots in Hanoi once again braced themselves for Vietminh retaliation. Once again Sainteny was dispatched from France to use his relationship with Ho to good effect; and once again he found himself teetering on a tight-rope, totally unsupported.

We are here to execute orders but these orders, first we need to receive them. France ought to know whether she wants to keep her Empire and how she expects to do this. Whether she is willing for a few moments to give up her preoccupation with parochial politicking and whether she is willing to give orders to those who are trying to hold it for her.

'There is not a moment to lose,' he added. The situation was far worse than in the previous year; in fact it was already beyond control. On 19 December, to pre-empt the sort of coup which had overtaken the Vietminh government in Saigon fourteen months earlier, the Vietnamese plunged Hanoi into darkness, severed most of its highways, and launched an all-out attack on French installations. Sainteny himself was badly wounded when the armoured car in which he was travelling hit a mine. But the French had been warned of trouble and were ready to respond. Fighting raged throughout the city for the rest of the month with the Vietnamese taking heavy casualties. The Vietminh moved out into the countryside, Ho and his government narrowly avoiding capture in the process. It would be six and half years before they regained their capital.

The Forgotten War

Given the parallels between the independence struggles of Indonesia and Vietnam, one might now have expected the Vietminh to launch an international crusade. After all, an effective and elected government of what even the French had recognised as a 'free state' had been overturned, its nationals killed and its territory infringed. Invoking the Atlantic and UN charters, appeals could have been directed to world opinion; delegates could have been sent to the UN, and recognition sought from sympathetic governments in India, the Philippines and the Middle East.

And what of the United States? It was only a year since the Vietminh, much to the envy of Sukarno's nationalists, had been receiving encouragement and even arms from Major Archimedes Patti and his colleagues of the China-based OSS, a forerunner of the CIA. Surely now was the moment to invite further US interest, if only to draw attention to the French use of American war *matériel* for colonial oppression. In Indonesia's case international opinion and US pressure would eventually cow the Dutch. Why not, then, the French?

The answer would seem to lie partly in the exclusive nature of French colonialism. In 1946 no one else cared about Indo-China because no one else had an interest in the country. Sixty years of the *mission civilisatrice*, of *mise en valeur* and *assimilation*, had created a society unused to looking beyond France and an economy wholly dependent on France. France's prestige, rather than the colony's commercial potential, had informed the acquisition of Indo-China, and to the creation of 'a France in Asia' a degree of isolation had always been conducive. French protectionism had therefore excluded foreign investors and restricted foreign trade. The country's rubber was controlled by the French and its rice, the largest export earner, mainly by Saigon's Chinese community. No international conglomerates were losing any sleep over the state of the Indo-Chinese market.

There was also the question of the Vietminh's Communist sympathies. While in Paris for the Fontainebleau conference, Ho had visited the US ambassador to assure him that the Vietminh were dedicated to independence within the French Union rather than to Communism. Although this was more than three years before the Communist triumph in China and the Truman doctrine of containment, the Communist or 'totalitarian' nature of the Tonkin Republic counted against it. The US State Department, while still distrusting colonialism, adhering to the idea of trusteeship, and urging a negotiated settlement, reserved its belief in intervention; but it was unable to decide on whose behalf to exercise it and as yet attached no global significance to the struggle.

This caution had much to do with the relative importance of France in western Europe. If the Netherlands had little choice but to accept and defer to American prompting, France was a very different proposition. The left-wing coalition of French socialists and Communists on which Ho had counted finally came to power just as the war in Tonkin broke out. It brought the Vietminh little consolation, even the Communists supporting the draft of more troops to Indo-China. But it left the US and its allies in no doubt as to the precarious nature of French politics. If the choice was between supporting Vietnamese independence and so embarrassing centrist opinion in France or ignoring the Vietnamese and so strengthening the centrist parties, the priority was obvious.

The Vietminh were not unrepresented abroad. Delegations in Bangkok and Paris voiced the party's grievances and appeals were indeed made to the United Nations. Only their timing was wrong. India, later an intermediary with the Vietminh government, would gain its independence in August 1947 – so just as the Dutch were launching their first 'police action' against the Jogja Republic but not until eight months after the battle for Hanoi. When a further appeal from the Vietminh government was received by the UN in September 1947, new political initiatives were underway.

Following the December 1946 capture of Hanoi, the French Expeditionary Force had been boosted to 115,000 men in a determined effort to effect a swift extinction of the inferior and isolated Vietminh forces. Pincer movements combining air, land and riverborne forces cut into the Vietminh-controlled zone immediately north of Hanoi. Their execution was copy-book correct but the enemy proved elusive. In a pattern which would become all too familiar, the Vietminh, and on one occasion Ho himself, melted into the jungle just as the 'paras' landed. By securing the Red River delta and Route Coloniale 4, which ran along the Chinese frontier in the north, the French intended to contain the Vietminh and then exterminate them. But instead of containment within the designated quadrangle of billowing forest, these pressure tactics, like pounding a pillow, resulted merely in diffusing the enemy. Lucien Bodard, in his classic account of *The Quicksand War*, put his finger on the problem.

> The war on the Chinese frontier might have been won if the French of 1947 had imitated their forefathers of the days of colonial conquest and had plunged into the jungle to fight the enemy hand to hand. But they clung to roads; they were the prisoners of their own cars and trucks; and they therefore condemned themselves to failure . . . The Expeditionary Force most bitterly experienced the truth of the first great rule of war in Indo-China, the rule which states that every undertaking which is not a total success is fated to become a total disaster.

'The forgotten war', as Bodard calls the pre-1950 phase, settled into a stalemate in which the fighting in the north flared as unpredictably and ubiquitously as it had for some years in the south. According to Giap 'the armed forces of the two sides were enmeshed, like hair in a comb'. The French preferred to talk about 'mopping-up operations' and 'pacification programmes'. If a military solution still looked remote, they had hopes of the new political initiative which was launched in late 1947.

This centred on the enigmatic figure of Bao Dai, the ex-Emperor. Having abdicated in favour of the Vietminh in the summer of 1945, he had been rewarded for this transfer of legitimacy by privileged access to Ho as his 'supreme adviser'. However in early 1946, while on a mission to China, Bao Dai absconded to Hong Kong. There, like Aguinaldo, Sun Yat-sen and Ho himself in earlier times, he succumbed to Kowloon's heady cocktail of sanctuary, celebrity and indulgence. In 1947 the American humourist S. J. Perelman tracked him down to a gaggle of hostesses in the alcove of a glitzy night-club.

> The royal exile, a short slippery-looking customer rather on the pudgy side and dipped in Crisco, wore a fixed, oily grin that was vaguely reptilian. Since he spoke almost no English [and Perelman only classroom French] . . . I inquired whether the pen of his uncle was in the garden.

Apparently the query was fraught with delicate implications involving the conflict in Indo-China, for he shrugged evasively and buried his nose in his whisky-and-soda.

Celebrity had its drawbacks. Scarcely a flight touched down at Hong Kong's Kai Tak airport without disgorging at least one traveller intent on disturbing His ex-Majesty's dalliance. Some came on behalf of the Vietminh who saw in a renewed understanding with Bao Dai the means of impressing Paris with their nationalist, non-ideological and hence impeccable credentials as the only people with whom to re-open negotiations. Most, however, were either French or their Vietnamese surrogates. They too saw in Bao Dai the acceptable, if glistening, face of Vietnamese nationalism. Around his ample figure it might just be possible to construct a tractable and non-Communist consensus, one which would wean moderate nationalist opinion from the Vietminh, win international, and especially American, support, and yet not be totally opposed to collaboration with the French.

For more than two years, Bao Dai, a genuine nationalist and a shrewd if lethargic operator, prevaricated. The price for his eventual co-operation, as enshrined in the Elysée agreements of March 1949, included the setting up of a central government for a united Vietnam (including Cochin-China) and the cession to it, albeit within the French Union, of 'independence', a word hitherto notably absent from French dialogue. Ho Chi Minh would have settled for less in 1946. In 1949, with Bao Dai's only discernible support coming from Paris, the promised independence would prove largely illusory and the promised central government insubstantial; it comprised little more than office-holders, most of them discredited. Yet on paper the terms were generous, indeed too generous for right-wing opinion in France and Saigon; yet anything less would neither have commanded international respect nor have tempted Bao Dai back.

Amongst the first to recognise the Bao Dai government was the United States. Washington had doubts about Bao Dai, as well it might. A monarchist scion heading an unrepresentative regime that proved to be neither popular nor effective, he should have been anathema. But he was also a nationalist beset by revolutionary Communist opponents. As such he was deemed even worthier of support than Sukarno. And since the French were his main sponsors, it was to the French that in 1950 those first shipments of C-47s and jeeps were directed. More would follow. Two years later it was for 'the maintenance [of] C-47s by 25–30 USAF personnel at Nha Trang on a temporary loan basis' that the State Department authorised the dispatch of the first US servicemen to Vietnam. Again, more would follow. Meanwhile the US financial contribution to the French war effort soared steadily towards over 80 per cent by 1954.

What had changed American perceptions of the war was of course Mao's Communist victory in China. The People's Liberation Army reached the Vietnamese frontier in December 1949. A month later both Moscow and Peking recognised Ho's Democratic Republic of Vietnam. The Vietminh's political and physical isolation was at an end. It meant awarding a higher priority to Communist orthodoxy within Vietminh controlled zones, but to Party members like Ho, Giap and Pham Van Dong, Ho's eventual successor, there was no contradiction between Marxist means and the nationalist end. For the safe havens, munitions and training facilities on offer in China, alignment with the Moscow-Peking axis was a small price to pay.

Washington saw it differently. Nationalism and Communism, despite the example of Yugoslavia, were considered incompatible. To the US Secretary of State Dean Acheson, Moscow's recognition gave the lie to Ho's nationalist credentials and revealed him 'in his true colors as the mortal enemy of native independence in Indo-China'. With the outbreak, two months later, of the Korean War and the enunciation of President Truman's doctrine of containing Communism throughout the world, the Cold War took a grip, gelling the ideological confrontation and so hardening US attitudes as to render the American commitment to the defeat of the Vietminh firmer even than that of France.

On the face of it this represented a triumph for French diplomacy. The leading critic of France's colonial empire in Asia had been manoeuvred into an open-ended commitment to support and finance its retention. Like Japan's raid on Pearl Harbor, the Communist victory in China had brought the US into line with European colonialism.

Untroubled Killing

Before 1949 the war had attracted little publicity. Lacking such features as notable battles, heroic figures, an obvious front line, or any recognisable logic, it had largely eluded the war correspondent. Mao's victory in China changed that too. The war without a front line became itself the front line as Indo-China lined up with Korea on Asia's ideological watershed. Correspondents, columnists, academics and pundits began to take notice. Colonial wars, to any but the colonising power, were mere column fillers; the potential flashpoint of the Third World War was headlines.

Facing Communist insurgency in Malaya, the British saw the fate of Indo-China as relevant to the future of all south-east Asia. In France diehard imperialists began to ask why the metropolitan economy was haemorrhaging, and why the cream of its officer corps was dying, in what was now revealed as America's global crusade against Communism. And in America itself Congress was keen to hear that its average annual contribution to the war of half a billion dollars was being used to good effect.

From 1950, and even more so after the Korean armistice in 1953, the Indo-China war was waged in a glare of publicity. News teams set up home in Saigon; editors eagerly commissioned articles from itinerant writers; columnists endeavoured to disentangle the essentials of a still confusing confrontation. Experienced journalists like Lucien Bodard, friend and mentor to the novelist Graham Greene, provided an introduction. There was a war in the cities, according to Bodard, a war in the mountains, a war in the mud of the deltas, and most notoriously a war in the jungle.

> In an area nearly the size of France each side fought in the twilight, without seeing the other; handfuls of men, lost in the enormous landscape, tried to creep up on one another through the darkness and the leaves, to kill at point-blank range. But it was not only the French and Vietminh who hunted one another down . . . The jungle turned into a chaos of hatred in which men varying in civilisation from the Stone Age to the utmost refinement of Buddhism wiped one another out. All the primitive enmities between clans and tribes were exploited, and between the imperialists and the Communists they exploded spontaneously.
>
> It was an inextricable tangle. Wars dating from every century were all going on at the same moment; the weapons ranged from blowpipes, spears and spells to machine guns and mortars.

It was a war, or wars, for harvests and for land, for salt and for opium, for commercial concessions and vice rackets, for sectarian and ethnic separatism, for social equality, security of tenure, and that Malayan panacea 'hearts and minds'. It was also about ideology, sovereignty, territory and communications.

From Saigon came lurid reports of bicycle bombers and of splintering glass as blooded *boulevardiers* reeled into the roadway, of sensational intrigue, corruption and racketeering plus the raunchiest vice in the East. Under Bao Dai's numerous ministries, the violence was increasingly contained within the crowded walls of interrogation centres; but corruption flourished and protection paid. War could be juicy as well as hideous, personally profitable as well as nationally crippling.

Venturing forth into the Cochin-China countryside, the world's press discovered a different scene. Minor roads were few and dangerous; the main arteries were safer and, as Norman Lewis discovered, you could tell them by the brick and bamboo watch-towers which, like mile posts, interrupted their monotony.

> It was better, said the driver, not to stop between the towers, and his method was to accelerate to about 65 mph until a tower was about two hundred yards away. He would then relax speed until we were past, and about the same distance on the other side. This confidence in the towers seemed not altogether well-founded.

Traffic moved mainly in convoys, never at night, and never stopped between towers. 'Anyone immobile on the road was condemned, given over to the men in black.' The fate which overtook Alden Pyle, Graham Greene's 'Quiet American', probably derived from Bodard's experience when his car broke down on the road from Mytho. He was only a couple of miles from Saigon and it was not yet dark. There was a tower in sight and its occupants were signalling to him. Then they opened fire.

> The bullets whipped past me. I reached the tower and darted up the ladder, which was instantly pulled up. The partisans laughed, and told me that I had been within a few seconds of being kidnapped. They had been firing at a group of Vietminh creeping up behind me.

Correspondents keen to file a report on *une opération française* had to venture still further afield, usually up to Tonkin. The arrangements were made by the military and were closely supervised. From Saigon a Dakota took the pressmen to an airstrip near Hanoi, whence they might venture to the city's Metropole Hotel or be whisked off to an officers' mess. From more military transport, a launch perhaps or another airplane, they observed the exercise, watched the drop, and then returned to base and to the ever optimistic briefing before flying back to Saigon.

There was no possibility of going north overland. Cochin-China, now increasingly referred to as south Vietnam, and Tonkin, now north Vietnam, were totally cut off from one another. The railway had not operated since the Allied bombings of 1945; and Route Coloniale 1 (RC1), the only north-south artery, was blocked by Vietminh zones in Annam. The northern half of this route was known as *La Rue Sans Joie*, 'The Street without Joy'. Here Bernard Fall, a French doctorate scholar and later author, observed a 1953 offensive to clear the Vietminh and open the road at least as far as Hue. The casualties lent credence to a bland statistic that estimated the cost of keeping roads open at 3–4 men per day per 100 kilometres.

RC4, the road along the Chinese frontier in the extreme north, was excluded from this calculation. By 1949 scarcely a convoy was getting through to the frontier posts intact. Then in 1950, hard on the arrival of Mao's People's Liberation Army across the border, the Vietminh launched a succession of devastating assaults on the road's strongpoints. Four thousand men of the French Expeditionary Force were lost at Caobang, vast quantities of guns and ammunition were abandoned at Lang Son.

In 1951 the situation was somewhat improved when General Jean de Lattre de Tassigny, the charismatic new commander-in-chief, repelled several Vietminh advances. His inspirational leadership, his introduction of napalm (supplied by the US), his recruitment of a Vietnamese army on Bao Dai's behalf, and his 'de Lattre Line' of concrete bunkers protecting the vital corridor from Hanoi to Haiphong briefly restored confidence in the idea of being able to retain Tonkin. But de Lattre died of cancer in early 1952, and by late that year French forces were again on the defensive.

In 1953 Giap, the now jungle-hardened genius of Vietminh strategy, switched the focus of the war from the Red River and its delta to the remote uplands of Tonkin whence he swept towards the Mekong valley in Laos. Although he then withdrew, the danger of the Vietminh thus reaching ill-defended Cambodia and Cochin-China by the back door and so linking up with their fellow guerrillas in the south had to be prevented. Hence the decision to establish a massive concentration of forces, which could only be supplied by air, on the strategic but isolated and often mist-shrouded Plain of Jars. The spot chosen was called Dien Bien Phu.

Surrounded from early 1954, the defensive complex at Dien Bien

Phu came under heavy Vietminh assault as of 13 March. As if to make up for the untidy nature of the war so far, it proved to be an epic and decisive encounter. The worsening plight of the French and the concentration of the Vietminh's normally elusive forces invited outside intervention. In Washington the Eisenhower administration was all for direct action, the minimum being massive bombing, the maximum the use of US ground troops and atomic weapons. But the British declined to become involved and, without the international backing of her allies, the US held her fire.

Instead, the West watched in disbelief as the cream of France's Expeditionary Force, a multi-racial army of Frenchmen and Vietnamese, Moroccans, Algerians and Senegalese, plus the Germans and Russians of the Foreign Legion, faced the fanatically dedicated cohorts of the Vietminh. Outnumbered and outgunned, the defenders surrendered on 7 May after eight weeks of unimaginable horror. Their losses were later put at 15,000 lives. Also lost were at least sixty aircraft, plus whatever prestige still clung to the mystique and the *mission* of France in Asia.

It was against the background of this unfolding tragedy that, under pressure from the US and the individual governments, further concessions on independence were made to the 'associate states' of Cambodia, Laos and Bao Dai's Vietnam. Had the French won at Dien Bien Phu, such concessions might have been reeled in or rendered worthless. But the surrender, coinciding as it did with the opening of the Vietnam phase of a four-power conference in Geneva, played into the hands of the Vietminh and then of the incoming ministry of Pierre Mendés-France in Paris. A radical socialist who had undertaken to effect a settlement within a month, Mendés-France agreed to the partitioning of Vietnam at the 17th parallel. All French forces were to be evacuated from the north, and elections were to be held to determine the future status of the whole country, both north and south. Although the United States declined to participate officially in what it regarded as a betrayal of the free world's commitment to resist Communist aggression, and although the Geneva accords were never ratified by either side, they effectively ended French involvement in Indo-China.

De Lattre had once declared of the war that not since the Crusades had France taken part in such a 'disinterested operation'. Hijacked by the super-powers, a long-standing struggle with colonial 'bandits' and revolutionaries had become a major and very 'dirty war' which threatened France's position both in Africa and in Europe. Despite eight years of fighting and 90,000 casualties, defeat now looked decidedly closer than victory. A negotiated settlement was the best that could be hoped for.

That it also meant imperial disengagement in Asia followed from the involvement of the United States. French authority had come to depend less on its own effectiveness and more on the fragility of Indo-China's would-be successor states. Bao Dai's Vietnam already owed its army and its various government programmes almost entirely to US munificence. With the US willing to continue bank-rolling the shaky regime in Saigon, there was no role for France. As an American diplomat reportedly put it, 'We [the United States] are the last French colonialists in Indo-China.'

14

On a Silver Platter

The Enemy Inside the Mosquito Net

The US government was not alone in seeing the 1954 Geneva accords between the French and the Vietminh as a defeat for the West in its global confrontation with Communism. Throughout Asia, wherever Communist insurgency was rife, in the Philippines, Malaya, Thailand and Burma, a similar disaster now seemed possible. Alerted by Washington, the alarm bells began to sound from London to Hong Kong, Singapore and Canberra.

Something had gone badly wrong with the long-term prognosis for the East. The prospect of a framework of newly independent nation states, each under a representative government which would collaborate with the Western allies in a mutually beneficial exchange of produce and security arrangements, was visibly receding. This was not how empire was supposed to end.

It was as if decolonisation, a fraught yet inevitable parting of the ways, was being traumatised by the onset of an unforeseen and deadly cancer. The cancer, of course, was Communism, and to its insidious attacks both subject nations and successor states seemed equally vulnerable. No respecter of race or religion, it assailed ruling élites, be they indigenous as in the Philippines, colonial as in Vietnam, or both as in the Malayan Federation. It could lurk benignly within a nationalist regime, as it had in Hanoi and would appear to be doing in Indonesia in the early 1960s, or it could malignantly oppose nationalist pretensions as in south Vietnam and later in Singapore.

'All the old problems are irrelevant,' wrote Donald Moore, a Singapore publisher, in 1955. 'All else, it now seems to us here, should be subservient to the containing of Communism.' The familiar antithesis of a recalcitrant colonialism and a resurgent nationalism, a sort of death and rebirth, suddenly began to look outdated. For the empires of the West there was to be no such thing as a natural demise. Weakened by war, troubled by failing faculties and distracted by domestic demands, the grizzled leviathans of empire unsteadily confronted their final challenge in the cancer of Communism.

But was it really a cancer, or had it been misdiagnosed? Perhaps the world was simply witnessing the dramatic effects of one of the new wonder-drugs, an antibiotic panacea. In Russia, in the space of a generation, this ideological kill-or-cure had sensationally transformed a moribund feudal society into a dynamic and industrialised super-power. The results were noted throughout the emergent world and would provide countries as dissimilar as India and Algeria with a developmental bench-mark.

Now an equally dramatic transformation was promised in Mao's China. If it worked there, argued nationalist intellectuals, it must also work in south-east Asia. As the deadly enemy of imperialism, Communism's credentials appeared even better than those of the liberty-loving United States; they also carried a reassuring promise of historical determinism. Washington might decry international Communism as the worst kind of enslavement, more insidious even than colonialism, but Moscow, echoed by Peking, insisted that Marxist-Leninist ideology alone guaranteed the robust immunity which would make national liberation unassailable. If the price was revolution, the prize – social justice as well as national resurgence – was glittering. Asian intelligentsias were dazzled.

The Vietminh's improbable successes in Tonkin seemed to prove the point. Ideological motivation, plus Mao's injunctions on the conduct of a 'people's war', were showing themselves to be an irresistible combination. Beleaguered revolutionaries elsewhere took heart. Nowhere would this be more true, or more ominous according to its anxious British community, than in Malaya. Six years into their own jungle war with 'Communist terrorists' (CTs), the British administrations in Malaya and Singapore would eye events in Vietnam with increasing concern.

Indo-China is the key to the entire situation in South-east Asia. If the Communist Vietminh forces succeed in that country, the Communist road of advance runs into Thailand, down through Malaya, into Indonesia and then points southwards to Australia.

According to Harry Miller, chief correspondent in Kuala Lumpur for the Singapore-based *Straits Times*, there was no need to invoke the domino theory. Communism was simply treading the trail blazed by Japanese hegemonism in 1937–42, first China, then Tonkin, Cochin-China, Malaya and so on.

Miller was writing just before Dien Bien Phu and the Geneva conference. For many of his fellow Britons in Malaya, the latter would prove to be the final straw. In Singapore Donald Moore, hearing of the outcome of the Geneva talks, wrote simply of his sense of betrayal. First the Dutch had decamped from the islands; now the French were pulling out of the mainland. Deserted by the other European powers, Albion was left to defy the onward march of Communism, standing alone in south-east Asia just as she had stood alone against Nazi Fascism in Europe. And as Moore noted in his diary, there was another parallel with pre-war Europe.

August 1 1954
The war in Indo-China ended yesterday, and, to many of us who have grown accustomed to living on the fringe of Communism, it was ended by an Eastern Munich. It seems to us that peace was bought at a price no less than that which Chamberlain, in his day, was obliged to pay to Hitler, and with no greater honour.

Like Hitler, Malaya's Communists could only be mightily encouraged. An escalation in their activities must be anticipated; their hitherto undecided compatriots would now surely pledge their support to the Party.

Similar scares had punctuated the whole course of the Malayan 'Emergency'. Amongst old Malaya hands there was a strong feeling that, but for such extraneous or fortuitous crises, plus a lamentable lack of support from London, the whole business could have been wound up in a matter of months. In fact, it might never have started. Bill Moran, who as a police lieutenant in the terrorist-ridden state of Perak was on the front line from the start, blamed 'the pacifist attitude of the British Labour Party'. Had British troops stayed on in Indo-China to support the French in 1946, he argued, the 'Malaya crisis' would never have developed. A united stand against Communist incursion by all the Western allies would have stopped it dead in its tracks.

In 1949, a year after the 'Emergency' had been officially declared as such, and just when the Kuala Lumpur government felt it was getting on top of the situation, it would be the Communist triumph in China which afforded to the insurgents, themselves largely Chinese Malayans, renewed encouragement. This, however, was as nothing, according to men like Moran, compared to their sense of betrayal when a year later the same appease-all Labour government in London would see fit to extend official recognition to Mao's new regime in Peking. It was tantamount, they argued, to endorsing the CTs' cause. Recognition meant that Mao's government could station its own consuls in each of the Malay states. According to Sir Henry Gurney, the Malayan Federation's High Commissioner, the consequent increment in propaganda and subversion potential could be compared to reinforcing the guerrillas with an entire division.

Although the consular issue would be shelved, the terrorists would indeed take heart. In 1950–1 there followed an upsurge of activity which climaxed in the murder of the High Commissioner himself. To Moore, the Singapore publisher, this was the worst outrage of the whole Emergency. Recalling it three years later, he was still so outraged that he seemingly forgot that in 1951 the British sovereign was still George VI.

> The case for co-existence fell to the ground the day the Communists murdered the High Commissioner . . . The crime would not have been in any way different if it had been Queen Elizabeth of England whose body they had shot to pieces. The High Commissioner was the representative of the Queen; the Queen was murdered by proxy.

Die-hard planters, long doubtful of the government's resolve, began to move out. Amongst them would be the Lucy family whose domestic arrangements habitually mirrored the times. Married by the Bishop of Singapore on the day before the Japanese landed on that island, Peter and Dorothy ('Tommy') Lucy had spent their honeymoon in an air-raid shelter and then been separated during three and half years of Japanese internment. Both had survived, returned to Malaya to manage a rubber estate and, despite the Emergency, remained 'absolutely determined that we were going to stay'. Several ambushes later Peter Lucy was still declaring that 'in no circumstances will I leave'. The circumstances included news that his name was on the local CT hit-list and that his wife was having twins. She went into labour while bent double inside a cast-iron bath as she repelled a terrorist attack with her trusty bren gun. They were again ambushed *en route* to the Kuala Lumpur hospital.

As we went down the drive we saw the 'bandits' ahead of us . . . so Peter put his foot down on the accelerator and we roared and bumped over this road. Why the twins didn't arrive in the armoured car I don't know, but as a final gesture of defiance I put my pistol through the louvres of the armoured car and fired a shot and yelled, 'That's for you. You devils.'

In one of the best-loved images of the Emergency, the Lucy twins, blonde and well-groomed toddlers, were later photographed playing in their nursery, its inner walls lined with sandbags and an armed constable on guard outside the window. Beyond, invisible in the picture, were more sandbags, observation posts, searchlights, a barbed-wire perimeter fence and two ferocious Alsatians. Yet by 1952 even the indomitable Lucys had had enough. On the advice of the new High Commissioner, the family emigrated to Kenya. (There too history dogged their quest for domestic tranquillity. They arrived just as another Emergency was declared, this time in response to the tactics of the Mau Mau.)

Two years later the British in Malaya would be convulsed over the French 'betrayal' at Geneva. Perhaps the Lucy family felt that their exodus had been vindicated. In this instance, though, the fears of a further escalation in the violence proved wholly unfounded. As will be seen, by 1954 the frequency of terrorist 'incidents' in Malaya was already declining and it would continue to do so. Eighteen months later the Malayan Communist Party's guerrilla leaders would be emerging from their jungle hide-outs to seek an end to hostilities. Although the talks would fail, the war had been won. Malaya was not to be another Vietnam, its peoples' rejection of Communism being every bit as emphatic as the triumph of its British-led security forces.

As in Vietnam significant political concessions would accompany the counter-insurgency measures. Malayans were co-opted into high office during the early 1950s, and the first nation-wide elections to seats in the Federation's Legislative Council were held in 1955. In the 1948 constitution, which had replaced that of the ill-fated post-war Malayan Union, there was specific mention of eventual self-rule. These political initiatives were not, therefore, seen as frantic window-dressing by a desperate colonial regime, as was the case in Vietnam. After conceding independence to India, London's sincerity about Malayan independence was never in doubt. While the French saw their 1946 'liberation' of Hanoi as completing the restoration of empire, their British equivalents had become accustomed to the idea of dismantling empire. For John Cross, an officer in the Gurkhas, having the imperial carpet pulled from under his boots had become an occupational hazard.

> We arrived in Malaya on 12 January [1948]. We'd left tribal territory on the North West Frontier in October 1947, we'd left Pakistan in November 1947, we'd left India in December 1947 and we'd left Burma in January 1948. Four months on the trot during which we'd seen nothing but our flag pulled down and being spat at et cetera; and it had all been very nasty. So we were delighted to get somewhere peaceful. Ha! Ha! Because in June 1948 the Emergency was declared!

With the British making a habit of withdrawal and with mainstream Malayan nationalism continuing to cold-shoulder Marxism, the dialogue of decolonisation could proceed in an atmosphere of genuine amity. The Emergency merely loosened tongues and strengthened hands, most notably those of the central, that is the Federation, government in Kuala Lumpur. To its usually more progressive approach to political reform the sultans and their individual state governments had increasingly to defer since they lacked the power and resources to tackle the insurgents on their own. Where Clementi, Gent and others had failed in their schemes to sideline the cumbersome autonomy of the Malay states, the Emergency succeeded.

For Tunku Abdul Rahman the conviviality of the head-to-head negotiations which proceeded fitfully throughout the early 1950s would later be a matter of some embarrassment. As the first premier of an independent Malaya, he would feel it essential to his nationalist credentials to project the image of an erstwhile freedom fighter. It was thus a matter of great regret to him that he had never, for instance, been gaoled like Nehru. Even treating the Communist cancer, or swatting what the Tunku called 'the enemy inside our own mosquito net', had meant cosying up to the British. 'Having the Communists as a common focus of hatred or discontent hastened independence for Malaya,' he conceded. But lest this admission be misconstrued as collaboration with colonialism, he quickly added that it was the British, dismayed by the Communist challenge, who elected to collaborate with Malay nationalism. 'And that's why I think in the end the British supported us.' This tortured logic found classic expression in his memoirs.

> [Malayan] Independence was served on a silver platter as a result of the British 'winds of change' policy, and people nowadays hardly realise how hard we had to fight for our freedom then.

In fact it was in a euphoric daze of mutual congratulation that Britain would concede, and Malaya celebrate, its 1957 independence. Six years later concerns over territorial integration, like those which had overshadowed the celebrations in Hanoi and Jakarta, would be satisfactorily met when Singapore, Sarawak and North Borneo joined the Malayan Federation in the creation of Malaysia; and even Singapore's subsequent secession occasioned only limited rancour. Although the transition could have been tidier, it stands out as perhaps the least fraught of all transfers of power from empire to independent nation state.

If there was any reluctance to sever the colonial tie, it would be discovered as much amongst Malayan nationals anxious about Chinese-Malay relations as amongst the British. British commercial interests were safeguarded and the country remained in the Commonwealth. Under the Anglo-Malayan defence pact some British troops stayed on and strategic British installations were retained; when the latter were finally closed it would be at the insistence not of Malaysia or Singapore but of the British Treasury.

The contrast with France's ignominious exit from Indo-China could hardly have been greater. Obvious parallels between the French and British confrontations with Asian Communism may have obsessed contemporaries but, in retrospect, it is the differences between the French experience in Indo-China and that of the British in Malaya which deserve attention. They apply across the board. The Communist Party in Malaya would find itself labouring under handicaps which even a Ho Chi Minh would have been pushed to surmount; the British authorities, whether from a wise appraisal of the situation or from a welcome rediscovery of their legendary pragmatism, would insist on regarding the insurgency as a civil disturbance and on promoting Malayan solidarity to oppose it; and finally, amongst Malayans of all races, the opportunities offered by a booming economy and imminent independence would comprehensively outweigh the sacrifices demanded by ideological struggle.

Two Stars Too Many

The Malayan Communist Party (MCP), founded in Singapore, was first heard of there in the 1930s. Its pre-war championship of industrial grievances, especially in Singapore, resulted in its proscription and the imprisonment or deportation of some of its members. This membership, and that of affiliated groupings like the bizarrely named 'Anti-Enemy Backing-up Society', drew its inspiration from China's Communists, the enemy-not-to-be-backed-up being the Japanese whose troops were then storming up the Yangtze. MCP recruitment was therefore almost entirely from Malaya's Chinese communities, the only notable exception being Lai Tek (Loi Tek), its leader, who, though Chinese, was born in Vietnam. Without Malay (as opposed to Malayan) support, Lai Tek's pretensions as the would-be Ho Chi Minh of Malaya were fatally flawed from the start. They were fatally flawed for other reasons too, but as yet the most obvious was that a broad-based nationalist consensus along the lines of the Vietminh was impossible without the collaboration of the Malays, still (but only just) the country's largest ethnic group and its indigenous élite.

The identification of the MCP with the Chinese communities in Malaya had been reinforced during the Japanese occupation. Treated more harshly than the Malays and subject to summary execution, it was almost entirely the Chinese who joined or supported the MCP-dominated guerrilla resistance against the Japanese. Armed and encouraged by British agents like John Davis and Spencer Chapman, this 'Malayan Peoples' Anti-Japanese Army' (MPAJA) never commanded the loyalties of more than one Malayan people, those of Chinese extraction. Although during the Emergency its anti-British successor would adopt the *tiga bintang* as its cap badge, its 'three stars', supposedly representing Malaya's Malay, Chinese and Indian communities, were mere wishful thinking. There were always two stars too many.

Come the Japanese surrender the MPAJA took revenge against the mainly Malay police who had occasionally betrayed it. Chinese-Malay conflict flared as a result, and there were communal massacres amongst the rubber trees before the British Military Administration managed to restore control. Although certainly the most organised political party in the country, the MCP with its limited appeal was in no position to speak for Malayan nationalism and made no bid for Malayan independence. While Ho Chi Minh's followers were forming the Democratic Republic of Vietnam's first government in Hanoi, Lai Tek's men were turning in their guns and queueing up to shake hands with Mountbatten.

Given the comradeship between the MPAJA and its wartime British contacts, the MCP was now allowed to operate freely within the political process. It welcomed the citizenship proposals contained in the Malayan Union constitution and reverted to its pre-war objectives of organising and politicising the industrial proletariat which, in Malaya's case, meant rubber tappers, tin miners and workers in the docks and processing industries. In early 1946 a succession of escalating strikes crippled Singapore and were due to climax with a one-day shut-down on 15 February. The date, the fourth anniversary of the British surrender to the Japanese, was intentionally provocative. What looked like being a celebration of the empire's worst defeat scandalised the administration and was duly banned. Nine party activists were detained.

The wily Lai Tek was not amongst them. He had led a charmed life under the Japanese, passing unsuspected through their security checks in his ostentatious limousine, and he now appeared equally capable of outwitting the British. Truly, it was said, Lai Tek must be possessed of exceptional powers. Just like 'Uncle' Ho, he was always a step ahead of his enemies; fortunate indeed was the Party to have such a consummate operator as its General Secretary.

Throughout 1946 the Party continued to espouse constitutional methods and to extend its influence over organised labour. The Malayan Union constitution was now in disarray and its promise of equal citizenship for Chinese Malayans was receding. Here was a ready-made grievance which the MCP might reasonably have exploited to win greater Chinese support. Yet it was Dato Onn's United Malay National Organisation (UMNO) that was making the running, spearheading the unexpected surge in Malay nationalism and hammering at the heavy-handed presumptions of British imperialism.

The MCP seemed to have missed its chance and in early 1947 Lai Tek's moderation came in for criticism. So did his leadership. When asked to account for both he suddenly disappeared, taking with him most of the Party's funds. Rumours that there had been more to his immunity from arrest than consummate guile had already surfaced. It was subsequently established that throughout his mercurial career he had been a double-agent serving first the French in Vietnam, then the British, then the Japanese, and recently the British once again. Heavily compromised from the start, the MCP now became positively paranoid about internal dissent while an exultant British Intelligence lapsed into dangerous complacency.

The 1947 unmasking of Lai Tek also cast suspicion on the gradualist policies he had advocated. Under the new leadership of

Chin Peng, the ex-MPAJA guerrilla leader who had been awarded an OBE, the Party immediately espoused greater militancy and authorised retaliatory violence against the imperialist oppressors and their running dogs. By early 1948 rubber factories and sawmills were being burned down and dock-workers were going on strike. The British responded with trades union legislation aimed at undermining MCP control of industrial disputes. More violence resulted.

Happily for the MCP this general escalation coincided with a somewhat ambiguous authorisation from Communism's international hierarchy for the adoption of armed struggle. Some MPAJA guerrillas were duly recalled for training; guns stashed away at the end of the war were dug up, and half-forgotten jungle hideouts refurbished. But it was not until the government, responding to the murders of three British planters in Perak, imposed a State of Emergency in June 1948 that the switch from urban incitement to rural revolution was made. Armed struggle now became a reality; and since the Emergency provisions included proscription of the Communist Party and its affiliates, the MCP had no option but to go underground. 'Underground' in Malaya meant into the jungle, where policemen like Bill Moran were expected to follow.

> I have seen one of those camps in the jungle. It had every detail from barracks – some married quarters, compound and school – down to a field hospital. It was considered just one of those things during the first years of the Emergency if a police jungle patrol of about 20 men had the misfortune to encounter a Communist guerrilla force of anything up to four hundred. . . . [The guerrillas] performed all the functions of a normal soldier, even to the extent of the flag ceremony at dawn and dusk.

Moran and the 14,000 men, mostly Malays, of the Royal Federation of Malaya Police bore the brunt of the fighting during the first two years. Heavily criticised for their inability to protect the country's scattered and often remote communities of plantation managers and mine overseers, they tended to exaggerate the strength of the enemy and to emphasise its professionalism. What could mere police, poorly armed and ill-informed, achieve against an experienced military machine which had successfully defied even the Japanese?

It was true that in the early stages of the Emergency whole regiments of what was now called the 'Malayan Peoples' Anti-British Army' were occasionally encountered. But at no point throughout the twelve years of the Emergency did the combined strength of what subsequently became the 'Malayan Races' Liberation Army' (MRLA) exceed 8,000. Against them, in due course, would be ranged regular troops, a Home Guard, special forces, a vastly expanded police force of Special Constables and auxiliaries, plus naval and air-force personnel, to the tune of 350,000. Yet over the twelve years barely 7,000 CTs were killed or captured, an undistinguished and possibly unprecedented strike rate, according to a contributor to Charles Allen's *Savage Wars of Peace*.

> I worked out that statistically, for every million man hours of effort in the jungle we only saw the bandits for a period of twenty seconds, which gives you a statistic that is horrific. And that's why one could go a whole year in the jungle without seeing anybody at all.

The problem, of course, lay in the unfathomable nature of the Malayan jungle or, nowadays, 'rain forest'. For the MRLA, however, it was not quite the congenial refuge it was made out to be for, though excellent cover, it provided few other aids to survival. Malaria probably inflicted as many insurgent casualties as did the security forces. Wounds festered in the clammy atmosphere and all food, as well as funds and medicines, had to be obtained from outside. Captured CTs, often sick, were invariably starving; for those who surrendered voluntarily the prospect of imminent nourishment appeared to be an important incentive.

Nor, unlike in Vietnam, was there any other escape for the insurgents from what their pursuers called 'this poxy green hell'. Malaya's only land border was with Thailand where the government was engaged in its own repression of Communist dissent. Whereas the Vietminh obtained substantial aid and armaments from the Chinese Communists and could periodically withdraw to neighbouring regions of China to recuperate, retrain and re-arm, the MRLA was on its own. Anticipated arms shipments and troop reinforcements from its brethren in China never materialised; nor did the diplomatic pressure and the international recognition which Moscow and Peking eventually mobilised on behalf of the Vietminh. For weapons, ammunition and even uniforms the Malayan guerrillas were dependent on what they had inherited from the MPAJA, what they purloined from the British, and what they could devise for themselves. Unlike the Vietminh, they had to manage without artillery, vehicles or wireless, let alone any anti-aircraft capacity against RAF bombing.

Documentation obtained from MRLA sources revealed that even when the tide of insurgency was running at its highest, in 1950–1, the MCP had no illusions about a military victory. While the British response steadily escalated with more weaponry being deployed, more troops arriving, more intelligence being amassed, and more jungle being penetrated, the story of the MRLA's struggle was one of strategies being continually revised downwards in the light of glaring failures. Early objectives, like the creation of 'liberated areas', had to be abandoned; intimidation was found to be counter-productive; so were indiscriminate ambushes; and the slashing of rubber trees and sabotaging of tin mines, while desirable ways of disrupting the imperialist economy, were found to alienate the large numbers of Malayans who depended on them for their liveli-hood. In short, the insurgents were fighting a losing battle from the start.

Fish Out of Water

It was also the wrong battle. Harried by hordes of police and troops, the MRLA increasingly found itself locked into a jungle war when it should have been out and about extending its support amongst the rural population outside. They, according to Maoist doctrine, were the water in which the fish, or 'the forces of armed struggle', were supposed to swim; people should be the guerrilla's camouflage, not trees. Perhaps because of its MPAJA origins, the MRLA was slow to absorb such dictums; and this despite the fact that initially the jungle fringes positively sparkled with inviting water-holes. In many areas whole communities were believed to support the guerrillas, a situa-tion which seemingly invited the sort of offensives mounted by the French against civilian targets in Vietnam.

No such formal offensives materialised in Malaya because, to the insurgents' chagrin, the British administration, unlike the French in Vietnam, recognised only an Emergency, not a war. Understating the situation always appealed to the British. Additionally they recog-nised an important distinction. It may have been lost on the belea-guered guerrillas when, in the final stages of the struggle, they found themselves the targets of bombing raids by Canberra jets and of search-and-destroy assaults by helicopter-borne commandos; but the point was that in Malaya, unlike in Vietnam, such firepower could never be deployed against civilian targets, however compromised, so long as the administration refused to concede a state of war.

It is also claimed that this reticence was in deference to commercial interests whose well-insured property, so often the target of enemy attack, would no longer have been covered for compensation if a state of war had been acknowledged. Howsoever, downgrading the struggle to a civil emergency, and thus endeavouring to wage it within the law (albeit Emergency law), meant that technically troops were used only in an auxiliary capacity and at the discretion of the civil power. This certainly diminished the risks of a gung-ho disregard for civilian sensitivities. Conversely it laid the administration open to accusations of not taking the situation sufficiently seriously. It also laid the security forces, whenever they did resort to strong-arm tactics, open to well-founded accusations of perpetrating atrocities.

More significantly, the refusal to dignify the conflict with the status of a war obliged the authorities to devise alternative and subtler tactics worthy of the peculiar challenge posed by Maoist struggle. In respect of the MRLA and its MCP leadership these included a belated but decisive emphasis on intelligence and undercover work which eventually yielded a comprehensive dossier on almost every known insurgent. Also introduced were a variety of propaganda initiatives aimed at undermining morale, plus generous incentives and amnesties to encourage defectors and informants. Dakotas showered the jungle with safe-conducts and enticing cash offers while MRLA deserters broadcast affidavits attesting their favourable treatment. Meanwhile extraordinary efforts were made to interdict the enemy's access to supplies and intelligence, thereby forcing them to forsake the jungle and so incur the risk of discovery or ambush. Ambushing those for whom the ambush was a trademark was particularly satisfying. But the operation of this policy of interdiction depended on neutralising those pro-Communist rural communities, generally characterised as 'squatters', on whom the MRLA depended for supplies. It was on the squatters, therefore, rather than MRLA combatants, that the new tactics focused.

During the recession of the 1930s and then during the Japanese occupation perhaps 400,000 workless Chinese (and some Indian) immigrants had sought survival in the occupation and cultivation of marginal land, much of it remote and on the fringes of the jungle. With no title to their holdings or to citizenship, these squatters had largely slipped beyond the reach of government. They were generally ignorant or suspicious of its intentions and they were also vulnerable to the Malay exclusivity practised by the state governments. Insecure and disaffected, sharing the anxieties of their Chinese brethren, and peculiarly receptive to promises of assured tenure and social redress, they were ready-made for Communist recruitment. Not all responded and some, mostly those whose family affiliations were with the Chinese Nationalists, staunchly resisted MRLA pressure. Of the roughly 3,000 civilian fatalities during the Emergency, by far the majority were Chinese Malayans killed by Chinese Malayans. But whether thus intimidated or whether genuinely sympathetic, many squatting communities did become MRLA collaborators, providing it with funds and supplies on demand and eventually with couriers and recruits. They were the water in which the armed fish of the MRLA might safely swim.

Removing the squatter settlements, or draining the water, was thus a British priority from the start. At first, though, resettlement was seen as a punitive exercise. Only those communities which were known to be assisting the enemy were targeted. Their settlements were duly surrounded and destroyed, and their inmates, assumed to be collectively guilty, were usually deported back to China. This soon ceased to be an option, partly because of the numbers involved and partly because Mao's China declined to receive them. Instead, the squatters were relocated in detention camps – or in new settlements which were indistinguishable from detention camps. The innocent there suffered along with the guilty and came to share their distrust of government. Soon there were more Communist sympathisers in the camps than there had been in the squatter settlements.

Resettlement nevertheless continued and was revised as an important constituent of the 1950 'Briggs Plan'. Lieutenant-General Sir Harold Briggs, the Emergency's first Director of Operations, also introduced a system of declaring insurgent-free areas 'white', so no longer subject to the Emergency's more tiresome restrictions, like the curfew. The idea, probably torn from the Maoist manual on 'liberated areas', was that 'white' areas would be progressively extended, thus rewarding loyal districts, encouraging others to aspire to their privileges, and enabling the security forces to be concentrated more effectively.

With a similar emphasis on incentive and on protecting squatters from MRLA intimidation rather than punishing them for it, the resettlement programme was relaunched, the object being now to relocate the entire squatter community in what became known as 'new villages'. These were designed to be desirable and economically viable as well as secure. In Johore, Cunyngham-Brown insisted that the squatters hailed their new quarters with delight, 'talking and singing and enjoying themselves as they built their houses'. Yet the harsh realities of dispossession remained. For the security forces it still meant dawn raids on unsuspecting settlements, the mass removal of wailing women, uncomprehending children and their pitiful effects, and then the destruction of all that remained. Coming across one of these abandoned settlements could be cause for sombre reflection.

> And there were the ruined huts and discarded implements gradually sinking down into the ground again – and I remember thinking as I walked through that village, I wonder what the Romans felt as they headed for Dubris in 410 and walked through the villages of Roman Britain. I wonder if they thought this is the end of the Empire.

The 'new villages' were ringed with fences and subject to security surveillance. But each family was to be given a title to its small-holding and compensation for any loss of property incurred in the move. As well as a police post, the villages were eventually to acquire health facilities and schools and to be encouraged to elect their own representatives and to provide their own guards. A similar relocation of plantation and mining labour resulted in a grand total of nearly three quarters of a million Chinese Malayans being concentrated in fenced and regulated settlements. It was an ambitious programme of population control, possibly the largest ever undertaken, and certainly the decisive measure in the defeat of the MRLA.

It was also extremely expensive. That it was ultimately realised was thanks mainly to the massive hike in government revenues which conveniently occurred in 1949–52, partly as a result of the demands of the Korean War. 'Malaya is as rubber does' went the popular adage. The MRLA's failure to cripple the country's tin and latex production, drive out more of its British management and engage the support of its mainly Chinese and Indian workforce probably owed as much to the bonanza conditions as to the steadfast opposition of the security forces. Wages rose and work opportunities beckoned as the government's revenues increased six-fold in the space of three years. The funds, and simultaneously the military and police reinforcements needed to conduct the operation, were channelled into defeating insurgency and above all resettling the squatters.

Most of the credit for its success went to Briggs' successor, who also succeeded the murdered Sir Henry Gurney as High Commissioner, thus combining the roles of civil and operational supremo. This was General Sir Gerald Templer, a dapper and inspirational figure with a frenetic manner, a pencil moustache, a penetrating stare, and a penchant for disconcerting language. 'Injecting the urgency into the Emergency', as he might have put it, from 1952 to 1954 Templer reorganised the command structure, travelled relentlessly, interfered at every level and created a legend of dynamic if controversial leadership. It was he who realised the Briggs Plan and he who captured its spirit in his injunction about 'winning the hearts and minds of the people'. Repeated with the regularity of a mantra, the words were soon drained of meaning and even he came to recognise them as 'that nauseating phrase'. Yet Templer's 'hearts and minds' crystallised the character of British decolonisation in the East just as Macmillan's 'wind of change' would later in Africa.

A Break in the Clouds

Of the nine directives issued to Templer on his taking up office, only three dealt with the conduct of the Emergency. The other six, which came first, were all concerned with the policies to be pursued so that Malaya 'should in due course become a fully self-governing nation'. To this end Templer was to encourage measures to mould 'a United Malayan Nation'. Nation-building therefore became one of his priorities. He forged ahead with a policy of democratisation from the bottom upwards, encouraging elections at village and municipal level, then state and federal level. At the top more Malayans were co-opted into the Federation's Executive and Legislative Councils and served as ministerial 'shadows'. The thorny issue of citizenship was again examined and qualifications relaxed to include more Malayans of Chinese and Indian extraction. By sponsoring the arts and crafts, founding museums and botanical gardens, and commissioning works on ornithology and archaeology he endeavoured to make good Malaya's lack of heritage and to instil in all its peoples a pride in their shared land. 'Independence is just around the corner' proclaimed his Information Service by way of encouragement.

Yet on independence Templer was ambiguous. No timetable had

yet been set and he preferred to emphasise the prerequisites, like defeating Communism, uniting Malay and Chinese, and accustoming them to democratic norms. Privately he believed independence was still distant. Most Malayans, he thought, had no desire for it; it was only the Communists and a few nationalist radicals who were forcing the pace; they and, of course, 'world opinion'. Although personally on good terms with Malaya's political leaders, his scant political experience, and even less patience, served him ill when confronted with their conflicting demands. This, however, suited the politicians well, a degree of intransigence being a desirable trait in a colonial regime from which they sought the credit for winning their freedom.

The principal protagonist of Malay nationalism was still UMNO, founded by Dato Onn bin Ja'afar to oppose the Malayan Union. But Onn, given to understand that the British would never transfer power to a party representing only one of Malaya's communities, had since undergone a conversion to inter-communal politics and, encouraged by the British, tried to persuade UMNO to open its membership to non-Malays. In this he made some progress until in 1951, his proposed addition of a two-letter syllable to the party's official title proved his undoing. Onn wanted to change the name from the United Malay National Organisation to the United Malayan National Organisation. No one was fooled by this apparently innocuous change, and Onn, threatening resignation once too often, suddenly found himself out of the party. He responded by forming a new inter-communal group known as the Independence of Malaya Party or later the Negara Party. Onn's '-an' had apparently split the Malay vote.

The British, including Templer, continued to expect much of Onn, who was also Chief Minister (*Mentri Besar*) of Johore state and Member (that is, Malayan understudy) for Home Affairs in the Federal government. In his new party many saw the potential for a genuinely non-communal, as well as non-Communist, pan-Malayan consensus along the lines of India's Congress Party. Onn retained his journalistic tag as 'the Malayan Gandhi' and Nehru's Congress provided the ideal model of nationalist unity within a plural society. But instead of this obsession with India, the British and Onn would have done better to recall the fiasco of the Malayan Union constitution. Malays were not disposed to jeopardise the primacy of their sultans, of their Islamic faith, and of their citizenship in order to unite, even in the cause of independence, with Chinese and Indian immigrants whose loyalties might still lie with their parent countries and whose presence in Malaya was considered essentially exploitative. Onn's new party thus struggled from the start and was comprehensively defeated in the 1952 municipal elections in Kuala Lumpur. The lesson of the Union had been repeated.

The victors in Kuala Lumpur and, more crucially, in the country-wide federal elections of 1955 were two communal parties, Onn's erstwhile UMNO and a newcomer, the Malayan Chinese Association (MCA), a moderate and well-funded grouping dedicated to protecting Chinese ethnic and business interests. Neither party had made concessions to inter-communal harmony beyond vague expressions of seeking improvements in Malay-Chinese relations. They had, though, most unexpectedly formed an electoral alliance; and to it they owed their success and their consequent interest to the British authorities. Malayan unity within a single party was out, but seemingly alliance, coalition and collaboration were possible. Soon after, the Malayan Indian Congress (MIC) joined the UMNO-MCA Alliance, thus completing the 'three-star' coalition. As described by the Malayan academic, B. Simandjuntak, the secret seemed to lie in some typically British pragmatism.

> The essence of the strategy was the recognition of the hard facts of communal living and communal thinking. Both in the cities and in the countryside the Malays and the Chinese were living in distinctly segregated localities. It was, therefore, correctly assumed that voting would follow the line of communalism. All that was needed then was to put up MCA candidates in the predominantly Chinese wards and UMNO men in predominantly Malay wards.

Although not the architect of the Alliance, the man who most appreciated its simplicity and became its leader for the next two decades was Tunku Abdul Rahman. He had succeeded Onn as the leader of UMNO but, if Onn was Malaya's Gandhi, the Tunku was emphatically not its Nehru. He was more like a Malayan Bao Dai. Given to endearing lapses of concentration, not renowned for his devotion to political struggle, and best known in the members' enclosures at Ascot and Epsom, he was the most improbable independence leader.

In 1955, just as the UMNO-MCA Alliance was sailing to victory in the federal elections, President Sukarno was hosting the first Asia-Africa Conference in Bandung. To it flew in an unprecedented galaxy of 'third world' leaders – Jawaharlal Nehru and Indira (the future Mrs Gandhi), Nasser of Egypt and Makarios of Cyprus, Chou En-lai from China and Pham Van Dong from North Vietnam, U Nu of Burma and Sihanouk of Cambodia. In all twenty-nine nations were represented, nearly all of them newly independent, outspoken in their anti-imperialism, and firmly wedded to socialist policies. The Tunku was not invited and, had he been, he would surely have declined. As a gentleman and a race-goer, he had nothing against the British, and as a Malay prince, the brother of the Sultan of Kedah, socialism scarcely figured in his thinking. The conference, he later admitted, 'was a shot in the arm to countries such as ourselves which were then working for independence'. That did not mean that he was sorry to have missed it.

For the Malay voter the Tunku's aristocratic standing, his transparent honesty, and his commitment to the defence of Malay rights were all that mattered. Constantly surprising even himself with flashes of inspiration, he developed an instinctive understanding of grass-roots opinion which soon commanded British respect. It was the Tunku who, after negotiations that almost turned nasty, secured British agreement to the idea of the federal legislature having a majority of its members chosen by electors. And it was he who then campaigned so vigorously that the Alliance, 'my magic lamp' as he called it, won 51 of the 52 elective seats and thus secured an overall majority. The Tunku was duly appointed Chief Minister and, as the head of a responsible and representative government, initiated discussions about independence with both the British government and the Malay sultans.

The latter were consoled with guarantees of local autonomy and a constitutional role whereby one of their number would be head of state on a rotational basis. With the British, negotiations were greatly assisted by the MRLA's timely decision to sue for peace. Although the talks collapsed in the face of the Tunku's steadfast refusal to countenance the MCP as a legitimate party, and although both insurgency and Emergency therefore rumbled on for another four years, it was generally accepted that the crisis was over. British troops and a residual British administrative presence were deemed necessary in the immediate future; but these and other defence provisos proved no obstacle in the constitutional talks. To the mutual satisfaction of all concerned these were concluded in early 1957 and Independence was set for 31 August 1957.

On that day, awaiting the sombre ritual of the 'Last Post' and then the joyous outburst that would greet the raising of the Malayan flag the Tunku sat on his balcony scanning the skies. The superstitious race-goer sought celestial guidance. What were his chances in the Independence stakes?

> Slowly the rain dropped away, and just before I left for the Merdeka stadium to attend the celebrations, the whole sky cleared. In between breaks in the clouds above, there appeared a wonderful sign: the sun's rays gleamed like a star in the morning sky. It was an unusual phenomenon, and in my quiet way, I gave thanks to God, praying that Merdeka Day would bring us all good luck.

Riding the Tiger

Only in Penang was there any opposition to Malayan independence. The offshore island, where 170 years earlier Francis Light had first hoisted the British flag in the region, had been one of the Straits Settlements until 1946. Despite objections, it had then been bundled into the Malayan Union and, despite further objections, in 1948 it was slotted into the Malayan Federation. Imminent independence prompted a final squeal of protest when in 1956 one of Penang's leaders demanded outright secession. The island, he insisted, wished to remain British. Like Singapore it cherished its free-trade status and like Singapore it looked to its British links for much of its employment. But unlike Singapore, Penang was now of little commercial value and even less strategic moment. Its protests elicited scant sympathy from London and none at all from Kuala Lumpur.

The distinct status of Singapore, on the other hand, had never been in doubt. Raffles' eye for strategic potential, his insistence on free-trade status, and his encouragement of Chinese immigration had fashioned a fortress-emporium like no other in the East. By 1954 its civil airport, though yet to remove to Changi, was the busiest in south-east Asia, its port was as usual packed with the shipping of all nations, and its skyline, though still limited to buildings of no more than twenty storeys, was already assuming a decidedly vertical profile. The only question was whether the fortress-emporium could continue to prosper as an independent city-state. Excluded from both the Malayan Union and the Federation, it remained a separate British colony, the key to Britain's global role east of Suez and the best guarantee of Malaya's security. With Hong Kong almost overwhelmed by the triumph of Communism in China and more exposed and indefensible than ever, Singapore was vital. Its naval and aviational reach was supposed to bar Communist encroachment into the Indian Ocean just as its communications and intelligence networks were supposed to block that 'Communist road of advance' to Indonesia and Australia. The island was also essential, as would soon appear, to the security of the British empire's residual territories in the east, notably in North Borneo.

These considerations did not preclude a gradual progression towards self-rule. Since 1948 a minority of seats in the colony's legislative chamber had been filled by elected members. In 1954 a constitutional commission widened the electorate and increased its representation. Then in 1955, while Sukarno was fêting that galaxy of post-colonial luminaries in Bandung and while the Tunku's UMNO-MCA Alliance was unexpectedly sweeping to power in the Federation, Singapore served notice of its own designs on independence. From its April elections a pro-independence grouping emerged victorious for the first time. A coalition of several socialist parties, it was led by David Marshall, a Eurasian barrister.

Even more sensational, however, were the dramatic gains made by the vociferously pro-independence People's Action Party (PAP). Apparently a crypto-Communist organisation, the PAP represented organised labour and was headed by another fiery barrister, Lee Kuan Yew. Each grouping – the socialist coalition and the PAP – now vied with the other in anti-colonial rhetoric; but while Marshall declared himself anti-Communist, Lee Kuan Yew was merely 'non-Communist'. 'If I had to choose between Colonialism and Communism, I would vote for Communism, and so should the great majority of the people,' Lee told the *Straits Times*.

Marshall's socialist grouping could not command the unchallenged majority enjoyed by the Tunku's coalition in Malaya, but it still entitled him to form a ministry. Marshall himself was duly installed as Chief Minister and, at the head of his elected government, he promptly began the process of dismantling colonial rule. Constitutional negotiations with the British government got underway; meanwhile the more draconian of the Emergency provisions (as introduced to quell Communist insurgency in 1948) were repealed. The British government played along with him. In these final years of empire it was happy to trade colonial rule for Communist rout, plus a regional role in the post-colonial world.

Thus, for example, to spare Marshall the discredit of having to extend the operation of the remaining Emergency regulations, the British Governor offered to accept responsibility and suffer the obloquy. If defeating Communism meant making empire the whipping boy of radical nationalists, then so be it.

Marshall bravely declined this offer and paid the price. In the face of mounting industrial unrest, he was obliged to reinstate nearly all the Emergency regulations. He finally resigned in April 1956 after all-party constitutional talks in London broke down. In the light of continued industrial and political unrest, the British were now insistent on retaining ultimate control over internal security as well as external affairs and defence.

Singapore's Communists, well concealed behind a host of innocuous-sounding organisations which ranged from the PAP to the 'Chinese Musical Gong Society', took heart. Subdued during the late 1940s and early 1950s by a number of Intelligence coups, plus the exodus of cadres to join the MRLA in the jungle, they had since reverted to their pre-Emergency priority of urban revolution. Infiltration of the trades unions had resumed, and a fertile recruiting ground amongst the less-privileged youth in the colony's Chinese-medium schools had been carefully cultivated. The collapse of the 1956 constitutional talks brought renewed unrest followed by a British clampdown on the schools and other Communist front organisations. This in turn precipitated widespread rioting.

The riots of October 1956 were potentially the most dangerous in Singapore's history. Seemingly the revolutionary confrontation, long dreaded, had at last materialised. For the first time, troops as well as police battled it out in the streets of the metropolis. Fatalities, however, did not exceed twenty; the security forces were deftly deployed and acted with restraint; and the Special Branch successfully swooped on the leaders and their principal sympathisers. In retrospect, it was the failure of the rising and the detention of its instigators which was most significant. When new constitutional talks got underway in 1957, the Singapore delegation, without the fire-breathing Communists at their backs, accepted terms not unlike those they had rejected a year earlier. Similarly encouraged, within the PAP Lee Kuan Yew finally came out against his Communist colleagues. Benefiting from the detention of many, he secured his own position within the party. Then, by canvassing for their release, he enhanced his popularity with the electorate. Of Lee it is often said that he alone rode the tiger (of Communism) and lived to subdue it. It was no mean achievement even if the tiger in question was a circus specimen, de-clawed by the Special Branch and cowed by the whip of the Emergency provisions.

Lee's debt to the British tiger-trainer would be acknowledged in his retention of a security and intelligence apparatus which later soured Singapore's credentials as a liberal democracy. More immediately, the brush with the tiger influenced the terms he now sought for 'independence through merger' with the Malayan Federation. There were sound economic reasons for merging with the Federation and there were grave doubts about Singapore's viability without it. Lee aired both on radio, and now television, with persuasive eloquence. Yet for him as for the British, the decisive argument centred on the security advantages of union with the strong and stable anti-Communist majority represented by the Tunku and his Alliance. On its own, Singapore would continue to be vulnerable to Peking's claims on the sympathies of its Chinese majority. It would suffer serious economic dislocation if Malaya developed its own port facilities and processing industries. And above all, its ability to cope with internal disorder would be dangerously exposed without British security guarantees. Conversely, its independence would be dangerously compromised with them. The answer therefore was to seek sanctuary within a Malaysian Federation whose conservative majority would bolster Lee's anti-Communist position in Singapore and whose mainly Malay police and remaining British troops would keep the tiger behind bars.

In 1959 Singapore's first elections on a universal franchise saw Lee returned with a crushing majority. Despite defections and a 1961 split within the PAP (when pro-Communist elements finally withdrew to form their own Socialist Front), Lee, now Prime Minister, pressed ahead with his overtures to Kuala Lumpur. The Tunku was at first unimpressed. Having just officially declared the end of the Emergency in Malaya, he was not anxious to embark on another anti-Communist struggle in Singapore; nor was he disposed to welcome 1 million Singapore Chinese who, added to the 2.3 million Malayan Chinese, would skew the Federation's delicate arithmetic and produce a Chinese majority; nor was he convinced by Lee Kuan Yew's apparent conversion from Communist stooge to free-market socialist. Both men had once read law at Cambridge University; but whereas the Tunku, his studies interrupted by the heavy demands of the racing calendar and the London season, had been content with a dismal pass degree, Lee had triumphed with a double first. Each in his way typified the attitudes of his community. The easy-going Malay aristocrat and the ruthless Chinese demagogue eyed one another with grave misgivings. A meeting of minds across the Johore Strait looked unlikely.

The Tunku, however, gradually came round, and in 1961, as if vouchsafed another favourable omen, officially endorsed the idea of Malaysia. Contemporary events in the Caribbean played some part in his conversion. Left to its own devices, an independent Singapore might well, he reasoned, succumb to Communism, like Cuba. With a Chinese Castro building missile silos in the Royal Navy's former dockyard, Malaya would become a front-line pawn in the Cold War. Better to pre-empt such a crisis by embracing the merger.

Better still to offset this merger with another. The British had always favoured some regional arrangement which would also take into account their remaining colonies of North Borneo (now Sabah), Sarawak and Brunei. All three had a part-Malay heritage and close commercial links with Singapore and the Federation. Raffles had planned some such Malay-based entity; James Brooke, inspired by his example, had acquired his raj in Sarawak in expectation of it; later Clementi and others had tried to expedite it; and, since the war, a British Commissioner-General for all the south-east Asian territories had foreshadowed it. This influential post, centrally located in Johore beside the Singapore causeway, was held from 1946 to 1955 by Malcolm MacDonald, son of Ramsay MacDonald, the first Labour Prime Minister. Unconventional and heartily disliked by martinets like Templer, MacDonald played a discreet and conciliatory role in promoting ethnic, party and eventually territorial compromise. The Tunku himself would generously acknowledge him as the real architect of Malaysia.

More immediately it was noted that in all three places – Sarawak, North Borneo and Brunei – people of Chinese extraction were in a minority. Incorporating the Borneo territories into Malaysia would therefore redress the demographic imbalance which the inclusion of Singapore's Chinese would occasion. Additionally Borneo would provide a useful outlet for Singapore's excess labour and capital. And finally, no insuperable objections were anticipated from the Bornean colonies themselves. Their politically unsophisticated peoples, it was argued, must surely recognise that the security and the economic advantages on offer within the Malaysian Federation could never be matched by staying outside it.

With this reasoning the British wholeheartedly concurred. They encouraged the Tunku's change of heart, urged Lee Kuan Yew to endorse the Bornean idea, and primed the local leaderships in the Borneo territories. With such thorough preparation the final act of imperial disengagement in south-east Asia should have been a mere formality. That it was nothing of the kind was not the fault of the British, although perhaps a certain arrogance of empire blinded them to the strident aspirations of the post-colonial world.

Not a Small Question

Nowhere were these aspirations more ambitious or the rhetoric more strident than across the Malacca Strait in Sukarno's Indonesia. It will be recalled that when the Dutch grudgingly accepted Indonesian independence at the 1949 Round Table Conference in The Hague, the western half of the island of New Guinea was withheld under Dutch rule pending further negotiations with Jakarta. The Dutch took this to mean that they might retain what they called West Papua until such time as its shy and elusive peoples had acquired an awareness of their island identity and an interest in handling its affairs. To the Indonesians, however, the agreement had merely signified that the arrangements and timing of the transfer of the territory had still to be determined. That it, like all the rest of the Netherlands East Indies, belonged to the successor state was taken for granted. For President Sukarno, in particular, West Irian, as Indonesians then called it, represented a personal challenge. As he put it in his Proclamation Day speech in 1950, 'this is not a small question'.

> The Irian question is a question of colonialism or not, a question of colonialism or freedom . . . because we have sworn that we will fight on till Doomsday so long as one bit of our country, even one island no bigger than an umbrella, is still not free.

When negotiations over the territory with the Dutch collapsed in 1951, Sukarno considered that the terms of the Round Table agreement had been broken. He could therefore abrogate its provisions concerning Indonesian federalism. Units like 'The Great East' were wound up, and the 'Republic of the United States of Indonesia' became the centralised 'Republic of Indonesia'. The first armed incursions into West Irian began three years later. Appeals to the United Nations followed, and in 1957, with Sukarno assuming dictatorial powers under the guise of 'guided democracy', retaliatory measures were taken, including the seizure of Dutch plantations and businesses. These climaxed with the severance of diplomatic ties with the Netherlands and a succession of guerrilla invasions of West Irian in 1961–2.

At this point US diplomatic pressure on the Netherlands again bore fruit. Under a face-saving agreement, the territory was made over to the United Nations for six months. Following this it was to be administered by Indonesia pending a plebiscite which, to no one's surprise, eventually confirmed Indonesian sovereignty. Sukarno, however, did not wait. In accordance with his revolutionary practice, he declared 1963 'The Year of Victory' and in May the *merah putih* (Indonesia's red and white flag) at last flew over the Irian capital. Once Hollandia and briefly MacArthur's home during his westward leap-frogging towards the Philippines, the town now became Sukarnopura (later Jayapura) while the territory became Irian Jaya ('Irian Victory').

None of this activity in a distant and pristine territory which geographers regarded as Australasian rather than Asian impinged on the counsels of Malaysia's would-be components. It did, though, resurrect debate in Jakarta about the ultimate extent of the territories encompassed in the concept of 'Indo-nesia'; and it also left President Sukarno casting about for a new crusade that was both worthy of his virtuosity as an anti-imperialist champion and capable of engrossing the attentions of his restless generals, his voluble allies in the Communist Party of Indonesia (PKI), and his increasingly impoverished people.

The voluntary association of three of Indonesia's once British neighbours did not immediately seem to offer the potential for such a crusade, and no objection was lodged when the concept of Malaysia was formulated in 1961. In fact the first protest came not from Jakarta at all but from Manila when in 1962 President Macapagal's government reminded a forgetful world of the outstanding Filipino claim to North Borneo. This stemmed from the extensive but uncertain sovereignty once exercised over the islands and adjacent littorals of the Sulu Sea by the sultanate of Sulu, now an integral part of the Philippines. Although in the eighteenth century

British pioneers like the redoubtable Alexander Dalrymple had apparently accepted the Sulu claim, it had since been studiously ignored by both the British North Borneo Company and the Colonial Office. Manila could scarcely expect to repossess itself of a territory which, before being incorporated in the British empire, had been freely traded on the international market, but it did expect to be consulted about its future and it had strong reservations about the place being engrossed by one of its regional rivals.

The Filipino case also raised another issue. Malaysia as now proposed could not be described simply as a successor state. Sarawak and North Borneo had never been part of the Malay Federation and were not even contiguous to it. In making decolonisation the occasion for redrawing international frontiers, a dangerous precedent would be set. Indonesians, for instance, might come to expect that if the Portuguese ever left East Timor, it should be incorporated into Indonesia. They might also, and soon did, question whether the states of north Borneo should not rather be part of Indonesia. All the rest of Borneo was already Indonesian and, more to the point, opinion in the north Borneo states was not unanimous in the support of Malaysia.

This became common knowledge when on 8 December 1962 Singapore's operational facilities for once served their imperial purpose by dispatching, at four hours' notice, a rapid reaction force of Gurkhas and commandos. Its task was to suppress a revolution, its improbable destination the pocket sultanate of Brunei. To Bruce Jackman, a newly arrived subaltern in the Gurkhas, it was all rather alarming.

> It wasn't our area, nobody had heard of Brunei, we didn't have any maps ... and even the ordnance department had to be broken into to get ammunition as the man who had the key was on holiday up-country. So there were a lot of people caught napping.

Luckily the Brunei revolution had equal difficulty getting off the ground. An attempt to kidnap the Sultan failed and the revolutionaries, otherwise the 'North Kalimantan Army', quickly slipped away into Indonesian territory. Meanwhile their leader, A. M. Azahari, said to have been a tireless organiser and a spell-binding speaker, had taken refuge in Manila. Thence, not evidently a gritty realist, he provided a vivid commentary on the wholly imaginary success of his coup.

Though born on the island of Labuan, Azahari had previously served with Indonesia's nationalist *pemuda*. Returning to Borneo, he had formed Brunei's first political party and, like Gerald MacBryan, Vyner Brooke's one-time *eminence grise*, had hit on the idea of reviving Brunei's authority over Sarawak and North Borneo. Whether he envisaged an independent 'Greater Brunei' or whether he was preparing the ground for its incorporation into Indonesia is not certain. He had, though, secured Indonesian support and assistance in the training of his troops. He had also been in close contact with the leaders of Singapore's Socialist Front (that is, the pro-Communist breakaways from Lee's PAP) and with various Communists and radical nationalists, like those responsible for Governor Stewart's assassination, in Sarawak and North Borneo.

Despite, therefore, the abject failure of Azahari's revolution, it did serve as a catalyst for anti-Malaysian sentiment. Exactly a month later Sukarno declared Malaysia a neo-colonial abomination and launched Indonesia's 'Konfrontasi' (Confrontation) with the proposed Federation. As in the Irian struggle, the Indonesian public was roused to a pitch of anti-British and anti-Malaysian fervour; training camps were established along the Indonesian frontier with Sarawak; and small-scale incursions were made into Sarawak and North Borneo territory. The UN was again called on to mediate but found against Sukarno's contention that Borneans were opposed to Malaysia. Thus in September 1963 the new federation of Malaysia was formally if belatedly inaugurated.

With British troops heavily committed in Borneo, with Sukarno denouncing Malaysia as a British stooge and dispatching his guerrillas even to the Malayan mainland, and with a chastened Brunei having elected to remain under British protection rather than join the new Federation, the end of empire in south-east Asia had turned out to be anything but tidy. Two years later, in 1965, Malaysia was itself looking decidedly ragged when Lee Kuan Yew's PAP attempted to mobilise opposition to the Tunku's UMNO-MCA Alliance, thus threatening to split the ethnic consensus on which the Federation rested. The Tunku hit back by effectively ejecting Singapore from the Federation. Despite agreements on defence and a programme of mutual assistance, Singaporeans disparaged what was left of Malaysia as a dozy Malay reservation while Malays scoffed at Singapore's prospects of going it alone. It looked as if Sukarno's heated denunciations of Malaysia as a neo-colonial nonsense might have substance.

The rhetoric of 'Konfrontasi' soared to even greater heights in 1964–5. This, declared Sukarno, was the 'Year of Living Dangerously'. Foreign commercial interests were seized, embassies attacked, and British and Malaysian property destroyed. For Sukarno 'living dangerously' meant confronting not only the entire Western world but also many Bandung friends (in what was now called the Non-Aligned Movement) who sympathised with the Tunku and Malaysia. Indonesia had already pulled out of the UN after it had failed to support it in Borneo. Now Sukarno's growing friendship with Peking and his dependence on the Indonesian Communist Party convinced many that he was himself a Communist.

Whether it convinced Indonesia's Communists is uncertain. Their attempted coup in late October 1965 may or may not have had Sukarno's blessing. Either way it failed, and the army's counter-coup succeeded. Perhaps a quarter of a million Indonesians, only some of them Communists, were massacred in the process. After a few months as a mere figurehead president, Sukarno himself would be removed by General Suharto. Sukarno too had ridden the tiger but, unlike Lee, he had failed to escape from the ring. With him would go the policy of 'Konfrontasi' and Indonesia's opposition to the existence of Malaysia.

This turmoil in Indonesia, plus the continuing war in Vietnam and upheavals in Thailand and Burma, shed new light on the state of affairs in Malaysia and Singapore. Unexpectedly the erstwhile British empire in south-east Asia was emerging as an oasis of stability, democracy and prosperity in a revolution-rent world. Singapore was no bastion of liberalism and Malaysia, as yet, no beacon of progress. Moreover, serious race riots, in Singapore in 1964 and in mainland Malaya in 1969, marred their cherished claims of ethnic harmony. Yet both Lee's PAP and the Tunku's Alliance retained a firm and lasting popularity. Though still suspicious of one another, they managed to collaborate, and in 1967 both became founder members of the anti-Communist Association of South East Asian Nations (ASEAN).

Devoted to regional collaboration rather than mutual defence, this organisation nevertheless relieved tensions as well as accelerating economic growth. Sheltering beneath the US defence umbrella and benefiting hugely from the US and Japanese investment on offer to sympathetic Asian economies, the ASEAN countries were well-placed to share in the 'Asian miracle' of the 1980s. It may be taken as a compliment to empire that when the British finally withdrew from all their defence commitments east of Suez in 1971, their presence was scarcely missed.

15

Twenty Years to Pay

Rainy Days in Hong Kong

Had bets been laid on which eastern territory would retain its colonial status for longest, the favourite would surely have been enigmatic Irian, or perhaps little-visited North Borneo. Hong Kong, on the other hand, an impertinent pimple on the rosy countenance of a resurgent and extremely populous China, would have been a rank outsider. Back in 1930 when Weihaiwei was 'retroceded', the odds against its sister territory surviving to become the last outpost of empire in the East would have been long enough. In the late 1930s, as Japanese forces overran the China treaty ports, they would have lengthened; and in the mid-1940s, as the war in the Pacific drew to its sudden end, it seemed quite probable that Hong Kong had already dropped out of the race. Well outside the operational remit of Mountbatten's South East Asia Command, the island and its adjacent New Territories looked destined for rapid occupation either by the Chinese Nationalists or the Americans. The Nationalists had long been demanding Hong Kong's restitution; and the Americans, in their anxiety to boost the prestige of the Nationalists at the expense of their Communist rivals, were all for handing it to them (as well as that operational role in northern Vietnam).

Even the British Foreign Office, whose deep dealings with China had been habitually compromised by the status and pretensions of the colony, was inclined to write it off. But the Colonial Office stood firm, and so did the newly elected British Labour government; both insisted that if Hong Kong was to be excluded from the general principle of restoring the pre-war situation, it could only be as part of a wider regional settlement which might also include Malaya, the Philippines and the Netherlands East Indies. Such a blueprint would

be long on the drawing board. More immediately, for both sentimental and operational reasons, General MacArthur favoured the
idea of British reoccupation and, on the understanding that this
would not preclude future negotiations on the colony's status,
President Truman reluctantly concurred.

These arrangements were not compromised, as in Java and
Vietnam, by any unforeseen developments in Hong Kong itself.
There Franklin Gimson, the pre-war Colonial Secretary, emerged
from the long years of internment decidedly tetchy but utterly committed to restoring an authority which though lately ineffective had,
in his opinion, never lapsed. In the absence of the Governor (who
had been interned in Manchuria) he immediately had himself sworn
into that office; and to Japanese protestations that perhaps they
should surrender to the Chinese rather than the British, he gave the
shortest possible shrift.

> I replied that this view was merely their expression of opinion with which
> I was not concerned. I intended to carry out these duties to which I had
> been appointed by His Majesty's Government.

A stickler for protocol, Gimson ignored the sudden efflorescence
of Kuomintang flags and for two weeks stuck to his self-appointed
task until white ensigns and Union Jacks announced the arrival of
Admiral Harcourt's Royal Navy squadron. Considering that at the
time (29 August 1945) Mountbatten's forces had yet to reach either
Singapore or Malaya, let alone Indo-China and the Indies, Harcourt
had made good speed. Detached from the British Pacific Fleet in
Sydney, and following a pause at Subic Bay in the Philippines for
details of US minelaying in Hong Kong waters, he steamed past the
wrecks that littered Victoria harbour to face some opposition from
Gimson and his threadbare administration but none at all from the
Chinese.

Despite Gimson's reservations, when Harcourt duly took the surrender of the Japanese forces he did so on behalf of both his own
government and the Nationalist government in Chungking. The
British could afford to be generous. They had adroitly pinched the
colony from Chungking's post-war operational sphere and so
baulked the Chinese of their best-yet chance to reclaim it.

Nevertheless, Washington continued to disparage its retention
and Chungking to demand its return. When two Nationalist armies
began converging on Kowloon in late 1945, the colony's military

administration went on alert while its Chinese population was reportedly convulsed by 'a general feeling of tension and anxiety'. In fact the armies in question were heading for a showdown with Mao's Communists in Manchuria. They were merely in transit, using the colony as a convenient port at which to board troopships. Moreover, the British administration, being quite incapable of opposing such a force, had given its agreement. Then, as ever after, resisting a Chinese army that was minded to enter the colony was not a serious option. The chances of Hong Kong outlasting its colonial rivals remained slim.

Worse, however, would have been the odds on its outshining its rivals as a dazzling example of economic enterprise. To its pre-war reputation as an excruciatingly drab enclave of British exclusivity were added in 1945 the post-war burdens of acute impoverishment and mass immigration. The latter was no novelty, although its scale was unprecedented. In early 1946 it was estimated that over 100,000 mainland Chinese, mostly refugees from civil strife, were entering the colony every month. Controlling this flood was beyond the capacity of the colony's makeshift administration. Eventually it resorted to 'an indirect deterrent' by withholding the issue of ration cards to unauthorised immigrants, a move which might well have hastened the very unrest that immigration control was supposed to pre-empt.

If no serious disturbances ensued, it was thanks to the priority given to two of Hong Kong's enduring obsessions: police and money. 'Freedom, food, law and order, and a stable currency' – though not necessarily in that order – were what Admiral Harcourt hoped to confer. While the procurement of such basics as rice and fuel was still on a hand-to-mouth log-to-fire basis, police recruitment proceeded apace. Chinese students were enlisted *en masse*, rates of pay were raised and, in an innovative move designed both to cut the incidence of crime and boost that of its detection, 700 Chinese gangsters were offered immunity and eventual escape in return for acting as temporary law enforcers. This arrangement, which appears to have been honoured by both parties, could be taken to imply that the line between organised crime and its organised prevention was ever a fine one in Hong Kong.

Meanwhile, to universal relief, Harcourt's 'most urgent task [which] so greatly overshadowed all other problems' had been completed: the currency had been stabilised. Along with the first troops to arrive from Mountbatten's SEAC had come freshly printed Hong Kong dollars. They were immediately released into circulation while yen notes, variously overprinted, were simultaneously withdrawn. F.S.V. Donnison, author of the official history of Britain's post-war military administrations, noted the somewhat dramatic effect.

> As a result nine-tenths of the population found themselves with no money and very little immediate prospect of obtaining any. It was perhaps fortunate that the next three days were rainy and unpropitious for protest or agitation.

Prices of everything, bar rationed rice, spiralled alarmingly. Yet government relief works and the indulgent attitude of the Hong-kong and Shanghai Bank mitigated the distress caused by such shock treatment, and after a few anxious weeks the panic began to subside. 'By November 1945 it was possible to lift government controls and restore a free-enterprise system.' According to Frank Welsh, the colony's biographer, this represented 'a post-war adjustment unparalleled elsewhere'. Fortunately, though neglected and anything but ship-shape, the dockyards, the expanded Kai Tak airport, the Kowloon-Canton railway, and most public buildings were found to be intact. They were soon operational and Hong Kong was back in business.

The only obvious difference was that the barriers of class and race were crumbling. A shortage of British personnel was remedied by the induction of more Chinese management; the compulsory recall of Gimson and his pre-war colleagues cleared the corridors for a younger officialdom less wedded to protocol and privilege. Bastions of exclusivity like the residential area of the Peak were triumphantly scaled by polite Chinese with well-behaved families and ever-ready cheque books. In the spirit of the times there was even talk of making government more representative and accountable. Given that the colony's population was now over 97 per cent Chinese, most of them too intent on survival to register an interest in politics, universal suffrage was out of the question. Sir Mark Young, who returned as Governor in May 1946, stressed responsibility rather than representation. As well as expanding the Legislative Council, he proposed devolving certain functions of government to a municipal council. It was this subordinate body which, with some of its members being elected on a carefully weighted constituency basis, was slated to become the showpiece of democracy in Hong Kong.

Though modest enough, the 'Young Plan' was subjected to pains-taking scrutiny as Whitehall took three years to offer a qualified approval. By then Young had been recalled and his successor was having second thoughts. The plan was still under discussion in Hong Kong in late 1949 when another flood of refugees began spilling across the frontier into the New Territories. This upset its arithmetic and gave pause for thought. Constitutional reform suddenly seemed even less pressing if not irrelevant; it might even be provocative. The only concessions to democracy were about to be shelved.

The rethink, like the new influx of refugees, was prompted by momentous events on the mainland. It was as if the needle of history had just jumped a track. After twenty years of inconclusive struggle, in 1949 in the space of a few months Peking, Nanking, Shanghai and Canton had been overrun by the People's Liberation Army. China had gone Communist and the pimple that was Hong Kong now defaced not a respected if nationalistic wartime ally but a slogan-singing bourgeois-bashing revolutionary People's Republic.

Before the border was closed by Peking in November 1949, another half a million Chinese citizens had crossed into Hong Kong territory; and after every subsequent convulsion within Mao's China a further tsunami of immigrants inundated the colony. Its 1938 population of 1 million had trebled by 1968 and would be well over 5 million by 1990. Many of the immediate pre- and post-war immigrants came from Shanghai whose relocated business houses and manufacturers soon lent a new industrial dimension to Hong Kong's economic profile. Just as the place had drawn its commercial brains from Canton in the 1840s so it acquired its sweatshop sinews from Shanghai a century later.

Some immigrants were Nationalists wanting sanctuary, a few Communists out to make trouble. Most simply wanted to make a living. The poor sought work and the rich sought opportunity (to become richer). Cheap labour and speculative capital, to the latter of which US, Japanese and European investors would soon add, were plentiful. Injected into Hong Kong's favourable growing medium of open markets and benignly *laissez-faire* government plus, of course, firm policing and a mostly stable currency, such spores produced an almost instant culture of rampant enterprise. The Asian miracle, less alchemy than science, was about to begin. Mao had done the colony a favour.

Nor was it the only favour. The 1950 British recognition of the new Chinese regime, though it found no supporters in Malaya, made a good impression in Peking. Because of that 99-year lease on the New Territories, it implied that the government of the People's Republic had a legitimate interest in Hong Kong and that the British would in due course negotiate with it rather than with the Nationalists now penned in Taiwan. There remained the danger of impatient anti-imperialists overruning the colony, or simply withholding the supplies on which it depended. But officially Peking played by the rules. No demands for the colony's immediate restitution were made. It would be the British who would eventually initiate negotiations for the final hand-over.

In the 1950s, with nearly half a century left on the lease, this indulgent attitude from Peking encouraged what by Hong Kong's standards amounted to stability. Were the New Territories' lease to run its full course, there was now a real possibility that Palmerston's once 'barren island' would indeed become the last outpost of empire. Peking was apparently resigned to its continuation and would soon have good economic reasons to be grateful for it; additionally, and thanks again to Mao, the United States had had a change of heart.

Obituary for Empire

When in late 1945 those two Nationalist armies had converged on Kowloon for the voyage to Manchuria, it was to board Liberty ships which flew the Stars and Stripes. To the post-war policing of east Asia the Americans had taken a more positive, even partisan, approach than had the British in south-east Asia. It was partly a question of continuity in that US support of Generalissimo Chiang Kai-shek and his Kuomintang Nationalists had long been unstinting. During the war China had been promoted as one of the four Allied powers, entitled to the financial backing of the US, its warmest approbation, and whatever supplies and munitions could be air-lifted into Chungking. After the war, despite growing evidence of ineptitude, corruption and possible collapse, the militaristic Kuomintang continued to enjoy US diplomatic and logistical support. Hence the Liberty ships and hence the US disparagement of the British presence in Hong Kong.

While pressuring London over the colony's restitution to China, American diplomats liked to evoke the 'Open Door' policy, arguably as pivotal and immutable a lode-star of US international relations as the Monroe Doctrine. Originally conceived in the 1890s as a way of ensuring US access to China's markets – markets which might otherwise have been monopolised by the European powers (of which Tsarist Russia had been one) – the 'Open Door' was now mythologised as a US commitment to restore and preserve the integrity of China. This not only meant winkling out the British. It also meant helping the Nationalists to overcome their Communist rivals whom Washington persisted in regarding as Moscow-backed subversives.

When, therefore, the needle skipped and the jack-booted Generalissimo and his cohorts were sent skidding into offshore exile across the Taiwan Strait, Washington was nonplussed. Not for the last time, US foreign policy makers had got it badly wrong. The Communist threat in Asia had been underestimated; not enough had been done to support the Nationalists; Chiang Kai-shek should never have been trusted with their leadership. There were many lessons to be learnt. In the meantime the US and her allies, confronted in eastern Europe by the massed tanks of the Red Army, now found themselves checked and menaced in eastern Asia by the swarming hordes of the 'Yellow Peril'. The pay-off for a century of painstaking diplomacy and a horrific war had been hijacked by Muscovite ideologues, and in one fell swoop the world's wealthiest and most developed economy had been deprived of what was potentially the world's greatest market for its exports and investment. While the British, anxious about Hong Kong's fate, hastened to recognise the new regime in Peking, the Americans would have nothing to do with it. According to Dean Rusk, the People's Republic of China was but a 'Slavic Manchoukuo' (in other words a Soviet puppet).

It was as a result of this new US thinking that Hong Kong, from being a hazardous piece of colonial flotsam adrift off the Pearl River, was suddenly identified as a bobbing float on the bulging net of Communist containment, vital as an indicator of Chinese intentions and as a source of and base for intelligence. 'Restoring the integrity of China' was no longer mentioned; it was more a question of 'restoring China' since the US persisted in recognising the Kuomintang in Taiwan as the only legitimate government.

A year later, in November 1950, the People's Republic of China entered the Korean War. No doubts could now be entertained about the expansionist ambitions of Communism in Asia. Wherever the net looked like bursting, wherever the 'free world' was under threat, Washington felt bound to intervene. Hence the decision to bank-roll the French war in Indo-China, to encourage the British in their Malayan 'Emergency', and to neutralise Communist-led insurgency in a country that was nearer both to Washington's heart and its pocket. This was the Republic of the Philippines, whose early independence America had proudly sponsored and which was now about to receive an early taste of post-imperial intervention. It would prove highly effective; but also fatally so, for from the success of interventionist tactics in the Philippines grew the confidence of success in Vietnam.

Many Americans might query the idea that their country's involvement in the Philippines in the early 1950s and subsequently in Vietnam has any place in a catalogue of empire. Both, like Korea, were about resisting Communist encroachment, upholding Western values and assisting legal but alarmingly vulnerable regimes. Either that or they were insane and highly divisive attempts to deny to Asian peoples their right of self-determination and so spite their would-be sponsors in Peking and Moscow. Whichever was the case, empire, except in the fevered imaginations of America's French surrogates in Indo-China prior to 1955, was not a factor. The sovereignty of the Philippines was never challenged and nor was that of Vietnam (although conceding quasi-sovereign status to South Vietnam might look that way to Hanoi). Nor was there any intention of reducing either country to colonial status. US policy-makers and spokesmen would be hyper-sensitive to imputations of colonial or neo-colonial behaviour and, not without pride, would invoke their past record. Was the United States not the champion of national liberation, sponsor of the UN charter, the first to concede independence to an Asian colony, and now the only great power in history to deny itself the easy pickings of dominion?

Herein, though, lay a catch. It was partly one of timing. The Communist challenge had found the French and the British still in possession of their empires and therefore responsible for dealing with the 'red menace'. Only after endeavouring to do so did they bid their colonies adieu. On the other hand American haste to be rid of the Philippines meant that there, technically, Communist insurgency was a matter for the government of the Republic of the Philippines. Despite its investments there and its bases, the US had no responsibility for the internal security of the Philippines and no right to intervene. It could only do so by a surreptitious retracing of foot-steps and then by effecting what might look like forced entry. MacArthur's 'I will return', a promise redeemed the first time around, came to sound like a threat revived when repeated.

And what possible responsibilities did the American people have to the Vietnamese? It was hard to imagine anywhere in Asia where American links were more tenuous or American interests less evident. Forcing entry into a previous residence, for example the Philippines, whose ever-obliging owner still stored some of one's effects was understandable. Barging in on a total stranger was not. In fact a willingness to intervene militarily in the affairs of remote and unfamiliar territories was the essence of empire. It might be well-intentioned; empire often was. It was nevertheless typically imperial-ist aggression.

Sixty years earlier, when the US had first intervened in the Philippines, it was supposedly to 'rescue' its people from the iniqui-ties of Spanish colonialism. Just so, there were those who would see intervention in Vietnam as a crusade to rescue the Vietnamese from French colonialism. There too, as McNutt might have put it, a glori-ous 'monument to American idealism and enterprise' awaited construction; there too, as MacArthur might have put it, another 'citadel of democracy in the East' might be raised. 'Manifest destiny' beckoned; misguided opponents like Aguinaldo or Ho Chi Minh must stand aside. Bolstered by its self-belief as the champion of anti-colonialism, Washington went about the business of imperialism with a clear conscience.

Empire was irrelevant only in the sense that the whole concept was now so outdated. 'The easy pickings of dominion' no longer required an elaborate system of administrative ring-fencing. In fact the flagging of empire so proudly pursued in the past – the colouring-in of world maps, the monarch's head on colonial curren-cies and postage stamps, the emblematic obeisance of subject peoples to a sovereign or republic 'over the seas' – was now frowned on. Commandeering territory in order to engross profitable trade routes, monopolise desirable commodities and corner promising markets seemed absurdly archaic, as well as unnecessarily costly and provocative, in an age of jet transport, global diversification and technological innovation; so did the idea of assuming administrative responsibility for peoples quite capable of managing their own affairs, indeed clamorously eager to do so; and so, it soon became apparent, did the gunship mentality of enforcing compliance in a global orthodoxy by military over-kill.

This would be the lesson of Vietnam for the West as of Afghanistan for the Soviet Union. But if the conceit of formal empire awaited its obituary in Vietnam, notice of its death had already been posted elsewhere, and particularly in the Philippines.

I'm Sticking to My Guy

In the spring of 1950, between the Maoist triumph in China and the outbreak of the Korean War, a delegation from Manila had visited Washington to lobby on behalf of Filipino veterans of the Pacific War. For Ramon Magsaysay, an expansive Filipino Congressman, it was the first visit to the US. Capitol Hill appealed little to him. An erstwhile trucking contractor from up-country Luzon, he lacked both education and finesse; but he liked Americans and in Lieutenant-Colonel Edward G. Lansdale of the newly created United States Air Force he met a man who seemed genuinely impressed by his unsophisticated background. They were introduced during the course of a dinner and immediately found much in common. Both were in their early forties, both irreverent newcomers to the political circuit, and both firm believers in individual initiative. Also, Lansdale had served in the Philippines at the end of the war and had evidently made it his business to probe deeply into rural conditions and political dissent. This naturally brought them to an exchange of views on the then escalating 'Huk' rebellion.

Repairing to the Colonel's rooms, they continued their discussion late into the night. Lansdale was attentive and incisive, Magsaysay voluble and receptive. Eventually the Filipino's prescription for combating Huk insurgency was tapped out, two-fingered, on the Colonel's portable typewriter. It corresponded almost word for word with a paper that Lansdale himself had just presented to his superiors. Such a congruence of opinion was highly satisfactory. Next day Lansdale would submit Magsaysay's ideas, then pilot him through a series of high-level interviews. His own mind was already made up.

> I decided he should be the guy to handle [the Huks] out in The Philippines because of his feelings toward the people and toward the enemy. He understood the problem, which very few Filipinos or Americans ever did.

Days later, for much the same reasons, it was decided that Lansdale should be the guy to handle Magsaysay. With a small staff he followed him back to the Philippines.

There President Roxas, General MacArthur's protégé, had died of a heart attack in 1948. His successor, Elpidio Quirino, now came under heavy pressure from US military staff to appoint Magsaysay as Secretary for Defense. A substantial US financial package for the Filipino defence forces depended on the appointment. The hard-pressed Quirino was therefore happy to oblige. This was in September 1950. Soon after, the new Defense Secretary moved into Lansdale's spacious villa on the outskirts of Manila. It was partly for his own security, partly because he so valued Lansdale's company. Draped across the upholstery, they could again talk into the small hours. According to P. C. Richards, the Reuter's correspondent in Manila, it was now the affable Lansdale who did most of the talking. 'Ed [Lansdale] was . . . telling Magsaysay what to do. There is no question of that. He was just someone you didn't notice.'

For a Filipino with Hollywood ideas of what an American colonel should look like, Edward G. Lansdale was it – a trim and boyish figure with short black hair, crisp moustache and a smile that bade homage to quality toothpaste. In *The Ugly American*, a late 1950s best-seller, authors William J. Lederer and Eugene Burdick barely disguised him as 'Edwin B. Hillandale', otherwise known as 'The Ragtime Kid' because of his virtuosity on the harmonica. Of a Saturday, they wrote, 'the kid' would slip out of Manila on his motor cycle, head for the hills, and spend the day winning hearts and minds in some disaffected *barrio* where no government troops dared venture. He took along his harmonica because he spoke no Tagalog and it helped to break down hostility. Lansdale later objected to this portrayal on the grounds that he never rode a motor cycle. The harmonica, however, was a Lansdale trade mark. According to his biographer, Cecil Currey, 'it was the one thing that brought him out of himself'. 'A regular guy' by any standards, he was inconspicuous because archetypal.

That he was also, in the opinion of the CIA Director William Colby, 'one of the greatest spies of all time' is now common knowledge. He lived until 1987, published an autobiography, and has been much studied as well as fictionalised. Whether his work and influence are better understood as a result is questionable. His wartime career in military intelligence and possibly with the OSS in China is still a mystery. He was, he explained, 'a sort of handyman', presumably an unskilled 'plumber'. After the war, though transferring to the USAF, he learnt no more of aviation than would any frequent traveller.

Instead he 'volunteered for Cold War duty' and, by the time he adopted Magsaysay, he was a senior operative in the Office of Policy Co-ordination. This was a shadowy organisation loosely linked to the new CIA but even more secretive and often in competition with its parent organisation. Lansdale, once a high-flyer in the advertising business, specialised in what he called 'psywar', that is psychological warfare techniques or 'dirty tricks'. They ranged from ambitious and laudable initiatives for redressing the social grievances on which Marxism thrived to hare-brained schemes for disseminating misinformation and discrediting the enemy. As no one appreciated better than Lansdale, the threat posed by 'people's wars' and 'liberation struggles' required a new and more innovative approach to warfare.

This he and Magsaysay now tried on the 'Huks', or the Hukbalahap, an abbreviation for *Hukbong Bayan Laban sa Hapon*. The Huks represented a post-war revival of the Filipino 'Anti-Japanese Army', another Communist-dominated guerrilla organisation that had, like the MPAJA in Malaya, defied Japanese rule. After the war MacArthur, unlike Mountbatten, acknowledged no debt to these guerrillas, many of whom espoused agrarian dissent which threatened the ascendancy of the Filipino élite, or *ilustrados*, with whom Americans had always dealt. When the Huks contested the elections in 1946 as a left-wing Democratic Alliance, their candidates were harassed and their supporters attacked. After one such incident, Luis Taruc, their leader, headed back to the hills and proclaimed the formation of a People's Liberation Army. Presidents Roxas and then Quirino outlawed the organisation but failed miserably to suppress it. In March 1950, when the Vietminh were switching from bombing outrages in Saigon to their devastating assault on RC4 and when the MRLA were building up to their worst year of terror in Malaya, the Huks were overrunning much of central Luzon and launching battalion-strength assaults on government convoys and garrisons. This was the background to Lansdale's meeting with Magsaysay and the challenge which the two men now embraced.

It was true that, compared to the MRLA or the Vietminh, the Huks, though numerous and dedicated, were novices in the ways of Communism. One of Lansdale's more imaginative wheezes was to get word to the Huk leadership that a Russian submarine was in Filipino waters waiting to make contact. He approached the US Navy about borrowing a suitable sub – 'That's a good idea you got,' replied Admiral Arleigh Burke: 'Whether it works or not, let's try it' – and he also began a crash course in Russian, the plan being that when the Huks rowed out for the rendezvous, a great-coated Lansdale would be on the submarine's deck to lull their suspicions with a fraternal '*Dobry Dyen Comrades*'; they would then be apprehended and their whole movement discredited because of its Soviet links. Even after Washington had vetoed the idea (querying their operative's sanity in the process), Lansdale remained convinced that it would have succeeded. Yet there is no conclusive evidence that the Huks ever had any direct dealings with Moscow or any other Communist directorates; nor that they would have welcomed such an approach. Luis Taruc, though influenced by his Marxist reading, was never a party member. The Huks' strength lay not in ideological orthodoxy or international solidarity but in the support they commanded among Luzon's oppressed peasant farmers and landless plantation workers.

To compete for this support Magsaysay and Lansdale, besides more gimmicky initiatives, set out to 'change the outlook of the government [in Manila] towards the people'. Their chosen instrument was not, as in Malaya, a vastly increased police force but Magsaysay's now vastly increased and heavily US-subsidised Filipino forces. Into them, on Lansdale's initiative, was injected a Civil Affairs Section designed to instil in the troops a sense of responsibility towards the community. 'We started with discipline and getting them to act helpful,' explained Lansdale in his autobiography. 'We started Civic Action which is now part of military actions in the US Army.'

Soldiers were directed to undertake public works projects, all of them heavily publicised; military attorneys offered their services free to peasants engaged in land suits; the purloining of villagers' stores, livestock and wives was discouraged. As in Malaya cash payments were made for information, while amnesties for rebels were accompanied by the promise of a home and land-holding, usually in distant Mindanao. There seemed no end to the bright ideas emanating from the new Defense chief and, though more notable for their hype than their results, they made an impact. So did more effective intelligence and more incisive operational deployment. By 1952 the tide was definitely turning in the government's favour and Magsaysay was being hailed as the saviour of what Americans liked to call the 'showcase of democracy in Asia'.

However, no credit for this tag, or anything else, went to President Quirino whose government, born of outrageous ballot-rigging, was now paralysed by venality and factionalism. Reviewing Quirino's dismal record of squandering US aid, Dean Acheson, President Truman's Secretary of State, was reminded of Chiang Kai-shek. America must not make the same mistake twice; Quirino, in short, must go. And who better to succeed him than the Huk-bashing Magsaysay? As the 1953 elections approached, Lansdale geared up for his greatest triumph.

By now the Defense chief and the Colonel were inseparable, bound alike by the mutual obligations of the Filipino *compadre* system and by the buddiness of an all-American adventure in which the butch and suggestible Magsaysay played Cassidy to 'The Ragtime Kid'. Magsaysay was not without credentials. Like Tunku Abdul Rahman, he enjoyed an effortless empathy with the Filipino masses. As one of them, he understood their love of personal contact and happily reciprocated, travelling widely and impressing all he met with his warmth and sincerity. But it was Lansdale who master-minded the operation. In 1952 he escorted his protégé to the States to collect the plaudits of the President and the media, thus establishing Magsaysay as 'America's candidate'. This endorsement, the kiss of death anywhere else in Asia, was reckoned an essential benediction in the Philippines. US press coverage, like *Time* magazine's fulsome homage to the 'Eisenhower of the Pacific', was then duly distributed by Lansdale and reprinted in the Manila papers.

Magsaysay's speeches were also generally reckoned to be Lansdale compositions; so was his slogan, the possibly ambiguous 'Magsaysay is My Guy'. His campaign song, however, the catchy 'Magsaysay Mambo', was written by Raul Manglapus, a young saxophonist and Magsaysay supporter who later represented the Philippines at the Bandung Conference. All of thirty years later still, he served as Foreign Secretary under Aquino and Ramos and led the negotiations which eventually terminated the US bases in the Philippines. Magsaysay would not have approved. He loved Americans, welcomed their continued involvement, and guessed correctly that most Filipinos felt the same. When the rattled Quirino blundered into a condemnation of him as a US puppet, 'My Guy's' victory was assured. It was recorded by Stanley Karnow, whose journalistic assignments included Manila and resulted in a notable television series on the Philippines.

> Magsaysay was aboard a US vessel [in Manila Bay] when the results flashed. He [had] won nearly seventy per cent of the vote, beating Quezon's record in the race for commonwealth president in 1935. It was also a triumph for America and for Lansdale – whom the Indian ambassador to Manila nicknamed 'Colonel Landslide'.

That Jawaharlal Nehru's ambassador should have so unerringly identified Lansdale as the architect of victory was wholly appropriate. The Indian Prime Minister had always been suspicious of Filipino independence. In words that must have rankled at the time but now seemed prescient, he had taken the occasion of the Philippine Republic's independence to sound a stern and disconcerting note.

> We hope that this really signifies independence for this word has become rather hackneyed and outworn and has been made to mean many things. Some countries that are called independent are far from free and are under the economic or military domination of some great power. Some so-called independent countries carry on with what might be termed 'puppet regimes' and are in a way client countries of some great power. We hope that is not so with the Philippines.

Puppets, though, even puppeteers, can be popular and, whatever else was wrong with the Magsaysay victory, it undeniably represented the will of the people. Sadly his presidency, of which so much was expected, proved something of an anti-climax. Taruc surrendered and the Huk uprising collapsed, but those of Magsaysay's supporters who looked to the new President for social and agrarian reform were largely disappointed. So was Washington. The consensus which would make the country proof against future Communist agitation failed to emerge. Worse still, Magsaysay, the most popular president the Philippines had ever had, was killed in a plane crash after only three years in office.

Possibly he might have achieved more if Lansdale had remained at his side. But for the Colonel a new and greater assignment beckoned. 'The Ragtime Kid' had bid farewell to Manila and Magsaysay in January 1954. Five months later, now 'The Quiet American', he made his Saigon début as confidant and side-kick to Ngo Dinh Diem.

We Have to Fight for Liberty

Nineteen fifty-four was the year of Dien Bien Phu and of the Geneva Conference. In the aftermath of the battle but while the cease-fire negotiations were still under way, Bao Dai, Vietnam's restored head of state, had invited Ngo Dinh Diem to head his government in Saigon. Both men were absentees. The ex-Emperor held court in a stately château near Cannes within a *wagon lit*'s ride of his Paris mistress and a chauffeured Rolls Royce's drive of the Monte Carlo gaming tables. Diem lived less well on boiled cabbage in a Belgian monastery. A Catholic of priestly habits, he had spent the previous two years in a seminary in New Jersey, 'washing dishes, scrubbing floors and praying' according to Stanley Karnow, while he cultivated American contacts. These included co-religionists like Cardinal Spellman and John F. Kennedy who were impressed by his piety and abstemious lifestyle as well as by his considerable political credentials. For, although Diem was the head of a powerful Vietnamese clan whose support had been sought by both the French and the Vietminh, his self-denial of the perquisites of office had left him with a reputation for nationalist integrity untainted by either colonial compromise or Communist collaboration. He was not 'America's candidate' because as yet America did not presume to have a candidate in Vietnam, but he might have been if she had.

In Bao Dai's estimation, this claim on Catholic American regard was Diem's principal qualification for office. To convince Washington that its generous aid was not subsidising a French puppet, and to ensure that it would continue to pump dollars into Saigon once the French had gone, Diem seemed the ideal prime minister. His appointment was announced, in France, on 18 June 1954.

'It was what Lansdale had been waiting for,' notes Cecil Currey. Flying into Saigon only weeks ahead of Diem, Lansdale was still busy organising his Saigon Military Mission, another 'psywar' agency. He nevertheless decided to go out to Tan Son Nhut to welcome the man who might be his Vietnamese Magsaysay.

Driven by 'Proc', a pistol-packing Filipino in dark glasses who also acted as his bodyguard, the Colonel's Citroën 2CV skidded over the *pavé* towards the airport. Then he changed his mind. Instead of greeting the new premier he would observe how the Vietnamese people greeted him. A curious crowd of modest proportions lined part of the route. They waited. Diem sped by invisible in a darkened limousine. Then they dispersed. It was not the ovation Lansdale had envisaged. That evening he compiled a list of priorities for the new premier and next morning, accompanied by a colleague who could speak French, he cheerfully marched into the Norodom Palace and tracked Diem to his office. Cecil Currey describes the meeting.

> With incredible chutzpah, Lansdale introduced himself. He was a Colonel in the United States Air Force, he worked at the embassy, and what could he do to help? After a few moments he handed his notes to the premier, suggesting that the notes could form the basis of their conference.

Unfortunately the colleague-interpreter had forgotten his glasses and Diem's English, for one who had recently spent two years in the United States, proved woeful. He laboured over Lansdale's notes with the help of an English-French dictionary, then in despair offered his own glasses to the interpreter. After that they got along fine.

Diem was clearly a rather different proposition to Magsaysay. Some thought him saintly, others merely humourless. Diminutive, ascetic and self-important, he wore a well-pressed suit, usually white, and talked non-stop. He could go on, lecturing and sermonising, for two to three hours. Those, principally Americans, who complained that he never listened to their advice admitted that this was partly because they got so little chance to tender it. Lansdale himself was no mean talker. To colleagues in Saigon and Washington he tirelessly drummed home the need to support those Vietnamese such as Diem who were willing to fight Communist domination. 'He preached (Oh, how he preached!),' recalled William Colby. But he was also a great listener and it was this quality that endeared him to Diem. Three weeks after their first meeting, Diem is said to have asked the Colonel to move into his Norodom Palace. Lansdale felt that this might compromise them both; but for the next eighteen months 'Proc' and the 2CV spent long evenings parked at the palace as Lansdale attended the premier. Magsaysay's *compadre* had become Diem's confessor.

The Lansdale charm had again worked its magic. A combination of heartwarming companionship, respectful solicitude, naïve presumption and lethal dedication, it was best captured by Graham Greene in *The Quiet American*. Greene always denied that Lansdale was the model for 'Alden Pyle' and, unlike Lederer and Burdick, he did not claim that his characters were based on real people. He did, however, know and apparently dislike Lansdale; there is, too, much circumstantial coincidence in the activities attributed to 'Pyle' and those undertaken by Lansdale; and significantly it is in the pages of Greene's novel that the Lansdale-Pyle character at last becomes a plausible figure.

As Magsaysay had discovered, here was a man who made all things possible. Never short of ideas, like a Raffles he flitted from one grandiose construction to the next; never easy to control, like a Garnier he frequently took unauthorised initiatives; and never totally candid, like all imperialists he made the imperatives for action sound deceptively simple. When, in Greene's novel, 'Pyle' is being tormented by the infuriatingly omniscient English journalist who is really Greene himself, the American quietly enunciates the bottom line. 'You have to fight for liberty,' he insists. America, like France, had a 'mission'; Communism, like barbarism, was a form of slavery and a challenge to civilisation; the Free World, like free trade, was something worth fighting for. Vietnam stood on the frontier of south-east Asia; and south-east Asia, as once Singapore, was the 'key' to India, the Middle East and the Pacific. As Lansdale saw it, the Third World War was already underway. If the US backed off in Vietnam 'all Asia would go down the drain'. As one of his colleagues recalled, Lansdale could always convince people. 'Of course he was an advertising man, a salesman, very soft-spoken, very quiet, very smooth.'

So it was 'foot in the door' empire, with no deposit and twenty years to pay. Only the tools and the trappings had changed. These days it was the enemy who had gun-boats (Hanoi's would eventually provide the pretext for direct US military action against North Vietnam). The super-powers had more sophisticated aids to 'untroubled killing' like atomic weapons, long-range bombers and, as Lansdale appreciated better than most, a stranglehold on the world's media and its offensive potential. His nearly three years in Vietnam, although no more critical in committing the US to a Vietnam war than those that preceded and followed them, would clearly betray the imperial presumption which underlay that fatal venture.

Running Someone Else's Country

Diem had arrived in Saigon, with no natural constituency of support and no experience of high office, to head the practically non-existent government of a supposedly short-term half-state (south Vietnam) that was neither sovereign nor legitimate. The French, whose troops were still on the spot and whose officers controlled the south Vietnamese army, were out to discredit him. A host of internal power groups, one of which controlled Saigon's police and *sûreté*, was determined to topple him. And while Bao Dai's support was remote and ambivalent, America's was provocative and contingent; it depended on Diem commanding the loyalties of a hopelessly divided people while asserting his negligible authority against the Vietminh, the French and his domestic rivals. Under the terms of Geneva, he was also expected to preside over an exchange of refugees with Hanoi and to ready the south for an all-Vietnam plebiscite which would decide the future complexion of the whole country – and which Hanoi would probably win. He was up against it.

On the other hand he had faith – in his God and in his own untried abilities. And then there was Lansdale. George Washington had fathered a people in the midst of adversity, said the ever upbeat Colonel. Diem could do the same. Even the refugee crisis could work to his advantage. Instead of encouraging an exodus of local Vietminh activists to the north, Lansdale wanted them to stay. He therefore bombarded them with directives, supposedly from Hanoi, urging all cadres heading north to bring warm clothing in case they had a chance to volunteer for railroad building in China. A Vietminh fighter who went north, according to the Colonel, was a vote lost, but every one that stayed might be a vote gained because he 'could be educated later'.

Similarly every refugee from the north was a potential Diem loyalist and so another vote won. They must be made welcome, given land, and provided with social services. Under cover of the shuttle of peoples, Lansdale sent his right-hand man into Hanoi, there to form 'stay-behind' groups who would destabilise Ho's government with disinformation and acts of sabotage. They were also to panic as many northerners as possible into moving south. Instead of Diem's expected 10,000, something like a million eventually headed down across the 17th parallel. Many were Catholics – whole villages coralled by their priests – who would probably have come anyway. Lansdale could still claim some credit. He had identified the opportunity and his, of course, was the slogan which filled the airwaves: 'the Virgin Mary is heading south'.

In Saigon itself Diem's position, though weak, was not completely hopeless. Rivals could be bought off, and some were; Lansdale arranged it. French interference could be eliminated by re-routeing US aid, and was; the last troops left in the course of 1955. Meanwhile Lansdale was secretly recruiting Vietnamese paramilitary units and importing counter-insurgency specialists furnished by Magsaysay in the Philippines. Under the Geneva terms, neither side was supposed to increase its forces or their foreign advisers. Lansdale's Vietnamese units were therefore smuggled out of the country for training at US bases in Saipan (Micronesia), then smuggled back in. The Filipinos, whose advertised role was to service the stockpiles of US machinery and weapons, came as 'technicians' under contract to the Freedom Company, later the Eastern Construction Company, both CIA fronts of which Lansdale was especially proud.

Nevertheless, Diem remained vulnerable and inexplicably supine. General J. Lawton Collins, a US Special Representative, tried to galvanise him and stayed for six months. 'One may see [Collins] as the first of the American pro-consuls,' writes Anthony Short in his seminal analysis of *The Origins of the Vietnam War.* 'Collins himself was taking on some of the normal functions of government.' Naturally Diem was suspicious and, disdaining the General's advice to broaden his government, heeded and rewarded only his near relatives. Meanwhile other vultures were gathering. Bao Dai, possibly prompted by the French, hinted at Diem's replacement, while his Chief of Staff, a Vietnamese with a French commission and French citizenship, was openly defiant. Lansdale beefed up the palace guard with Filipino 'instructors'; the Chief of Staff was packed off to Paris. But in April 1955 a coalition of warlords spearheaded by the Mafia-like Binh Xuyen put troops on the streets and demanded that Diem step down. Besides controlling Saigon's protection rackets (including the dice-and-vice city that was Le Grand Monde), the Binh Xuyen also ran the city's police; its godfather was Bao Dai's appointee as head of the *sûreté*. With the Norodom Palace surrounded, Collins advised that Diem was doomed. Eisenhower had no choice but to disown him; instructions to that effect were duly drafted.

Lansdale, though, remained loyal, and it was a telegram from him to John Foster Dulles, the US Secretary of State, which saved Diem. The latter, after Lansdale had failed to deny the rumours that Washington was to dump him, had at last bestirred himself. In a gesture of exasperation he ordered the few troops available to him to engage and repel the Binh Xuyen. Whether they were strong enough was doubtful and whether they would remain loyal, even more so. Lansdale, busy at work behind the scenes, thought they had a chance and cabled Washington to this effect. Dulles, trusting Lansdale, decided to wait. Within days the Binh Xuyen were fleeing the city.

Suddenly the doomed Diem became the hero of the hour. Washington reinstated its support and Diem began his seven-year stint as America's surrogate in south Vietnam. Later in 1955, with Lansdale's help, he won a scandalous 98 per cent of the vote in a referendum to depose Bao Dai; Diem now became President and South Vietnam a republic. But of that other poll, the one to be held throughout Vietnam as per the Geneva accords, little was heard. Since neither the USA nor Saigon had been signatories at Geneva, they did not feel bound by it. They laughed at the idea of a free and fair vote being possible in the north. (Hanoi, with good reason, felt the same way about the south). And anyway it was out of the question because the Communists would probably win.

Henceforth Diem's difficulties stemmed less from the destabilising ambiguities of his own position and more from those of his half-country. In that a strong and stable South Vietnam was as much America's objective as it was Diem's, there was cause for hope. They differed, though, over the kind of state they were trying to create and over their priorities in creating it. Diem, for instance, thought an autocratic government essential and accorded top priority to the stability of his regime; the US wanted a more liberal and democratic power structure and were obsessed with the elimination of the ideological challenge.

Such differences served only to underline the lopsided character of their patron-client relationship. As well as being South Vietnam's sponsor and protector, the US provided over half of its total revenue in the form of direct aid. This was, of course, a reversal of the received idea of a colonial relationship and could be seen to justify an even more interventionist attitude. Yet, as Short observes, such intervention inexorably undermined the original objective, namely creating a strong and stable state.

> From the beginning [the Washington-Saigon relationship] was a connexion which entirely transcended the alliance of one sovereign state with another. In the first place, South Vietnam, as an integral nation state, had still to be created; and ... the question which arose from the US assumption that the Vietnamese could not be left to themselves was whether the

US had the aptitude and capability for such a neo-colonial enterprise: here defined as the privilege and responsibility of running someone else's country.

Pay Any Price, Bear Any Burden

Ten years elapsed between the Eisenhower administration's decision to back Diem and the Johnson administration's decision to send the first large consignments of US combat troops to Vietnam. During the first five, 1955–60, the 'neo-colonial enterprise' appeared to be working. Advisers, both military and civilian, descended on the country much as they had after the US obliteration of Aguinaldo's first republic in the Philippines fifty years earlier. There their efforts in education, agriculture, medicine, engineering and all the other skills essential to a modern society had worked wonders. They made less impression in Vietnam, mainly because instead of succeeding and replacing military intervention they preceded and presaged it. In the Philippines pacification prepared the way for nation-building; in South Vietnam nation-building was seen as a prerequisite for pacification. Predictably the military assistance programme transcended all others and was much the most successful, duly equipping the country with a large and occasionally effective army.

Additional programmes for land redistribution, for rural development, and for resettlement along the lines of Malaya's 'new villages' were also foisted on the Diem government and were received with less enthusiasm. In that insurgency was being contained, however, even the partial and grudging implementation of such reforms appeared to be having an effect. It was difficult to measure, of course, and anything like optimism would soon be discredited; yet, in view of what followed, the 'Diem years' would come to be remembered as something of a golden age in the US-Vietnam relationship.

The Kennedy victory of 1960 promised even greater involvement. Although Vietnam was probably not in the forefront of his mind, the new President's pledge to 'pay any price, bear any burden, meet any hardship . . . to assure the survival and success of liberty' afforded encouragement all round. Lansdale, now back in Washington, heartily approved. If Graham Greene's American had not been so 'quiet', these surely were the fine phrases which would have silenced his cynical English adversary. Lansdale was particularly troubled by the inept handling of Diem by his successors in Saigon. The

Vietnamese President had been allowed to indulge the ambitions of his family, especially Ngo Dinh Nhu, his obsessive brother, and Madame Nhu, the latter's decorative but dangerously outspoken consort. Nhu, in his attempts to shore up the regime with an eccentric ideology and a variety of semi-secret organisations, was creating what Lansdale called a 'fascistic state'. The contradiction implicit in basing the defence of the 'free world' and its liberal values on a one-party police state was discomforting. Increasingly it also appeared to be counter-productive.

A crisis in Laos, ever the unregarded source of Indo-Chinese alarms and excursions, very nearly brought a full-scale American invasion in 1961. Soviet support for the Pathet Lao had suddenly polarised that country's dynastic confusion and prejudiced US interests. Only the Bay of Pigs fiasco in Cuba kept the B-29s on base. In swallowing its wrath, Washington was at pains to emphasise that it had no intention of being so accommodating over Vietnam.

Meanwhile, in 1960, for reasons that remain obscure, the remnants of the Vietminh in the south, now called by Saigon the Vietcong (Vietnamese Communists), had chosen to re-adopt a limited form of armed struggle. The frequency of terrorist incidents increased markedly and, though Hanoi seemed lukewarm about the decision, some of those guerrillas who had gone north in 1954 began returning south to join their colleagues. The Vietcong also increased the political pressure on Diem by forming, with other assorted nationalists, a National Liberation Front. This eventually spawned a provisional government in hiding based in the jungles along the Cambodian frontier.

Kennedy, much concerned by a gloomy report from Lansdale and then by the deteriorating security situation, authorised further increases in the size of the Vietnamese army and sent to Saigon fact-finding missions and further US advisers. These included more service personnel whose number would rise to 17,000 over the next three years. Although most were concerned with training Vietnamese troops and maintaining equipment, they were already becoming engaged in combat, sometimes unavoidably, sometimes not. Additionally, in 1961 the first combat troops to be acknowledged as such, a Special Forces team of 400 men, were dispatched for covert counter-insurgency operations. They were soon followed by US aircrews for 'reconnaissance' operations.

As for Diem, Lansdale's advice to afford him more support and encouragement was readily adopted despite evidence of mounting dissatisfaction with his family's monopoly of power. To reinforce the message of support Vice-President Johnson was sent to Saigon and, with scant regard for Anglo-American relations, obligingly lauded the desiccated and utterly dependent Diem as 'the Winston Churchill of south-east Asia'. Gratified, Diem must have found this acclaim hard to square with US demands a few months later to admit American participation and personnel at every level of government. Had South Vietnam had a legitimate claim to sovereignty, this would have represented a clear infringement of it. The President of the country was in effect being demoted to a status comparable to that of one of the pre-Federation Malay sultans. Kennedy's pledge to, amongst other things, 'bear any burden' looked to include taking up that of the White Man as spelled out by Rudyard Kipling.

Other parallels with Malaya, where the Emergency had just ended with a comprehensive defeat for the Malayan Communist Party, were more acceptable in Saigon. In 1961–2 Sir Robert Thompson, the security chief under 'hearts and minds' Templer, was invited to advise Diem on counter-insurgency. An ambitious new programme of resettlement was adopted. The 'new villages' of Malaya, promoted as 'agrovilles' in Vietnam by the likes of Lansdale back in 1955, now became 'strategic hamlets'. A thousand a month were supposedly being established during 1962. According to Diem, 7 million people had been resettled in less than a year. This was impressive and seems to have given the Vietcong cause for concern. But it was vitiated by the Diem government's tendency to exaggerate the numbers and to skimp on efforts to win their confidence. One of the senior directors of the programme was later found to have been a Vietcong agent, while Thompson's insistence on the wooing of hearts and suasion of minds eventually fell foul of what he regarded as American impetuosity. There was, in truth, reasonable doubt about the relevance of the Malayan experience. The British had enjoyed, besides the support of the entire Malay population, the inestimable advantage of a well-established administrative framework. As Lansdale had often bemoaned, no such thing existed in Vietnam. The only kind of government official known to the Vietnamese farmer was a tax-gatherer.

Relocation also encouraged Diem's crazed brother Nhu to foist his brand of 'fascistic' indoctrination on the resettled. It was, however, another brother, commanding the family fief in Hue, who precipitated the collapse of the regime. Discriminating in favour of the local Catholic population, he provoked Hue's Buddhists into protest and, by strong-armed repression, finally into acts of self-immolation. Film footage of robed monks and nuns being terrorised by the American-trained and American-armed storm-troopers of Washington's Saigon surrogate was profoundly embarrassing. When the same Buddhist exponents of non-violence were seen burning themselves – or 'barbecue-ing' themselves as the inimitable Madame Nhu preferred – Diem's fate was sealed. Notwithstanding denials at the time, American complicity in the coup which finally toppled him in November 1963 is now well established. His subsequent murder, and that of the Nhus, was not part of the plan. But, as US officials had been known to quip when afforded a solo audience with Diem, 'no Nhus is good news'.

With Diem gone, American policy-makers sought a new collaborator. They, and particularly the US military who through the Defense Secretary Robert McNamara were increasingly in the ascendant, chose one created in their own image, the Vietnamese military. Diem's successors as president and prime minister would be mostly generals or air marshals; the few civilians who held high office only did so with their support. None of them lasted very long. During the next two years the government changed hands six times until it was eventually cornered by an uneasy duumvirate of Air Vice Marshal Ky and General Thieu at the head of an Armed Forces Council. Military rule for a country that was now on a war footing was perhaps appropriate. By dressing the colonial enterprise in battle fatigues, the war also obscured the absence of political freedoms and effective government.

That a war was taking place in Vietnam and that the USA was involved became apparent in 1965. Kennedy's assassination in November 1963, only twenty-one days after that of Diem, had brought Lyndon Johnson to the White House. With an eye to re-election in 1964, Johnson at first fought shy of the vast commitment demanded by the worsening situation in Vietnam. When naval incidents in the Gulf of Tonkin provided a pretext for action, the first bombing of North Vietnam was nicely calculated to show presidential resolve without panicking the electorate with thoughts of war. Once the election was won, the continuous bombing of the North began in earnest. Initially retaliation for Vietcong attacks on US bases in the South, it became a concerted blitz to destroy the North's infrastructure, to prevent the concentration and movement of troops into the South, and to effect such a collapse in morale that Hanoi would call off the struggle in the South. It failed in all respects despite continuing, except for the occasional moratorium, for eight years and depositing on North Vietnam a tonnage of explosives estimated to be three times the grand total dropped worldwide during the Second World War.

Within weeks of the first regular bombing the first large consignment of US combat troops, 3,500 Marines, swept ashore at Da Nang. They were needed to protect US naval and airforce installations. The Saigon government had not requested this assistance and had not been consulted about it. Such formalities had become as irrelevant now as they had been 120 years earlier when the USS *Constitution* had first given Da Nang (then Tourane) a taste of American firepower. In 1965 the Marines were met with smiles and garlands in a carefully staged welcome. Greeting their successors in comparable style was not always possible. By the end of the year the 3,500 had become 200,000. By the end of the next year it had topped 400,000; and in 1968 it passed half a million.

To keep the world's most favoured troops appropriately supplied with munitions, transport, gadgetry and five-star amenities required a logistical effort of sensational proportions. Just as after Diem the government in Saigon was increasingly sidelined, so the economy of South Vietnam was now virtually submerged in that of the US armed forces. The coast of what was once Cochin-China, a slight and shrinking enclave of the south-east Asian mainland, found itself hosting one of the largest concentrations of Westerners, and certainly the most intrusive, in the history of empire.

Hostilities also escalated, most notably during the 1968 Tet offensive. The cost to the US Treasury soared into tens of billions of dollars per year and US fatalities edged towards their final tally of 58,000. Meanwhile Vietnamese casualties ran into millions. Hanoi insisted that it was fighting to liberate the South from US imperialism, a claim vociferously supported by Peking and Moscow despite their increasing divergence. Washington, supported by the Western allies, clung to the idea that it was holding the line against international Communism in south-east Asia. Less was heard of South Vietnam's endangered sovereignty and its democratic credentials, more of the irreparable blow to US prestige if Hanoi prevailed.

It was not Hanoi but US public opinion which would prevail. In

1965 Johnson had enjoyed almost total support in Congress and in the country for his escalation of the war. Thereafter every news story, every draft paper and every body bag slowly tipped the scales of opinion. By 1968 Americans were more divided over Vietnam than they had been over any other issue in the century. Reluctantly Johnson was persuaded against further escalation and offered to talk with Hanoi. Partly to ensure a free hand, he also declined to go for re-election.

Richard Nixon won the 1968 election with a promise, amongst others, to 'end the war and win the peace'. Troop withdrawals began in 1969 but the fighting continued, the bombing rumbled on and was secretly extended into Cambodia, and the campus protests in America registered their first fatalities. It took Henry Kissinger until 1972 to end the war, by which time winning the peace was out of the question. In their anxiety for an agreement that would permit military disengagement without the stigma of defeat, Kissinger and his team accepted Hanoi's refusal to withdraw its troops from the South, thus in effect sacrificing the country and the cause for which the US had been fighting. As Karnow puts it, 'having fought a war to defend South Vietnam's independence, the United States was now denying its legitimacy'.

Three years later, in late April 1975, the combined forces of the Vietcong and the Democratic Republic of Vietnam (that is, the Hanoi government) converged on Saigon for the final kill – or the crowning triumph of their thirty-year struggle. In Cambodia Phnom Penh had fallen earlier in the month with Americans and other foreigners being airlifted out by helicopter while its mystified citizens, like Hamelin's children, followed the pied fighters of the Khmer Rouge out into the killing fields. Saigon's Americans, still numbering about 6,000, and their countless Vietnamese agents and employees posed a greater logistical challenge. Fifty thousand were up-lifted by air and sea before the shells started raining in on the city. With only hours to go and all other routes closed, a further 7,000 were taken out by a fleet of seventy helicopters shuttling between the beleaguered city and warships lying offshore.

Commissioned to pen a scenario for empire's end, no script writer could have improved on the spectacle at the US embassy on 29–30 April. To the improvised helipad on the flat roof of the three-storey chancery building the evacuees clambered up a ladder which bent under their weight. Crowds waited on a lower roof to make the climb; more camped on the ground below. Outside the locked and heavily guarded gates surged a disappointed mob. There was no time for the niceties of leave-taking. To the chomp of chopper blades, a sound which would ever after symbolise the Vietnam War, the flag was lowered. Tucked under the arm of Ambassador Martin who, like the captain of a sinking ship, was amongst the last to leave, it was whisked into the air, over the delta, and out into the South China Sea.

Last Outpost

Footprints in the Alluvium

The US could, of course, have won the Vietnam War, even without drawing on its nuclear arsenal; indeed it probably was winning at least until 1970. For the peoples of the East, the lesson of Vietnam was not that the West was impotent but that the exercise of its power to create and uphold the cumbersome edifices of empire was no longer acceptable to Western opinion. In an age of instant exposure and global transmission the costs were too readily apparent and the cause too easily discredited. Like the smokestack industries which had once sustained it, empire was a relic of the past.

Although many of the newly independent nations of the East would continue to avail themselves of the remote protection afforded by US satellite surveillance and the nuclear umbrella, on the ground they sought a more appropriate political technology, less tainted with imperialism and ideological rivalry, with which to manage regional relationships and satisfy domestic demands. Happily they did not have far to seek. A familiar but much revised model of regional co-operation was making a dramatic comeback. Tokyo no longer had a long-winded name for it, and membership was now entirely voluntary; otherwise it was the Greater East Asia Co-Prosperity Sphere once again.

Japan's post-war recovery in the 1950s and 1960s had already reinstated its regional primacy; as its economy continued to mushroom through the next two decades it resumed its historic role of leading the East towards the grail of Asian co-prosperity. At first its newly independent neighbours looked on with that same mixture of pride and envy with which they had followed the rise of Japan at the turn of the century. Some owed their first taste of independence to the

Japanese occupation during the Second World War; and as General Yamamoto had hoped when handing independence to the Indonesians, most were 'not, at least, anti-Japanese'. Nor now were the Western powers, who readily endorsed a regional model which advertised prosperity as the best defence against dissent and Communism. For the recipients, here was an opportunity for development without the strings of empire; it was too good to miss. As of the mid-1970s a barrage of Japanese investment, aid and technological expertise rained down on the ex-colonial entrepôts of the East.

The capacity of Japan's manufacturing industries to absorb the raw materials of south-east Asia was also undiminished, but the impact of this regional diversification was most immediately felt in South Korea and in the smaller and more responsive 'karaoke economies' of Taiwan, Hong Kong and Singapore. These became the 'little tigers' whose double-digit growth rates made them the envy of the West and soon enabled them to compete with Japan in regional investment. Thus in Indonesia, Taiwan had overtaken Tokyo as the leading investor by the mid-1980s. Reversing the domino theory of Communist encroachment, the 'Asian' or 'Pacific miracle' was rippling rapidly outwards to Thailand, Malaysia and Indonesia and then rolling on towards the coasts of China and Vietnam.

Amidst all this excitement the ignominy of empire could be easily forgotten. By 1980 the majority of the region's population had no personal recollection of foreign rule. Except in Hong Kong, Europe's leviathans had long since slunk away; even the American colossus was still reeling from its bruising encounter in Indo-China. Yet in their business houses and financial corporations, their tele towers and their banks, the Western empires retained a Brobdingnagian presence. Crowding many an Asian skyline, these structures testified to commercial and financial expertise, to resource development and processing skills, and to the reinvention of communications which had integrated the East into the global economy. Without disparaging the dynamic impetus of independence, it seemed not unreasonable to claim that empire had helped to make the 'Pacific miracle' possible.

And there was another, less obvious, legacy. If, in 1980, one carefully scrutinised each successor state, it remained possible to detect in the region's still soft political alluvium the distinctive imprint of each imperial dinosaur.

In the Indies, for instance, where Governor de Jonge had once relished another 300 club-wielding years of Dutch rule, General (now President) Suharto was just completing his first fifteen years in office with another fifteen plus to go. A worthy disciple of Dutch authoritarianism, his quasi-military regime emphasised discipline, development and political decorum. Dissent was audible only in the outlying extremities of the archipelago: at the northern tip of Sumatra, Islamic Aceh contested Jakarta's pretensions much as it once had Batavia's; and three thousand miles away at the eastern end of the archipelago, separatists occasionally challenged Jakarta's 1963 incorporation of Irian Jaya, while freedom-fighters in East Timor mounted a marathon resistance against Indonesia's 1976 seizure of their ex-Portuguese enclave.

Otherwise the Indonesian Republic, like the Netherlands East Indies, lay low, its political pulse rate imperceptible and its international profile unremarkable. The Suharto regime, masking its authoritarian excesses with a bland paternalism, sought to promote economic growth while evading human rights' scrutiny. *Rust en ordre*, that distinctively Dutch ideal of peace and quiet through law and order, prevailed.

No such decorum was evident in the Philippines where by 1980, amidst a deafening crescendo of revolt, economic collapse and international ballyhoo, another autocrat was halfway through his second decade in power. To extend his presidency after two terms in office, Ferdinand Marcos had introduced martial law in 1972. This was ostensibly because of the internal perils that beset his regime. By magnifying the challenge from Muslim separatists and from a revived Communist movement, he pretended to as good a claim on Washington's indulgence as had Ngo Dinh Diem. Indeed he stage-managed terrorist outrages on behalf of his Communist opponents, thus ensuring a rush of American sympathy or forbearance just when it was most needed. Meanwhile the inimitable Imelda spent generously as she melted hearts and warped minds in support of 'Western values'.

Such had been the chronic corruption of democratic procedures in the Philippines that most Filipinos had at first welcomed martial law's promise of firm government. As Marcos, Imelda and their cronies turned government into an exercise in personal enrichment, most Filipinos had second thoughts. So, publicly, did Washington. American pride in Marcos, once described as 'another Magsaysay', and in Manila, recently 'the showcase of democracy in Asia', could not but be dented by the imposition of martial rule. Yet successive US administrations continued to lend Marcos their support, finding a protégé with a doubtful mandate doubly amenable and decidedly better than no protégé at all. Not until the 1986 triumph of 'People Power' under the leadership of Corazon Aquino did Washington rediscover its commitment to Filipino democracy. Now Marcos, like Diem, had to go. Marooned in the Malacanang Palace amidst a sea of yellow bunting, he appeared to imitate MacArthur at Corregidor, first protesting his willingness to fight on, then asserting his determination to return. As he was spirited away from Manila (and justice) by a US Air Force helicopter, the more obvious analogy was with Saigon's discredited evacuees exactly ten years earlier.

Vietnam continued to haunt the American imagination. If the war there had predisposed Washington to support the Marcos' 'conjugal autocracy', the war's end merely underscored this commitment. For, in Indo-China, the peace that followed the fall of Saigon had brought few dividends. Laos slipped back into obscurity as a Marxist satellite of Vietnam while Cambodia, anxious to avoid a similar fate, regressed into virtual oblivion. Adopting a national brand of Maoist fundamentalism, the Khmer Rouge set the clock back to 'the year zero', outlawed every conceivable manifestation of civilisation and, with a brutality of which the Stone Age would have been ashamed, reorganised society into prehistoric labour communes.

Even Vietnam, though at last united, continued to churn with revolutionary zeal. What Osbert Sitwell had called the 'tags' of France's Third Republic – *Liberté, Egalité, Fraternité* – still 'ticketed' the fading stucco of many a public building, challenged neither by the neon of an enterprise economy nor by the tired rhetoric of Hanoi's ideologues. Most of Vietnam's leaders and intellectuals had studied either in France or in French institutions in Vietnam. French was still their second language, English-speaking Vietnamese having mostly left with the Americans in whose service they had acquired it. Hanoi preached Marxist abstractions and enjoined national reconciliation. But its disregard of the regional sensibilities of the south Vietnamese, its 're-education' programmes for those tainted with American collaboration, its cavalier treatment of even the Vietcong, and its subsequent conflicts with its erstwhile allies in China and Cambodia betrayed a jealous and unforgiving side of the revolution that seemed to owe as much to Robespierre and the Jacobins as to Marx and Communist solidarity.

For a rosier picture, critics of America's 'showcase' in the Philippines might turn to Malaysia and Singapore. There, despite the Communist challenge and Malaysia's chronic racial divide, genuine multi-party democracy seemed to have taken root. A brief suspension of parliament had followed race riots in Kuala Lumpur in 1969; and the Malaysian leadership was often accused of a partisan paternalism in its promotion of Malay, as opposed to (mainly Chinese) Malaysian, interests. Likewise there was no hiding the authoritarian streak in Lee Kuan Yew's People's Action Party in Singapore. Provisions for detention without trial were retained; the press was subject to a variety of constraints; and opposition parties, though not outlawed, rarely secured a single seat. Yet both there and in Malaysia elections were for the most part free and fair. Following the retirement of the Tunku in 1970, Malaysian democracy weathered a succession of leadership changes from which Dr Mahathir emerged in 1981 to lead the country into the dynamic 1980s and the prosperous 1990s. Lee Kuan Yew remained in office until 1990, thus dethroning Raffles as Singapore's founding father and as the embodiment of its sensational economic growth. If his 'fortress-emporium' appeared to be an excessively regulated one-party state, that was evidently how most Singaporeans wanted it.

Sensational economic growth was also the lot of Hong Kong. Possessed of the finest deep-water harbour on the China coast, of the best handling facilities, the busiest airport, the speediest communications, the strongest currency and, since the demise of Shanghai, the most liberal economic regime, Hong Kong engrossed the China trade just as Canton had in the early nineteenth century. Theoretically the US embargo of Communist China, which lasted throughout the 1950s and 1960s, should have shut off this re-export trade. In fact, like a partially closed valve, it merely increased the pressure and diffused the flow. A business community spawned on opium smuggling and the secretive networking of China's family-based enterprises found ways round the embargo as Hong Kong itself became a manufacturing centre within whose embargo-free environment Chinese labour and capital eagerly relocated.

When the embargo was lifted in 1971, re-exports recovered, and then boomed when in 1978–9 Peking adopted more liberal economic policies. For the newly formed Special Economic Zones on the

Chinese mainland, Hong Kong provided the model and showed the way. Now, as banker, purchasing agent, shop window and freight handler to a vast but backward economy which appeared poised to perform the most dramatic and lucrative transformation in world history, Hong Kong looked to be on the threshold of an even greater bonanza.

Whether its success owed more to this unique relationship with China or to its Western-style capitalism plus colonialism's low-cost, *laissez-faire* management is debatable. Either way, empire could take some credit. Since the place was still under British rule, its staggering growth flatly contradicted the notion that empire necessarily disadvantaged its subjects. Likewise it disposed of the myth that the 'Asian miracle' owed everything to the dynamism engendered by decolonisation, self-determination and representative government. For Hong Kong, now a clear winner as the last colony in the East, enjoyed none of these things. While the British could, and did, congratulate themselves on having bestowed such benefits on their erstwhile colonies in south-east Asia, they had cheerfully withheld all such concessions in Hong Kong. The people of Hong Kong did not seem to want them, the international community did not seem to require them, and Peking was bitterly opposed to them.

'When the Time is Ripe'

In retrospect it appears fairly obvious that the people of Hong Kong, by failing to register an interest in self-government before their future came up for discussion in the 1980s, had already forfeited any chance of an independent post-colonial identity. But if the default was theirs, the fault was not. For two generations China had been demanding the return not just of the colony's leased New Territories, which would anyway revert in 1997, but also of its original ceded territories, principally Hong Kong Island. The New Territories comprised 92 per cent of the colony's land area; and ethnic Chinese, many of them first-generation immigrants from neighbouring regions of the mainland, now comprised 97 per cent of the colony's total population. Peking's claim to post-1997 sovereignty over the 92 per cent was incontestable, and its claim on the allegiance of the 97 per cent was formidable. However the British chose to manage their last imperial exodus, most of Hong Kong would become Chinese territory when they left and most of its population would become Chinese citizens.

The only legal question mark lay over the future of the 8 per cent of the colony's land area, namely the valuable real estate of Hong Kong Island and the peninsula of Kowloon, which had been ceded outright by the treaties of 1842 and 1860. However 'unequal' these treaties, and hence objectionable to Peking, they were probably valid in international law and theoretically entitled the British to stay on indefinitely. Thus Margaret Thatcher, the champion of a seemingly lost colonial cause in the Falklands Islands, would dearly have liked to strike another iron posture athwart Victoria harbour. But even she had reluctantly to concede that Hong Kong without the New Territories was unworkable. It would be like severing Manhattan from a probably hostile New York. Indefensible and deprived of the people, the provisions, the water, the power, the communications and the industry on which it depended, the island would at best moulder into an irrelevant liability, like Macao. Most important of all, it would also poison relations between London and Peking to the detriment of the trade which made the colony what it was.

Uniquely in British experience, therefore, the end of empire in Hong Kong would be dictated by demands from outside, namely Peking, rather than from within. And given that Peking, like Hanoi, remained Communist and, like Hanoi, continued to insist that the foreign enclave on its southern coastline was an integral part of its territory, the obvious parallel was with Vietnam rather than with Malaysia or Singapore. This was not an encouraging thought. Besides avoiding a military confrontation which would be even more hopeless than those waged by the French and the Americans in Indo-China, it was essential to pre-empt the ignominy and chaos of the political débâcle which had followed the US withdrawal from Vietnam. The British must therefore negotiate with Peking and must continue negotiating, however distasteful and unrewarding, until they secured guarantees of Hong Kong's future status and prosperity which would be acceptable to its people and so a fitting finale to British empire in the East.

The best guarantee for Hong Kong's future would, of course, have been some arrangement for the continuance of British rule. Ever since Clementi's idea of trading Weihaiwei for outright cession of the New Territories had fallen on deaf ears in the 1920s, the chances of prolonging British rule beyond 1997 had looked dim; indeed its survival until 1997 had looked highly doubtful. But when, despite US censure in the late 1940s, the Korean War and Mao's pressure tactics in the 1950s, and finally the turmoil of the Cultural Revolution in the late 1960s, the colony still remained miraculously intact, the British became more sanguine of seeing out their term and even began to explore the possibility of a post-1997 presence. The New Territories would inevitably lapse, but perhaps Peking, in return for the transfer to it of sovereignty over the other 8 per cent, could be persuaded to let the British continue to administer the whole territory.

Such was the uphill challenge which the British set themselves in 1982 when talks between London and Peking got underway; and such was the slope on which the talks immediately stalled. Deng Xiaoping's negotiators would have none of it. In Chinese eyes the British occupation of any part of Hong Kong was illegal because of those 'unequal' treaties. The British therefore had no sovereign rights to trade, and there could be no question of a continued British role in Hong Kong's administration. It was the British who had requested a negotiated agreement; they had anticipated a general decline in business confidence unless some reassurance about the colony's future could be obtained; and more specifically they had professed anxiety about the status of sub-leases on development land in the New Territories, sub-leases whose sale constituted a significant source of government revenue which was now threatened by doubts about their post-1997 legality. Peking appreciated these difficulties and had agreed to talks aimed at providing just such reassurance and ensuring a smooth transition. It was unthinkable that they should also include discussion of sovereignty or administration which, according to Peking, were indivisible aspects of the same thing.

The British negotiators pressed hard, but got nowhere. Rebuffed by the great wall of Chinese intransigence, they explored other approaches. They liked to think of it as 'finessing their position'; a weak hand well played could still win the rubber; the main thing was that the game, or the talks, went on, which they did for two years. But if the British were playing bridge, for the Chinese it was chess. And with their opponent reduced to pawns, they were always going to win.

Failing a continued British role in Hong Kong, the next best guarantee of its future status looked to be some form of international supervision or involvement. The British position in Hong Kong was covered by what London considered valid international treaties but which, in accordance with the UN charter, and with an exemplary regard for the interests of its colonial subjects, it was willing to relinquish. In Indonesia, Indo-China and elsewhere the UN had played a role in facilitating the decolonising process. The Thatcher government dearly wished to invoke its help in Hong Kong's decolonisation, thereby restraining Peking's ambitions.

Unfortunately for Whitehall, though, and largely unnoticed by the British public, Hong Kong had in theory already been decolonised. Ten years earlier, in 1972, Peking had written to the UN to inform its relevant committee that Hong Kong and Macao were, and always had been, part of Chinese territory. Therefore, according to the letter, these places did 'not at all fall under the ordinary category of colonial territories [and] should not be included in the [UN's] list of colonial territories covered by the declaration on the granting of independence to colonial countries and peoples'. Their future, in other words, was an internal Chinese matter; it would be resolved 'when the time is ripe'; the UN had no jurisdiction over it.

At the time, which was evidently not 'ripe', President Nixon's visit to Peking had just opened the way to a normalisation of Sino-US relations; London and Peking were about to upgrade their diplomatic links to full ambassadorial level; and in Hong Kong itself the prospect of Peking no longer being treated as an international pariah had triggered a sensational boom with the Hang Seng index rocketing into four figures. Under the circumstances, and possibly by prior agreement with Peking, London had therefore decided not to contest this redefinition of Hong Kong's status. The Chinese letter had been duly noted by the UN, Hong Kong had been removed from the UN's list of colonies and the British in due course obligingly began to refer to the place as 'the Territory of Hong Kong' rather than 'the Colony of Hong Kong'.

However desirable, then, in 1982 there remained no grounds for UN supervision. London had to think again. Unable to offer the people of Hong Kong either British or international guarantees for their future, the Foreign Office negotiators now concentrated on exploring the most favourable and binding terms of offer from Peking. As with Weihaiwei, the Chinese were proposing to make Hong Kong a Special Administrative Region within the People's Republic. What this would imply in terms of local autonomy – political, judicial, commercial, fiscal and financial – was uncertain, but it was encouraging that the Chinese saw Hong Kong as an opportunity to demonstrate their new commitment to 'one country, two systems' (in which socialism and capitalism might co-exist). It was also encouraging that they saw the resumption of authority in Hong Kong as a blueprint for that over Taiwan. If Hong Kong could be reabsorbed without prejudicing its prosperity or panicking its people, Peking hoped that Chiang Kai-shek's Nationalist descendants in Taiwan might be reassured about their own ineluctable reversion when 'the time was ripe'.

Here at last, in the mutual desire to lull Hong Kong's fears and safeguard its success, was the glimmer of a shared objective. The British, relishing the chance to explain how the place worked and what made it so successful, introduced into the discussions a mass of detail. From it their Chinese counterparts, under pressure from their own deadline, discarded anything they regarded as infringing their sovereignty while accepting, often by default, most of what did not. The result, embodied in the 1984 Joint Declaration, had something for everyone: Peking got Hong Kong, Hong Kong got a fifty-year transitional period during which to manage its own affairs with minimal interference from Peking, and London got a deal which it was not ashamed to put before Parliament. Much further detail remained to be sorted out but the agreement was widely hailed as a triumph for all concerned.

Pessimists noted two obvious omissions: there were no guarantees that both parties would respect the terms, and there were no sanctions if they did not. Such fears, largely ignored amidst the late 1980s euphoria about economic and possible political liberalisation in China, became unpleasantly relevant when in June 1989 the tanks of the People's Liberation Army ceased kow-towing to the pro-democracy demonstrators around Tiananmen Square and the machine guns opened fire. In the People's Republic 'People Power' proved powerless. The advocates of accountability were called to account, and the China to which Hong Kong was returning was revealed as the authoritarian, centrist, socialist, one-party tyranny of Mao's day. A hob-nailed regime capable of grinding underfoot its own unarmed subjects was not going to tip-toe round the sensibilities of a renegade enclave, however 'special' its administrative status and however explicit the Joint Agreement and the subsequent 'Basic Law' which defined this status.

Massive Hong Kong support for the pro-democracy demonstrators in Peking gave way to massive protests over their massacre and detention. The Joint Declaration came in for ferocious criticism and, to the ill-disguised horror of those who had negotiated it, both British and Chinese, a new guarantee of Hong Kong's future status was sought. Under the vigorous direction of Chris Patten, a politician rather than a diplomat who in 1992 became the territory's last governor, proposals were launched, albeit belatedly, for democratising the Hong Kong administration. Now it was the people of the territory who were to become their own best guarantee. In a complicated series of reforms, a third of the seats in the Legislative Council were to be filled by directly elected members, and other members were to be chosen by a vastly widened electorate.

China was invited to comment and did so, lambasting the proposals as a breach of the Joint Declaration and Patten as a monster of perfidy. The latter, more accustomed to contumely than his diplomatic predecessors, also proved more robust. To Peking it was pointed out that the Joint Declaration clearly envisaged a future legislature constituted by election; the British government had undertaken moves in this direction both before and during the negotiations; and the British Parliament had enthusiastically endorsed the idea.

Peking was not reassured. Patten was called even nastier names and China's collaboration in the construction of the territory's new airport was threatened. Nevertheless, with some modifications, the proposals went ahead and, in the 1995 elections held under the new dispensation, pro-democracy candidates performed impressively to emerge as the largest party.

Whether, by such a late autumnal sowing of democratic procedures, the British have given Hong Kong a source of winter sustenance, or whether they have merely lumbered its people with a horticultural liability, remains to be seen. Contrary to the gloomy predictions of the British Foreign Office, Peking did not tear up the Joint Declaration. Although it continued to threaten a speedy disbandment of the new Legislative Council, the airport project continued and Sino-British discussions about the formalities of the 1997 hand-over eventually resumed.

Meanwhile the British, applauded by the US and others for their staunch promotion of Western values, began to feel distinctly better about the hand-over. For the Chinese, 30 June 1997 would undoubtedly be a day of celebration. For the British it might have been a Weihaiwei wake. Now they too had contrived something worth memorialising. Hong Kong could go on its way with the priceless benediction of representative government. Patten could go home to resume, if he cared to, a political career that would no doubt be enhanced by his championship of Asian democracy. The British government could go to the country in 1997 claiming to have done everything possible for the people of Hong Kong (short of offering them the politically unthinkable opportunity of asylum in Britain). And empire could go out, if not with a fanfare of glory, at least with the solemn dignity of a last 'Last Post'.

Glossary of Place Names

Aceh	Acheh, Acheen
Amoy	Xiamen
Badung	Denpasar
Bantam	Banten
Batavia	Jakarta
Bengkulu	Benkulen
Buleleng	Singaraja
Canton	Guangzhou
Chefoo	Yantai
Chungking	Chonqing
Chusan	Zhoushan
Foochow	Fuzhou
Formosa	Taiwan
Fukien	Fujian
Hangchow	Hangzhou
Hollandia	Sukarnopura, Jayapura
Hopei	Hebei
Ichang	Yichang
Kiaochow	Jiaozhou Wan
Kwangchow	Leizhou
Liaotung	Liaodong
Makassar	Ujung Pandang
Malacca	Melaka
Moluccas	Maluku
Mukden	Shenyang
Nanking	Nanjing
Ningpo	Ningbo
North Borneo	Sabah
Peking	Beijing
Port Arthur	Lushun

Port Swettenham	Pelabuhan Kelang
Riau islands	Rhio islands
Saigon	Ho Chi Minh
Shantung	Shandong
Swatow	Shantou
Szechwan	Sichuan
Tientsin	Tianjin
Tourane	Da Nang
Tsingtao	Qingdao
West Irian	Irian Jaya
Whangpoo River	Huangpu Jiang
Yangtze River	Chang Jiang

Bibliography

To anyone disappointed by the absence of source notes the author offers his apologies. Spattering a narrative history with numbered references, whilst it may invite scholarly regard, is inhibiting for the writer and can be irritating for the reader. In this case, the facts of the story are mostly beyond dispute, and the emphasis, analysis and opinions are mostly those of the author. Quoted extracts are sourced in the text. The full titles and publication details of works quoted will be found in the following bibliography.

Other sources include:

Abdul Rahman, Tunku, 'End of Empire' transcripts in Rhodes House Library, Oxford

Broome, Richard, transcripts in Imperial War Museum Sound Archive, London

Cao Xuan Pho, transcripts of BBC and personal interviews

Cunyngham-Brown, Sjovald, 'End of Empire' transcripts in Rhodes House Library, Oxford (Mss Brit. Emp. 8527/9)

Davis, John, 'End of Empire' transcripts in Rhodes House Library, Oxford

Ide Anak Agung Gde Agung, transcripts of BBC and personal interviews

Johnston, Sir R. F., letters in the possession of Mrs Sarah Markham and letters in J. H. Stewart Lockhart Collection (see below)

Lockhart, J. H. Stewart, papers in the National Library of Scotland, Edinburgh, by kind permission of George Watson's College and the Merchant Company Education Board

Sadao Oba, in Nish, I. (ed), see Bibliography

Sheppard, Tan Sri Dato Mubin [Mervyn], 'End of Empire' transcripts in Rhodes House Library, Oxford

Stewart, Duncan, private diary in the possession of his heirs

General

Allen, Charles, *Tales from the South China Sea*, Abacus, London, 1983

Butcher, J. G., *The British in Malaya, 1880–1941*, Oxford University Press, Kuala Lumpur, 1979

Cady, J., *The Roots of French Imperialism in East Asia*, Cornell University Press, Ithaca, 1954

Cross, Colin, *The Fall of the British Empire*, Hodder & Stoughton, London, 1968

Cunyngham-Brown, Sjovald, *Crowded Hour*, John Murray, London, 1975

Davis, John, quoted in Allen, Charles, *Tales from the South China Sea*, Abacus, London, 1983

Emerson, Rupert, *Malaysia, A Study in Direct and Indirect Rule*, Macmillan, New York, 1937

Fieldhouse, D. K., *The Colonial Empires*, Macmillan, London, 1982

Fitzgerald, C. P., *A Concise History of East Asia*, Penguin, London, 1974

Gallagher, John, *The Decline, Revival and Fall of the British Empire*, Cambridge University Press, Cambridge, 1982

Gullick, John, *Malaysia*, Benn, London, 1981

Kahin, G. McT., *Nationalism and Revolution in Indonesia*, Cornell University Press, Ithaca, 1972

Karnow, Stanley, *In Our Image*, Century, London, 1990

——*Vietnam, A History*, Century, London, 1983

Kennedy, J., *A History of Malaya*, Macmillan, London, 1962

Lancaster, Donald, *Emancipation of French Indo-China*, Oxford University Press, London, 1961

Lightfoot, Keith, *The Philippines*, Benn, London, 1973

Louis, W. R., *Imperialism: The Robinson and Gallagher Controversy*, Oxford University Press, London, 1976

Low, D. A., *Eclipse of Empire*, Cambridge University Press, Cambridge, 1991

McAlister, J. T., *Vietnam, The Origins of Revolution*, Allen Lane, London, 1969

McNutt, Paul V., quoted in Karnow, Stanley, *In Our Image*, Century, London, 1990

Malcolm, G. A., *First Malayan Republic: The Story of the Philippines*, Christopher, Boston, 1951

Mehden, F. R. von der, *South-east Asia, 1930–1970: The Legacy of Colonialism and Nationalism*, Thames and Hudson, London, 1974

Morris, James, *Farewell the Trumpets*, Penguin, London, 1979

Morris, Jan, *Hong Kong: Xianggang*, Viking, London, 1988

Reece, R. H. W., *The Name of Brooke: The End of White Rajah Rule in Sarawak*, Oxford University Press, Kuala Lumpur, 1982

Ricklefs, M. C., *A History of Modern Indonesia*, Macmillan, London, 1981

Runciman, Steven, *The White Rajahs: A History of Sarawak, 1841–1946*, Cambridge University Press, Cambridge, 1960

Tarling, N. (ed.), *The Cambridge History of Southeast Asia*, vol. 2, Cambridge University Press, Cambridge, 1992

——*The Fall of Imperial Britain in Southeast Asia*, Oxford University Press, Singapore, 1993

Tate, D. J. M., *The Making of Modern South East Asia*, 3 vols., Oxford University Press, Kuala Lumpur, 1979

Thomson, J. C., Stanley, P. W., and Perry, J. C., *Sentimental Imperialists, The American Expansion in East Asia*, Harper Row, New York, 1981

Tregonning, K. G., *Under Charter Company Rule: North Borneo*, University of Malaya, Singapore, 1958

——*A History of Modern Malaya*, University of London, London, 1964

Welsh, Frank, *A History of Hong Kong*, Collins, London, 1993

Wesley-Smith, Peter, *Unequal Treaty 1898–1997*, Oxford University Press, Hong Kong, 1980

Winstedt, Richard, *Malaya and Its History*, Hutchinson, London, 1953
Woodcock, George, *Who Killed the British Empire?*, Jonathan Cape, London, 1974

Part One

Adams, Henry, quoted in Wolff, Leon, *Little Brown Brother*, Longman, London, 1961
Airlie, Shiona, *The Thistle and the Bamboo: The Life and Times of Sir James Stewart Lockhart*,
   Oxford University Press, Hong Kong, 1989
Atwell, Pamela, *British Mandarins and Chinese Reformers: The British Administration of
   Weihaiwei (1898–1930) and the Territory's Return to Chinese Rule*, Oxford University
   Press, Hong Kong, 1985
Benson, Stella, *Some Letters of Stella Benson*, ed. C. Clarabut, Libra, Hong Kong, 1978
Burchett, Wilfred, *North of the 17th Parallel*, Red River, Hanoi, 1957
Dekker, E. D. ('Multatuli'), *Max Havelaar; or The Coffee Auctions of the Dutch Trading
   Company*, Edmonstone and Douglas, Edinburgh, 1868; trans. R. Edwards and
   reprinted Massachusetts University Press, Amherst, 1982
Fairbank, J. K., *Trade and Diplomacy on the China Coast*, Stanford University Press,
   Stanford, 1964
Freith, H., and Castles, L. (eds.), *Indonesian Political Thinking, 1945–1965*, Cornell
   University Press, Ithaca, 1970
Furnivall, J. S., *Netherlands India*, Cambridge University Press, Cambridge, 1939
Gorer, Geoffrey, *Bali and Angkhor*, Macmillan, London, 1936
Grant, Joy, *Stella Benson*, Macmillan, London, 1987
Hanna, W. A., and Star, B., *Bali*, Apa (HK), Hong Kong, 1983
Hoe, Susanna, *The Private Life of Old Hong Kong*, Oxford University Press, Hong
   Kong, 1991
Holt, Claire (ed.), *Culture and Politics in Indonesia*, Cornell University Press, Ithaca,
   1972
Innes, James, quoted in Fairbank, J. K., *Trade and Diplomacy on the China Coast*,
   Stanford University Press, Stanford, 1964
Johnston, R. F., *The Lion and the Dragon in Northern China*, 1910, reprinted Oxford
   University Press, Hong Kong, 1986
——*Twilight in the Forbidden City*, 1934, reprinted Oxford University Press, Hong
   Kong, 1983
Keay, John, *The Honourable Company: A History of the English East India Company*,
   HarperCollins, London, 1991
——*Indonesia: From Sabang to Merauke*, Boxtree, London, 1994
Lacouture, J., *Ho Chi Minh, A Political Biography*, Penguin, London, 1968
Lethbridge, H. J., *Hong Kong: Stability and Change*, Oxford University Press, Hong
   Kong, 1978
Lockhart, James Stewart, quoted in Airlie, Shiona, *The Thistle and the Bamboo: The Life
   and Times of Sir James Stewart Lockhart*, Oxford University Press, Hong Kong,
   1989
Lulofs, Madelon H., *Rubber, A Romance of the Dutch East Indies*, London, 1933,
   reprinted Oxford University Press, Singapore, 1987
Lyautey, Hubert, *Intimate Letters from Tonquin*, trans. A. Le Blond, Bodley Head,
   London, 1932

Maugham, W. Somerset, *The Circle*, Heinemann, London, 1921
——*The Painted Veil*, Heinemann, London, 1925
——*The Casuarina Tree*, Heinemann, London, 1926
——*The Summing Up*, Heinemann, London, 1938
——*A Writer's Notebook*, Heinemann, London, 1949
Mills, L. A., *British Rule in East Asia*, Oxford University Press, London, 1942
Money, J. W. B., *Java, Or How to Manage a Colony*, 1861, reprinted Oxford University Press, Singapore, 1985
Powell, Hickman, *The Last Paradise*, Cape, London, 1930
Pramoedya Ananta Toer, *House of Glass*, trans. Max Lane, Penguin, Melbourne, 1992
Sitwell, Osbert, *Escape With Me!*, Macmillan, London, 1939
Sjahrir, S., *Our Struggle*, Cornell University Press, Ithaca, 1968
Spence, J. D., *The Gate of Heavenly Peace*, Faber, London, 1982
Stanley, P. W., *A Nation in the Making: The Philippines and the United States, 1899–1921*, Harvard University Press, Cambridge, Mass., 1974
Sukarno, quoted in Freith, H., and Castles, L. (eds.), *Indonesian Political Thinking, 1945–1965*, Cornell University Press, Ithaca, 1970
Székely, Ladislao, *Tropic Fever*, 1937, reprinted Oxford University Press, Kuala Lumpur, 1979
Tarling, B., 'Sir Cecil Clementi and the Federation of British Borneo' in *Journal of the Malaysian Branch of the Royal Asiatic Society*, vol. xliv, pt. 2, December 1971, Kuala Lumpur
Tate, D. J. M. (ed.), *Rajah Brooke's Borneo*, Nicholson, Hong Kong, 1988
Twain, Mark, quoted in Wolff, Leon, *Little Brown Brother*, Longman, London, 1961
Van Leur, J. C., quoted in Furnivall, J. S., *Netherlands India*, Cambridge University Press, Cambridge, 1939
Vickers, A., *Bali: A Paradise Created*, Periplus, Singapore, 1989
——(ed.), *Travelling to Bali: Four Hundred Years of Journeys*, Oxford University Press, Kuala Lumpur, 1994
Winstedt, Sir R. O., *Start from Alif: Count from One*, Oxford University Press, Kuala Lumpur, 1969
Wolff, Leon, *Little Brown Brother*, Longman, London, 1961
Woodcock, George, *The British in the Far East*, Weidenfeld and Nicolson, London, 1969

Part Two

Allen, G. C., and Donnithorpe, A. G., *Western Enterprise in Indonesia and Malaya*, Allen and Unwin, London, 1954
Allen, Louis, *Singapore, 1941–1942*, Cass, London, 1993
Anderson, B. R. O'G., *Java in a Time of Revolution: Occupation and Resistance, 1944–1946*, Cornell University Press, Ithaca, 1972
Anon., *All About Shanghai: A Standard Guide Book*, The University Press, Shanghai, 1935
Barber, Noel, *Sinister Twilight: The Fall of Singapore*, Collins, London, 1968
Chapman, F. Spencer, *The Jungle is Neutral*, Chatto, London, 1953
Cook, Christopher, *The Lion and the Dragon*, Elm Tree, London, 1985

Bibliography

Elsbree, W. H., *Japan's Role in South-east Asian Nationalist Movements*, Harvard University Press, Cambridge, Mass., 1953

Flower, R., *Mutiara, A Perspective of Penang*, Treasury, Singapore, 1989

Gardner, Mona, *Menacing Sun*, Travel Book Club, London, 1940

Gautier, G., *La Fin de l'Indochine*, SPL, Paris, 1978

Hammer, Ellen J., *The Struggle for Indochina, 1940–1955*, Stanford University Press, Stanford, 1966

Iriye, Akira, *Power and Culture: The Japanese-American War, 1941–1945*, Harvard University Press, Cambridge, Mass., 1981

James, D. Clayton, *The Years of MacArthur*, Leo Cooper, London, 1970

Keith, Agnes, *Land Below the Wind*, Michael Joseph, London, 1939

——*Three Came Home*, Michael Joseph, London, 1948

Keswick, Maggie, *The Thistle and the Jade*, Octopus, London, 1980

Klestadt, Albert, *The Sea Was Kind*, Constable, London, 1959

K'tut Tantri, *Revolt in Paradise*, Harper and Brothers, New York, 1960

Legge, J. D., *Sukarno: A Political Biography*, Allen and Unwin, Sydney, 1972

Lockhart, R. H. Bruce, *Return to Malaya*, Putnam, New York, 1936

Louis, W. R., *British Strategy in the Far East, 1919–1939*, Clarendon Press, Oxford, 1971

——*Imperialism at Bay, 1941–1945*, Oxford University Press, London, 1977

MacArthur, Douglas, quoted in James, D. Clayton, *The Years of MacArthur*, Leo Cooper, London, 1970

Mackie, R. C. H., *This Was Singapore*, Angus and Robertson, Sydney, 1942

Mountbatten, Louis, *Personal Diary, 1943–1946*, ed. Philip Ziegler, Collins, London, 1988

Nish, I. (ed.), *The Indonesian Experience, The Role of Japan and Britain*, London School of Economics, London, 1979

Owen, Frank, *The Fall of Singapore*, London, 1960

Parkin, Ray, *Out of the Smoke*, Hogarth, London, 1960

Peh-T'i Wei, Betty, *Old Shanghai*, Oxford University Press, Hong Kong, 1993

Sergeant, Harriet, *Shanghai*, Cape, London, 1991

Sternberg, Josef von, *Fun in a Chinese Laundry*, Macmillan, New York, 1965

Torrible, Graham, quoted in Cook, Christopher, *The Lion and the Dragon*, Elm Tree, London, 1985

van Mook, H. J., *The Stakes of Democracy in South-east Asia*, Allen and Unwin, London, 1950

Yong Mun Cheong, *H. J. van Mook and Indonesian Independence*, M. Nijhoff, The Hague, 1962

Part Three

Allen, Charles, *Savage Wars of Peace: Soldiers' Voices, 1945–1989*, Michael Joseph, London, 1990

Allen, Louis, *The End of the War in Asia*, Hart-Davis, London, 1976

Barber, Noel, *The War of the Running Dogs*, Collins, London, 1971

Blascheck, Charles, quoted in Dunn, P. M., *The First Vietnam War*, C. Hurst and Co., London, 1985

Bodard, Lucien, *The Quicksand War: Prelude to Vietnam*, Faber, London, 1967

Bogarde, Dirk, *Backcloth*, Viking, London, 1986

Bibliography

Bonavia, David, *Hong Kong 1997, The Final Settlement*, Columbus, Bromley, 1985

Cady, J., *The History of Post-War South East Asia*, Ohio University Press, Athens, Ohio, 1974

Chan Lau, K. C., *China, Britain and Hong Kong, 1895–1945*, Chinese University Press, Hong Kong, 1990

Cloake, John, *Templer, Tiger of Malaya*, Harrap, London, 1985

Clutterbuck, Richard, *Conflict and Violence in Singapore and Malaysia*, Brash, Singapore, 1984

Cole, Allan B., *Conflict in Indo-China*, Cornell University Press, Ithaca, 1956

Cotterell, Arthur, *East Asia*, John Murray, London, 1993

Cottrell, Robert, *The End of Hong Kong*, John Murray, London, 1993

Crisswell, C. N., *The End of the Brooke Raj*, Paul Strachan/Kiscadale, Gartmore UK, 1994

Cross, John, quoted in Allen, Charles, *Savage Wars of Peace*, Michael Joseph, London, 1990

Currey, Cecil, *Shadows, The Story of Edward Gray Lansdale*, Houghton Mifflin, New York, 1988

Dalloz, Jacques, *The War in Indo-China, 1945–1954*, Barnes and Noble, New York, 1990

Dennis, Peter, *Troubled Days of Peace: Mountbatten and South East Asia Command, 1945–1946*, Manchester University Press, Manchester, 1987

Donnison, F. S. V., *British Military Administration in the Far East, 1943–1946*, HMSO, London, 1956

Dunn, P. M., *The First Vietnam War*, C. Hurst and Co., London, 1985

Endacott, G. B., and Birch, A., *Hong Kong Eclipse*, Oxford University Press, Hong Kong, 1978

Fall, B. B., *Street Without Joy: Insurgency in Indo-China*, Pall Mall Press, London, 1966

Fusayama, Takeo, *A Japanese Memoir of Sumatra, 1945–1946*, Cornell University Press, Ithaca, 1993

Gimson, Franklin, quoted in Welsh, Frank, *A History of Hong Kong*, Collins, London, 1993

Greene, Graham, *The Quiet American*, 1955, reprinted Penguin, London, 1981

Hatta, Mohammed, quoted in Wehl, David, *The Birth of Indonesia*, Allen and Unwin, London, 1948

Idrus, 'Surabaya' in *Indonesia*, No. 5, Cornell University Press, Ithaca, April 1968

Jackman, Bruce, quoted in Allen Charles, *The Savage Wars of Peace*, Michael Joseph, London 1990

Josey, Alex, *Lee Kuan Yew: The Struggle for Singapore*, Angus and Robertson, Sydney, 1974

Kahin, A. R. (ed.), *Regional Dynamics of the Indonesian Revolution*, Hawaii University Press, Honolulu, 1985

Kahin, G. McT., and Lewis, J. W., *The US in Vietnam*, New York, 1967

Koke, L. G., *Our Hotel in Bali*, Jeremy Brooks, Wellington NZ, 1987

Lapping, Brian, *End of Empire*, Granada, London, 1985

Lederer, W., and Burdick, E., *The Ugly American*, Norton, New York, 1958

Lewis, Norman, *A Dragon Apparent*, Cape, London, 1951

Lucy, Dorothy, quoted in Allen, Charles, *The Savage Wars of Peace*, Michael Joseph, London, 1996

Mackenzie, Compton, *All Over the Place*, Chatto, London, 1948

Bibliography

Mackie, R. C. H., *Malaysia in Focus*, London, 1963

MacMahon, R. J., *Colonialism and Cold War: The US and the Struggle for Indonesian Independence*, Cornell University Press, Ithaca, 1981

Marshall, D. Bruce, *The French Colonial Myth and Constitution Making in the Fourth Republic*, Yale University Press, New Haven, 1973

Means, Gordon P., *Malaysian Politics*, University of London Press, London, 1970

Michener, James A., *Voices of Asia*, Secker and Warburg, London, 1952

Miers, Richard, *Shoot to Kill*, Faber, London, 1959

Miller, Harry, *Menace in Malaya*, Harrap, London, 1954

Moore, D., *We Live in Singapore*, Hodder, London, 1955

Moran, J. W. G., *Spearhead in Malaya*, Peter Davies, London, 1959

Nehru, Jarwaharlal, quoted in Tarling, N. (ed.), *The Cambridge History of Southeast Asia*, vol. 2, Cambridge University Press, Cambridge, 1992

O'Ballance, E., *Malaya: The Communist Insurgent War, 1948–1960*, Faber, London, 1966

Parrot, J. G. A., 'Who Killed Mallaby?' in *Indonesia*, No. 20, Cornell University Press, Ithaca, October 1978

Perelman, S. J., *Westward Ha*, Simon and Schuster, New York, 1948

Purcell, Victor, *Memoirs of a Malayan Official*, Cassell, London, 1965

Rafferty, Kevin, *City on the Rocks*, Viking, London, 1989

Rahman, Tunku Abdul, *Looking Back*, Heinemann, Kuala Lumpur, 1977

——*Viewpoints*, Heinemann, Kuala Lumpur, 1978

Reid, A. J. S., *The Indonesian National Revolution, 1945–1950*, Longman, Victoria (Australia), 1974

Roff, W. R., *The Origins of Malay Nationalism*, Yale University Press, London, 1967

Sainteny, J. *Histoire d'une Paix Manquée: Indochine, 1945–1947*, Amiot-Dumont, Paris, 1953

Short, Anthony, *The Origins of the Vietnam War*, Longman, London, 1989

——*The Communist Insurrection in Malaya, 1948–1960*, Muller, London, 1975

Simandjuntak, B., *Malayan Federalism, 1945–1963*, Oxford University Press, Kuala Lumpur, 1969

Stockwell, A. J., *British Policy and Malay Politics during the Malay Union Experiment*, Malaysian Branch of the Royal Asiatic Society, Kuala Lumpur, 1976

Stubbs, Richard, *Hearts and Minds: The Malayan Emergency, 1948–1960*, Oxford University Press, Singapore, 1989

Thompson, Sir Robert, *Defeating Communist Insurgency*, Chatto, London, 1967

Truong Nhu Tang, *Journal of a Vietcong*, Cape, London, 1986

Van der Post, Laurens, *The Night of the New Moon*, Hogarth Press, London, 1970

——*Yet Being Someone Other*, Hogarth Press, London, 1982

——*A Walk with a White Bushman*, Chatto & Windus, London, 1986

Wehl, David, *The Birth of Indonesia*, Allen and Unwin, London, 1948

Wolf, Charles, Jr., *The Indonesia Story*, J. Day, New York, 1948

Index

Index

Index